Messianic Thought Outside Theology

Messianic Thought Outside Theology

Edited by

ANNA GLAZOVA AND PAUL NORTH

FORDHAM UNIVERSITY PRESS

New York 2014

Library of Congress Cataloging-in-Publication Data

Messianic thought outside theology / edited by Anna Glazova and
Paul North.
    pages cm
  Includes bibliographical references and index.
  ISBN 978-0-8232-5671-6 (cloth : alk. paper) —
ISBN 978-0-8232-5672-3 (pbk. : alk. paper)
    1. Messianism.   2. Messianism in literature.   3. Political
messianism.   4. Philosophy, Modern—20th century.
5. Philosophy, European—20th century.   6. Popular culture—
Philosophy.   I. Glazova, Anna   II. North, Paul, 1971–
  BL475.B444 2014
  206'.1—dc23
                                                2013046185

Printed in the United States of America
16 15 14   5 4 3 2 1
First edition

CONTENTS

MESSIANIC THOUGHT
OUTSIDE THEOLOGY

Introduction:
Saving Hope, the Wager of Messianism

Anna Glazova and Paul North

The Messianic Remainder

A minor genre has been taking shape in cultural theory and philosophy: essays and books have been being written whose centerpiece is talk about messiahs. This development will not seem so surprising if the new genre is assimilated to the "turn to" or "return of" religion that has come to be thought of as a key to understanding our contemporary situation.[1] Taken as part of this larger movement, messianic theory—or, as it might be called, epimessianic theory,[2] since it purports to come after traditional messianisms and to resolve some of the dilemmas posed by them—can be studied alongside other theologoumena and religious phenomena such as faith, ritual, scripture, and so forth, themes and concepts that have come back to critical consciousness within the framework of the return of religion. This essay collection is then part of the return to religion and part of its analysis, which began at least a decade ago.[3] It is part of it and not part of it. As part of it, the collection analyzes or summarizes a sub-concern within the broader field: It tracks attempts to redeem messianic figures from defunct theological constructs and it shows how the theological or the religious in fact persisted throughout the so-called secular and survived into what is sometimes now called the postsecular age. Indeed, some of the essays do this. Essays in this collection, on the whole, provide insight into the presuppositions and purposes of more and less explicit attempts to salvage messiahs and messianisms in the nineteenth and twentieth centuries. Yet alongside this scholarly act, many of the essays also divulge a secret. The new genre cannot comfortably be classed within religion's return or its analysis. This is due, as far as we can see, to messianism's special historical status. Messianic theory in its recent form—epimessianism—stands at the virtual limit of the recent "return," insofar as it pushes the concept of return to its breaking point. This is because it recognizes the trouble with returns. That is, talk of a "return" adduces a history that is by and large messianic. As soon as one says, "Messianism is back," one steps into a paradox or vicious circle—whether in good or bad faith, it doesn't much matter. It seems as though, from the start, any critique or reevaluation of messianic thought depends on what it wants to critique and thus a priori fails. And so "analysis" is not the best methodological term for what many of the essays in this book attempt to do.

Of all the possible theologoumena and religious phenomena that could return, messianism and its variants are perhaps the most vexing. Messiahs do this: They come back. Moreover, they are the quintessence of what comes exactly as predicted. In this way, messianic hopes open time as the horizon within which all other events, including returns, become possible. Messiahs guarantee the existence and also the continuation, so to speak, of the temporal continuum by setting its outermost limits. In some accounts this is called the "structure" of time. Messianic hope gives time a structure, starting with a beginning and an end, and moving on to something like directionality and movement and inner divisions. Within a messianic understanding of time, any end of anything becomes a quotation of the end of all endings. A messiah makes up, in this way, the reason for religion's arrival as well as for its ultimate departure and dissolution. An intellectual return to religion is thus itself in some way already messianic, and the exposition of this trend has its roots deep in the same belief. Built on a basic tenet of messianic thinking, the return of or to religion, along with its prophecies and commentaries, are caught up in a logic that can hardly be fathomed from within the confines of the messianic idea. Epimessianic theory does not avoid this vicious circle; the best examples of it make the circle manifest. From this perspective, epimessianic thought stands alongside the return of or to religion, as a sort of inassimilable remainder of recent intellectual and spiritual history. God may have absconded; religion and the secular may come and go, supersede one another, and return again, but they do so under the auspices of a messianicity that exceeds them both and belongs to neither. As the most general condition of all perceptible origins and ends (including shifts in intellectual paradigms), messianicity itself—rather disturbingly—is subject neither to origin nor to end. And so, more than simply thematizing the return of another religious phenomenon or a theologoumenon repressed by the secular age, the new genre that has been taking shape, for a century or more—messianic theory outside theology—focuses instead on the concept or concepts of history in which something like a return becomes intelligible. The genre treats, in short, the meaning of historical time, as it is constituted by messianicity and in the hope that this messianic component *could possibly* be thought otherwise.

According to its status as a remainder, messianic thinking does not technically return, but it also is not simply present. It exists rather in a kind of intellectual purgatory, in which name and concept hang around indefinitely, ever ready to be called into service again. If this is the case, what can possibly be done about it? The messianic theories treated in this collection respond in different ways to messianism's special conundrum. Each takes an extreme approach; each tries to transcend the boundaries of the question as traditionally asked. Even where an epimessianic theorist resurrects the term and some of its meanings, even where he rebaptizes its logic, in the most general terms, the epimessianist attempts to deflect or destroy one or more of the intransigent aspects of messianism, so that it cannot return as the same, so that it brings with it a different conception of history, so that it abrogates the fatefulness and also the comfort of the tradition. Kant does this, and Marx of course as well, as do Benjamin and Derrida, but then also others who belong less obviously to post-theological dealings with messianism, such as Baudelaire, Kafka, and Paul Celan.[4]

This is the conceptual kernel of epimessianism: It tries to reform the messianic concept of history by keeping some messianic elements and discarding others. One could argue that if messianism arises in or before a historical crisis, then epimessianism, or critical messianism—writing that adjudicates among concepts of the messianic in order to condemn some and redeem others—arises in the aftermath of the disappointment, responding perhaps to a secondary crisis produced by leftover, unsatiated providential fervor. What is nineteenth-century radical politics if not the melancholic attempt to resuscitate the dead messiahs of the French Revolution? In most cases epimessianism retains a part of the original hope, hope in this figure and in the powers it is supposed to wield. Epimessianic writing is thus not totally divorced from certain ticks and traits common to discourse about the return of religion—a good example of which is Charles Taylor's *A Secular Age*. Throughout this book, Taylor charges that secularization has produced an emptiness in our world that calls for fulfillment. This is of course already a messianic claim, available to him under the already accepted principle of a messianic time. In its special perpetuity, messianism is always available, now, again, for use. It is in fact rather repetitive. Without addressing the messianic as such, Taylor, in his particular repetition, nevertheless argues along messianic lines: The core of our problem today is the loss of a certain model of loss, the loss of a loss that can be redeemed.[5] The hopeful thought that what is broken can be restored, that what has been lost can be found, has itself vanished in the rational model of the secular world, and Taylor gently but firmly urges us to return to belief in this first-order loss, in order to fill the void left by its absence. The absence of meaningful loss would seem to have little to do with the recent economical crisis in the United States. Yet, when credit is suddenly withdrawn, it is clear that the most desired commodity is still hope, hope that springs up when loss is found again. In this instance the hope was for a renewed faith that might be stronger than the weakened and controversial old faith in the market. Hope: a modality that in times of crisis seems more attractive than incredulity, critique, or despair. Even though this economic phenomenon may have little of dogmatic or institutional religion about it, the messianic thought is not far away: Faced with loss, we tend to choose hope over everything else, even if hope hardly alleviates the present crisis—even if, indeed, it helps perpetuate it. Instead of throwing out bad institutions, one does everything possible to reimagine their failure as structural, as destined, as belonging essentially to us and to our world. We become desperate only when we anticipate a possible loss of the messianic model of loss. This may explain why saving the messiah demands altering him, almost—but not quite—beyond recognition. This gambit, epimessianism's wager, may be seen as a symptom of this desperation, a last and most desperate attempt to return to the idea of loss as the redeemable.

Let us say, provisionally, that there are two strands of epimessianism. Both believe that the messiah can be redeemed from dogmatic religion as well as from a simplistic secularism, by means of modification or critique. One stresses the finiteness and fallenness of the world, the other stresses the coming age. These two emphases, which at times blend into one another almost to the point of duplicity, correspond to two kinds of eschatological dreams. In one, the end of the world brings the total annihilation of everything that ever was; it destroys the non-messianic, fallen middle. In the other, it brings the glorious restitution of the same. Both apocalypses, however—destruction and restitution—are violent. Preparation for the coming glory requires, to use the Apostle Paul's terminology, *kenosis*, emptying out. Emptying and its companions, sacrifice, asceticism, delay, hope, charity, and so forth, do violence to the world until the end for the sake of the end. Kenosis is slower, but finally as destructive as Armageddon. When we speak of a messianic potential, then, we should be careful not to dwell only on its restorative or revolutionary power, when the destructive dimension is part and parcel of it. Yet this threatens to lead to confusion. Messianicity is both the most hopeful and the most nihilistic thought, calling for destruction and restitution alike. Insofar as messianism and epimessianism often make political claims, this duplicity can be seen as a political duplicity. Hope for a revolution that both destroys and creates is its classical form. With this in mind, we hope that this collection of essays revives discussion of an old riddle: why in politics—even and especially in contemporary politics—political hope and political violence seem so intimately and so intransigently conjoined.

The "secular age" is done with religion and theology, and yet both, it goes without saying, continue to exist and to transmute and extend themselves, exerting enormous influence on the public as well as the private spheres. The messianic elements of certain religions, it could be argued, have only gotten stronger. At the same time, messianicities have continued to influence the so-called secular in more and less self-conscious ways—to name just two, in democratic, some would say demagogic, discourse, and in critical cultural theory and philosophy. It seems safe to say, without impugning either for the faults of the other, that in both cases, democracy and philosophy, messianic talk produces hope for restitution while at the same time threatening longstanding institutions. Whether it is hope for a better day or hope for a better theory, a messianic impulse remains, even in attitudes toward "the messianic." The messianic remainder, whose stubbornness the essays in this book address, the residue of messianic thought that taints secular operations as well as critical ones, such as theory and philosophy—the messianic remainder is, to say the least, an equivocal thing.

Transformations of the Messianic

The end of the eighteenth century would be a singular turning point in a nontheological history of messianism. At this point, the more traditional eschatological images and narratives associated with monotheism fall under two strong bans: a political ban and an intellectual ban. If the French Revolution didn't put an end to human history as abruptly and completely as a messiah would have, it nevertheless did discredit certain Christian messianisms as the sole guarantee of history's order and purpose. The revolution shook the idea of the state built upon monarchy and blessed by God, a shaking comparable to the one the Lisbon earthquake had given Christian faith in God's mercy in 1755. Both catastrophes, the natural and the political, called for a reformation of the idea of providence and made hopes in divine salvation appear not so much fruitless as insufficient when faced with disastrous events. Catastrophe, one could argue, had entered history as a noncausal and atelic force, though not necessarily a non-messianic one; catastrophe calls for a transformation of messianic hopes when religious dogmas become destabilized.

Whereas the French Revolution reshaped politics and society, Kant's *Critique of Pure Reason* brought about a revolution in thinking no less radical than the political drama. Reason precedes us, reason poses the most significant, unanswerable questions, reason arrives to transform human experience. One could argue that Kant's purification of metaphysics took the sovereign status away from the messiah and reassigned it to reason.[6] And yet he did not break with messianism as radically as the thinker himself believed. Just as the liberal ideals of the French Revolution banned the theopolitical sovereignty of the monarch and promoted an idea of popular sovereignty, Kant commended the fate of the world into the hands of rational humanity. Kant's hope, in this one way in accord with the hopes of the revolutionaries, was that nondogmatic reason would allow society to give itself its own laws.

After Kant, religion no longer provided the first premises for philosophical arguments about politics, morality, and knowledge. Therefore, when Ludwig Feuerbach reduced religion to an anthropological phenomenon,[7] an expression of a particular stage in the progress of rationality, his view was in line with the ideas that pervaded the intellectual atmosphere of the Left Hegelians and indeed of the time. Karl Marx, with his rejection of idealism and its role in history, went one step further and denied religion any positive value. When Marx reformulated human history as the progress of productive forces, he denied even the theological cliché to which Feuerbach had still been committed, the transcendental subject.[8] Human beings are not subjects of but subjected to history; their fate is decided by the productive forces that develop through them but nonetheless also, until the revolution at least, stand largely outside their control. This idea makes Marx's model of history appear at times more rather than less messianic; class society lives toward an event in the history of productive forces that it cannot foresee. At most moments Marx believed this event to be the proletarian revolution and its driving force the class with nothing to lose—i.e., the one free of possessions. In some respects this class can seem like Marx's messiah, the one that does not act at all in history except to bring it to an end.[9] Antitheological as it was, Marx's model of history nevertheless at times relies on and often seems to prefer an extra-historical, eschatological force.

A necessary—but often unforeseen—result of the apparent secularization of thought is the need to come up with an alternative model of temporality. Mere certainty that the future will succeed the present, since the present succeeded the past, doesn't seem to suffice any longer. Even Kant, who postulated that time was a pure form of intuition and the basis of all experience, still faced the necessity to think through "The End of All Things."[10] In the essay by this name, Kant concludes that the thought of an end of the world follows from our need to rationalize duration; for a world without duration would seem meaningless to us. The thought of an end of the world gives meaning to its whole history. It is not at all surprising, given the destructive and creative poles of messianic thought, that Kant's essay ends with opposing depictions of the world's future. In one the world is a free Christian state; in the other Christianity has become discredited and its dogmas turned upon themselves in an anti-Christian theocracy.

Once eschatological certainty is depleted or shaken, the messianic entrance into eternity asks to be rethought or replaced. Two possibilities readily present themselves: either to understand history as a gradual process of fulfillment without reference to a supernatural order or to posit history as constitutionally lacking a purpose. The latter possibility leads to the nihilistic thought of "bad perpetuation." In it eternity is reduced to an endless succession of events, a perpetuation of the finite as its negative double, infinity, whose affective corollary is pessimism about history and about human history in particular. Schopenhauer, having grasped this abysmal thought to its fullest, concluded that, under these existential conditions, the wisest strategy and the most welcome state of mind was to will nothing.[11] Schopenhauer's insight makes clear why the idea of history devoid of an inner purpose is troubling. If the world is seen as an endless perpetuation of itself and any single life leads to nothing except death, there is not only no hope for any one of us; the world itself is hopeless. It begins to appear as though the idea of continuous, infinite time actually excludes hope; one might even go as far as to say that discontinuity comes to be the only hope for history, and that messianism is in effect a species of discontinuity. The problem that arises with the end of theological messianism takes the form, then, of an odd dilemma: Either we abandon a temporal continuum or we abandon hope. At this point the two seem mutually exclusive.

Epimessianism's Two Poles

The dilemma—a choice, really (put coarsely: between hope and continuous, infinite, progressive time)—can and frequently does resolve itself into a distinction between life and history. Messianism's great power and attraction lies in its promise to resolve the tension between our everyday experience of temporal continuity, what some call daily life or else a lifetime, and our desire for larger-scale discontinuity, the in-breaking messianic redemption of all finite lifetimes. This tension and this desire express themselves as hope, as an everyday hope for a greater eschatological hope.[12] When Marx reformulates history as dialectical progress—that is, as a complex historical continuity that absorbs all life into it—he nevertheless sees the enabling limit to progress in a discontinuation; the suffering of the proletariat will terminate in a violent and redemptive interruption, whereupon daily life and individual lifetimes, otherwise consigned to suffering and ultimately to perdition, will be once and for all vindicated and relieved. There are other ways to maintain a spark of hope, however: One way is to reject the continuum of lifetimes—that is, to deny the self-consistency of history even before the messianic event. In the twentieth century, Walter Benjamin and Jacques Derrida do something like this.[13] Each in a different way confronts the tension between hope and continuity in theories of history, and at the same time refuses to conceal the messianic remainder in his thought.

Derrida and Benjamin seem motivated by a desire to, at one and the same time, redeem hope from Abrahamic religions and save it from reductive and dissimulating secular messianisms. For Benjamin, hope is stuck somewhere between past and present; for Derrida, it is stuck in a future that, when it arrives, postpones itself again, though not without affecting us now. The future is behind Benjamin's angel of history, who with his staring gaze receives the hope flashed to him out of the past, be it only as weakly messianic as a reflection from the deserted Garden of Eden. Derrida, conversely, saves hope by projecting it into a future that never fully comes. Though neither pretends to capture and hold it, both show the straightened conditions under which hope is still possible. Benjamin reverses its direction, whereas Derrida, while postponing it indefinitely, indicates that it nevertheless and in this very postponement still governs our acts here and now. This is the meaning of "to-come" for Derrida: not a deferral to a future that does not yet affect us, but the most urgent and poignant effect on us of what is and never will be fully here.[14] The critical moment in the epimessianic thought of both philosophers is the peculiar shape temporality takes so that hope can be preserved.

In other discourses, hope names the affective, faintly epistemological correlate of a belief that what is hoped for will necessarily arrive, after a proper delay. It will come, but not now. Hope is thus usually at bottom a hope for future history, a form of expectation, a wish for a return of the same. Both Derrida and Benjamin seek to cancel expectation and undermine the continuum idea on which it depends. What then is the new time of hope? For Derrida it looks like indeterminacy. The future is indeterminate, but this also means that the act or attitude of hope becomes indeterminate as well. It is not only indeterminate, for that too is highly determined. It is, instead, "undetermined"—absolutely so. "This absolutely undetermined messianic hope" is the right disposition to receive the emptied-out messiah, facing "an alterity that cannot be anticipated."[15] Hope without a specifiable horizon, hope for no messiah, hope that the messianic figure will be an absolute surprise, a devious hope turned against itself, more like a loving rejection than a hot caress of the desired future, Derrida's hope is meant to insure that a history, in which something can happen—an event, a singularity—and which would not have been predictable from inside its course, has the possibility to occur. This is a task, according to Derrida, for all of us, all the time, as well as for all time.

Only what Benjamin calls a "historical materialist" has "the gift" "to fan the sparks of hope in past things."[16] It is left unambiguous in this sentence precisely where hope resides: It resides in past things, not in the historian. The historian is just the one who increases it. Whatever the historical materialist is or does, and he is and does many different things in the drafts of the theses entitled on one typescript "On the Concept of History," written most likely between 1938 and 1940, one thing is for certain: The historical materialist cannot reawaken an entire past, or even part of it, since there is no entirety of the past, and thus also no parts. First, in direction, hope is reversed. Hope points from the past toward us, and we must train ourselves to become receptive to it. Second, hope disintegrates; it breaks the continuum down into particles that collide. As recipients of hope, we can at most strike up a contiguum, a juxtaposition—and a transient and interested one at that. Historians are potentially messiahs, "weak" in that they do not end history but only disturb its apparent flow.

Both these theories are as destructive of our hopes in messianism as they are redemptive of facets of the messianic thought. The hope residing in past things that can be rekindled, in Benjamin's vision of history, may be "for us," but succumbing to it does not bind us to any larger unity. We are in effect singularized by it, in our momentary, violent, and peculiar collision with something that is no longer, that never was, until we fulfilled its hope for a future. Nothing more can be redeemed by someone than a few shapes that culture has previously taken, and then only the ones that speak to him or to his conception of his time. Benjamin's weak messianic force "saves," if saving means a minor material resistance to total loss. Simultaneously, however, it condemns any collective based on a whole or universally shared cultural memory. An antihistorical force, hope is there only for those rare things and those rare historians who no longer have hope in anything more transcendent. In contrast, Derrida's hope is more grandiose than Benjamin's seems to be, although it is no less destructive. Derridean hope is "for us," for everyone, a universal structure, an absolute, but it is also "hope in" an other who can never be specified, called to, called on, or even, perhaps, when it comes to it, be recognized as the object of this tainted hope. Today, messianic thought outside theology seems to take a stand most strongly between these two poles, which are also the orientation points of our project.

In Part I, "Critiques of Messianic Thought," Lisa Marie Anderson discovers configurations of the messianic in a famous 1930s debate between philosopher Georg Lukács and Ernst Bloch about political aesthetics. Thomas Macho discusses Jacob Taubes's critical stance toward Gershom Scholem's views on Jewish messianism in the post–Second World War era. Nicole Pepperell examines Derrida's *Specters of Marx* and suggests that Marx periodically departs from his own commitment to dialectical history. David Ferris compares three moments of messianic thought outside theology in Derrida, Benjamin, and Giorgio Agamben. And Vivian Liska presents the messianic as a question of the teleological assumptions underlying the epic genre. In her essay, a detailed exposition of Agamben's theory of prose is followed by a critique of his notion of messianism.

In Part II, "Inverted Messianism," Catharine Diehl argues that despite scholarly arguments to the contrary, Kant's essay "The End of All Things" connects teleological and eschatological "ends," providing the groundwork for a theory of historical time and collective action. Joshua Wilner offers a reading of Baudelaire's sonnet "Bohémiens en voyage," a poem that offers itself as both a meditation on and an instantiation of what Benjamin will write of as the "weak messianic power." To do this, Wilner reads the poem in relation to an etching by Callot, where the bohemian revolutionary encounters biblical prophecy. Anna Glazova analyzes a gesture in Paul Celan's poem "Unter die Haut deiner Hände genäht," with which the poet both invokes and distances himself from a Jewish ritualistic practice of circumcision of the word in prayer. And Peter Fenves, in his "'When Christianity Is Finally Over': Images of Messianic Mobility in Heine and Benjamin," suggests that there is a messianic potential in language's impenetrability, be it the language of Neapolitans or church stones.

Finally, in Part III, "Negating the Messiah," Oleg Gelikman proposes that the posthumous text with the mock apocalyptic beginning "Le monde va finir" is the one place in Baudelaire's corpus where a reckoning with the messianic takes place. Paul North analyzes the shift between Franz Kafka's remarks about messiahs in early winter 1917. He shows how, in a principle of messianism, if the meaning of messianicity should be also "to come," messianic thought is at best incoherent. And Werner Hamacher, in his essay entitled "Messianic Not," based loosely on a fragment from Jean-Luc Nancy's *La pensée dérobée*, attempts to think through the notion of the messianic by analyzing it alongside its nondialectical counterpart, the *a*-messianic.

PART I

Critiques of Messianic Thought

Of Theory, Aesthetics, and Politics: Configuring the Messianic in Early Twentieth-Century Europe

Lisa Marie Anderson

How do we account for the recent spate of interest, particularly among the humanities, in the messianic? Surely one explanation is the prevalence of messianic tensions at the intersections of religion and global politics in the contemporary world—tensions that are inspiring a wealth of scholarship. The four-hundred-year debate that Mark Lilla traces in *The Stillborn God*, for example, was set off by a distaste for politically motivated "messianic passions," and ended with the development of "a modern political theology" that aimed to "revive the messianic impulse in Western life."[1] Messianism takes its place here as the alpha and the omega of modernity's debate about religion and politics, an ancient puzzle that even secular culture struggles—often unsuccessfully, it would seem—to leave behind.

This essay interrogates a very limited cross-section of modern preoccupation with messianism, a historical period in which a remarkable concentration of messianic desire persisted even alongside a strong cultural resistance to it. I hope to demonstrate that the early twentieth-century art, literature, and philosophy of German-speaking Europe offer a unique perspective from which to consider the very notion of redemption, or the arrival of a new age. The decades on which I will focus—the 1910s, 1920s, and 1930s—were, as we now know, caught between a turn-of-the-century taste for sweeping renewal (Zionist or otherwise) and the terror of a regime whose deployment of millenarian ideology compelled a radical caesura in philosophical engagement with religion and politics. As it happened, this interstice was also defined in large measure by a global conflict of newly violent and destructive proportions, feeding a fervor to break constitutively with the past and forge a redemptive future out of the apocalyptic flames of war. These and other factors converged to create a Central Europe struggling with its own desire for the renewal and, in fact, the salvation of humankind, for the interruption of history and the advent of a new order. As a result, diverse ways of thinking the messianic came into contact with each other, all of them shaped by the Jewish and Christian traditions from which they drew, as well as by contemporary forces of pacifism, Marxism, and fascism. The picture of messianism that emerges from this era is thus both multifaceted and contentious enough to be especially relevant to the questions we ask of the messianic today— namely, what it is, how it functions, and how it should or should not be employed.

Messianic Desire in the Age of German Expressionism

The Expressionist movement in art and literature (roughly 1905 to 1925 in German-speaking Europe) is characterized by its exceptionally overt and ecstatic articulations of messianic desire, by its unrelenting calls for the renewal and redemption of humankind. Many of the movement's adherents placed their faith specifically in new forms of human expression, and thus of relation to the divine, as a means to salvation. In his essay "Concerning the Spiritual in Art" (1910), Wassily Kandinsky wrote of an emerging movement that was not only artistic but also spiritual, and that would create "the new intellectual realm" and would "arrive in many despairing hearts now wrapped in the darkness of night as a sounding of redemption," "a hand that points the way and offers relief."[2] Ernst Bloch used similar imagery when writing in the same era about music, claiming that "the great work of art is a reflection, a star of anticipation and a song of consolation on the way home through the darkness."[3] I will have more to say below about this conception of the power of art, particularly as articulated by Bloch. But first it is important to note that the reception of Expressionist art exhibited an equally ecstatic mood. Critics were prompted to characterize the movement as "not so much the business of art . . . as a spiritual event that has reached into . . . the cosmos, altering the world and humanity itself."[4]

A number of literary Expressionists, too, believed that their creations would facilitate a new and redemptive reality in society and for humanity. The messianic drive behind Expressionist poetry, for example, is self-evident in the title of the 1919 anthology *Menschheitsdämmerung*—a title that is at once eschatological (the end for humanity; its twilight) and millenarian (the advent of a new humanity; its dawning). The twenty-three poets represented in *Menschheitsdämmerung* evince what the anthologist Kurt Pinthus would unapologetically call the "messianic leitmotif of Expressionism," a "fanatical belief in a new beginning in the arts, in the life of the individual and in the human community."[5]

In one of the volume's best illustrations of this fanaticism, Johannes R. Becher concludes his poem "Decay," which has catalogued images of burials and decomposing bodies, with an extended image of expectant hope: "One day I will stand on the path,/Lost in my gaze upon a great city./Golden winds wafting around me./Light falls faintly through the fleeing clouds./Rapturous figures, wrapped in white . . . /My hands stir/Toward heaven, filled with gold,/Opening itself like miraculous doors." But this enthusiastic expectancy is also an impatient and apocalyptic one: "When will you appear, eternal day?/Or must we wait?/When will you resound, clangorous horn,/You arduous cry of the tides?/From thicket, moor, grave and thorns/Calling the slumberers forth?" (40–42). Moreover, it is the role of the poet to fulfill this messianic longing by awakening the slumberers; this is indicated in another poem, "Preparation," in which Becher writes that the poet "blows the tubas and beats the shrill drum," "reawakens the people with his hacked up sentences" (a reference to one of the stylistic idiosyncrasies of Expressionist literature) and "sketches" the "new world/like this: blotting out the old, the mystical, the world of anguish. . . . Paradise begins" (213).[6]

The playwrights of Expressionism embraced a similar confidence that their own innovations would interrupt the flow of history and bring about a radically different future. They posited the Expressionist stage as "the tribune from which the poets will proclaim a new confraternity of humanity."[7] Their striving toward this goal is borne out by the number of Expressionist dramas characterized either as station plays, proclamation plays, conversion plays, martyr plays, or some combination of the above. One of the most emblematic of such dramas, Ernst Toller's *The Transformation* (1917), is animated by its hero's "radiant visions" of "youth strid[ing] ahead, eternally giving birth to [it]self,/eternally destroying the old,/creat[ing] life full of blazing spirit."[8] Birth and rebirth imagery is an important tool in the Expressionist mission to refashion the world, one whose innumerable applications in the literature of the age require relatively little explication, given the centrality of rebirth in the culturally familiar Pauline configuration of salvation. Equally crucial, though, is the temporal dialectic of this Expressionist refashioning, which is most conspicuous in this passage. The destruction of the old order is an eternal process, requisite for the equally eternal process of rebirth, for which humankind is responsible to itself. And yet the process remains a vision prefigured in the literary imagination, until a fundamental break in history can catalyze it in actuality.

More strongly even than the poet Becher, the Expressionist playwrights claimed that it was their literary visions that would lead others to Paradise. Georg Kaiser, one of the most widely performed Expressionist dramatists, wrote of the "vision" that "takes unto itself heaven and earth," the vision "of the renewal of humankind."[9] It was the fervent belief in this renewal which breathed life into Expressionism, "the greatest age in art," Kaiser wrote, and which constituted "the construction of the cathedral whose foundations are deep within the earthly kingdom, but whose spire thrusts into heaven" (4:571–72).

This kind of absolute faith in the efficacy of a new aesthetic movement as a vehicle for radical change was rejected by a particular group of writers during the Expressionist period, who argued instead for a more political approach to societal redemption. Calling themselves the Activists and following the leadership primarily of the pacifist journalist Kurt Hiller, they denounced those who would reduce salvation to "a matter of lyrical dreams,"[10] since the artist's "intellectual activity [was] in and of itself too little."[11] They insisted instead on pacifist, socialist, or communist activism as the most effective means toward their admittedly no less chiliastic ends. The Activist Rudolf Leonhard wrote that "while earlier Chiliasts rejected action for the sake of forbearance, the Activist has rejected both forbearance and suffering for the sake of required action."[12] The projected results of this action were cast in explicitly messianic terms and included the "construction of a new world," the "realization of prophecy," and the restoration of Paradise.[13]

While the messianic desire coursing through these decades—whether more aesthetically or more politically conceived—was far-reaching, it also met with strong resistance. The prose of Thomas Mann and Robert Musil, for example, reminds us that the longing for redemption and renewal via a messiah-figure (whether personal or notional) was already a controversial sort of enthusiasm. So do other luminaries of the age. Sigmund Freud wrote in 1921 that the "socialistic tie" was replacing "the religious one," with "the same intolerance towards outsiders as in the age of the Wars of

Religion."[14] And Max Weber, in his celebrated 1918 lecture "Science as a Vocation," warned of a kind of ersatz devotion corrupting the German academy: "Some of our young people are making the mistake of seeking something else in the professor, . . . —a *leader* and not a *teacher.*" If no "prophet or savior" is to be found, Weber said, "or if his proclamations are no longer believed, then he will certainly not be willed into the world by the attempts of thousands of professors . . . to relieve him of his role in their lecture halls."[15]

The Dialectics of Messianism: Bloch, Lukács, and the Expressionism Debate

By the time Weber delivered those cautionary remarks, he had spent the prewar and war years in Heidelberg as the leader of an intellectual circle that met regularly at his home and included such luminaries as Georg Simmel and Ernst Troeltsch. Also among this circle during the prewar years were Ernst Bloch and Georg Lukács, young philosophers attracting increasing attention, and also intimate friends. Two decades later, they would lead a crucial debate about the heritage of Expressionism: about its aesthetic legacy and its relationship to National Socialism. Before engaging that particular debate, I would like to establish some of the relationships between the young Bloch, the young Lukács, Expressionism, and messianism.

Theodor W. Adorno has called Blochian philosophy, with its focus on the utopian and the messianic, "that of Expressionism itself."[16] While Bloch remained active until his death in 1977, it was during his involvement in the Weber circle that his early thought took shape, particularly in his grand volume (written in typically Expressionist style) *The Spirit of Utopia* (1918). Philosophy, Bloch wrote there, contains an a priori "synthetically expanding messianism" and thus bears the responsibility to create "the kingdom of the second truth," "to seek, to accelerate, to complete . . . the traces . . . of utopia."[17] These traces are found not in philosophy itself but in the experience of great art as foretaste of the kingdom to come. Among the arts, music contains a particularly messianic force, on the basis of its "power of somnambulic revelation of the *innermost being of the world*" (195), its capacity to "bring us into the warm, deep, gothic chamber of interiority, which alone still shines in the midst of the muddy darkness," and which "will be, on the last morning, nothing other than the kingdom of heaven revealed" (208). This, then, is the link Adorno identifies between Bloch and his Expressionist contemporaries: a shared desire "to break through the encrusted surface of life," to "protest . . . against the reification of the world" in the name of a new and eventually realizable utopian truth—and to do so in stubbornly aesthetic terms.[18]

Lukács, meanwhile, was working out his pre-Marxist aesthetic theory, primarily in 1916's *The Theory of the Novel*. The centrality of the messianic in his thinking at the time is apparent in the preparatory work for that volume, especially in the "Notes on Dostoevsky" (1914–15), which are concerned with Jewish messianism, with chiliasm and its relationship to revolution, and with the problem of redemption itself.[19] In a lecture delivered soon afterward, Lukács challenged his audience to realize the Kingdom of God on earth.[20] But it was in "Bolshevism as a Moral Problem" (1918) that Lukács's most significant formulation emerged. This brief essay used explicitly messianic language to set the scene of a Europe gripped by revolution and to underscore the "moment of decision that has now arrived." In this moment, socialism represented nothing less than "the *ethical objective* of a coming world order," such that the proletariat was taking its place as "the agent of the social salvation of mankind, the messianic class of world history." It was their activity, Lukács said, that would now bridge the "dualistic separation of the soulless empirical reality and the human—that is, the utopian, the ethical—objective."[21]

Both Bloch and Lukács left Heidelberg during the war, and a stark divergence developed in their respective aesthetic theories during the postwar years, reaching its crest in their debate about Expressionism, carried out in a series of essays in the 1930s. In 1934, Lukács published "Expressionism: Its Significance and Decline," examining "the historical destiny of expressionism" in order "to disclose the social basis of the movement and the premises of the world outlook that derive from" it.[22] Naturally, the Marxist orientation Lukács had been developing since his Heidelberg days informed this enterprise to the fullest. It was partly on the basis of Lenin's writings that Lukács lamented the lack of any dialectic in the foundations of Expressionism (107). The intellectuals of that age may have "honestly attempted, at least subjectively, either a critique of German political and social conditions, or even a critique of the capitalist system"; but this critique remained "unclear, confused, and unable to offer a dialectical solution to the divorce between objective basis and subjective intention, simply patching this up eclectically" (82). Thus Lukács perceived in Expressionist literature, as well as in Hiller's Activism, a "reactionary and utopian sham radicalism," a kind of "preaching" that was in fact "counter-revolutionary" (100). Because their methods had been based in "isolation, tearing apart, the destruction of all connections" (102), the Expressionist generation was guilty of "the deliberate ignoring of the determinations whose richness, linkage, entwining, interaction, sub- and superordination, in a dynamic system, are what form the foundation of all portrayal or reality" (107). As Lukács's views gained acceptance, others too began to question whether the Expressionists' dialectic had been dialectical enough, or whether their complete and uncompromising rejection of the old had compromised their vision of the radically new.

This criticism from Lukács and his disciples brought Bloch into the fray as a defender of the Expressionist heritage. In his essay "Discussing Expressionism" (1938), Bloch engaged what he saw as Lukács's rejection of "any attempt on the part of artists to shatter any image of the world," of the Expressionists' striving "to exploit the *real* fissures in surface inter-relations and to discover the new in their crevices." Bloch asked instead whether there might not be "dialectical links between growth and decay," whether the "confusion, immaturity and incomprehensibility" with which Expressionism had been charged might not be "part of the transition from the old world to the new? Or at least be part of the struggle leading to that transition?"[23] Bloch even lamented the lack of a dialectic in Lukács's own "black-and-white approach," in which "almost all forms of opposition to the ruling class which are not communist from the outset are lumped together with the ruling class itself" (21).

In his reply, "Realism in the Balance" (1938), Lukács continued to deny that there had been any dialectical or transitional impulse in Expressionism. He could not endorse an ethos that saw "revolutions only as ruptures and catastrophes that destroy all that is past" and thus discounted "the living dialectical unity of continuity and discontinuity, of evolution and revolution."[24] Seeing in the avant-garde movement a foil for the realist writers whose politically productive work he vastly preferred, Lukács attacked Expressionism finally on grounds that lie at the heart of its messianic ambition: "Modernism has not, nor has it ever had, anything to do with the creation of 'prophetic figures' or with the genuine anticipation of future developments" (48–49). The Expressionists remained for Lukács mere "ideologues" with "highflown pretensions to leadership" and "a pseudo-profundity" (51), since "even the most passionate determination, the most intense sense of conviction that one has revolutionized art and created something 'radically new,' will not suffice to turn a writer into someone who can truly anticipate future trends, if determination and conviction are his sole qualifications" (49).

The reading of Expressionist art and literature put forth in the first section of this essay—as an ecstatic articulation of a sweeping desire for renewal and redemption—would not have been a foreign one to Bloch or to Lukács, particularly given the concern for the messianic that both show in their own writings from that period. Direct references to messianism abound there, and yet not one appears within the confines of the Expressionism Debate. Nonetheless, Bloch and Lukács would seem to be arguing here about the proper dialectic for messianic thinking: Lukács's condemnation of the Expressionists' particular apocalypticism (their indiscriminate destructiveness and refusal of any connection to the past) stems from his conviction that a redemptive future depends on "continuity" and "evolution"; Bloch defends what he prefers to call the Expressionists' "shattering of images" or "exploiting of fissures," methods that contribute to a thoroughly dialectical process of transition from the present world to a better one. Their debate, then, is as much about the dialectics of messianism as a construct as it is about Expressionism or any other aesthetic program.

Derrida, Benjamin, and the Incalculability of the Messianic

Debates about messianism are complicated further still by the inclusion of models of the messianic that rest on a far less dialectical structure. Such models exist and flourish in our time, and were present also during the Expressionist age, though in more nascent form. They have always depended principally on a conception of the messianic as something that is, above all, inherently aporetic. Among the wealth of contemporary theory concerned with messianism, the adoption of such a supposition is evidenced most centrally and sustainedly in the work of Jacques Derrida, for whom the messianic is a category or mode of being based on *"the opening to the future or to the coming of the other as the advent of justice."*[25] Recalling the careers of Bloch and Lukács, one can be sure that this, at least, was a concern held in common. And when Derrida goes on to ground the messianic in *"possibilities that both open and can always interrupt history,"* he would seem to be coming down on the side of the Expressionists' radicalism, against Lukács's more evolutionary view of human history. But Derrida also stresses that what he is treating here is *"messianicity without messianism,"* an opening to the future *"without horizon or expectation and without prophetic prefiguration"* (17). In a later essay, Derrida calls this messianicity "a universal structure of experience . . . which cannot be reduced to religious messianism of any stripe" and which "refers, in every here-now, . . . to the most irreducibly heterogeneous otherness."[26] Here too Derrida emphasizes "a waiting without expectation," an "exposure without horizon," "a way of thinking the event 'before' or independently of all ontology" (249). While this may seem more in line with Lukács's insistence that prophesying even a redemptive future is neither possible nor productive and that it leaves one mired in mere ideology, by Derrida's lights, Lukács too has already done just that, since his progressive model of human history as evolution already posits a particular, predetermined futurity, even if its incipience is not a revolutionary fissure. For Derrida, by contrast, the messianic is not assimilable to any human expectation: *"The coming of the other can only emerge as a singular event when no anticipation sees it coming, . . . interrupting or tearing history itself apart."*[27] Thus, Derrida would reject both Lukács's model and that of Bloch and the Expressionists, positing instead a messianic futurity with an aporetic rather than dialectical relationship to the present.

Of course I have leapt ahead by a number of decades in bringing Derrida to bear on 1930s debates about early twentieth-century configurations of messianism. Yet that period, too, provided its own model for an understanding of messianism that tends more toward the aporetic—in the writings of Walter Benjamin. A contemporary of Bloch, Lukács, and the Expressionists, Benjamin kept an intractable paradox at the center of the critical project he built on the messianic destinies of both language and history.[28]

On one side of this paradox is the redemption whose promise is contained in language itself. Mankind first received language, Benjamin writes, when "in man God freely released the language which had served *him* as the medium of creation." Thus the very essence of humanity is "the language in which creation took place."[29] But with the Fall comes the loss of the unity that had been bestowed in divine language. Benjamin writes that "the Fall is the birth of the *human word*" (2:152), and from then on, "the infinity of all human language remains of an always limited and analytical nature in comparison with the absolute, unlimited and creative infinity of the divine word" (2:149). But it is the task of language to work toward the restoration of this lost unity between God and man. As they approach a utopian unfolding of God's word, the diverse languages of nature and of humans (for Benjamin, language is never limited to humans) also approach the original divine language, and thus ultimate redemption (2:157).

On the other side of the paradox, there is for Benjamin always an irreducible incalculability in play even as human languages "grow to the messianic end of their history," since the task of reaching that end "seems never soluble," and since the "realm of the reconciliation and fulfillment of languages" is simultaneously "predestined" and "withheld" (4:14–15). This may be the intractable problem at the heart of the messianic, this paradox between predestination and withholding—or, to put it in more Derridean terms, the aporia of a promise that has been made but that is also held in suspension. The incalculability of the messianic, then, is already in Benjamin precisely a divine incalculability, as it is God who suspends or at least withholds the fulfillment of a promise that humanity has as yet been unable to realize of its own volition. The promise having been extended, however, humanity will continue to try.

To return again to the Expressionists: It is certainly a fair argument that they failed to grasp just this incalculability that informs Benjamin's thought. To quote Richard Wolin, works of art can be for Benjamin *"pre-figurements* of reconciled life," or can at least "yield affinities with a state of redeemed life," but "they nonetheless stop short of providing an ontological guarantee of this possibility."[30] Many Expressionists, by contrast, seem to have persisted in the naïve belief that their works of art could be enough of a gesture toward redemption, that the mere words they wrote could inspire a revolutionary change in the course of history. But if this naivete missed the kind of aporia already inherent in Benjamin's understanding of messianism, it also depended absolutely on the foundational tenet of that understanding—namely, that language is something with a redemptory power gravely lost and now to be reclaimed.

The Expressionists were willing to give credence to such a salvific possibility in language—which is to say in literature and the arts as a form of communication—partly because they also believed they were experiencing an era of such extreme degeneration and corruption that the only viable solution was a radical break in the historical continuum. While this may represent a simplification of his theories of time and history, it too coincides in many respects with Benjamin, according to whom a messianic rupture is always at least conceivably immanent, as history unfolds not in the "homogenous and empty time" implied by capitalist and historicist notions of progress, but rather in "now-time." Now-time, by contrast, subsumes, "as a model of messianic time, and in a tremendous abbreviation, the history of all mankind," such that it is "shot through with splinters of messianic time."[31]

Here too, though, the incalculability of the messianic, at least from a human perspective, cannot be ignored. Benjamin writes: "Only the Messiah himself completes all history, in that he is the first and only one who redeems, completes, creates its relationship to the messianic itself" (2:203). Thus history does not complete its own relationship to its terminus, and human attempts to "force the end," while perhaps a necessary part of striving toward redemption, will always run headlong into the unmitigated "secrecy" of the "index" that directs us toward redemption—hence the "weak-

ness" of the "messianic power" in "every generation" (1:693–94). This is
what makes the messianic in Benjamin, as Wolin argues, very much like an
Idea in the Kantian sense, "an absolute end in itself unobtainable, which
nevertheless serves as a binding guide for ethical conduct"—or, as Michael P. Steinberg puts it, a "heuristic necessit[y] but forbidden realit[y]."[32]

Two clarifying points must be made here. First, during the later stage of
Benjamin's career, during which he was influenced at least as much by historical materialism as by the theological concern for messianism that had
characterized his early work, he chose to call his method of criticism "dialectic at a standstill."[33] Thus it is clear that Benjamin was by no means aiming away from *all* dialectic in thinking the messianic. Still, a relationship
can be traced here between the moment at which dialectic comes to a halt
(temporary or not) and the emergence of a more aporetic understanding
of a claim on the messianic promise. This returns us to Derrida and brings
me to my second clarification. While Derrida writes that Benjamin's idea
of a "*weak* messianic power" is "consonant . . . , despite many differences
and keeping relative proportions in mind," with his own thinking about the
"messianic without messianism,"[34] he resists strongly the absolute assimilation made by some commentators between Benjamin's "weak" and his own
"without,"[35] an assimilation that seems to disregard his caveat about differences and proportions and to enable the charge that his messianicity is essentially utopianism.[36] Yet even while bearing in mind Derrida's insistence
that a resemblance between *a* and *b* does not allow for a reduction of *a* to
b,[37] one can still discern at the heart of the consonance between Benjamin
and Derrida an inherently aporetic framework for thinking the messianic.
Both refuse, throughout their careers, to conjure away by any means the
limits of human calculation regarding the coming of something (or someone) radically and in fact structurally heterogeneous to any current order.

Dialectic or Aporia? The Messianism of Expressionism and the Rise of Fascism

In order to draw a fuller contrast between the dialectical and aporetic
models of messianism I have traced, I would like to conclude by returning
to the Expressionism Debate, and to highlight an aspect of it that has not
yet been in focus here—namely, the claim that Expressionism contributed
directly to the rise of fascism in Germany. As I have argued, it was in large
measure the dialectical temporality of the messianic that facilitated Expressionism's self-transformation from a band of artists rebelling against
earlier conventions into a movement defined by its shattering of those

conventions in the name of the redemptive and eternal future that might arrive at any moment. And as I have further argued, a differently dialectical view like that of Lukács animated a potent critique of a messianic ideology that seemed to destroy recklessly any possible heritage from the past.

As the 1930s unfolded, Lukács's critique supported the argument that the vacuous rhetoric of modernist irrationalism was essentially assimilable with—even an enabler of—fascism. Lukács called Expressionism "undoubtedly only one of the many tendencies in bourgeois ideology that [would] grow later into fascism," "a subordinate element" "in the fascist 'synthesis'" but an element of it nonetheless. While fascist ideology was not identical to Expressionism's "pseudo-critical, abstractly distorting and mythologizing variety of imperialist sham opposition," "anyone who gives the devil of imperialist parasitism even his little finger" eventually gives " his whole hand."[38] This line of argumentation supported the claim that Expressionism amounted to the logical forerunner of fascism. (It did not help matters that a number of Expressionist writers, including Gottfried Benn, Arnold Bronnen, Reinhard Goering, and Hanns Johst, became active in Nazi politics and ideology.) Unquestionably, Expressionism's messianic fervor had abutted the ascent of a radical millenarian ideology; many now identified a causal relationship alongside the chronological one.

A balanced assessment of the relationship between Expressionism and fascism in Germany must acknowledge at least one crucial difference: The former "related the millennium to all mankind," while the latter "confined [it] to their own nation."[39] The humanism and universality of Expressionism—its dream of the whole human community living in a redeemed state—should not be underappreciated, particularly in contrast with Nazism.

And yet, if one follows Benjamin's definition of fascism as "the aestheticization of politics," one observes a process by which, in Steinberg's paraphrase, the "aesthetic gains cultural power as the instrument that inherits from religion the task of the reenchantment of the world."[40] The parallel between this structure and the aggrandized role of art in the Expressionist vision is too striking to be ignored or explained easily away. Moreover, Benjamin has already provided a still clearer lens through which to examine the link between Expressionism and fascism: In their respective co-optations of messianic and millenarian expectation from Jewish and Christian models, both sustain an exclusive focus on human agency, taking no real account of the incalculability—the secrecy, even—that is absolutely central to those models. That is, while the temporal structure of messianism in both religious traditions most certainly yields a dialectical construct (restoration and renewal, the eschaton and the new age), the aporetic is never absent either. Those who strive—however patiently or impatiently—toward a particular fulfillment of the messianic promise, even in the face of a persistently reticent divinity, can attest to this.

CHAPTER 2

On the Price of Messianism: The Intellectual Rift between Gershom Scholem and Jacob Taubes

Thomas Macho

Preliminary Biographical Remarks

The history of the relationship between Gershom Scholem and Jacob Taubes can be structured into several stages: However, it is essentially the story of a personal and intellectual rift. The rift occurred after Taubes spent several semesters as Scholem's pupil, and even confidante, in Jerusalem in the early 1950s. Scholem alludes to the cause of the breach in one of his letters,[1] published in the compendium of his correspondence, even though the exchange of letters preceding it and his former pupil's replies or later written attempts at contact (with the exception of a single, much-abridged exception in the recently published third volume of letters) have not been documented.[2] The written correspondence of Scholem and Taubes thus remains largely unpublished. All the more surprising, then, is editor Thomas Sparr's strangely derogatory comment in the introduction to the second volume of letters: "We feel justified in our decision to print Gerschom Scholem's 1952 letter to Jacob Taubes. Its incisiveness goes beyond the personal conflict to shed light on Jacob Taubes, whose personality, even more than his oeuvre, became very influential in the 1960s."[3] This comment requires correcting on at least three points: The letter in question is from 1951; it sheds light on Scholem as well as on Taubes; and one cannot speak of his being merely "influential in the 1960s"—that is, not only after the colloquia on religious theory and political theology, but also after the publication of a new edition of his dissertation as *Occidental Eschatology* (1991), after the Heidelberg *Lectures on St. Paul* (1993) and the collected essays on the history of religion and spirituality (1996), and after the publication of the Italian translations the *Scritti su Carl Schmitt* (1996, by Quodlibet) and the *Escatologia occidentale* (1997, by Garzanti). Evidently, Taubes's (notoriously slender) oeuvre has reentered the discourse, and indeed in contexts that were not stamped by his "personality" as teacher and orator.

I will speculate here just as little on the legitimacy of the rift that Scholem evinces in his letter of October 7, 1951, as on the numerous critical comments that he formulates about Taubes in letters to other interlocutors (from Leo Strauss to George Lichtheim). Evidently, this is about an indiscretion that Scholem could not forgive, since he had committed it once himself. Taubes, at any rate, left Jerusalem, only to return after a quarter of a century for a talk on the occasion of the Jewish World Congress of 1979. The congress organizers first rejected the proposed talk (only to accept it with minor title changes), said to be perhaps the most "radical critique that Gerschom Scholem has encountered during his lifetime."[4] The former pupil had been traveling from Berlin, where he was professor of Judaism, sociology of religion, and hermeneutics at the Freie Universität from 1966 until his death on March 21, 1987. Taubes had long ago recast the personal breach as an intellectual conflict and had wanted to carry it out publicly already two years before the World Congress; however, his attempt to publish a critical Festschrift on the occasion of Scholem's eightieth birthday— *contrary to* and *with* the celebrant—failed entirely. His letter of over twenty pages dated March 16, 1977, in which he had intended to convey a desire for conflict as well as for reconciliation, received a brief and withering response: "What has irreparably separated us for twenty-five years hardly belongs to the 'vanity of academic life.' Rather, it belongs to the existential decisions of my life (not academic but rather *moral* life, if I may be permitted to use the word this once), along with the experiences I have had in the course of long years of effort to understand Jewish people and phenomena. I won't go into the contents of your letter. It is a free country, and you can write as many critiques of my propositions, essays, or books as you please. But I wish to state unequivocally that I will not participate in any book that deals with me critically, approvingly or politely, in which you, Mr. Taubes, act as an editor or publisher. You made your decisions over twenty-five years ago, and I made mine. I have no intentions of changing these. 'Look at each where he stands / and where he stands, that he does not fall.'" [5]

Those who understand the severity of this letter must begin to doubt the legitimacy of reconstructing an intellectual break with such strong bio-graphical connotations, especially on the occasion of Scholem's hundredth birthday. But pious silence—and this constitutes my first apology—does not honor living or deceased combatants but at best a questionable cult interest. Silence serves a desire for ceremony, one that is rarely felt by the individuals concerned, at the occasion of birthdays and anniversaries. In his letter thanking Theodor W. Adorno for an article on the occasion of Scholem's seventieth birthday, published on December 2, 1967, in the *Neue Zürcher Zeitung*, Scholem was particularly pleased that Adorno praised his "lack of ceremony": It is "a quality that means a lot to me," and he signed the letter "the untrustworthy birthday child." [6]

Shrouding rifts and conflicts in silence (irrespective of the considerations) does honor not to living or deceased combatants but instead to their audience, and this cannot be justified as soon as it involves discussions of an intellectual and a scientist. Argument—and this is to serve as a second justification for the audacious remembrance of a conflict's anniversary—is a basic intellectual discipline; someone lacking in serious opponents is unlikely to have defended a finely delineated position. The value and intellectual potential of an idea takes shape by being submitted to a process of criticism; it is the sharpness of differentiation and dissociation that characterizes every serious effort of reception that is not mere praise. It is no secret that Scholem—no less than Taubes himself—was a master of such polemical work, as evinced by numerous letters. It is no secret that the exceptionally crude letters that Scholem addressed to Georg Lichtheim (dated January 28 and October 21, 1968) contain a series of bitter comments on Taubes's "moral" character and writings. [7] I will not give my view of these reproaches and comments (and their largely unknown contexts) but shall speak, as aforementioned, exclusively about the guise of the *intellectual* irreconcilability between Scholem and Taubes; in so doing, I will attempt to extract the breach from its biographical contingency and to represent it as the figure of the *memory* of unresolved (and possibly irresolvable) problems.

"Internal" and "External" Redemption

On the very first page of his seminal text *The Messianic Idea in Judaism and Other Essays on Jewish Spirituality* (1959), Scholem states a quintessential distinction between the Judaic and the Christian concepts of redemption.

Although this distinction is well known, I will allow myself to quote it nonetheless:

> Judaism, in all of its forms and manifestations, has always maintained a concept of redemption as an event that takes place publicly, on the stage of history and with the community. It is an occurrence that takes place in the visible world and cannot be conceived apart from such a visible appearance. In contrast, Christianity conceives of redemption as an event in the spiritual and unseen realm, an event which is reflected in the soul, in the private world of each individual, and which effects an inner transformation that need not correspond to anything outside.[8] The line of demarcation between the two notions of redemption is drawn by means of numerous concepts that virtually form a series of polar opposites. The series of *external redemption* is characterized by the ideas of the public, history, society, the world, and visibility; the series of *internal redemption*, by the ideas of privacy, the soul, individuality, the spiritual, and the invisible. The apocalyptic transformation of the world and of life itself (in the literal sense of *apokalypsis* as revelation and disclosure) stands in contrast with *concealed* transformation, which can be sensed or comprehended neither in the world nor in the body of the redeemed.

Helmut Gollwitzer protested against the bluntness of this distinction in a review of Jonachan Bloch's book *The Indecent People* (1964),[9] remarking that, for the Christian, the distinction between these concepts of redemption indeed has the value of disturbing the complacency in which he had held his tradition to be the naturally superior one, in that he perceives that exactly what was customarily held to be the glory of Christianity and the stain of Judaism appears exactly the other way around to the Jew. If, however, a Christian is expected not only to recognize himself in the ascribed image but also to elevate it to his program, then his commitment to the scriptures will ensure that he can speedily divest himself of this straitjacket he has been forced to don. It is precisely for this reason that he must prompt his Jewish partner to reject such clichés, which are only approximations, even in a historical sense, and mostly represent only distorting simplifications, and shove them out via a process of dialogue."[10] Gollwitzer's critique rests on shaky ground, however, for while it suggests a change in perspective, it also—in a strange exaggeration of the paradigm shift that factually reverses a centuries-long history of pogroms and theological disputes—seems to lament the "straitjackets," clichés, and simplifications to which Christians rather than Jews have been subjected (he leaves open by whom). It is obvious that, in the face of such an "exhortation" for a Judeo-Christian "partnership," Scholem was "shoved" beyond "dialogue" into polemic. Revised extracts of his (now also published) answer to Gollwitzer were printed as "From a Protestant Theologian's Letter," or "supplementary remarks" to the new edition of the volume accompanying the Eranos lectures, "On some basic concepts of Judaism" (1970).[11]

In the lecture for the abovementioned 1979 Jewish World Congress, Taubes opted for a different line of criticism, though it was published only after Scholem's death in 1982. His core objection did not relate to Scholem's attempt to contrast Judaism with Christianity but focused much more on the assumptions and consequences of this strict differentiation "declaimed with great authority": that is, it presumes an ahistorical view of the intellectual history of messianism, and even of Judaism itself. Taubes claimed that Scholem's method enabled "no insight into the inner dynamics of the messianic idea when actualized in a concrete historical setting." It appeared to him to be "a hangover from the classic Jewish–Christian controversy of the Middle Ages," "obfuscating the concrete dynamics of the messianic idea itself." Indeed one must consider the dialectic in the messianic experience of a group at the moment when prophecy of redemption fails. The "world" does not thereby fall into ruin, but the hope for redemption crumbles. If, however, the messianic community does not falter thanks to its inner conviction, then the messianic experience must turn inward; redemption is bound to be conceived as an event that takes place in the spiritual realm, reflected in the human soul. Interiorization is not a dividing line between "Judaism" and "Christianity," but instead signifies a crisis within Jewish eschatology itself—i.e., Pauline Christianity as well as in the Sabbatian movement of the seventeenth century. How else can redemption be defined after the Messiah has failed to redeem the external world except through a displacement into interiority?[12]

The argument applies to the entire series of Scholem's "polar opposites." Taubes does not restrict his criticism to the "static contrast" of external and internal but includes the confrontation of the visible and the invisible, world and soul, history and spirituality, community and individuality. He reminds us that the reality of the external world, according to its Jewish conception, can in no way be derived from nature and its legality, but instead solely from the Torah, the divine law. This means, moreover, that an apocalyptic anticosmism must consistently be articulated as antinomianism. Taubes underscores the historic impact and the community-forming influence of this Pauline "internalization," which extended to coaxing the "evil spirit" of Hitler to want to exterminate conscience itself as a "Jewish invention."[13] In a word: The messianic crisis is—as Taubes states—"an inner Jewish event."[14] In opposition to both Scholem and Gollwitzer, then, Taubes not only associated "interiority" with "Jewish," but by extension cast Christianity—better put: its Pauline and the Marcionite interpretations—as a symptomatic expression of a question central to Judaic messianism. On the occasion of his return to the Holy City, Taubes's proposed lecture, following twenty-five years of his banishment "from Jerusalem to Berlin," was indeed highly provocative. It culminated in the thesis according to which "by removing the roadblock of interiorization that Scholem has erected to preserve in dogmatic fashion an 'essential' difference between the '-isms'—Judaism and Christianity—a more coherent reading of the inner logic of the messianic idea becomes possible. Internalization, or opening the inward realm, belongs essentially to the career of that 'idea.'"[15] Theopolitical disappointments such as the destruction of Jerusalem after the Romano–Jewish war or the defeat of the Bar-Kochba uprising are followed historically by a retreat to the "inner worlds" of redemption. But, argues Taubes, this retreat into ahistorical zones cannot be separated from their historical preconditions. In other words, the Apostle Paul, and even Marcion himself (whom Taubes occasionally describes as a Jewish anti-Jewish intellectual) must be perceived as figures of an unresolved question of Judaism.

In line with a statement by Leo Festinger, Taubes put forward a dialectical schema of the "career" of messianic ideas: *When prophecy fails*, the possibilities of apocalypticism increase, and when apocalypticism fails, the possibilities for interiorization and Gnosis increase.[16] In a conversation, Christoph Schulte once suggested that the intellectual history of the past half century be analyzed in the light of this model: a first phase of "prophecy" (namely, the Adventism of "New Man" and the transition to a peaceful, socialist society, effected by the student movements of the late 1960s and early 1970s) is followed by a phase of "apocalypticism" (in the guise of the prognosis of nuclear Armageddon in the late 1970s and early 1980s), and finally comes a phase of Gnostic "internalization" (in effect since the early 1990s). Admittedly, the status of this schema remains unclear. Should the messianic process be defined as an "anthropological constant" of the history of religion or as simply a series of contingent events, revealed only in historicist research? In his lecture at the Jewish World Congress, Taubes sketched the alternative as an "inescapable" dilemma. "Either messianism is nonsense, and dangerous nonsense at that, but the historical study of messianism is a scientific pursuit, and in the case of Scholem itself scientific research at its best; or messianism, and not only the historic research of the 'messianic idea' is meaningful, inasmuch as it discloses a significant facet of human experience."[17]

The dilemma was projected onto Scholem: anthropology of religion or philosophy of history. It is impossible to characterize the one horn of the dilemma more concisely than by Saul Liebermann's "alarming expression" from his *Jewish Theological Seminary:* "Nonsense is nonsense. The history of nonsense, however, is science." Taubes quoted this, adding the following comment: "This formula is not an apocryphal aperçu, but was chosen by Gerschom Scholem as the introductory sentence to his second lecture on his research, held at the established stronghold of the American *Academy of Science of Judaism* in the late 1950s. Scholem spoke about the results of 'Jewish Gnosticism, Merkabah Mysticism, and the Talmudic Tradition,' results which, in my opinion, refute late-classicist concepts of religious history."[18] The other horn of the dilemma results from the necessity to recognize the outlined developmental logic of the transition from prophecy to apocalypse and from apocalypse to Gnosis; this, however, entails "seeing internalization as a legitimate consequence in the career of the messianic idea itself."[19] Taubes ended his lecture by concluding that the revision of the secession of "internal" and "external" redemption suggested itself with increasing urgency, for "every attempt to bring about redemption on the level of history without a transfiguration of the messianic idea leads straight into the abyss." In other words: "If the messianic idea in Judaism is not interiorized, it can turn the 'landscape of redemption'"—described by Scholem in his treatise *The Messianic Idea in Judaism*[20]—"into a blazing apocalypse."[21]

Messianism and Theocracy

The dilemma was indeed projected onto Scholem; even so, it was and remains a true dilemma, an unresolved and perhaps irresolvable problem. It is a simple result of the complexity of messianic logic, of the necessity either to conceive of the appearing Messiah as figure of the sublation of messianism (the Pauline conception) or to dismiss this figure of the Messiah on principle as "false" (that is, rendered "false" by the fact that and because he appears—thus simultaneously demanding the transformation of history of philosophy to anthropology or aesthetics). In line with his attempt to cleanse the Jewish notion of redemption from all notions of "internalization" (to avoid potential "Christian" infection), but without reducing messianism to a politically contingent utopianism, Scholem postulated an identification of messianism and apocalypticism. He converted (Christian) interiority to (secular, Marxist) "innerworldliness," and closely cleaved the messianic idea to the apocalypse in order to portray the motif of unpredictable redemption as "exit" from history: The Bible and the apocalyptic writers know of no progress in history leading to the redemption. The redemption is not the product of immanent developments such as we find it in modern Western reinterpretations of Messianism since the Enlightenment where, secularized as the belief in progress, Messianism still displayed unbroken and immense vigor. It is rather transcendence breaking in upon history, an intrusion in which history itself perishes, transformed in its ruins because it is struck by a beam of light shining into it from an outside source. The constructions of history in which the apocalyptists (as opposed to the prophets of the Bible) revel have nothing to do with modern conceptions of development or progress, and if there is anything which, in the view of these seers, history deserves, it can only be to perish.[22]

Messianism is now thought of as a term in a sophisticated *quaternio terminorum:* on the one hand, it is the longed-for appearance of the Messiah and the dawn of the messianic era; on the other, however, it is conceived of as this event itself, and thus as the suspension of all yearning and expectation of a break in time. Scholem argues toward the end of his treatise that Judaism paid a tremendous price for such an initial construal of the ahistoricity of messianism:

> The magnitude of the Messianic idea corresponds to the endless powerlessness in Jewish history across the centuries of exile, when it was not prepared to come forward onto the plane of world history. . . . There is something grand about living in hope, but at the same time there is something profoundly unreal about it. It diminishes the singular worth of the individual, and he can never fulfill himself because the incompleteness of his endeavors eliminates precisely what constitutes its highest value. Thus in Judaism the Messianic idea has compelled a *life lived in deferment,* in which nothing can be done definitely, nothing can be irrevocably accomplished. One may say, perhaps, that the messianic idea is in fact *the* anti-existentialist idea. Precisely understood, there is nothing concrete that can be accomplished by the unredeemed. This makes for the greatness of messianism, but also for its constitutional weakness.[23] The expected and wished-for suspension of history through the appearing Messiah is thus effectively projected back into history, so that history itself can be disclaimed as a powerless deferring of its own annulment.

It is pretty obvious that Taubes—the author of a dissertation on Occidental eschatology, interpreted as the history of the influence of Judaic apocalypticism—could not concur with such a suspension of the historical. For him, Judaism appeared almost as the site of the beginning of all history: "Israel breaks through the cycle of this endless repetition, opening up the world as history for the first time. History is for Israel the pivot around which everything revolves."[24] In opposition to Scholem, he asserts that not messianism but the rabbinic Judaism of the halacha propagated and completed the exit from history: Every endeavor to actualize the messianic idea was an attempt to jump into history, however derailed the attempt may have been. It is simply not the case that messianic fantasy and the formation of historical reality stand at opposite poles. . . . If Jewish history in exile was "a life lived in deferment," this life in suspension was due to the rabbinical hegemony. Retreat from history was in fact the rabbinical stance, the outlook that set itself against all messianic lay movements and cursed all messianic discharge a priori with the stigma of "pseudo-messianic."[25] In a typescript titled *Messianism: Zionist or Marxist*, a text that in large parts consists of a late essay on Walter Benjamin (and on Scholem's interpretation of the *Theological-Political Fragment*), Taubes continued to claim that "the religious anarchist Gerschom Scholem summons the history of Jewish mysticism to charge the bastion of rabbinic Judaism. This bastion has been in the lee of history from the very outset as it was the rabbis' intention to extract the Jewish religious community from the trajectory of history."[26] This paragraph is missing from the published text; and while the line of thought is continued in the typescript—with the question "But which God does Scholem 'believe' in? He must believe in the God of Israel, who, as attested by history and tradition (notwithstanding the crisis of tradition) has chosen us and, through his 'commandments,' 'sanctified' us to become a 'holy people'"—the printed version is far coarser: "Which God does Scholem believe in? Even the devil believes in God! He must believe in the God of Israel who, as demonstrated historically and traditionally—crisis of tradition notwithstanding—has chosen us and, through his 'commandments,' 'sanctified' us to become a 'holy people.' Then, however, 'theocracy' is on the horizon at least virtually."[27]

Taubes links his support of secular messianism with his commitment to the historico-philosophical definition of the messianic idea, and this endorsement is based around the linchpin of the concept of "theocracy." In *Occidental Eschatology*, Taubes had already qualified theocracy as a necessary consequence of eschatology (even before the proclamation of the state of Israel); for even the "the first tremors of eschatology can be traced to this dispute over divine or earthly rule." Theocracy is built on the "anarchical ground of Israel's soul"; in it is expressed the "human desire to be free from all human, earthly ties and to be in covenant with God." The theocratic concept can be raised to a "passion for the act." Thus, "viewed in terms of immanence, theocracy is a utopian community"; indeed, Taubes under-scores Israel's "decisive part" in the revolutionary movements of world history, from the Taborites to the Puritans, from Marx to Trotsky, from Moses Hess to Eduard Bernstein, from Ferdinand Lassalle to Rosa Lux-emburg.[28] In his later works, Taubes does not use such a "radiant" concept of theocracy but merely refers to the "religious war" in the "state of Is-rael, where theocracy gains a brutal, historically factual meaning, which only illusionists can permit themselves to cover up."[29] Whereas Scholem attempted to end his text *The Messianic Idea in Judaism* with references to the "overtones of messianism" that, though audible in the "retreat to Zion," are not submerged in the "at least virtually evoked" "crisis of mes-sianic expectation,"[30] Taubes warned of a "phrase" that, were it to be taken more seriously, could only compromise the Zionist idea in a catastrophic manner.[31]

In other words: The perspectives were again reversed. Whereas Scholem regarded messianism as an "exit from history" but was willing to recognize theocracy as only a "virtual" risk for the State of Israel, Taubes emphasized the historico-revolutionary potential of the messianic idea, at once criti-cizing the "political aspect" of theocracy as a deep, almost spectral danger to Israel. The radicality of the distinction that Scholem upheld between Jewish and Christian notions of redemption was mirrored by the radical-ity with which Taubes defended the distinction between a political and a religious-mythical concept of theocracy. There is more at stake here than just a question about the adequate interpretation of Walter Benjamin's phi-losophy of history—nonetheless this question is also at stake, and it is a question that exemplifies the intellectual rift between Scholem and Taubes just as well as their dispute over Zionism. It is well known that Taubes refused to view Benjamin's *Theological-Political Fragment* in a chronologi-cal proximity to the later *Theses on the Philosophy of History*. The point of the matter was the affirmation and rehabilitation of a theoretical position that promised not only to retain the dilemma of messianism—the apo-ria between historicity and ahistoricity—but also permitted him to argue against any position that aestheticized redemption (i.e., against Adorno)[32] or that politicized theocracy (i.e., against Scholem). I do not wish here to discuss the clear-sighted passages of the Heidelberg *Lectures on St. Paul*, in which Taubes attempted to link the *Fragment* and the eighth chapter of Romans. Decisive for my reconstruction of the intellectual rift with Scholem is rather Taubes's repeated appeal to Benjamin's statement that theocracy "does not possess political, but merely theological meaning. The greatest merit of Bloch's *Spirit of Utopia* was its extremely strong disclaiming of the political import of theocracy."[33]

Models of Jewish Dissidence

In the Heidelberg *Lectures on St Paul*, Taubes recounts a short verbal exchange with Scholem, evidently from the time prior to their rift. "When we still communicated daily, I once allowed myself to question Scholem jokingly: 'Listen, for this Nathan of Gaza, one receives a full professorial salary.' I meant his. 'And for St. Paul at the Hebrew University, not even a lectureship!'"[34] Regardless of whether this "joke" led (as Taubes claimed) to a professorship's being estbalished for David Flusser, it informs us over the deeply divergent understanding of Jewish dissidence, a divergence that certainly exacerbated the breach between Scholem and Taubes. Put simply: Scholem regarded the question of Jewish dissidence as an internal Jewish problem—like the tension between messianic awakening and rabbinic orthodoxy, and perhaps also like the difference between Jewish mysticism and a historical "science of Judaism." Taubes, by contrast, consistently interpreted the same question as an expression of a Jewish preoccupation with the boundaries of Judaism, including their experimental transgression, whether in founding a new religion (as in the case of St. Paul and Marcion), or in converting to another religion (as in the case of the Marranos, but also the Sabbatai Zwi), or in the sense of the Enlightenment and the secularization of messianism into the history of philosophy (from Maimonides to Spinoza and from Marx to the "mystical Marxists" Bloch and Benjamin). In his draft for the article on Walter Benjamin, Taubes refers to the "Jewish 'self-criticism' that flares up from time to time in eras of crisis—it is a constellation that is first linked to the name Elischa ben Abuja, a contemporary and companion of the great Akiba, who established the tradition of Orthodox rabbinic Judaism, and that flares up in times of Jewish crisis: Spinoza, Marx, and Simone Weil can be seen as representatives of stages of Jewish self-criticism that belong to the darkest chapters of Jewish spiritual history."[35]

In a recorded and transcribed conversation with Peter Sloterdijk in January 1987, a few weeks before Taubes's death, Taubes recounted his various differences with Scholem, which are all articulated by their fundamentally differing appreciation of the possible modes of expression of Jewish dissidence. In the transcript he states:

> I have suppressed it [the experience of a "pneumatic" succession—effectively, an "apostolate"], as I wanted to identify myself as a Jew, but they noticed it didn't work; for years I have gone through the world wearing a mask, and have suppressed it in myself. I'll say something spiritual now, there was a small chance between Scholem and me, because Scholem understood all that without its having to be expressed in words, I couldn't fool him, there was no chance. The following happened, and again it was an issue that made it clear to me that it wouldn't work: I was at Scholem's, and he was horribly angry at a lady, whose name I'd never heard of, and he hadn't either until four weeks previously—namely, Simone Weil. And he ranted and raved, and recounted in rants that Simone Weil's books got him so angry—the first French editions from back then—that he'd thrown them in the rubbish. And the way he told the story about the woman, oh dear, I left and went to the rubbish bin and took the books out, and the end of the story was that Susan Taubes wrote a dissertation on Simone Weil. There were states of tension. Scholem knew what pneumatic meant; he knew what ecstasy and mysticism are. He never confused himself with a mystic, and all these attempts to turn him into one he refused with good reason. He wanted something else; he wanted the renaissance of Jewish experience, cost what it may and whatever was in it, be it the shabbiest type of Kabbalism, if it comes out of us, it is something.[36]

Scholem remained a historian, a fact that Taubes often lamented; even in his diary Scholem described mysticism as "short-circuit thinking" (June 15, 1948).[37] The historian called for a reconstruction of the concealed history of Judaism, whereas Taubes thought it possible to make "a promise for the future of the as yet unplumbed depths of the Mysterium Judaicum"; for "this story has not yet ended, in fact, it hasn't even started, so far there have only been mere skirmishes."[38] Taubes was counting on a "post-Judaic situation,"[39] while Scholem was still systematically "recovering" the ancient Greeks and Egyptians—as Harold Bloom confirmed in a gracious anecdote:

> According to Scholem's wishes, the Kabbalah should have been completely Gnostic while simultaneously being completely Jewish. This was the reason for his audaciously ingenious insistence on the Jewish roots of Gnosticism. . . . As I once visited Scholem in his house in Jerusalem,

I had the opportunity to listen to his captivating, learned discourse on these matters. When I tried to object that Gnosticism appeared to be a false reading of Plato as much as of the Hebrew Bible, so that in a somewhat strange manner Gnosticism and neo-Platonism could be both derived from Plato, Scholem answered triumphantly: "Exactly. And where does Plato get it from? From Egypt, and they have everything from us!"[40] Scholem remained a historian—admittedly not without epistemico-political interest. It was just this interest that Taubes mistrusted, notably when it related to the appreciation of the Sabbatians and Frankists. As he wrote in the draft of his article on Walter Benjamin: "Gerschom Scholem's masterpiece on the Messias Saabatai Zwi is understood and received *nolens volens* as a piece of Zionism's prehistory. History is not a sort of *art pour l'art* but is rendered contemporary 'for us' by the historian. Thus, Gerschom Scholem becomes, perhaps against his liberal, European, humanistically molded and therefore anti-messianistic understanding of reason, a witness to the new messianic constellation of Israel in the medium of history; and thus also a witness to the trend-reversal that, over the last months, has so astonished and shocked the public."[41]

Postscript on the Philosophy of History

The divergences between Scholem and Taubes cannot be reduced to the conflict between apocalypticism and mysticism, between messianism and halacha, between spiritual and political theocracy. Even the question in which sense Christianity can be deduced from the ambitions of Jewish dissidence (with Taubes: from Marcion to Simone Weil)—and thus interpreted as a product of "internal Judaic conflict"—need not fundamentally separate the historian of Sabbatism and the occasional Marxist and later "Paulinian." A more decisive role was played by the methodological and even literary differences between a historico-anthropological approach to theology, as Scholem seemed to practice it at the time of the Eranos circle (enabling his friendships to Henri Corbin and Mircea Eliade), and Taubes's position as a philosopher of history, a position that he took up during his dissertation and never relinquished despite multiple changes in his stance. From this viewpoint it may be bold, but not implausible, to view the conflict that Taubes engaged in with Odo Marquard regarding the latter's book *In Praise of Polytheism*.[42] Taubes wanted to defend the unity of monotheism and the historico-philosophical (or, more accurately, *messianic*) vision and argued with vehemence against the attempt to enact a *posthistoire* religious "separation of powers." Is Marquard a "mask" of Scholem? Taubes held the philosophy of history to be the most valuable legacy of Western thought; and he polemicized fiercely against every attempt to exchange this inheritance for the more general terms of mythology and symbolism. At this point the interpretation of Walter Benjamin's writings became a particularly virulent bone of contention with Scholem; not for nothing did Taubes substantially contribute to the distribution of a (previously unknown) letter of Benjamin's to Carl Schmitt.[43] The issue at hand did not restrict itself to philology and the politics of ideas but extended to correcting certain interpretations of Benjamin, ones that Scholem had strongly supported.

I am coming to a close. What I wanted to demonstrate, in necessary brevity, was the—at least partially aporetic—profile of a rift and conflict that cannot be reduced to idiosyncrasies or biographical anecdotes but gained its fervor from the questions and issues on which it is based. Thus, undertaking to discuss such rifts and conflicts may be permissible even on birthdays and anniversaries, though this may well lessen gratitude and hinder the person's elevation to the status of an author, or even a classic. In his lecture on *The Price of Messianism*, Taubes rightly drew attention to the fact that proclamations—especially messianic ones—must be validated by interpretations and not by biographical tales. There is comfort in this. In 1977, the same year that Taubes planned to publish the critical Festschrift on Scholem—as his postcard to Manfred Schlosser dated March 18 attests—he wrote a birthday article, which was printed in the daily newspaper *Die Welt* on December 10, 1977, in reasonably good time for Scholem's eightieth birthday. This article ended with a story, told by the poet S. J. Agnon and which Scholem related; Taubes included this in his birthday missive, after repeating well-known points of criticism. The story runs as follows:

> If the Baal Schem had to undertake a particularly difficult task, a secret task benefiting the creatures, he went to a particular place in the woods, lit a fire, and, sunk in mystic meditation, spoke prayers. If, a generation later, the Maggid of Mesritsch had to undertake the same task, he also went to that place in the woods and said, "Although we can no longer light the fire, we can still say the prayers'—and everything happened according to his will. Yet another generation later, the Rabbi Moshe Leib also had to undertake the same task. He also went into the woods and said, "We can no longer light a fire, we no longer remember the secret meditations that bring the prayer to life, but we know the place

in the woods where it must be done, and this must be enough"—and it was enough. Another generation later, it was the Rabbi Israel of Rischin's turn. He sat in his palace on his golden chair and said, "We can no longer light the fire, we can no longer say the prayers, and we no longer know the place, but we can tell the story." And, the pious narrator of this "anecdote" added—the rabbi's tale alone had the same effect as the deeds of the other three.[44]

CHAPTER 3

Impure Inheritances:
Spectral Materiality in Derrida and Marx

Nicole Pepperell

Written in the aftermath of the collapse of the Soviet Union, in a period of the apparently unchallenged ascendance of liberal market ideals and institutions, Derrida's *Specters of Marx* questions the triumphalist declaration that Marx's ideas are dead, and insists that the specter of communism, and the spirit of Marx, continue to haunt a present that remains out of joint.[1] The recent global financial crisis has cast into stark relief the prescience of Derrida's claim. It has also underscored the importance of the question that informs *Specters*: How are we to inherit Marx today?

Derrida asks whether a certain spirit of Marx might be summoned to challenge the dominance of market liberalism without encouraging dogmatic and totalitarian impulses. He then effects such a summons through a curious material transformation of Marx's text: He excises a single sentence from the pivotal passage in which Marx christens the commodity fetish. This excision subtly transforms the meaning of Marx's text—and positions the act of interpretation as an active, transformative, selective appropriation of the past, rather than as a passive reception of materials inexorably transmitted from history.

Here I explore the way in which Derrida foreshadows and then effects this excision from Marx's text. In doing so, I both highlight the distinctive understanding of transformative inheritance at the heart of Derrida's work and pose the question of why Derrida should effect this particular transformation when he searches for nondogmatic impulses in Marx's critique.

After examining Derrida's transformation of Marx's text, I explore an alternative interpretation of the same passages from *Capital*, focusing on the book's unusual narrative strategy. I argue that the various ontological claims put forward overtly in *Capital*—which Derrida reads as straightforward declarations of Marx's own stance—can instead be read as set pieces designed to portray the conflicting claims of political economic theory. The text as a whole can be read as a play in which personifications of contradictory tenets of political economic discourse stride successively onto *Capital*'s economic "stage." Through the succession of such performances, Marx enacts an immanent critique of political economic discourse, showing how it is possible to mine moments from within this discourse, in order to achieve critical insights into the limitations and internal contradictions of the discourse as a whole. While many different ontological claims are displayed in the course of these performances, the narrative logic of the text implies that Marx endorses none of them. Instead, the narrative structure of *Capital* as a whole operates to destabilize and, ultimately, relativize the ontological claims with which the text opens, revealing them to have been the targets of the critique all along.

This unusual presentational strategy means that *Capital* can be read productively as an immanent critique of political economic discourse, which does not require a purportedly external, "objective" standpoint—material or otherwise. This immanent critique will ultimately undermine the ontological stances with which the text opens, such that Marx—as much as Derrida—can be shown to distrust claims founded on the notion of a disenchanted, secular, "material" world. It may therefore be easier than *Specters* suggests to inherit a certain deconstructive spirit of Marx.

Impure Inheritances

Derrida's reading of the commodity-fetishism passage hinges on the interpretation that Marx aims to decontaminate material reproduction. Derrida sees *Capital* as motivated by the desire to free the objective, intrinsic, material elements of material production—use-value, labor, technology (in orthodox Marxist vocabulary, the forces of production)—from the spectralizing and contingent social contagions of money and exchange (the productive relations). Derrida thus positions Marx as grounding his critique in a particular kind of ontology, in which privileged access to a supposedly pure "material world" provides a standpoint from which to evaluate "merely social" phenomena.

While reading Marx in this way, Derrida attempts to open the possibility to inherit him otherwise. In Derrida's account, what we inherit from our time is not fully determined by the weight of history bearing down upon us. Inheritance does not take the form of a passive, faithful reception of contents transmitted in pure and undistorted form—nor is faithful inheritance some sort of regulative ideal to which we should aspire. Inheritance is instead an active, performative act (54–55). We—the heirs—initiate it; we select those aspects of the past that shall remain relevant to our time. In selecting, we form a specific constellation with one among many possible pasts: We determine, retroactively, which elements of our potential pasts will have been determining upon us, precisely by enacting those elements of the past as our own ongoing concern.[2]

This performative act need not be undertaken consciously or with deliberation. Nevertheless, the possibility—the inevitability—of such a selective inheritance shatters any notion of history as a progression of modalized presents that lead inexorably from one to the next: No potential future "realizes" the pure essence of the past better or more faithfully than any other; the dead cannot bury their own dead—it is up to us, the heirs, to decide when and how their remains shall be interred.[3] Our present is haunted precisely because we face a choice among multiple pasts we could inherit, precisely because we sit at the nexus of many futures we might create. What comes next is not predetermined by the present time; the future we create will, in turn, open potentials and possibilities we cannot currently foresee.

In the final chapter of *Specters*, Derrida applies this concept of selective inheritance in a particularly literal way to the pivotal passage in which Marx christens the commodity fetish, by excising a single sentence from Marx's original text. This excision is heavily foreshadowed in earlier chapters of Derrida's work, most directly in a discussion of a passage from Valéry in which Hamlet examines illustrious skulls and finds, in the skull of Kant, a line of inheritance that runs from Kant to Hegel, and then from Hegel to Marx. Derrida notes that Valéry quotes this same passage in a later work, reproducing it in its original form—except for a single line. Derrida lingers over this point, drawing the reader's attention to the omission, noting:

At this point, Valéry quotes himself. He reproduces the page of "the European Hamlet," the one we have just cited. Curiously, with the errant but infallible assurance of a sleepwalker, he then omits from it only *one* sentence, *just one*, without even signaling the omission by an ellipsis: the one that names Marx, in the very skull of Kant. (5)

In a subsequent discussion of Blanchot's "Marx's Three Voices," Derrida draws attention once more to the figure of the ellipsis, characterizing Blanchot's work in terms of a "very powerful ellipsis" that amounts to an "almost tacit declaration" (35). Ellipses—marked and tacit—are therefore foregrounded in the early chapters of *Specters* as significant features of texts and traditions. The chapter in which Derrida effects the excision of Marx's sentence is then titled "Apparition of the Inapparent"—subtitled "The Phenomenological 'Conjuring Trick'" (125). The text thus prepares the reader for the appearance of an absence: It warns us of the ellipsis to come.

Leading into his discussion of commodity fetishism, Derrida presents a detailed analysis of Marx's critique of Stirner in *The German Ideology*. Derrida characterizes this work as a "whirling dance of ghosts" in which both Stirner and Marx share a common wish "to have done with the revenant" through a "reappropriation of life in a body proper" (129). Marx and Stirner thus share the goal, Derrida argues, of exorcising the ghost. Where they differ is simply over the means through which this exorcism must be performed: Stirner seeks an immediate reappropriation of the spectral into an egological body; Marx declares Stirner's concept of an egological body itself to be a ghost. This stance does not render Marx any more friendly to spirits. Marx's objection is, instead, that Stirner obscures the means to achieve a true exorcism, in the form of a reappropriation of the spectral that must take place—not immediately, as in Stirner's egological reappropriation—but rather through the mediation of work, through a labor of thought and practice that takes into account all the social mediations constitutive of the specters that throw the time out of joint, and that therefore must be exorcised (129–31). In Derrida's account, Stirner thus stands criticized for attempting to destroy, in thought alone, a spectrality that, because it does not originate in thought, could never be abolished there. Instead, the exorcism can be effected only in practice:

> Marx denounces a surplus of hallucination and a capitalization of the ghost: what is really (*wirklich*) destroyed are merely the representations in their form as representation (*Vorstellung*). The youth may indeed destroy his hallucinations or the phantomatic appearance of the

bodies—of the Emperor, the State, the Fatherland. He does not actually (*wirklich*) destroy them. And if he stops relating to these realities through the prostheses of his representation and the "spectacles of his fantasy [*durch die Brille seiner Phantasie*]," if he stops transforming these realities into objects, objects of theoretical intuition, that is, into a spectacle, then he will have to take into account the "practical structure" of the world: Work, production, actualization, techniques. Only this practicality, only this actuality (work, the *Wirken* or the *Wirkung* of this *Wirklichkeit*) can get to the bottom of a purely imaginary or spectral flesh (*phantastiche . . . gespenstige Leibhaftigkeit*). (130)

As Derrida sees this argument, then, Marx seeks, like Stirner, to abolish spectrality. Marx believes, however, that this abolition can be achieved only through a process that transforms the "practical structure of the world," a transformation effected specifically, in Derrida's reading, through the mediation of labor (130–31). On this reading, labor figures as a despectralizing form of action—and production, actualization, and technique are positioned as forms of practice that can effect an exorcism, abolish the ghost that renders the time out of joint, and set the time right, once and for all, by constituting a self-identical present moment that is rationally and transparently in control of its own emancipatory possibilities (130–31).

Derrida finds a similar logic in Marx's argument about commodity fetishism (148). His representation of the commodity-fetishism passage both accentuates his interpretation that the passage reenacts Marx's critique of Stirner and prepares to interrupt this reenactment, to prevent it from being performed again in the same way.

Noting that the commodity-fetishism passage is so familiar to us that it is difficult to interpret, Derrida sets himself the goal of carrying out an "ingenuous reading" (149)—a goal that, Derrida notes, the text itself immediately begins to undermine. Marx warns us, from the first sentence of the fetishism passage, that we cannot take the commodity at first sight (149). Derrida reads this warning as a statement that performatively institutes a distinction between what Derrida calls the "phenomenological good sense of the thing itself" and the "metaphysical" and "theological" dimensions of the commodity (150). This distinction is at the core of what troubles Derrida about the passage—and is therefore one of the things he seeks to subvert.

Derrida interprets "phenomenological good sense" as adequate, in Marx's account, for the interpretation of use-value, whose qualities might be perceptible "at first sight" (150). He argues that Marx associates this phenomenological good sense—and use-value—with an Enlightened perception, citing Marx's comment that "use-value has nothing at all 'mysterious' about it" (150). Derrida takes use-value, then, as the standpoint from which Marx hopes to pierce various forms of mystification, by holding them up against an ideal of what is "proper to man, to the properties of man"—what is naturally meet for human needs (150).

The naturalness of use value operates, in Derrida's reading, to secure use value as a kind of firm ontological anchor for Marx's critical ideals. Significantly, Derrida contrasts the category of use-value to the category of the commodity—thus positioning use-value as an external standpoint from which Marx effects his critique of the commodity-form. This firm ontological anchor is then haunted by something spectral—by the commodity, a supersensible social thing that has been only contingently grafted onto its natural base.

Derrida draws attention here to Marx's theatrical language, and analyzes in evocative detail the "Table-Thing" with which Marx introduces the commodity-fetishism section, finding in this image a horror of prosthesis, of artificial life, of mechanical autonomy (150–54). In Derrida's reading, Marx locates the spectral qualities of the commodity firmly in the market—outside of use-value, outside of the material, outside of *hulē* (155). This attempt to locate—to ontologize—the specter allows Marx to open up the possibility for its exorcism: for the abolition of the fetish. For Derrida, such an exorcism is predicated on the notion that spectrality is contingent and dispensable—that spectrality interrupts the coming to presence of essence, which would otherwise enable some underlying material reality to express itself, openly, in human history. This underlying material reality, Derrida argues, is labor—the truth of the social character of labor, disguised by the artifice of market exchange (156–57).

Without flagging his strategy directly, Derrida begins here to sunder the presentational structure of the passage in which Marx christens the fetish—separating the elements of Marx's original presentation in time and place, overtly amending the passages—and then eventually excising a sentence. A brief digression into Marx's original passage will help cast into relief how Derrida actively modifies the original text.

Social Objectivity

Before introducing the term *fetishism* in the opening chapter of *Capital*, Marx leads the reader through two analogies, representing two different sorts of relationships—one, a physical relationship between physical things, and the second, an intersubjective relationship among persons.[4] He contrasts both of these sorts of relationship with the peculiar relationship he is trying to grasp through the concept of commodity fetishism, which he introduces in the following way:

> The mysterious character of the commodity-form consists therefore simply in the fact that the commodity reflects the social characteristics of men's own labour as objective characteristics of the products of labour themselves, as the socio-natural properties of these things. Hence it also reflects the social relation of the producers to the sum total of labour as a social relation between objects, a relation which exists apart from and outside the producers. Through this substitution, the products of labour become commodities, sensuous things which are at the same time supra-sensible or social.[5]

To begin to clarify how this happens, Marx then introduces his first analogy—an optical analogy—which describes the physical relation between an object and the eye: "In the same way, the impression made by a thing on the optic nerve is perceived not as a subjective excitation of that nerve but as the objective form of a thing outside the eye" (165). Marx argues here that a relation in which the object and the eye are both active participants is interpreted in perception as though the eye is just a passive entity, receiving impressions that originate in the external object alone. Implicitly, Marx treats the process of perception as a process best grasped as actively constituted by all elements involved in the interaction, rather than as a purely objective or purely subjective phenomenon.

This optical analogy is then distinguished from the phenomenon Marx is trying to grasp, on the grounds that the relation between the eye and the objects it perceives is a purely physical one:

> In the act of seeing, of course, light is really transmitted from one thing, the external object, to another thing, the eye. It is a physical relation between physical things. As against this, the commodity-form, and the value-relation of the products of labour within which it appears, have absolutely no connection with the physical nature of the commodity and the material [*dinglich*] relations arising out of this. It is nothing but the definite social relation between men which assumes here, for them, the fantastic form of a relation between things. (165)

It is at this point that Marx introduces his second, religious analogy—specifically in order to pick out the social character of the commodity fetish:

> In order, therefore, to find an analogy, we must take flight into the
> misty realm of religion. There the products of the human brain appear
> as autonomous figures endowed with a life of their own, which enter
> into relations both with each other and with the human race. (165)

While the relations constituted by religious practice and belief are social—arising solely from human interaction and therefore historically
contingent—these relations arise, in Marx's formulation, in "the human
brain." In more contemporary language, these relations are intersubjective, relying on shared beliefs and frameworks of meaning. By contrast,
Marx does not believe commodity fetishism arises from shared intersubjective frameworks—commodity fetishism is not, in other words, an ideology or a mere false belief. As a consequence, he distinguishes religion from
the phenomenon that interests him here by saying, "So it is in the world of
commodities with the products of men's hands" (165).

"So it is" that the products of human practice appear autonomous from
the humans who create them—but with the important exception that, with
commodity fetishism, it is not intersubjective relations that generate this
apparently objective phenomenon but rather a peculiar historical form of
interaction between humans and their physical world.

It is at this point, having thus carefully distinguished this phenomenon
from two apparently similar sorts of relations, that Marx finally christens
the commodity fetish: "I call this the fetishism which attaches itself to the
products of labour as soon as they are produced as commodities, and is
therefore inseparable from the production of commodities" (165). Neither an objective physical relation nor an intersubjective one, commodity fetishism instead arises through historically specific and transformable
sorts of interactions between humans and other objects. The analysis of
commodity fetishism is therefore a critique of a non-intersubjective, but
nevertheless social, environment that strikes the social actors who create it
as an autonomous material world.

I will explore in further detail below how Marx develops this analysis
into a critique of a peculiar social form of materiality that is mistakenly
interpreted as a secular, disenchanted, "objective" material realm. First,
however, it is important to capture how Derrida hears this passage, and
thereby understand why Derrida might conclude that a specific material
transformation of the text would be required to inherit Marx's theory in a
deconstructive form.

Prestidigitation

Derrida subtly disturbs the order of Marx's discussion of the fetish—separating in time and space his discussion of different moments of this passage, in a way that both privileges the textual importance of the religious analogy and obscures how the two analogies work together to clarify the concept of commodity fetishism in Marx's text.

To do this, Derrida staggers his presentation of the fetishism passage. He discusses the "optical analogy" in isolation and returns to the religious analogy only some nine pages later.[6] This sundering of Marx's original presentation suggests a much more proximate relationship between the religious analogy and his concept of commodity fetishism than it does between the optical analogy and the commodity-fetishism concept. It thereby implies that commodity fetishism should be understood as an ideology or false belief, and thus suggests a strong link between the commodity-fetishism argument and the critique of religion Derrida had earlier discussed in relation to *The German Ideology*.

Derrida then interpolates, between these two analogies, an extended reflection on what he takes to be a paradox in Marx's account: *Capital*'s constant tendency to reiterate, on the one hand, that commodities are passive, inert, material things, which must be commanded by human will; and, on the other hand, gestures that seem to undermine these claims—by, for example, speculating about what commodities might say or do if only they could speak or did possess will.[7] Derrida finds these recurrent counterfactuals peculiar and notes a number of examples, including the passage in which Marx quite literally places words in commodities' mouths, making them actors—citing Shakespeare's *Much Ado about Nothing* to underscore the theatrical resonance.[8] Derrida writes:

> This rhetorical artifice is abyssal. Marx is going to claim right away
> that the economist naively reflects or reproduces this fictive or spectral
> speech of the commodity and lets himself be in some way ventrilo-
> quized by it: he "speaks" from the depths of the soul of the commodities
> (*aus den Warenseele heraus*). But in saying "if commodities could speak"
> (*Könnten die Waren sprechen*), Marx implies that they cannot speak. (157)

Derrida draws similar attention to the ambivalence of the claim that commodities have no will. In his (somewhat exasperated) words:

> Since commodities do not walk in order to take themselves willingly,
> spontaneously, to market, their "guardians" and "possessors" pretend

to inhabit these things. Their "will" begins to "inhabit" (*hausen*) commodities. The difference between *inhabit* and *haunt* becomes here more ungraspable than ever. (158)

Once again, the order in which Derrida introduces these textual dilemmas breaks with Marx's own presentation: The passage in which Marx discusses what commodities would say if they could speak is the culminating passage of the first chapter of *Capital*—it takes place well after the presentation of both the optical and the religious analogies, rather than interposing itself between the two; the passage in which Marx discusses the commodities' lack of will opens the second chapter of *Capital* and therefore follows a considerable distance after the analysis of the fetish.[9]

By not flagging the broken order of presentation, Derrida subtly transforms our sense of how the original text operates. This strategy is of course fully consistent with Derrida's notion of selective inheritance. His transformation of the text should be understood as a demonstration and illustration of concepts he has outlined previously, rather than as an attempt to distort our understanding of Marx: By choosing to attend to certain elements in the text, we can bring certain potentials of the argument more clearly into view and render these potentials more accessible. But what potentials are Derrida attempting to grasp?

Derrida unspools them over the next several pages, developing his argument that *Capital* presents use-value as an originary, untainted, self-identical ontological state, which comes to be contaminated and haunted by an external and more contingent social process. In Derrida's reading, Marx presents the ghost—the haunting, mysterious qualities of the commodity—as something that "comes on stage"—something that is introduced at some point after the presence of the secure, objective materiality that is use-value.[10] For Derrida, this is reminiscent of strategies Marx criticized in Stirner, and Derrida asks whether Marx, like Stirner, was "a man who became frightened of his own ghost, a constitutive fear of the concept that he formed of himself, and thus of his whole history as a man" (159). Here Derrida begins to deploy his critique. In what sense, he asks, can we presuppose some pure materiality? Where is this untainted starting point, such that the contamination of exchange can take place only somewhere downstream (159–60)?

Derrida argues that use-value can operate only as a kind of limit concept—a concept that makes sense only in contradistinction to its other, and therefore a concept that is always already contaminated by its other. Use-value therefore cannot precede the commodity's coming on stage. Rather, it is the commodity that provides the condition of possibility for use-value as a limit concept. The ghost of the commodity—like the ghost of Hamlet's father, whom Derrida has analyzed earlier in the text—returns only at the moment where it seems to arrive on stage for the first time. Its coming is already anticipated by the category of use-value itself—a category that would make no sense without the bifurcation introduced by the spectrality of the haunting (160–61). It is with the first introduction of use-value—rather than with the introduction of commodity fetishism—that the haunting properly begins.

Derrida expands on this discussion—which by itself could be taken as an analysis of the concept of use-value rather than as an analysis of use-value "itself"—to discuss how the practices associated with material reproduction are implicated in the constitution of iterability, exchange, and prosthesis (162). The phenomena traditionally lined up with the "forces of production" in orthodox Marxism cannot be seen as self-identical or untainted. Already within these processes are all of the potentials for temporal disjoint that Derrida believes Marx attempts to locate exclusively in the social process of exchange.

In these passages, Derrida worries about Marx's claim that the spectrality of commodity fetishism could be abolished:

> Let us not forget that everything we have just read there was Marx's point of view on a *finite delirium*. It was his discourse on a madness destined, according to him, to come to an end, on a general incorporation of abstract human labor that is still translated, but for a finite time, into the language of madness, into a delirium (*Verrücktheit*) of expression. We *will have to*, Marx declares, and *we will be able to, we will have to be able to* put an end to what appears in 'this absurd form' (*in dieser verrückten Form*). We will *see* (translate: *we will see come*) the end of this delirium and of these ghosts, Marx obviously thinks. (163–64)

Derrida then gives voice to his driving fear—that it is spectrality as such that Marx seeks to abolish: "'This madness here?' he asks, 'Those ghosts there? Or spectrality in general?'" (164).

Interpreting Marx as a theorist whose critique is grounded in a privileged access to an objective material reality, it is difficult for Derrida not to conclude that Marx seeks to abolish spectrality in general. This Marx, Derrida fears, is what has been inherited by oppressive parties and totalitarian states. This Marx must be shown not to be an intrinsic, "essential" Marx whom loyal heirs must faithfully inherit. To inherit Marx in some other way, Derrida returns to the commodity-fetishism passage—seeking, in the most literal sense, to rewrite history.

Derrida introduces the passage in which Marx christens the commodity fetish by revisiting the concepts of exorcism and conjuration (164–65). Thinking, Derrida suggests, relies on conjuration. The question is therefore not how we shall abolish conjuration but rather: What kind of conjuration shall we perform? Derrida has just presented Marx as someone who wants to conjure away spectrality. He has also refused to exempt himself from the dynamic of conjuration. We can therefore expect what follows to be a conjuration of its own, an exorcism in its own right. We are forewarned, then, on a number of explicit and tacit levels, to expect prestidigitation in the pages that follow—enjoined to pay attention to the absence of what will be conjured away.

Derrida now finally introduces the religious analogy, telling us that it is only through this analogy that one can explain the autonomy of the ideological—a claim that is more persuasive precisely because the structure of Marx's argument has been broken apart in Derrida's re-presentation. Continuing to equate the argument about commodity fetishism with an argument about "ideology," Derrida stresses the uniqueness of the links Marx makes with religion: "only the reference to the religious world," "only the religious analogy," "the only analogy possible" (165). Derrida repeats these phrases as if they are an incantation—just after drawing attention to the mantra-like "ritual, obsessional" "formulas" involved in conjuration (165).

It is at this point that Derrida quotes the passage from *Capital* that seems to secure this interpretation:

> There [in the religious world] the products of the human brain [of the head, once again, of men: *des menschlichen Kopfes*, analogous to the wooden head of the table capable of engendering chimera—in its head, outside of its head—once, that is, *as soon as*, its form can become commodity-form] appear as autonomous figures endowed with a life of their own, which enter into relations both with each other and with the human race. . . . I call this the fetishism which attaches itself [*anklebt*] to the products of labour as soon as they are produced as commodities, and is therefore inseparable from the production of commodities.
>
> As the foregoing analysis has already demonstrated, this fetishism of the world of commodities arises from the peculiar social character of the labour which produces them.[11]

The text that is omitted here—only a single sentence, marked by an ellipsis—is where Marx *distinguishes* commodity fetishism from religion. The excised sentence is the one where Marx declares: "So it is in the world of commodities with the products of men's hands."[12]

As Derrida has invited us to ask, by asking the same of Valéry: "Why this omission, the only one?"[13]

Derrida presents Marx as a theorist whose stance is grounded in the forces of production—in use-values as a potential objective "outside" from the standpoint of which the merely contingent social relations of market exchange can be criticized. Derrida has voiced the fear that Marx is undertaking the critique not of some specific dimension of social experience but of spectrality as such. In Derrida's reading, the commodity-fetishism argument operates as a kind of unveiling—a piercing of an ideological illusion, to reveal the material reality occluded underneath—of a hidden material reality whose revelation would tell us how we "ought" to live, finally, in order for social life to become self-identical and fully transparent. In Derrida's reading, the desire to make this move is tantamount to the desire to abolish the conditions of possibility for any future nonidentity of the present with itself. This desire, for Derrida, has manifested itself in the spirit of Marx that has been inherited in dogmatic and totalitarian forms.

At this point, Derrida attempts an exorcism. He edits out the moment where, in his reading, Marx whisks away the veil and reveals a "materialist" principle as the secret truth that lies behind the spectral illusion. In Derrida's transformative citation of Marx's text, the moment of revelation never comes—the illusion is never pierced, the standpoint of objective reality is never seized, the specter is left to haunt. What Derrida attempts to exorcize in this passage is exorcism itself: He seeks to banish the moment in which Marx seems to tear aside the curtain separating us from a privileged material standpoint that will abolish spectrality and inaugurate a society that has become self-identical and fully present to itself.

This potential—of a Marxism that does not ground itself in its privileged access to a transparent materiality—is a spirit of Marx that Derrida puts forward as compatible with a certain spirit of deconstruction. Imagine what it would have been like—Derrida invites us to conjecture—if Marx had not understood critique as the abolition of all spectrality. We, as Marx's heirs, have the power to make it so.

Putting Capital *into Play*

Is Derrida's intervention, however, the only means to wield this kind of power? Here I want to explore a different path to summoning a certain deconstructive spirit in Marx's work. In this interpretation I join a small number of authors who have argued that understanding the substantive claims in *Capital* requires keeping track of a range of literary devices that the text itself deploys—in particular, devices related to irony, satire, and the sarcastic performative enactment of the positions being criticized.[14] This body of scholarship strongly suggests that many previous interpretations of Marx have suffered from an over-literal reading strategy that has overlooked the role played in Marx's text by "literary" features such as voice and tone, character, dramatic structure, and plot. By failing to attend to such literary strategies, many interpretations of *Capital* have missed the ironic, satirical character of the text and thereby failed to capture how *Capital* undermines and destabilizes claims that it originally seems to endorse.

To give a sense of the sorts of readings that become possible once *Capital*'s literary structure is brought into view, let me turn briefly to two works written prior to *Specters:* John Seery's *Political Returns* and Dominick LaCapra's *Rethinking Intellectual History.*[15] Both of these works effectively highlight the ironic, satirical character of Marx's work in a way that frames the interpretation of *Capital*'s opening chapter that I present in the sections to come.

Seery focuses on the earliest stages of Marx's work, examining the foreword for Marx's doctoral dissertation, which addresses the problem of how philosophy is possible after Hegel.[16] According to Seery, Marx argues that philosophy is possible after Hegel—but only if it assumes an ironic form (244–45). Seery traces the way in which this theme plays itself out in subterranean form in Marx's doctoral dissertation, which focuses on the difference between Democritus's deterministic materialism and Epicurus's materialism—the latter of which Marx sees as accommodating the potential for a "swerve" that deviates from strict determination (245–49). Seery then argues:

> The foreword begins with the question of how it is at all possible to philosophize after Hegel's total triumph, how, as it were, one can "swerve" from Hegelianism. Traditionally, scholars have interpreted the young Marx as still enraptured at this time with Hegel and Hegelianism. . . . I suggest, however, that a careful reading of the foreword along with the dissertation reveals that Marx is thoroughly distancing himself from Hegel while at the same time he is informing us that his alternative stance will nonetheless *resemble* Hegelianism in outward form. (250)

In Seery's interpretation, the parallels between Marx's method and Hegel's must be understood in a deeply ironic light—as a citation of the forms of Hegel's work in order to effect a fundamental internal transformation of

Hegel's system. Seery argues that Marx's embrace of irony is a specific response to the question of how we can escape from totalizing philosophies:

> In particular, Marx wishes to show why, in the wake of totalizing philosophies, it is necessary for the subjective form of philosophy to wear "disguises" and "character masks" . . . and why, by extension, Marx will *apparently* embrace Hegelianism. . . .
>
>   In order to philosophize after Hegel . . . to "live at all after a total philosophy," Marx is saying that we need "ironists," or those who are able to break with totalizing views of reality, and then can act on their own, like the self-initiating motion of Epicurus' swerving atom. But because Hegel's triumph is so encompassing, according to Marx, post-Hegelian ironists will need to couch their subjective philosophies in Hegelian terminology, nonetheless. (250–51)

Seery thus finds in Marx an anti-totalizing impulse, ironically expressed in the rhetoric of a totalizing philosophy. I would suggest that a very similar impulse informs Marx's later work. If the early Marx was striving to break away from the dominance of a seemingly omnipresent totalizing philosophical discourse, the later Marx confronts a social system that, seen from certain angles, can also appear totalizing. In both cases, I suggest, Marx opts for irony as his critical tool of choice, as the technique by which he expresses the possibility for the "swerve" that will burst apart the totality from within.

As a presentational strategy, however, irony can have strange effects on the reader's experience of the text—particularly when, as is the case in *Capital*, the technique is not explicitly announced in advance. As Seery notes: "Compounding the problem of discovering Marx's 'ironic' outlook is that Marx would be, according to his dissertation, an ironist *on the sly*, a writer who *conceals* his ironic view of things. Is all hope lost of pinning Marx down?"[17] Seery recommends specific reading strategies to overcome this problem: "I suggest that we can discern Marx's 'irony' by indirection, by disclosing its deep presence through elimination, by smoking it out of hiding" (253).

While Seery limits his discussion to Marx's early works, LaCapra suggests that these same reading strategies are required for *Capital*—a point he attempts to demonstrate through what he calls a "fictionalized reconstruction of the 'phenomenology' of reading Capital."[18] In this reconstruction, LaCapra notes that the way readers approach *Capital*'s opening passages generally determines how they understand the claims made in the rest of the text. When these passages are read as straightforward definitional claims, readers tend to fall into overly literal interpretations of the opening passages. As LaCapra puts it:

> Reading these opening sections for the first time, one is struck by the seemingly abstract delineation of concepts to analyze the commodity form (use value, exchange value, abstract labor power, and so on). Marx seems to conform to the image of the pure scientist, indeed the theorist who, in the afterword to the second German edition, seems to invert Hegel by collapsing positivism and the dialectic into a purely objectivist notion of the laws of motion of the capitalist economy. A positivistic dialectic appears to be revealed as "the rational kernel within the mystical shell." The first three sections of the principal text also seem to fall neatly within this "problematic." (333)

LaCapra suggests, however, that as the text progresses it calls into question this first impression—starting, in LaCapra's reading, with the section on the fetish character of the commodity, which

> causes a rupture in the text and disorients one's expectations about it. One is led to reread the earlier sections in its light and to notice the evidence of "double-voicing" or of "internal dialogization" operating to disfigure their seemingly placid positivistic façade. (333)

LaCapra's "heuristic" observations on the experience of reading the text come very close to characterizing the interpretive approach I would also recommend: Reading *Capital* requires an interpretive strategy that involves the constant reevaluation of earlier claims in light of new perspectives introduced later in the text. This process helps bring into view what LaCapra calls double-voicing, and sensitizes us to the presence of internal dialogues as a way of making sense of the complex presentational strategy playing out in the main text. In the process, it becomes easier to see how apparently firm ontological distinctions that are introduced in the opening passages of *Capital* are progressively destabilized as the text moves forward. In the coming sections, I will put this sort of reading strategy into play in order to reinterpret the opening chapter of *Capital*.

Marx's Three Voices

In the opening sentence of *Capital*, Marx quotes himself, referencing his own earlier work: "The wealth of societies in which the capitalist mode of production prevails," he tells us, "appears as 'an immense accumulation of commodities.'"[19] This gesture is peculiar. Having opened the text and set about reading, we would generally assume that we are immediately engaging with Marx's argument about capital. Only a handful of words in, however, we are confronted with a curious problem: If we are already reading Marx, then why does the text need to quote him? Has he not been speaking all along? Keenan captures the effect well:

> The immediate question is, Why? Why the gesture of quoting oneself, from an earlier and suppressed draft, for two words, with the apparatus of quotation marks, footnotes, etc.? The question itself functions as a monster or a ghost, an uncanny visitor accumulated from another text.[20]

Marx's self-quotation suggests a distance between the voice expressed in the text and Marx's own citable positions. It hints that the voice speaking to us in the opening sentence of *Capital* is somehow not fully identical to Marx's voice, such that the intrusion of Marx himself into the text must be explicitly marked in the form of a quotation. Somehow the argument being made in the opening sentence references Marx. It positions Marx within the opening declarations about how the wealth of capitalist society "appears"—but, at the same time, the very act of quotation seems to suggest that the main text is somehow disjointed from Marx's position. What the distinction might be between the Marx who is quoted and the voice otherwise speaking in the main text remains at this point quite unclear. How should we make sense of this bifurcation, this play within a play, or Marx within a Marx, in the opening sentence of *Capital*?

A few sentences later, we stumble across another peculiar gesture. In the main body of the text, we are told, "The discovery . . . of the manifold uses of things is the work of history."[21] The language implies a passive, contemplative relationship between humans and material objects: Humans discover material properties that have always been inherent to particular objects; at the point of their discovery, these material properties shift from being latent to being manifest in human history. A footnote provides a citation to Barbon—a quotation that seems to support the claim being made in the main text: "Things have an intrinsick vertue," Marx quotes, "which in all places have the same vertue; as the loadstone to attract iron" (125n3). Marx seems, however, somehow to disagree with the link Barbon draws between use-value and intrinsic properties, dryly observing that "the magnet's property of attracting iron only became useful once it had led to the discovery of magnetic polarity" (125n3). For Marx, then, use-value would seem to have a more troubled relation to intrinsic material properties than Barbon's quotation—and, by extension, the main text—suggests.

Yet what is the nature of Marx's objection? Even more perplexing, why whisper the objection in a footnote, while placing a contrary position in a much more eye-catching location in the main text? Why does Marx appear marginalized and bracketed—footnoted and quoted but nevertheless strangely distanced from the main body of his own text?

This problem only deepens as we move forward. The opening paragraphs tell us that "first of all" the commodity is an "external object" that satisfies our changeable needs through its own intrinsic material properties:

> The commodity is, first of all, an external object, a thing which
> through its qualities satisfies human needs of whatever kind. . . . Every
> useful thing is a whole composed of many properties; it can therefore
> be useful in various ways. The discovery of these ways and hence of the
> manifold uses of things is the work of history. (125)

We discover material properties—given time and effort—but these properties themselves subsist outside us: They are objects of our contemplation. Use-value, bound as it is to material properties, is also in some sense essential: the text describes it as a transhistorical substance of wealth, as contrasted with the more transient and socially specific form of wealth, which in capitalism happens to be exchange-value. "They [use-values] constitute the material content of wealth, whatever its social form may be. In the form of society to be considered here they are also the material bearers [*Träger*] of . . . exchange-value" (126). Exchange-value is then itself described as a purely relative form—as an expression of the ways in which quantities of commodities may be equated to one another—without a substantive content specific or intrinsic to itself:

> Exchange-value appears first of all as the quantitative relation. . . . This
> relation changes constantly with time and place. Hence exchange-value
> appears to be something accidental and purely relative, and conse-
> quently an intrinsic value, i.e., an exchange-value that is inseparably
> connected with the commodity, inherent in it, seems a contradiction in
> terms. (126)

Much of this passage seems consonant with Derrida's interpretation: Use-value seems plausibly associated with what Derrida calls "phenomenological good sense"; the term is directly associated in the text with a context-transcendent materiality; and exchange-value appears to be a contingent social phenomenon. If we disregard the puzzling marginal notes and self-references—whose meaning is, at any rate, difficult to discern at this point—little in the first pages of *Capital* seems to trouble Derrida's reading. Moreover, if we were to stop reading at this point, we might be justified in thinking that we know what the commodity is: It is an external object, a unity of sensible properties that include both intrinsic material qualities and socially conventional rates of exchange.

Just as we seem to have all this settled, a second character intrudes, contesting whether this conception of the commodity is adequate to grasp the wealth of capitalist societies.[22] This new character tells us that a commodity's characteristics are not exhausted by reference to its sensible properties alone. Commodities are exchanged in a process that treats them as equivalent to one another. In order for this to happen, however, they must share some property in common:

> A given commodity, a quarter of wheat for example, is exchanged
> for x boot-polish, y silk or z gold, etc. In short, it is exchanged for
> other commodities in the most diverse proportions. . . . x boot polish,
> y silk or z gold, etc., must, as exchange-values, be mutually replaceable
> or of identical magnitude. It follows from this that, firstly, the valid
> exchange-values of a particular commodity express something equal,
> and secondly, exchange-value cannot be anything other than a mode
> of expression, the "form of appearance," of a content distinguishable
> from it.[23]

This common property, however, cannot be anything in the commodity's sensible form, because sensible properties vary from one commodity to the next. It must therefore be something that transcends sensuousness entirely—a supersensible property whose existence can be intuited by reason but to which our sensory perception remains sadly blind.

To get us to this point, the second character engages in a virtuoso demonstration of its deductive acumen, dazzling us with a bit of geometry (127) and then walking us through a sort of transcendental deduction of the existence of the supersensible category of value. It derives the determination of value by labor time and then argues that the labor whose expenditure is measured is some strange entity the text calls "human labour in the abstract" (127–31).

The supersensible categories of value and abstract labor are presented as something like transcendental conditions of possibility for commodity exchange. Such transcendental conditions were invisible from the perspective of the opening "empiricist" character, which doggedly held fast to what could be perceived directly by the senses, and therefore overlooked the intangible properties of the commodity.

When these supersensible properties are brought into view, the apparently arbitrary and contingent appearance of exchange-value is dispelled. Exchange-value, it turns out, does have an intrinsic content—an essence—albeit an intangible essence that cannot be directly perceived by the senses: value (129–31). Moreover, the proportions in which commodities exchange no longer appear purely arbitrary and conventional but rather exhibit lawlike properties: The determination of value by socially necessary labor time emerges as an immanent order behind the apparently random motion of goods that we can immediately perceive.

This second voice is the one Derrida seems to associate with exchange-value—and therefore with the commodity proper. Yet the category of the commodity has already been introduced—in the very first sentence of *Capital*. Both use-value and exchange-value are introduced as moments of the commodity—and yet both are also introduced *prior* to this discussion of the supersensible dimension of the commodity-form. Derrida wants to identify this supersensible dimension with exchange and thus to convict Marx of asserting that "phenomenological good sense" is adequate for grasping use-value alone. The text, however, introduces both use-value and exchange-value as sensuous phenomena *before* it brings on stage the notion of supersensible properties. These supersensible properties are not identified with exchange-value but are instead presented as residing *behind* it. But if this move to the supersensible is *not* a movement from use-value to exchange-value, how should we understand it? Was the first, empiricist character something like a straw man that Marx has defeated through his logical acumen? Is this second, "transcendental" character Marx's proper entry onto the main stage of *Capital*?

The transition to the third section of the chapter strongly suggests that this is not the case. In this transition, Marx begins explicitly to portray both the empiricist and the transcendental characters as actors in a farce. He invokes the image of Dame Quickly, tacitly impugning the analytical virility of the political economists by suggesting that they do not know how to bed down their categories:

> The objectivity of commodities as values differs from Dame Quickly in the sense that "a man knows not where to have it." Not an atom of matter enters into the objectivity of commodities as values; in this it is the direct opposite of the coarsely sensuous objectivity of commodities as

physical objects. We may twist and turn a single commodity as we wish; it remains impossible to grasp it as a thing possessing value. (138)

At this point, the text introduces a third character, which enters the stage speaking in a "dialectical" voice. This character argues that commodities cannot be understood fully through either empiricist or transcendental analysis but must be grasped through a dialectical analysis of their *social* interactions:

> However, let us remember that commodities possess an objective character as values only in so far as they are all expressions of an identical social substance, human labour, that their objective character as values is therefore purely social. From this it follows self-evidently that it can only appear in the social relation between commodity and commodity. (139)

This dialectical analysis, we are told, follows "self-evidently" from the nature of commodity exchange. This character sounds confident of its results. Its predecessors, however, were equally self-assured: The opening "empiricist" character launched boldly into its series of descriptive definitions, telling us what the commodity is "first of all" (125). Its argument sounded persuasive until we reached the following page where the text advised, "Let us consider the matter more closely" (126), and then broke into the presentation of the "transcendental" character, which claimed to illustrate its points with logical deductions, equations, and "simple" examples (127). What is the purpose of these performances? Why does *Capital* stage multiple interpretations of the wealth of capitalist societies?

The Phenomenology of Capital

Here, I suggest, it helps to know that Hegel has staged something like this play before.[24] A comparison of the opening chapter of *Capital* with the early chapters of Hegel's *Phenomenology of Spirit* suggests that Marx is adapting an earlier work—appropriating and turning to his own ends a narrative arc that structures Hegel''s chapters "Perception" and "Force & Understanding."[25]

When these sections of the *Phenomenology* are read against the opening sections of the first chapter of *Capital*, a number of striking parallels leap out. In these early chapters, Hegel follows consciousness as it assumes a series of shapes in its search for certain knowledge of its object. Hegel traces a shape of consciousness—he calls it Perception—that in one of its configurations takes its object to be an external thing that is a collection of sensible properties. Consciousness takes this thing to be more essential than itself and adopts a contemplative stance toward it.[26]

In Hegel's account, Perception fails to achieve the certainty consciousness seeks, and consciousness finds itself driven toward a new shape, which Hegel calls Understanding. Understanding attempts to reach beyond Perception, by taking its object to be supersensible universals. It therefore searches for certain knowledge that transcends the sensible realm but can be intuited by reason (72, 74, 90).

For Hegel, Understanding opens up the lawlike regularities that lie behind the apparent randomness of what can be perceived by the senses. It falls into the error, however, of presupposing that these laws subsist in some separate substance or world that lies behind the flux perceptible to the senses, thus replicating in a new form the separation, of consciousness from its object, that has plagued Perception. This new shape of consciousness is therefore also unstable, leading in Hegel's narrative to a restless oscillation through which it finally confronts what Hegel calls an "inverted world" (90–91).

Within the *Phenomenology*, consciousness's confrontation with the inverted world provides one of the major dramatic pivots of the text. Through this confrontation, consciousness realizes that what it had taken to be a realm of flux and appearance is generative of lawlike regularity, and that what it had taken to be a realm of law and timeless essence is generative of flux. In the process, consciousness comes face-to-face with the instability of the ontological divisions and hierarchies into which it had previously attempted to carve its world. What consciousness had taken to be separate substances or worlds now come, through the confrontation with the inverted world, to be grasped instead as mutually implicated and interpenetrating moments of the very same dynamic relation. This relation, moreover, implicates consciousness as one of its moments, such that consciousness comes to realize that it can no longer position itself as external to its object but finally grasps that it has been its own object all along. At this point in Hegel's drama, consciousness achieves Self-Consciousness (96).

This dramatic arc in Hegel's narrative, in which consciousness moves from Perception, through Understanding, to Self-Consciousness, is subtly spoofed by the characters introduced in *Capital*'s opening chapter. The first, empiricist, character expresses the sensibilities Hegel associates with Perception. The transcendental character aligns with Hegel's Understanding. The dialectical character strides onto the stage, I suggest, as a parallel to Hegel himself. The text in *Capital*'s third section explicitly runs through what are called a set of dialectical "inversions"—after which Marx opens the section titled "The Fetishism of Commodities and Its Secret."[27] The narrative arc of the first chapter of *Capital* thus inserts the commodity-fetishism discussion at the point where Hegel's *Phenomenology* draws aside the curtain that has been separating consciousness from its object, to reveal that consciousness has been its own object all along.

Like Hegel's grand drama of how consciousness struggles to attain certainty of its object, in the process gradually transforming its conception of its object, and thereby itself, the first chapter of *Capital* also stages a struggle over "where to have" an object (138). In the case of *Capital*, however, this elusive object is the commodity, and the production takes the form not of a grand metaphysical construction but of a burlesque squabble over how to grasp the wealth of capitalist society.

Marx is suggesting, through the very structure of the chapter, that the "metaphysical subtleties and theological niceties" that emerge in Hegel's narrative already arise in a much more everyday and indeed crass context: in the course of commodity production and exchange. The most basic, most common, most apparently self-evident object of our economic experience—the commodity—has in this chapter been shown capable of generating great ontological confusion. What is a commodity, this chapter asks? A collection of sensible properties? A transcendental unity that lies behind sensible experience? A dynamic relation with mutually implicated parts? All of these positions, unfolded originally in the course of Hegel's high metaphysical drama, reemerge here in *Capital* in a sort of debauched parody of Hegel's work.

This parody, I suggest, involves a form of selective inheritance very similar to the one Derrida endorses in *Specters*. In my reading, many claims that Derrida attributes to Marx can be more productively read as claims put forward originally by political economy. *Capital* reenacts such claims in a farcical form, repositioning them as set pieces in an ironic Hegelian drama that seeks to undermine the ontological basis of these claims from within. In this way, the text attempts to show that there is no ontological impediment to making history in ways that would seem to be barred by the forms of empiricism, transcendental thought, or dialectical analysis initially put forward in the text.

Let me now explore how this reading transforms what we can inherit in Marx's commodity-fetishism passage.

Turning the Tables

Marx begins his discussion of commodity fetishism with the line that Derrida interprets as a declaration about the accessibility of use-value to "phenomenological good sense": "A commodity appears at first sight an extremely obvious, trivial thing."[28] This sentence, I suggest, is intended to refer back to the chapter's first paragraphs, in which the opening, empiricist character literally takes the commodity "at first sight," equates the commodity with its empirically sensible properties, and therefore views the commodity as "an extremely obvious, trivial thing." The text does not speak nostalgically about this kind of empiricism—it does not, as Derrida fears, seek to return to some self-evident, transparent materiality. Instead, it marks out this form of empiricism as one of the targets of its critique, quickly dismisses it, and moves on.

In the next line, Marx encompasses the perspectives opened up by the transcendental and dialectical interpretations: "But its analysis brings out that it is a very strange thing, abounding in metaphysical subtleties and theological niceties" (163). At this point, as Keenan argues, it becomes clear that "the *phantasmagorische Form* of fetishism is an exact description of the story we have just been reading."[29] Marx here explicitly tips his hand and reveals the satirical nature of the previous sections of the chapter.

Derrida worries that Marx's concern with the "metaphysical" and "theological" properties of the commodity might reflect a nostalgic desire for a self-identical present in which all objects would be transparently whatever they are. I would suggest, instead, that Marx's concern is a more straightforwardly deflationary one: For Marx, it is the political economists who are confident that they know the intrinsic properties of the material world; Marx's analysis seeks to show that what the political economists take to be "objective," "material" qualities can instead be shown to be *produced*—contingently, and only in very specific circumstances. The purpose of this kind of critique is not to search for an even purer, more objective vision of materiality but rather to demonstrate the potential for a more selective inheritance of our historical experience than political economy's ontology would allow.

The passage on the dancing table underscores this point. Having revealed that the kinds of analysis performed in the earlier sections are, in some unspecified sense, the targets of his critique, Marx introduces this evocative image:

> So far as it is use-value, there is nothing mysterious about it. . . . But as
> soon as it emerges as a commodity, it changes into a thing that tran-
> scends sensuousness. It not only stands with its feet on the ground, but,
> in relation to all other commodities, it stands on its head, and evolves
> out of its wooden brain grotesque ideas, far more wonderful than if it
> were to begin dancing of its own free will.
>
> The mystical character of the commodity therefore does not derive
> from its use-value.[30]

The point of this passage would seem to be very clear: Use-value, Marx
tells us, has nothing to do with what he will call the fetish character of the
commodity. We have earlier been told that the commodity is a unity of
use-value and exchange-value. This leads Derrida to decide that, if the use-
value dimension of the commodity does not account for the fetish, then
the *other* dimension of the commodity—the exchange-value dimension—
must account for the phenomenon. The next line, however, undermines
this conclusion. In an exact parallel to the preceding discussion of use-
value, *Capital* claims that "just as little does it proceed from the nature of
the determinants of value" (164).

What is Marx saying here? The fetish character of the commodity does
not arise from the determining factors of use-value—that much is clear. But
apparently this character also does not arise from the determining factors of
value. None of the component moments of the commodity would appear, on
this analysis, to account for the fetish character of the commodity. If none of
the components of the commodity explains the fetish, then what else remains?
Marx asks the same question—and gives a particularly cryptic answer:

> Whence, then, arises the enigmatic character of the product of labour,
> so soon as it assumes the form of a commodity? Clearly, it arises from
> this form itself. (164)

But what does it mean to say that the "form" of the commodity explains
its fetish character, while also insisting that the component parts within
that form, taken by themselves, do not?

What Marx is trying to express, I suggest, is that the fetish character of
the commodity is what we would call, in more contemporary vocabulary,
an *emergent* phenomenon. He is arguing that the component parts of the
commodity are currently arrayed in an overarching assemblage that generates a distinctive consequence—the fetish character of the commodity—
that would not be produced by any of those parts taken in isolation or

assembled into other wholes. Marx claims here that, if you could abstract use-value from the commodity relation, nothing about its components would generate consequences that would render "socially valid" the sorts of "metaphysical subtleties and theological niceties" expressed in the interpretations Marx has brought on stage earlier in this chapter. If you could abstract the determinants of value from the commodity relation, those parts would not generate such consequences *either*. Only the aggregate effect of combining all of these parts, into this historically and socially specific whole, accounts for the fetish character of the commodity.

Marx provides further textual evidence for this interpretation toward the end of the chapter, where he runs through a quick series of examples. Each example, I suggest, reassembles the various parts that are also found in the commodity-form, in order to demonstrate that the same emergent effects do not arise when these parts are assembled into a different configuration.

Marx begins by exploring the hypothetical example of Robinson Crusoe on his island. He argues that the relations between Crusoe and the wealth he creates are "simple and transparent," even though "those relations contain all the essential determinants of value" (170). No fetish character arises in this example, because the "essential determinants of value" are not able—owing to Crusoe's social isolation—to operate in tandem with other sorts of social phenomena. These determinants therefore do not generate any sort of indirect, emergent effect, and so their consequences can be derived from the direct observation of each determinant by itself. As a result, the relations between Crusoe and the wealth he produces are, in Marx's terms, "simple and transparent"—a phrase that, in this context, does not imply a nostalgia for self-identity but simply picks out that these relations generate no emergent effects and therefore possess no fetish character.

Marx immediately extends this same form of analysis into properly social examples, examining a form of feudal production in medieval Europe, a patriarchal peasant family, and, "for a change," an association of laborers working freely together and owning the means of production in common (170–72). In each case, Marx reassembles some of the raw materials also found in the commodity-form, placing these materials into new configurations in order to show that the fetish character does not arise—the emergent effects are not generated. Significantly, not all of the scenarios are "good," and even the example of laborers working in common is chosen "for the sake of a parallel with the production of commodities" (172). The point of these demonstrations is not to recommend some specific alternative form of production but instead to illustrate an analytical strategy—involving both historical research and speculative extrapolation—for assessing the likely consequences of extracting specific parts of the assemblage that currently reproduces capital and reassembling these parts into some very different whole.

In the section on the fetish character of the commodity, Marx begins to hint, very subtly, that the strange, layered, conflictual presentation of his text is meant to express the actual characteristics of our social world, which is characterized by many different layers of practical experience, each of which generates divergent potentials for the future development of capitalist societies. Specific potentials can be selectively inherited by disaggregating the complex whole, adapting some of the practices that currently contribute to the reproduction of capital into new forms, which generate new consequences. *Capital*'s presentational strategy performatively demonstrates this potential for creative appropriation and selective inheritance, by deconstructing the various practices and discourses associated with the reproduction of capital.

Socializing the Material

Right after telling us that the metaphysical and theological character of the commodity derives not from its parts but from the relation into which those parts are suspended, Marx moves into a dense series of paragraphs that culminate in the naming of the fetish. First he argues that

> the equality of the kinds of human labour takes on a physical form in
> the equal objectivity of the products of labour as values; the measure
> of the expenditure of human labour-power by its duration, takes on
> the form of the magnitude of the value of the products of labour; and
> finally the relationships between the producers, within which the social
> characteristics of their labours are manifested, take on the form of a
> social relation between the products of labour. (164)

These sentences are very compressed and difficult to unpack. What Marx wants to analyze is a peculiar social process by which certain characteristics are conferred on human labor. Generally, he suggests, social characteristics are enacted through some sort of intersubjectively meaningful process, such as a long-standing cultural tradition, custom, or law. If the social characteristics listed above were to be conferred on human labor through such an intersubjective means, this might take the form, for example, of an intersubjectively meaningful custom of treating all different forms of human labor as equal, or of a law that dictates that the expenditure of labor-power must be measured by the socially average duration that would be required under normal conditions of production.

These sorts of intersubjective processes, Marx argues, are *not* involved in the constitution of the social characteristics of commodity-producing labor (164–65). Instead, the social characteristics of commodity-producing labor arise unintentionally and also indirectly, as implications of what Marx calls a "social relation between the products of labour." Thus the equality of various kinds of human labor is constituted *implicitly* by a process that seems asocial, because it manifests itself only in relations between the goods this labor produces. Similarly, the measure of human labor power by its duration is *implicitly* generated by a process that is more directly manifest in the relationships among material goods.

Translating these claims back into the vocabulary of emergence: The "social characteristics" of labor should be understood as emergent effects—patterns of social behavior that arise as unintentional consequences of aggregate social practices. An emergent pattern of social behavior manifests itself as a *trend* that plays out, over time, in and through the flux of ordinary social practices. Marx describes the operation of one such trend with a typically vivid image a bit later in this chapter:

> In the midst of the accidental and ever-fluctuating exchange relations between the products, the labour-time socially necessary to produce them asserts itself as a regulative law of nature. In the same way, the law of gravity asserts itself when a person's home collapses on top of him. The determination of the magnitude of value by labour-time is therefore a secret hidden under the apparent movements in the relative values of commodities. (168)

This emergent pattern is "supersensible" because it cannot be immediately observed by examining the individual social practices that produce it, or even the aggregate state of all social practices at any given moment in time. It therefore cannot be sensed directly but can only be deduced, by intuiting the existence of nonrandom trends that emerge in and through the apparently random movements of material goods. The pattern appears "objective" because social actors do not deliberately create it, and nothing about their practices suggests the possibility to generate this sort of emergent result. Since the result has no immediately obvious social origin and is originally discovered as a pattern flowing through the apparently random flux of the movements of material goods, the pattern plausibly appears to arise spontaneously owing to the inherent characteristics of this material realm.

It is at this point that Marx runs through the two analogies—one to optics, and one to religion—whose relation Derrida sunders. Marx uses these analogies to pick out more clearly the peculiar character of the social phenomenon he is trying to analyze, by distinguishing it from two apparently similar phenomena: physical relations that arise from interactions between humans and natural phenomena, and intersubjectively shared beliefs that arise from interactions between humans and their own ideational creations. The phenomenon that interests Marx, by contrast, is neither genuinely asocial nor, in its origins, intersubjective: It is instead a phenomenon that contingently arises from human practice and is therefore social; at the same time, it is a very peculiar sort of social phenomenon, because it is disembedded from intersubjective frameworks and therefore confronts the social actors who create it as though it were a sui generis phenomenon. It is at this moment, having run through these analogies and distinguished from both the phenomenon that interests him, that Marx finally christens the fetish:

> I call this the fetishism of commodities which attaches itself to the
> products of labour as soon as they are produced as commodities, and is
> therefore inseparable from the production of commodities. (165)

Derrida rightly senses that this christening is also an exorcism. What is being exorcised, however, is not spectrality but the myth of Enlightenment: the belief that we can look out onto the material world with a fully disenchanted gaze. The distinctive fetish of capitalist society is the belief that we can look out onto material nature without anthropomorphic projection. It is precisely this belief in disenchantment, Marx suggests, that is the anthropomorphism of our time—one that wears the perfect asocial disguise.

A certain spirit of deconstruction can make it easier to recognize the satirical form of Marx's critique of political economy and the burlesque character of his analysis of the fetish character of the commodity. This deconstructive spirit, however, is partially abridged in Derrida's reading— thus driving Derrida to summon, by means of an exorcism, a relation to spectrality that was already haunting Marx's text without this intervention. To preserve the spectral in Marx's text, to allow nonidentity to continue to haunt the present time, what is required is not the excision of lines from Marx's text. Instead, what is required is an ability to cite Marx's text in more of its moments, inheriting a much more multifaceted and layered understanding of *Capital*'s narrative structure. By recognizing the self-deconstructive presentational strategy through which the text gradually destabilizes and relativizes its opening positions, we can better inherit what Derrida hoped to create: a Marxian critique of ahistorical materialisms that attempt to assert a transparent and unproblematic access to a disenchanted material world.

CHAPTER 4

Agamben and the Messianic:
The Slightest of Differences

David Ferris

First, Benjamin's retelling of Scholem's story about the messianic kingdom. This version comes from Benjamin's "In the Sun" (1932):

> The *Hassidim* tell a story about the world to come that says everything there will be just as it is here. Just as our room is now, so it will be in the world to come; where our baby sleeps now, there too will it sleep in the other world. And the clothes we wear in this world, those too we will wear there. Everything will be as it is now, just a little different.[1]

Like this story's account of the messianic kingdom, the difference between theological and non-theological messianicity may be so slight that it may never be recognizable. Yet, such a difference is crucial if not unavoidable in an age that has so exhausted the sense of its modernity that it can experience the present only as an unending recurrence of ends and limits: the end of politics, the end of history, the limit of thought—to name a few. The possibility of a difference that arrests these limits without reproducing them yet again has constituted what can be called the messianic turn, a turn that emerges with Benjamin's weak messianic power and then becomes more pronounced in the later twentieth century, particularly when we are confronted by claims such as Derrida's "messianicity without messianism," or with Agamben's attempt to reinterpret Carl Schmitt's state of exception in relation to the messianic (a reinterpretation that becomes the basis for Agamben's claims on behalf of law, politics, and a community no longer organized around states of exception). While both Agamben and Derrida reflect a messianic turn in their work after the early 1990s, there is a distinct difference in what each of them calls upon as the messianic as well as in the way that they relate the messianic to larger political and existential claims. The task of this essay will be to clearly delineate the specific force of Agamben's messianic turn in the context not just of Derrida's remarks on the messianic but specifically of the extent to which the hesitations Derrida gives voice to in the early 1990s indicate a fundamental problem that no authentic or genuine messianic tradition—such as that claimed by Agamben—can sweep aside without attempting to master the slightest of differences in which the possibility of the messianic is invested.

Before I present this problem, consideration is first due to why the messianic has had such an unmistakable attraction for the philosophical imagination of the later twentieth century. This attraction is both a historical and a philosophical issue. Philosophical because it involves the question of the possibility of thought at a time when philosophy has become the experience of itself as a limit; historical, because what is being played out at this limit is the fate of an era, of a secular modernity that defines itself in contrast to theological claims. Within this philosophical and historical context, the messianic turn appears as an effort to extend secular thought beyond the limits of its Enlightenment origins—in other words, this turn announces a project to reconfigure modernity through the reinterpretation of the religious perspective against which modernity defined itself. Thus what is at stake in the messianic turn is the relation of the religious and the secular in terms other than those pursued by the Enlightenment and its organization of history and thought according to progressive, rational principles.

Accordingly, one of the claims inherent in this turn is that the messianic is rescued from any restrictive religious context, that it is rescued from any discourse in which it has been embodied in a figure who returns—in short, a messiah. Here, the messianic turn becomes a renegotiation of the terms in which secular thought sought to displace its teleological anxiety about human history by proclaiming unending progress in the place of transcendent belief. To recover a different understanding from religion is the claim of a project that has refused the historical definitions of the religious and the secular in favor of another understanding that no longer adheres to the narratives of modernity. It is here that the messianic comes on the scene with the promise of making a difference to the entrenched histories in which the religious and the secular have been cast. Yet, as Derrida has remarked, the arrival of the messianic turn is not unproblematic, even though his later work will show less recognition of this problem as he too embraces this turn more strongly. This initial hesitation is not only instructive with respect to this later embrace but, at the same time, it recognizes a state that Agamben does not address—namely, that the force of the messianic lies less in the recovery of an authentic tradition than in its constant divorce from all other traditions or forms of thought, as if it were the exception to which all states of exception aspire.

Already in Derrida's phrase "messianicity without messianism," a sense of the problem posed by the messianic as well as by the tradition it would be an exception to can be discerned. The claim for such an exception is expressed through the privative effect of the preposition "without," which defines the relation of these two words.[2] For the messianic to emerge it must be deprived of the messianism practiced by religion. The means by which this exception is expressed also has its tradition, even though its context has little to do with messianic thought. The most significant moment for this exception in modern thought takes place in *The Critique of Judgment* when Kant is compelled to account for a teleology of some kind for aesthetic judgment. Kant characterizes such a "teleology" in the well-known phrase "purposiveness without purpose." Here, Kant's need to take exception into his own thought and his reliance on this formula to do so (adjectival noun deprived of its noun) establishes a recourse that returns almost two hundred years later as contemporary thought takes up the question of founding politics, law, and democracy, on what cannot be determined in advance and does not lay claim to a transcendent event such as the arrival of the messiah or a suprasensible rationality. In the avoidance of an event, the necessity of an exception arrives.

In the case of Derrida's phrase, "messianicity without messianism," what is aimed at is the possibility of thinking something other than religion from within religion itself. At the same time, this "messianicity without messianism" is also the attempt to shift the secular with respect to itself so that the secular remains open to something other than the restricted, progressive sense of history to which it has been committed. To rescue the messianic from messianism is, in this context, to recognize messianism as the form in which messianicity has been sheltered. Derrida clearly formulates such messianism as a condition of messianicity:

The events of revelation, the biblical traditions, the Jewish, Christian and Islamic traditions, have been absolute events, irreducible events which have unveiled this messianicity. We would not know what messianicity is without messianism, without those events which were Abraham, Moses, and Jesus Christ, and so on. In that case singular events would have unveiled or revealed these universal possibilities and it is only on that condition that we can describe messianicity.

"Roundtable," 23–24

To speak of unveiling and revelation is to evoke a language Heidegger was not shy to turn to in his account of how truth, or *aletheia*, happens. Yet, as Derrida indicates, there is a difference to note here. Derrida speaks of what is unveiled in terms of a reiterated conditionality: "*In that case* singular events *would* have unveiled or revealed." This conditionality is far removed from Heideggers's reinterpretation of *aletheia*, or the double movement in which truth happens in a way that makes it both unconcealed and concealed in the same event.[3] Holding on to this conditionality will be crucial for Derrida if the messianic is to avoid becoming an absolute event in its own right. (According to what Derrida says here, only messianism can claim such an event, but it can do so only in the name of a particular religion, thereby limiting the universal claim of its messiah.) The recognition of this limit becomes the condition of both knowing and describing the messianic, but it is a condition that can offer knowledge of the messianic only because it limits the messiah to a singular, absolute occurrence or figure such as those embodied by Abraham, Moses, and Jesus Christ. Thus, rather than reveal the messiah, this messianism reveals what is *like* the messiah (messianicity, the messianic)—that is, it reveals the time in which the messiah is still always to come but without having come. For Derrida, this not having come (which is distinguished from the simple negation of not coming—in the sense of not ever coming) carries the force of an openness that history, politics, religion, and philosophy are unable to close but that is nevertheless disclosed in the failed claim of each to achieve the absolute event of the messiah.

A consequence of Derrida's account of messianism is that the religious, biblical context in which it occurs is the possibility of something other than the fulfillment of that context. Derrida offers two interpretations of this possibility: the one just given, which sees messianicity as being produced as a consequence of messianism, and the possibility that sees messianicity as the condition of messianism and its religions. Derrida characterizes this other account of messianicity as "the groundless ground on which religions have been made possible" ("Roundtable," 23). Where the first account sees messianicity as being unveiled as "universal possibility" in all the conditionality of a present moment, the second equates messianicity with "the fundamental ontological conditions of possibilities of religions" ("Roundtable," 23). As Derrida notes, this other account is Heideggerian in style to the extent that it brings religion within the project of recalling a fundamental ontology that the history of religion is destined to forget. Although Derrida will give more space to the former (messianicity as a universal possibility revealed by religious messianism), he refuses, at the time of this roundtable discussion in 1994, to choose either of these accounts, thereby suspending messianicity in a hesitation when he says, "I confess that I hesitate between these two possibilities" ("Roundtable," 23). But this is not Derrida's only hesitation at this point.

Derrida's hesitation between two accounts of messianicity is accompanied by a hesitation about messianicity itself. This more fundamental hesitation, also expressed in his "Roundtable" (1994), poses the question of the extent to which the significance of the messianic turn remains strategic— that is, the extent to which it belongs to a history rather than bringing about the arrest of history. This hesitation is expressed as follows:

> Between the two possibilities I must confess I oscillate and I think some other scheme must be constructed to understand the two at the same time, to do justice to the two possibilities. That is why—and perhaps this is not a good reason, perhaps one day I will give up this—for the time being I keep the word "messianic." Even if it is different from messianism, messianic refers to the word Messiah; it does not simply belong to a certain culture, a Jewish or Christian culture. I think that for the time being I need this word, not to teach, but to let people understand what I am trying to say when I speak of messianicity.
>
> "Roundtable," 24

Derrida's hesitation about a decision that would validate either one of these possibilities poses the question of another understanding that would, in effect, do justice to this oscillation or hesitation. The problem Derrida points to here involves how to justify this oscillation not as two discrete moments, whose separateness requires that a decision is made for one or the other, but as moments belonging to a single time. The problem addressed here can be discerned if the character of the two possibilities is recalled. According to the first possibility, messianicity is a general structure of experience, a groundless ground on which the revelations of "religions have been made possible." According to the second, messianicity is what issues from the revelations of religion. The problem to be addressed is why each possibility is forced to take exception to itself, to deprive itself of what constitutes it in order to claim significance. This exception is present in the first possibility when it is characterized as a ground without ground ("groundless ground"); the second possibility is the phrase already discussed, "messianicity without messianism."

Is the difference inserted by this self-exception the difference that Benjamin speaks of, "the slightest of differences," when he recalls Scholem's story about the difference between the messianic kingdom to come and the world as it is now? Does the recourse to exception in each of the possibilities Derrida describes depend on a sense of messianic difference despite his question about some other scheme other than the messianic? If not, then what is the difference or scheme that is something other than *the* messianic in this case? It is with these questions in mind that we can now turn to Agamben's recourse to the messianic as a guiding figure for the various theoretical positions he has claimed on behalf of law and politics in his writings. The issue to be addressed is whether, as Agamben claims and without hesitation, there is a genuine messianic tradition that sustains his accounts of politics, law, a coming community, and so on. Or, if not, by what means and on what grounds has Agamben claimed such a tradition?

By strategically positioning messianicity in a different relation to the Messiah, Derrida, as he admits, is attempting to refer to a word whose significance religions have limited to a specific universality. To avoid a simple lapse into such a specific universality, Derrida describes this reference as both necessary and temporally limited ("I think that *for the time being I need* this word"). Messianicity cannot, in this case, possess significance beyond a reference that remains historical. It is on this last point that the significance of Derrida's treatment of messianicity has its most crucial relation to Agamben's claims about the messianic. These claims first emerge prominently in Agamben's work with an essay adapted from a lecture he delivered in 1992, "The Messiah and the Sovereign: The Problem of Law in Walter Benjamin."[4] It is between this essay and the later commentary on Paul's letter to the Romans, *The Time That Remains* (first published in 2000), that Agamben's messianic turn can be positioned. It should not be overlooked here that Derrida's hesitations about the messianic, from the 1994 "Roundtable," are expressed between the dates, 1992 and 2000, of these two Agamben texts. Thus, when considering how Agamben picks up and deploys the messianic in his work, the question posed by Derrida's hesitations cannot be put aside. Not only does such an issue have consequences for any claim made on behalf of the messianic, but it also draws attention to how such claims return to the "slightest of differences" in which the contemporary significance of the messianic has been invested after Benjamin and Scholem. It becomes a question of whether such differences can be sustained as a condition that is itself historical and therefore locatable within an "authentic" tradition. Or does such a condition have only strategic significance?

As both Derrida's and Agamben's writings are witness to, the emergence of the messianic as a topos for contemporary thought owes much to Benjamin's the second thesis of Benjamin's last work, "On the Concept of History," where he identifies a weak messianic power. The crucial sentences from this thesis are as follows:

> The past carries with it a secret index by which it is referred to redemption. Doesn't a breath of the air that pervaded earlier days caress us as well? In the voices we hear, isn't there an echo of now silent ones? Don't the women we court have sisters they no longer recognize? If so, then there is a secret agreement between past generations and the present one. Then our coming was expected on earth. Then, like every generation before us, we carry along with us a weak messianic power, a power on which the past has a claim.
>
> *SW* 4:390; translation modified

The significance of the first sentence quoted here can be discerned if the assumptions informing the rhetorical questions by which it is followed are unpacked: The first question states that there is a secret agreement between generations; the second question states that the coming of another generation is expected; the third question states that each generation is endowed with a weak messianic power. What makes Benjamin's thinking cohere in this thesis is the secret agreement that allows a later generation to become the index of a preceding one although never in the actual form or voice of the earlier but only as the echo of what is silent. The demand made by this agreement is that the later generation must recognize that it is also subject to this agreement, that it cannot redeem the past but only become the means by which a future generation may refer to redemption. No generation can become the messiah of history, since it is only an index to the redemption invested in such a figure. As an index, the redemption associated with each generation is weak, since it can only refer to redemption without achieving it. This is the agreement and the messianic power that traverses generations for Benjamin.

While Derrida claims something "consonant" with as well as "many differences" with Benjamin's weak messianism, Agamben embarks on a course that will elaborate this weak messianic power in relation to Carl Schmitt's "state of exception" in order to establish fundamental claims about the nature of law, religion, and politics.[5] To do this, the central thesis of Agamben's "The Messiah and the Sovereign" reconfigures the messianic as follows: "The thesis I would like to advance is that the messianic kingdom is not one category among others within religious experience but is, rather, its limit concept" ("Messiah," *Potentialities*, 163). This notion of a limit is precisely the ground on which Derrida expressed his hesitation with Benjamin's understanding of the messianic, as such a notion establishes the messianic within a specific horizon, thereby defining it as either "infinite progress or a waiting and awaiting" for something to be experienced at the limit.[6] In this context, when Agamben calls the messianic a "limit concept," is he attaching a more restricted sense of suspension to the messianic, a sense that is already specifically adapted to what his thesis seeks to establish—that is, a transformation of Carl Schmitt's "state of exception"? But, when Agamben develops this understanding in a remark on how Benjamin uses Schmitt's language in Thesis 2 from "On the Concept of History," what emerges as crucial is less the promise of such a transformation than the manner in which Agamben attempts to precipitate it:

> In defining the messianic kingdom with the terms of Schmitt's theory
> of sovereignty, Benjamin appears to establish a parallelism between
> the arrival of the Messiah and the limit concept of State power. In the
> days of the Messiah, which are also "the 'state of exception' in which we
> live," the hidden foundation of the law comes to light, and the law itself
> enters into a state of perpetual suspension.[7]

Agamben first states that Benjamin "appears to establish" this parallelism ("Benjamin sembra istituire un parallelo.")[8] However, the hesitation of "sembra" disappears quickly as Agamben, immediately after the sentence just cited, declares that "in establishing this analogy [stabilendo questa analogia ("Il messia," 13)], Benjamin does nothing other than bring a genuine messianic tradition to the most extreme point of its development" (*Potentialities*, 162). Despite what Agamben says here, Benjamin's concern in the thesis referred to is with a different political tradition, one that is already socially and historically embedded:

> The tradition of the oppressed teaches us that the "state of emergency"
> in which we live is not the exception but the rule. We must attain to

a conception of history that accords with this insight. Then we will clearly see that it is our task to bring about a real state of emergency, and this will improve our position in the struggle against fascism.

Thesis 8, *SW* 4:392

Agamben's framing of Benjamin in terms of a genuine messianic tradition has more to do with establishing Benjamin as having brought Carl Schmitt and the messianic to a common point that exposes what Agamben calls the "hidden foundation of law." By means of what Benjamin *appears* to say, Agamben creates a suggestion that is then repeated as if it has all the force of an established certainty. This pattern is not restricted to this example. Immediately after claiming that Benjamin actually establishes what Agamben first says he had only appeared to establish, Agamben goes on to make another suggestive hesitation before quickly overcoming any reservation about that hesitation. Agamben first writes: "The essential character of messianism is *perhaps* precisely its particular relation to the law" [Il carattere *forse* essenziale del messianismo è precisamente il suo particolare rapporto con la Legge (emphasis added; "Il messia," 13; "Messiah," 162). Then, once more and almost immediately this time, the hesitation of *forse* ("perhaps") disappears as Agamben not only states but emphasizes in italics the following restatement of his putative thesis: *"The Messiah is, in other words, the figure through which religion confronts the problem of the Law, decisively reckoning with it"* ("Messiah," 163).[9]

What was "perhaps essential" is now decisively so for Agamben. The suggestion introduced by these hesitations is affirmed as if the hesitation had never occurred.[10] At the same time, the question is not raised whether Benjamin's parallelism/analogy is in effect an evocation of the messianic that follows the parallels Agamben wishes to pursue. If this were to be raised, one would have to turn back to Thesis 6 of Benjamin's text to recover his actual reference to the messiah. In Thesis 6, Benjamin states, "The Messiah comes not only as the redeemer, he comes as the victor over the Antichrist."[11] Characteristically for Benjamin, this sentence has an intrusive and arresting effect, and, as its context (Benjamin's remarks on the task of the present-day historian) makes clear, this arrest places the messiah in contrast to the plight of the historian. No messianic kingdom is invoked here. Rather, the focus is on the historian who, in the sentence following the reference to the messiah, is described as follows: "The only historian capable of fanning the spark of hope in the past is the one who is firmly convinced that *even the dead* will not be safe from the enemy if he is victorious. And this enemy has never ceased to be victorious" (*SW* 4:391).

Such a historian makes no messianic claim. Rather, the task of such a historian is to recognize that redemption, if at all possible, is not only fragmentary and momentary but also incapable of an enduring historical presence
for any generation. Here, the selectivity of Agamben's reading of Benjamin
seeks to displace the former's agency in configuring the messianic as the
exception to Schmitt's state of exception. This selectivity continues in the
thesis Agamben uses to claim an analogy between Benjamin and Schmitt
on the grounds of the messianic:

> The tradition of the oppressed teaches us that the "state of emergency"
> in which we live is not the exception but the rule. We must attain to
> a conception of history that accords with this insight. Then we will
> clearly see that it is our task to bring about a real state of emergency,
> and this will improve our position in the struggle against fascism.
>
> *SW* 4:392

Here Benjamin's language may evoke a parallel to Schmitt, but what Benjamin says reveals an intention different from what Agamben sees only
as a citation and falsification. Agamben writes: "It is this last sentence
[of Schmitt] that Benjamin both cites and falsifies in the Eighth Thesis.
Instead of 'the rule as such lives off the exception alone,' he writes: 'the
"state of exception" in which we live is the rule'" ("Messiah," 162). Where
Agamben will inflect the rule back into the exception, Benjamin seeks an
exception that will mark its difference to rule. That this difference is at
stake for Benjamin is already enough to indicate how much Agamben will
reread Benjamin's words as if their only object was Schmitt. Rather than
falsify Schmitt, Benjamin rewrites his terms to conceive of an exception
different from the one Schmitt adheres to—namely, a state of emergency
that will not become its own rule. What is important to retain here is that
Benjamin's language may be evocative of Schmitt but that such evocation
is not ipso facto a parallelism or analogy in thought. Benjamin's evocation
of Schmitt's language does not seek authority in the messianic, nor does it
seek to overcome fascism and to establish a different political community.
It is simply part of the struggle against fascism and a struggle against "an
enemy that has never ceased to be victorious" (*SW* 4:391).

Despite these differences, Agamben will state unequivocally that it is by
returning to Benjamin's Eighth thesis (in which the parallelism he claims
is not exactly made) that the legitimacy and coherence of his claim for a
parallelism is to be found: "If we now return to our point of departure, that
is, to Benjamin's Eighth Thesis, the comparison he makes between messianic time and the state of exception shows its legitimacy and its coherence"

("Messiah," 169). This claim reveals a tendency to a "post hoc ergo propter hoc" style of argument whereby the return becomes legitimate and coherent because of where one returns from. In so doing, it appears to establish a cause and effect between Benjamin's text and Agamben's thesis while erasing the preceding hesitancy ("appears to establish," "perhaps")—a pattern in which suggestiveness is erased by what it suggests.

In this return to the point of departure, Agamben claims to have expressed not just the "proper meaning" of Benjamin's eighth thesis from "On the Concept of History" but also "Benjamin's theses" overall. Agamben's escalation of the significance of his reading of Benjamin from a selection to all of the theses is accompanied by the articulation of what is really at stake in this reading of Benjamin—the authority to make the following claim:

> Today, everywhere, in Europe as in Asia, in industrialized countries
> as in those of the "Third World," we live in the ban of a tradition that
> is permanently in a state of exception. And all power, whether demo-
> cratic or totalitarian, traditional or revolutionary, has entered into a
> legitimation crisis in which the state of exception, which was the hidden
> foundation of the system, has fully come to light. . . . The entire planet
> has now become the exception that law must contain in its ban. Today
> we live in this messianic paradox, and every aspect of our existence
> bears its marks.
>
> *Potentialities*, 170

"Everywhere," "all power," "the entire planet," "every aspect of our existence"—with these words Agamben has generalized Benjamin's "citation and falsification" of Schmitt into a condition of existence, a condition that lies as the "hidden foundation of the system." What permits this generalized move is the analogy between the messianic and the state of exception. Remember, Agamben claims that "in establishing this analogy, Benjamin does nothing other than bring a genuine messianic tradition to the most extreme point of its development" ("Messiah," 162). This extreme point is the "limit concept" of religious experience, just as the state of exception is the limit concept of law; it is the point at which the law remains "in force but does not signify anything," or, again citing Agamben, it is the moment of "the self-suspension of the law," when the law "applies to the individual case in no longer applying" ("Messiah," 170). These moments are what constitute the "messianic paradox," which, Agamben asserts, marks "every aspect of our existence." This paradox has a consistent structure that is at once self-reflexive and self-negating. As in the example that Agamben is fond of citing, the law applies in its negation of its application or validity or, to put this another way, it applies *without* applying. Since, according to Agamben's thesis ("Messianic," 162), the messianic is the figure that decisively reckons with the problem of law. The messianic is *the* example of this paradox.[12]

In his treatment of sovereignty and law, subjects that are both central to "The Messiah and the Sovereign," Agamben establishes this paradox by evoking a history that takes the form of a symmetrical inversion of the concept of sovereignty:

> If the paradox of sovereignty once had the form of the proposition "There is nothing outside the law," it takes on a perfectly symmetrical form in our time, when the exception has become the rule: "There is nothing inside the law"; everything—every law—is outside law.
>
> "Messiah," 170

The perfect extremity of relation between the two possibilities that establish the law creates the limit concept through which Agamben articulates what the law, the sovereign, the messianic, Benjamin, and Schmitt have in common. Agamben articulates this limit through a phrase he uses to summarize Benjamin's and Scholem's 1934 correspondence on Kafka: "*being in force without significance* (Geltung ohne Bedeutung)" (*Potentialities*, 169)—a phrase he calls "an exemplary figure."[13] What remains at stake here is that there should be such an example and that this example should fulfill its role as a structural analogy. Only on the basis of such an analogy can Agamben claim that the law in its original state is tied to the state of exception. Agamben writes that "in this light we can also seek to clarify the structural analogy that ties law in its original state to the state of exception" ("Messiah," 169). The light referred to is the "legitimacy and coherency" that arise from "the return to our point of departure"—that is, to the return discussed above, the return of Agamben to his point of departure.

Agamben, by turning here to "original state" and "hidden foundation," as well as by returning to his initial claim that Benjamin in the Eighth Thesis compares "messianic time" and Schmitt's "state of exception," already indicates that his sense of the messianic has more in common with the first of the messianic possibilities described by Derrida: the fundamental condition of a "groundless ground" that Derrida characterized as Heideggerian in gesture. But there is also a difference here, and it runs like a thread through Agamben's subsequent treatment of the messianic tradition with respect to both Benjamin and the status of law that Agamben takes up again in the first section of *Homo Sacer*. This difference resides in the importance

Agamben attaches to what he calls "genuine messianic tradition" ("Messiah," 162).[14] For Agamben, only genuine messianic traditions can offer the limit concept that articulates the point at which religion, philosophy, law, politics, and the state are confronted with what they cannot account for.

That the messianic is a privileged place for the articulation of this limit is affirmed by Agamben in *The Time That Remains*, where in his long commentary on Paul's letter to the Romans he states that his goal is "to restore Paul's letters to the status of the fundamental messianic text for the Western tradition" (*Time*, 1). By claiming that this is not just any messianic text but the decisively fundamental one, Agamben not only raises the stakes of his reading of Paul's letters but also indicates that his treatment of Paul and the messianic is guided by the conviction that a specific text can be fundamental and that, in some way, the experience of the messianic is linked to the textual. In his commentary, Agamben will attempt to affirm these convictions by emphasizing "an aporia that concerns the very structure of Messianic time" (*Time*, 1). As this emphasis unfolds, it becomes clear that what Agamben is undertaking is to document the aporetic as the index to his sense of the messianic as a time that remains. Consequently, although not itself messianic time, the aporetic must be accounted for as a time that happens to coincide with the existence of the messianic. The aporetic thus becomes an index to the slightest of differences and is measured here as the difference between two experiences of time that happen to occur in the same time. Two things are then at stake: to establish a temporal coincidence between messianic time and the time of historical existence, and to account for the slightest of differences as the hidden foundation of this coincidence. Both of these, Agamben asserts, depend on what in the essay "The Messiah and the Sovereign" he had called the "proper meaning" of a text.[15] Here such a meaning issues from a contextual restoration:

> The possibility of understanding the Pauline message coincides fully
> with the experience of such a time; without this, it runs the risk of
> remaining a dead letter. The restoration of Paul to his messianic
> context therefore suggests, above all, that we attempt to understand
> the meaning and internal form of the time he defines as *ho nyn kairos*,
> the "time of the now." Only after this can we raise the question of how
> something like a messianic community is in fact possible.
>
> *Time*, 2

Here the possibility of understanding the Pauline message does not simply coincide but must coincide *fully* with the experience of messianic time if Agamben's thesis is to be sustained. This emphasis on "fully" leaves no room for any noncoincidence between messianic time and the Pauline message. In this case, the understanding at stake is one that must coincide fully with a time that that understanding already is. As a result, the question that remains for Agamben is how to keep messianic time and his understanding of the Pauline message separate enough for them to coincide, while at the same time claiming a level of coincidence ("fully") that suggests they are inseparable. In effect, Agamben will need to show that their separateness is their coincidence. Agamben's answer to this question is to recall how Benjamin concludes his version of Scholem's story about the messianic kingdom: "Everything will be as it is now, just a little different." For Agamben, what is embedded in Benjamin's words is a structural relation that amounts to the following understanding: the same without being the same.

Agamben's frequent recourse to such a structure in his work reveals not only that the extent to which his thought is formed by and seeks to uncover this structure as the hidden foundation on which the whole of modern experience as a state of exception rests but also that such a foundation is capable of producing a transformation of that experience. To make such a prophetic claim is to invest in the aporias of modern experience and modern history as being both aporetic and nonaporetic at the same time. It is aporetic because in Agamben's thought history, tradition, ethics, politics, etc. must be brought to a state of exception, and it is nonaporetic because the aporia must also be the index of something other than that exception.[16] In the case of *The Time That Remains*, Agamben refers to this something else as a "messianic community" that is itself a variant on what he had earlier called the "coming community" in a text of the same title that also gives prominence to Benjamin's retelling of Scholem.[17] The political purpose of such a community and of its links to the messianic is made even more explicit in his volume *Means Without End* (1995), where Agamben gives preeminence to messianism as the source of a future politics. There he writes that "the task that messianism has assigned to modern politics—to think a human a community that would not have (only) the figure of the law—still awaits the minds that might undertake it."[18] Agamben's interpretation of this distinction identifies messianism as the place of aporia and paradox, and, on the strength of this identification, he postulates a "messianic event" that simultaneously transgresses and fulfills messianism.[19]

How this argument by paradox works can be seen clearly when Agamben refers to the concept of a people in an earlier part of *Means Without End*:

[Concept of the people] is what cannot be included in the whole of
which it is a part as well as what cannot belong to the whole in which it
is always already included.

Hence the contradictions and aporias that such a concept creates
every time it is invoked and brought in to play on the political stage. It
is what always already is, as well as what is to be realized.

Means, 32

For Agamben, the paradox is the effect of a contradiction defined by the
terms of a law that demands that what is true has to be one thing or another but not both—in effect, Aristotle's principle of noncontradiction.
What Agamben does here is to overstate this contradiction as if it were a
self-evident absolute limit, so that it establishes the reality of "what always
already is." The stake of this argument by conflation lies in the necessity
of producing closed, impassable events—that is, conditions inviting the
intervention of Schmitt's "state of exception." As a result, what articulates
Agamben's theoretical claims on behalf of a coming messianic community
as well as Agamben's other claims on behalf of politics is the desire to force
metaphysical thinking to fulfill its claims. This desire produces limit concepts in the form of aporia, paradox, contradiction, etc., which are then
claimed as other to or transgressive of the tradition, messianic or otherwise,
within which they occur. Such a claim is already a limited reading of that
tradition as well as a failure to recognize that these concepts are produced,
defined, and set to work within such a tradition. As Heidegger repeatedly
insists in his reading of Nietzsche, transforming metaphysics by attempting to fulfill it only allows this tradition to continue through an inversion
that grants metaphysics the power to contradict itself and through that
power sustain itself.[20] That Agamben understands the paradoxes he emphasizes as fulfillment clearly comes to the fore in the following sentences
from *Means Without End*: "The paradoxes of messianism which Sabbatai
Zevi expressed by saying: 'The fulfillment of the Torah is its transgression'
and which Christ expressed (more soberly than Paul) in the formula: 'I did
not come to destroy the law but to fulfill it'" (*Means*, 135).

The necessity of this drive in Agamben to produce fulfillment, with
respect both to the concept of the people and to the messianism referred
to here, is not an advance beyond the problem Nietzsche bequeathed to
our modernity when he proclaimed himself "the first accomplished nihilist of Europe"; rather, it remains its repetition.[21] Although Agamben has
never referred to himself as a nihilist in the Nietzschean sense, this drive to

fulfill reiterates strongly the way in which Nietzsche sought to transform nihilism by attempting to fulfill it.[22] In Nietzsche's case, this attempt rests on a distinction he makes between two nihilisms, one passive or reactive, and the other active. Having made this distinction, Nietzsche initiates a project that would fulfill the first one so that it will be transformed into the second. What the example of Nietzsche shows here is a structural pattern to which Agamben also succumbs.

This pattern emerges nowhere more forcefully than in "The Messiah and the Sovereign." At a decisive stage in this essay's argument, Agamben not only seeks a similar fulfillment (or perfection) but does so on the back of distinguishing between two nihilisms, each of which he equates with two forms of messianism:

> We will have to distinguish two forms of messianism or nihilism: a first
> form (which we may call imperfect nihilism) that nullifies the law but
> maintains the Nothing in a perpetual and infinitely deferred state of
> validity, and a second form, a perfect nihilism that does not even let
> validity survive beyond its meaning but instead, as Benjamin writes
> of Kafka, "succeeds in finding redemption in the overturning of the
> Nothing."
>
> "Messiah," 171

For Agamben, the possibility of a trangressive messianism turns on the existence of these two nihilisms.[23] The first he characterizes as imperfect because, in a phrase Agamben coins to summarize Scholem, it is a nothingness or messianism that retains its value despite having become meaninglessness. As such, this first nihilism becomes the reference through which the second ("the overturning of Nothing") is realized. What Agamben decides in this manner is a nothing that is more than a nothing without meaning—when it has no meaning it has the meaning of force. This decision reveals how crucial such a distinction is—not only for Agamben's dispatch of nihilism but also for the possibility of realizing a messianism that stands beyond the state of exception articulated by Schmitt. (Like nothing, the law remains in force in Schmitt's state of exception despite having become meaningless through contradiction and paradox.)

Agamben has no doubt about the difference between these two nihilisms or messianisms, no matter how slight the difference between two nothings must be. In this respect, Agamben's messianic thinking repeats the strategy of Nietzsche but does so by claiming a difference whose slightness Nietzsche left as something yet to be attained. Ignoring Nietzsche's suspension, Agamben proceeds as if what Nietzsche left as something to be accomplished has been accomplished. Without this slightest of differences—in this case, the difference between two nihilisms or messianisms—Agamben's messianic thinking runs the risk of being merely insignificant, and hence the persistence to which his writing returns to eliciting "the slightest of differences" across a range of texts that articulate this difference on the basis of an absolutized limit such as Schmitt's state of exception. Here, the pernicious attraction of Schmitt for modern political thought and its critique of secular liberalism comes to the fore in a project that attempts to think with Schmitt and then resist the consequences of that attempt lest sovereignty in whatever form is inadvertently affirmed. To resist those consequences on the slightest of differences runs the risk of making no difference at all, especially when, as Vattimo has shown, this distinction between two nihilisms on which the possibility of fulfilling metaphysics rests is not as clear or as sustainable as it appears in Nietzsche.[24] In this case, the question to pose is first: What is at stake in insisting on such a difference as Agamben does? And, second: For whom is this insistence articulated?

The first of these questions points emphatically to a need to discern a structure that is specifically and unchangeably messianic. This need is not a religious need. Religion is not at stake here, as Agamben reveals through his repeated insistence on religion as a limited account of the messianic (which gives rise to the restriction of religion to messianism). What is at stake for Agamben is revealed in *The Time That Remains* when he states as a given fact that "the messianic world is nothing other than the secular world" (*Time*, 56). With this remark it becomes clear that, for Agamben, the turn to the messianic is the continued assertion of the secular at the very limit of its historical significance. This is why the "limit concept" is so crucial to Agamben and also why it is the product of the kind of fulfillment offered by Carl Schmitt as the condition of the "state of exception." The turn to the messianic then becomes a secularizing of religion that seeks to differentiate the secular enough in order to distinguish it from the tradition of liberal politics—with whose limitation the name "Schmitt" has now become synonymous. What this aims to produce is nothing less than a secularity without secularism, a secularity in which religion and the secular are both present by virtue of a difference so slight that one may be taken for the other. The difference at stake here, already present in the phrase that most accurately describes it, "secularity without secularism," is precisely what Agamben would locate in the kind of messianism he calls a "genuine, authentic tradition."

In his commitment to such a tradition, which he proclaims to be the Pauline message, Agamben, would redress the aporias that secular thought now rehearses as both its provenance and its limit. But Agamben's redress, by taking the form of a transgressive fulfillment of this secular thought, does not question the extent to which such a fulfillment occurs under what Mallarmé called "a false appearance of the present." If the messianic is a hidden foundation of both messianism and our secular age, as Agamben contends, then, according to his claims, neither religion nor the secular can be fulfilled. Their "fulfillment" can only be reiterated in the form of their limit: the paradox of being fulfilled by not being fulfilled—in other words, maintained by the limit that assures the domain of their effectiveness. To argue for such a fulfillment is to demand, at the very least, a time in which this limit or this slightest of differences can take place. This is why, in a text such as *The Time That Remains*, Agamben is so focused on the recognition of a time that is not quite the time of history. Agamben asserts that such a time occurs, to use a phrase he puts tremendous weight on, "as not" history—that is, both *as* and at the same time *not* the time of history. Agamben identifies this "as not" as what is properly messianic. So strong is this identification that Agamben will go so far as to claim that to be messianic is to exist *as* this "as not": "To be messianic, to live in the Messiah, signifies the expropriation of each and every juridical-factical property (circumcised/uncircumcised; free/slave; man/woman) under the form of the *as not*" (*Time*, 26). Messianic being is being that exists under a form. What remains can be given only as this form, or, in Agamben's formula, it is given *as not* object. The significance of this lies in the claim that it cannot exist as an object, only as an *as-not-object*. As such, it would retain the force of an object while lacking the material existence of such an object.

The importance of this recognition is that it defines Agamben's theoretical project as the reiterated attempt to give a form to a difference slighter than all other difference. Yet, it can do so only in a form that is essentially privative. In this respect, Agamben is restricted to the endless activity of giving form to what exists without object—a restriction that accounts for the repeated turn to recondite examples rescued from their textual and historical contexts. This overpowering recourse to example, over and beyond a testimony to Agamben's historical textual knowledge, indicates the extent to which what remains is what has to be affirmed over and over again. In other words, it marks the limit against which Agamben's thought continually positions itself. Here, Agamben's thinking as the ceaseless performance of its own limit, as the sign of the prophet who guards the limit of his prophecy at the very edge of secular metaphysics. Agamben has no hesitation about positioning his thought at this edge, which remains thoroughly messianic for him. It is in this sense that we can speak of an Agamben messianic, of an Agamben who holds the promise of a repeated limit before our eyes as if it were the threshold of the coming community, the threshold of a politics no longer haunted by the specter of bare life at the very limit of its existence.

With such promise in mind, it is instructive to recall Derrida's hesitation in 1994 between two messianic possibilities, not to discern which one Agamben has chosen but rather to document the necessity of a choice that this hesitation precipitated in both. Where Agamben asserts the messianic as something to which Paul can be restored, he claims a groundless ground, what Derrida called a "general structure of messianicity," yet for Derrida what Agamben claims remains a problem and an enigma—namely, Derrida asks, whether messianicity is the condition of religions.[25] In this remark, Derrida characterizes his choice as one between a hypothesis that remains enigmatic and a hypothesis that displaces this enigma into a future that will define the experience of the present as a waiting (but not a simple waiting for an appointed arrival, since that would be nothing more than a messianism without messianicity). This waiting, as Derrida describes it in an interview in 2004, would be nothing less than a "waiting without waiting, without horizon for the event to come, the democracy to come with all its contradictions."[26] On this occasion, the more fundamental hesitation, about the messianic as a category, that Derrida had expressed in the 1990s does not recur. Instead it is replaced by an admission that Agamben could never make despite his own need to give force and form to the "as not." Derrida states: "And I believe we must seek today, very cautiously, to give force and form to this messianicity, without giving in to the old concepts of politics (sovereignism, territorialised nation-state), without giving in to the Churches or to the religious powers, theologico-political or theocratic of all orders, whether they be the theocracies of the Islamic Middle East, or whether they be, disguised, the theocracies of the West" ("Justice to Come," 7). With the certainty of a belief that is also a necessity ("I believe we *must*"), Derrida ultimately adheres to the second messianic possibility he had elaborated in 1994. Not only has Derrida's hesitation between these two accounts gone, but so has the more fundamental hesitation about whether messianicity is an adequate rubric under which to think an alternative to the "old concepts of politics." In the context of Derrida's remarks just cited, Agamben's overcoming of any hesitation by embracing the messianic is not a matter of prescience; rather, it is a matter of mistaking a paradox for a contradiction that has always already come. And this contradiction, before it becomes a paradox, is the form in which Agamben's messianicity conceals his hesitation about the messianic itself.

This is its weakness: Messianicity is not what waits but, rather, it is the name of the hesitation in which our secular age survives the experience of its own end. The limit of the secular now resides in its recourse to a messianism in which the present is experienced as a perpetual hesitation about a past refigured in the form of a future that will always have come without coming.

CHAPTER 5

Messianic Language and the Idea of Prose: Benjamin and Agamben

Vivian Liska

> And the entire lengthy volume [in which] the hand of the
> scribe had crammed with characters was nothing other
> than the attempt to represent the perfectly bare writing
> tablet on which nothing had yet been written.
>
> —GIORGIO AGAMBEN, *Idea of Prose*

> The white page is poisoned. The book that doesn't tell
> any story kills. The absence of story signifies death.
>
> —TZVETAN TODOROV

Whoever has once—in a dream or daydream—dwelled in the redeemed world and whoever, like a figure in a fragment by Franz Kafka, has had a near-death experience from which he comes back certainly has rich stories to tell. One can, Kafka writes, learn many a thing from him, but what really occurs after death or—in our case—after the end of history, and whether this is a realm where stories are being told, that he cannot tell.[1]

The question whether there will be stories in a redeemed world and, if there will be, what they will be like and in what kind of language they will be told must seem futile to anyone for whom messianic redemption is itself nothing but a story that has outlived itself. Paradoxically, such a death certification only confirms the continuing life of this *grand récit*, in that it announces, like all messianisms, the end of an age-old story—the story of the eschatological imagination itself. If we accept, however, Walter Benjamin's dictum that every story legitimately invites the question "How does it continue?"[2] then asking about the fate of stories after the end of times is as legitimate as wondering what follows after the *grands récits* themselves. A possible variation of this continuation can be read in the current reception of Walter Benjamin's ideas about the relationship between language, epic forms, and messianic expectations.

Giorgio Agamben—for decades the Italian editor of Benjamin's collected works and a leading figure in contemporary Continental thought—performs one of the most radical recoveries of his messianic thinking to date. In his references to Benjamin, which permeate his work from his early theoretical studies on aesthetics and language to his later juridical and political texts, Agamben forcefully wrenches Benjamin away from the views of his former milieu, especially from Gershom Scholem and Theodor W. Adorno, as well as from his later readers, foremost among them Jacques Derrida. For Agamben, the constitutive inability of Derridean deconstruction to reach closure partakes in perpetuating the prevailing dismal condition of humanity through an attitude that he terms "a petrified or paralyzed messianism."[3] Agamben rejects Derrida's exhortation of an endless "expectation without expectation" and his definition of the messianic as an existential structure of infinite deferral and radical openness toward an incalculable, unpredictable future. Against Derrida, Agamben recovers aspects of Benjamin's messianic thinking that foreground the urgency to terminate deferral. This approach has significant consequences on his reading of Benjamin's reflections on messianic language.

Between 1982 and 1992, Giorgio Agamben wrote several essays on Benjamin's messianism that emphasize a redemptive reversal occurring at a "point of indifference," an empty spatial and temporal spot where beginning and end fall together and the course of history as a Hegelian "bad infinity" is brought to an end. A recurrent motif of these essays is a critique of various traditions of thought that rest on the structure of an infinite deferral. This critique becomes most concrete in the essay entitled "Language and History: Linguistic Categories and Historical Categories in Benjamin's Thought," originally published in Italian in 1983.[4] In this essay, Agamben addresses Benjamin's messianic concepts of a universal history and the universal language that corresponds to it. Basing himself on Benjamin's understanding that history was born along with meaning, Agamben develops Benjamin's idea of a pure language in its correlation with the end of history. In the course of his argumentation, Agamben rejects various manifestations of the structure of deferral that, he believes, run counter to Benjamin's messianism. At first sight these opposing theories, which reach from Kabbalistic speculations to contemporary French thought, seem to have little in common, but they all imply a form of "infinite task," an *unendliche Aufgabe*.

One of the concepts of a universal language that Agamben, along with Benjamin, rejects is the attempt to artificially construct such a language as Ludwig Zamenhof did in 1887 with Esperanto. According to Agamben, Benjamin rejects this language because it maintains a conception of language as a sign system based on an infinite conservation of signification and meaning. Benjamin's rejection is mostly politically motivated: Esperanto is, in his eyes, a false construction because it prematurely claims a universality before universal justice—the only authentic manifestation of redemption—has been established. Agamben's mistrust of Esperanto is of a more linguistic-philosophical nature. Another avatar of infinite deferral negated by Agamben is a hermeneutics of infinite meaning, for which universal language is merely a regulative ideal. Agamben objects to Hans-Georg Gadamer's view that "all human speaking is finite in such a way that there is laid up within it an infinity of meaning to be explicated and laid out."[5] Agamben rightly refers to Benjamin's own critique of an approach to interpretation as an "infinite task." Benjamin's idea of textual interpretation, the "mortification of the work" which ought to occur in the face of the danger of the respective historical moment, is succinctly described by Agamben as the opposite of a Gadamerian hermeneutics directed toward the merging of the horizons of past and present. It remains, however, questionable whether Agamben's alternative to Gadamer, which he derives from Heidegger—namely, a definitive "saying of the work" that captures its essence stripped of mediating comments and philological explanations—could, and should, for Benjamin, be practiced in an unredeemed world.

The third possible interpretation of universal language rejected by Agamben stems from the tradition he sees extending from the Kabbalah via Gershom Scholem to Derrida and deconstruction. Common to them is the primacy of writing and its infinite deferral of true meaning. Instead, Agamben insists on the messianic necessity to bring the "infinite task" to an end and reach the point where language will be finally free of all presupposition and mediation and is emptied out of all meaning, saying nothing but itself. In all these examples of Agamben's rejection of infinite deferral it remains unclear whether the correspondence between pure language and messianic redemption is one of precondition, analogy, causality, or any other mode of relation.[6] It is likely—as is suggested in Benjamin's *Theological-Political Fragment*—that this other mode of relation will itself come into being only with the coming of the messiah, and that his coming is this absence of relation itself.

In what follows I shall examine Agamben's reading of one passage by Benjamin and point out the correlation between Agamben's rejection of deferral—generally associated with Jewish messianism and explicitly described by Scholem as the characteristic mode of Jewish existence in a "Leben im Aufschub" (a life in deferral)—and his transformation if not outright demise of the ethical and political dimension of Benjamin's messianism.

Preamble: Hegel's Aesthetics

Agamben's "Language and History" interprets a single passage from Benjamin's paralipomena to his "On the Concept of History." It focuses on the link Benjamin establishes between "pure language" and "universal history" and retraces the correspondences that exist for Benjamin between the genres of narration, history, and redemption. These correspondences arise out of a revision of Hegel's theory of aesthetics. In the traditional triadic scheme developed by Hegel, the epic, in which human experience is grasped in its unity and totality, stands at the beginning. The epic, the most ancient account of history told in the form of heroic song, was later sublated into poetry, which was in turn sublated into disenchanted and no-longer-integral prose. In Hegel's progressive scheme, prose aims at regaining the original totality corresponding to the ancient epic, the genre in which universal history is to be told. For Benjamin, the conception of a constantly progressing and developing history, which in the end comes to itself in pure self-recognition, is just as much in crisis as is continuous narration. His messianic thought is also modeled on the triad of Paradise, Fall, and still-pending Redemption, but it is marked by discontinuities, which also characterize his theory of narration. But in modern times the genre of a continuously flowing, all-encompassing narrative has lost its validity. From now on, narration must either signal the impossibility of its own continuity or mark its status as a mere model for the historiography of a messianic age that is yet to come.

Benjamin gave no clear answer to the question "what the situation of a 'redeemed humanity' might actually be, what conditions are required for the development of such a situation, and when this development can be expected to occur" (*in welcher Verfassung sich die "erlöste Menschheit" befindet, welchen Bedingungen das Eintreten dieser Verfassung unterworfen ist und wann man mit ihm rechnen kann*).[7] Instead, he recovers scattered messianic fragments that point to anticipatory forms of this future state. These can be found in Benjamin's work in various experiences and figures: from Proust's *mémoire involontaire* to a *leibhaftige Geistesgegenwart* (embodied presence of mind), from the *flâneur* to the collector, from the translator to the materialist historian, from Kafka's seemingly insignificant assistants to the righteous man. This heterogeneous group includes the chronicler and his secularized alter ego, the storyteller. Benjamin's essay "The Storyteller" ("Der Erzähler") contains few messianic echoes, but the note written in preparation for his "On the Concept of History" provides clues about the condition of redeemed mankind that also concern the question of narration in a messianic world:[8]

> The messianic world is the world of total and integral actuality. In it alone is there universal history. What goes by the name of universal history today can only be a kind of Esperanto. Nothing can correspond to it as long as the confusion originating in the Tower of Babel is not smoothed out. It presupposes the language into which every text of a living or dead language must be translated in full. Or rather, it is itself this language. Not though, as written, but as festively celebrated. This celebration is purified of every ceremony; it knows no celebratory songs. Its language is the idea of prose itself, which is understood by all men as is the language of birds by Sunday's children.[9]

Other versions of this fragment in Benjamin's paralipomena to "On the Concept of History" end with the following remark: "The idea of prose coincides with the messianic idea of universal history. (Compare the passage in 'The Storyteller.')"[10] And the most extensive variant of the note contains an additional reference to "the types of artistic prose as the spectrum of universal historical types—in 'The Storyteller.'"[11] It may not be an exaggeration to see in Benjamin's note a prismatic spectrum that brings together all the messianic sparks relating to history, language, and narration that are scattered in his work.

Benjamin's fragment projects the condition of redeemed humankind as a comprehensive, fulfilled presence of language and history. Only in a messianic world, only at the end of time and from its end, can history be recounted in its entirety. Benjamin is here criticizing the narrative historicism of the nineteenth century, which deludes itself in claiming that it can still tell history in an epic form.[12] For Benjamin, this conception of history creates the illusion of an intact world, sides with the victors, and does not take account of the oppression of humankind. The prerequisite of a rightful and just universal history, which only falls to redeemed humankind, is the healing of the confusion of tongues through a universal language "understood by all men," which is reminiscent of Benjamin's early essay "On Language as Such and On the Language of Men" ("Über Sprache überhaupt und über die Sprache der Menschen")[13] and "The Task of the Translator" ("Die Aufgabe des Übersetzers").[14] Integral actuality—fulfilled concurrence of all events—is expressed in a language freed of mediation and difference, of writing and signs, a language of immediacy that will eventually deliver nature from its dumb sorrow and reconcile it with humankind. With the concept of the "idea of prose," which refers to Benjamin's doctoral thesis, "The Concept of Criticism in German Romanticism" ("Der Begriff der Kunstkritik in der deutschen Romantik") and the reference to the storyteller essay, this passage, in addition to the essays on language, takes up two early texts that are less about language than about epic forms.[15] But how can the messianic hope for immediacy and "integral actuality" go together with narrative, which always also presumes tension, difference, deferral, and mediation?

White Light

Benjamin's addendum to the note, which after mentioning the messianic "idea of prose" refers to the "the types of artistic prose as the spectrum of universal historical types—in the 'Storyteller,'"[16] suggests a passage in the storyteller essay, in which Benjamin presents history as "the creative indifference between all forms of the epic."[17] Then, Benjamin continues, "written history would bear the same relationship to the epic forms as white light bears to the colors of the spectrum."[18] The concept of "creative indifference"—the possibility of creatively reconciling polarities and contrasts—signifies in Benjamin an alternative, romantically inflected form of sublation, which evades Hegel's idea of progress and avoids its dialectical loss of the concrete. The white light of history-writing, in which all epic forms are inherent just as all poetic forms are inherent in prose, would only appear to be uniform. The purity of this light would not be an emptiness, no absence of colors, but instead an absolute fullness. Benjamin elucidates this figure of thought echoing Hegel's definition of types:

> For if . . . the writing of history constitutes the creative matrix [*schöp-ferische Indifferenz*] of the various epic forms (just as great prose is the creative matrix of the various metrical forms), its oldest form, the epic, by virtue of being a kind of common denominator [*eine Art von Indif-ferenz*], includes the story and the novel.[19]

In this vertical stratification, in contrast to Hegel's, all the lower forms are preserved without loss in the higher ones. For Benjamin, the epic contains both the novel and the story, but in his distinction between story and novel it is clearly the story that, as secularized form of chronicle, points forward to a messianic, "full" prose. The "idea of prose," which Benjamin introduces in his note as a form of universal history, appears as the last in this series of sublations. It is not reached through a Hegelian teleological advance but in messianic fulfillment. In the "idea of prose" the potentials of all the forms absorbed in it continue to have an effect. Accordingly, in the all-encompassing light of the messianic idea of universal history, which coincides with the "idea of prose," the story is also preserved as one of the colors of its spectrum.

The metaphor of the white light and the spectrum, of the invisible fullness of colors it contains, corresponds to what Benjamin in his dissertation on Romanticism defined as the Romantic "idea of art" as an "absolute medium of reflection" (*Reflexionsmedium*, GS 1.1:87). There, prose is called "the idea of poetry."[20] For the Romantics it represents the highest form of poetry, containing all its possibilities and liberating poetry from its codifications. In prose, "all metrical rhythms pass over into one another" and "combine in a new unity."[21] This is characterized by "sobriety" (*Nüchternheit*) and corresponds to a successful disenchantment of the epic and its festive songs. If in Benjamin's dissertation prose is the "idea of poetry," in which all poetic forms are liberated, then the messianic "idea of prose"—corresponding to this model of "creative indifference"—is its highest stage: It is "universal history," which contains all varieties of art prose within itself, just as the "white light" of "written history" contains the spectral colors of all the epic forms. It encompasses everything that has ever occurred and frees it from its codified bonds, indeed from its own artificiality itself. This messianic feast of freedom contains no festive songs, therefore, and does not return unchanged to the heroic songs of the epic: It is sober and "general," like the prose described in the dissertation. This "idea of prose" encompasses all other forms of art and, as universal narrative, takes in and preserves all the experience of creation.

Sheherazade and the Dying Man

In the storyteller essay, to which the addendum to Benjamin's note refers, two opposing figures vouch for storytelling. One is taken from literature: Sheherazade. She is the one who thinks of a new story whenever her tale comes to a stop and resides, in one form or another, in every storyteller. The second, opposite figure is taken from life: the dying man. In Benjamin's exposition, both figures take on a messianic dimension, which brings them into line with the idea of a universal history at the end of times. Sheherazade, while embodying that "unmessianic" movement of narrative that defers the end, is for Benjamin also the guardian of epic memory, who creates the web that all stories form together in the end. The narrative of the dying man, on the other hand, comes into being as retrospection. The stuff his stories are made of, Benjamin writes, are "his lived life" (*gelebtes Leben*). The gift of the storyteller, like that of the dying man, is "the ability to recount his *entire* life" (*sein* ganzes *Leben erzählen zu können*).[22] Universal history is the collective analogy to that narrative: It relates the *entire* history of all creatures on earth from its messianic end point. As with the dying man, even if he is "the poorest wretch," the storyteller recovers the past in its totality and all hierarchical differences are dissolved. Sheherazade and the dying man together embody messianic figures who preserve in the spectrum of the "idea of prose" the double movement of deferral and retrospection, infinity and closure, "hope and memory."[23] In the concept of the "idea of prose" there is contained not only the pure, perfect, and, in itself, complete *idea* but also the idea of *prose* as the general, the manifold and worldly story of all creation. In Benjamin's messianic world, the *restitutio in integrum* of the past is fulfilled in the shape of a web of stories spun from the matter of "lived life." At the conclusion of the storyteller essay, Benjamin defines the storyteller as the "advocate of all creation" on the day of the Last Judgment. The integral prose he uses has the task of preserving the particularity of each individual phenomenon in its entirety and of doing justice to all creatures. It would be a language of names to the extent that it no longer denotes arbitrarily but evokes and vivifies authentically what it names: Benjamin's messianic ethics of narration is founded in the desire for a complete narrativity, which, with this highest form of attentiveness, calls things by their name.

The Enjambment and the Expressionless

An initial insight into the difference between the two writers' "idea of prose" is provided by Agamben's text of the same name in his volume of poetic-philosophical short texts, which likewise bears this title.[24] Like Benjamin in his early study of art criticism in the Romantic period, in this short text Agamben, too, develops the essence of prose from its relation to poetry. But whereas Benjamin, in line with Schlegel, calls prose the "idea of poetry" and, through the metaphor of the white light, sees contained in it "all the possibilities and forms of poetry," Agamben situates the relationship of prose and poetry at the interface *between* them. Agamben describes the specificity of poetry as the divergence between rhythm and meaning. The location of this divergence is the enjambment, the continuation of a syntactic unit from one line or couplet of a poem to the next with no pause, which Agamben calls "the distinguishing characteristic of poetic discourse."[25] It is the point where poetry and prose are at the same time most radically different and yet united to an almost indistinguishable degree. In the enjambment, verse introduces the syntax of prose and, paradoxically, becomes poetry at the very point where it disavows the metrical language of poetry. It is also at this point that the "idea of language," which is "neither poetry nor prose, but their middle," occurs.[26] Unlike Benjamin's metaphor of the white light, which, even if invisible, contains the fullness of all spectral colors, this middle—a mere interruption in the flow of the poetic sentence, a blank space on the page—is empty.

Agamben elucidates the relationship between language and history in terms of the discrepancy between the original language of names and the historically mediated, always already transmitted and hence inauthentic language of communication between human beings. According to Agamben's explication of Benjamin's note, names always already precede all speech as original signs and cannot be grasped or circumvented. By contrast, thought without presuppositions is not possible in a language of signs. The mediation to which names are subject through history determines an endless chain of presuppositions, which place thought and human beings under a ban. Agamben transfers this conception of language as an imaginary prison to Benjamin's philosophy of history. Because history came into being at the same time as the Fall of language from its original unmediated state, the end of history coincides with the end of the communicative language of signs and with the restitution of the Adamic language of names. To Agamben, Benjamin's "idea of prose" aims at the messianic end of a history understood as fate and therefore as unfreedom. This corresponds in many respects to the understanding of history in Benjamin's note. Since, however, Agamben does not take into consideration the reference to the storyteller essay and the significance of prose as epic form and identifies the "idea of prose" entirely with the "idea of language," his conception of the term leads to an aesthetic of emptiness and an ethics of disconnectedness, to which Benjamin would hardly have subscribed. This can be shown in exemplary fashion by way of the difference between the conceptions of the "expressionless" (*das Ausdruckslose*) in Agamben and in Benjamin.

In his essay on Goethe's *Elective Affinities,* Benjamin links the "expressionless"—a feature of language that has no meaning in itself but interrupts a falsely harmonious continuity—to Friedrich Hölderlin's concept of the "caesura." For Hölderlin, this hesitation in the poetic meter produces a "counter-rhythmical interruption" (*gegenrhythmische Unterbre-*

chung), a resistance to the flowing rhythm of the hymns.[27] While Benjamin insists on the function of this interruption as a rupture of the illusion of wholeness, Agamben considers it as the event itself. In "Idea of the Caesura," another short text in *Idea of Prose*, Agamben refers to the same Hölderlin passage about the caesura as Benjamin and comments: "What does the interruption of the rhythmic transport in the poem reveal? . . . The rhythmic transport, which bears the momentum of the poem, is empty and bears only itself. It is the caesura, which as *pure* word, thinks this emptiness—for a while. . . . The poet . . . awakes and for a moment studies the inspiration which bears him; he thinks only of his voice."[28] This reading of the Hölderlin quotation, which flows into an awareness of the voice, bears the traces of Agamben's earlier book *Language and Death*, the starting point of which is Heidegger's *On the Essence of Language*.[29] In Agamben's book, voice plays a crucial role, and it reveals the origins of his own ethics implied in his understanding of the "idea of prose": "The Voice, as we know, says nothing; it does not mean or want to say any significant proposition. Rather, it indicates and means the pure taking place of language and it is as such a purely *logical* dimension." In this sense, Agamben continues, language as Voice is "the original ethical dimension in which man pronounces his 'yes' to language." And it is this affirmation of language that "opens up to man the possibility for the marvel of being and the terror of nothingness."[30] This ethics also determines Agamben's later interpretation of Benjamin's "idea of prose." There, pure "saying" is not only the task of the philosopher but becomes the ethical task as such: "It is . . . the actual construction of this relation and this region [of pure language] that constitutes the true task of the philosopher and the translator, the historian and the critic, and, in the final analysis, the ethical engagement of every speaking being."[31]

Agamben's "idea of prose" calls for an integral actuality—that is, of a fulfilled now-time without tension, displacement, and deferral. While Benjamin's *Jetztzeit* contains worldly splinters pointing to a messianic fulfillment, Agamben's *now* can be understood as an attempt to think a "pure" interruption, free of all mediation, conception, and precondition, uninfected by a world that presents itself as one continuous catastrophe. The urgency, however, which is constantly conjured up in Agamben's thinking, stands in curious contrast to the emptiness that is simultaneously appealed to. At its center stands the absence of a word that is very much present in the sphere of Benjamin's "Concept of History": the revolution as true, "lived" interruption of catastrophe. Contrary to Benjamin's revolutionary thrust, Agamben's hypostatization and, one might say, the "de-functionalization" of the interruption itself create a break in the bridge between Agamben's linguistic philosophy and his political thought. There is no path here that leads from "the marvel of being and the terror of nothingness" to an ethics and politics of justice. That impasse lies in the nature of a thinking that is concerned not with paths but with cuts, thresholds, and empty spaces, which no longer stand in any relation to what they interrupt. Ultimately it becomes a matter of the theoretical enthronement of discontinuity itself.

The messianic forces that, for Benjamin, interrupt the time continuum and point toward a redeemed world are, for Agamben, rendered absolute and empty to the point where they are no longer redeeming bearers of hope and signals for the cessation of a false continuity. Instead, interruption becomes an end in itself, eliding the experiential content and the worldly bearings of Benjamin's messianic figures. His sparks and splinters, poetic metaphors of a profane illumination, whose luster indicates the path of redemption, become abstract locations of discontinuity: the threshold, the limit point, the interface, "the in-between" as such. Perhaps in an increasingly complex post-revolutionary age their emptiness can be perceived as the only possible form in which to save the radicalism of Benjamin's political-theological legacy, but what is in danger of being lost is the very thing that is to be saved: lived, worldly life itself.

Coda

For Benjamin, the origin of storytelling is imbued with the authority of the dying man whose stories derive from the material of his "lived life." In "Idea of Matter," the first text in Agamben's *Idea of Prose*, Agamben indicates the place from which stories emerge. The text starts with a description of "the decisive experience" that is "so difficult to talk about." It is, Agamben continues, "not even an experience. It is nothing more than the point at which we touch the limits of language. . . . Where language stops is not where the unsayable occurs, but rather where the matter of words begins. Those who have not reached, as in a dream, the wooden substance of language . . . are prisoners of representations, even when they keep silent."

The liberation from this imprisonment is illustrated by Agamben in a comparison with a near-death experience:

> It is the same for those who return to life after a near-death experience. They did not really die (otherwise they would not have returned), nor have they liberated themselves from the necessity to die one day. But they have freed themselves from the representation of death. That is

why, when asked to tell what happened to them, they can say nothing about death, but they find rich material to tell stories and relate exquisite tales about their life.[32]

To have been there, near the place of death, liberates from representation and its presuppositions. But the stories generated by this experience are not, as in Benjamin, made of the stuff of lived life but of "the matter of the word."

A fragment from Kafka's diaries—obviously the model for Agamben's text—speaks of the experience of near-death and its relation to storytelling. Also for Kafka, "whoever has once experienced near-death, can tell terrifying things about it, but how it is after death, that he cannot say."[33] That he cannot say it has, however, less to do with the limits of language and more with the limited experience of death of the one who has come back. He has, Kafka contends,

> not even been closer to death than anyone else, he has merely lived something exceptional and not this exceptional but common life has become more valuable to him. It is the same with everyone who has lived something exceptional. Moses, for example, has certainly lived something extraordinary on Mount Sinai, but rather than surrendering to this exceptional experience he rushed down the mount and had valuable things to tell and loved the humans to whom he fled even more than before. One can learn a lot from both the one who returned from near death and the one who returned from Sinai, but the decisive one cannot learn from them because they themselves have not experienced it. And if they had experienced it, they would not have come back.[34]

The rupture, the exceptional, is, for Kafka as for Benjamin, mainly to be seen in function of the everyday, the common, the lived life. The place of the rupture, of the exceptional, the revelation—whether death or Sinai—is as manifold as it is indifferent in and of itself. Whoever has been there has "obviously valuable stories to tell," but "the decisive"—*das Entscheidende*—cannot be learned from them. "But," Kafka adds, "in truth, we don't even want to know it."

PART II

Inverted Messianism

CHAPTER 6

The Demand for an End: Kant and the Negative Conception of History

Catharine Diehl

Six years after the death of the Enlightenment king Friedrich II, Immanuel Kant considered the possibility of an end to the world. Yet Kant understood this end in light of the demands of practical rationality. "The End of All Things," published in the June 1794 edition of the *Berlin Monatsschrift*, was the last text he would publish on a religious topic before the new emperor of Prussia, Friedrich Wilhelm II, issued an edict barring him from writing on theology.[1] In this essay, Kant considers several possibilities for conceiving of an end of all things, concluding that this notion is meaningful only as a practical guide to action rather than as a theoretical prediction concerning some future state: It tells us neither about objects as appearances nor about things in themselves but can testify only to the structure of our practical rationality. If it purported to be *cognition* (*Erkenntnis*) concerning the end of the world—and thus the end of the sensible conditions of knowledge—eschatology would clearly violate the limits placed on theoretical knowledge by transcendental philosophy.[2] Yet, Kant argues, these eschatological doctrines have a practical significance when we understand them through the notion of a moral disposition (*Gesinnung*) outside space and time that forms the basis for the agent's free acts in the world of phenomena: We conceive of an "end" that would correlate to the original but freely acquired principle of all our actions.

Kant's essay plays a central role in a discussion concerning the nature and purpose of the "last things." The protagonists include Hans Urs von Balthasar, Jürgen Moltmann, Jacob Taubes, Ludwig Landgrebe, and Pope Benedict XVI.[3] Despite the importance of the essay for twentieth-century theology, however, "The End of All Things" occupies only a marginal place within Kant scholarship and is rarely considered important for Kant's philosophy of history.[4] In the theological tradition, on the other hand, the essay is regarded as a contribution to the philosophy of history—but then dismissed as lacking. In contrast, I will claim that this text suggests a unique critical philosophy of history.[5] In order to do this, however, I will first turn to Kant's theological critics and investigate how they have interpreted Kant's essay. In their seminal texts, Balthasar and Moltmann argue that Kant inaugurates a new doctrine of "transcendental eschatology" by conjoining the principle of the origin of action—the original, freely acquired disposition—with the notion of an "end" in order to internalize both within an individual subject. For Balthasar and Moltmann, as well as for many subsequent commentators, Kant's doctrine constitutes the locus classicus of a fruitful but insufficient conception of the end, a doctrine that must be overcome in order to achieve the messianic potential implicit in the idea of an end time. Moreover, as we will see, they consider it necessary to go beyond Kant's account in order to formulate an adequate conception of history. On this interpretation, Kant's essay exemplifies a moment of de-historicization and internalization in which the infinite demand for an end is sundered from any context and the transcendental is thereby *substituted for* the properly historical.[6]

Such an analysis, however, does not account for the specific conception of history that Kant develops in "The End of All Things." Rather than eliding the idea of history, as critics often claim, Kant argues that the time of mathematical natural science is insufficient for historical temporality; instead, he develops a theory of history from the tensions generated by the relation between the subject's noumenal disposition and the actions of the temporally bound phenomenal self. This negative conception of historical time is a consequence of Kant's rejection in the Antinomies of Pure Reason of the possibility of positive knowledge of the totality of events in time. Furthermore, the conception of historical time Kant introduces in "The End of all Things" provides, I will argue, the possibility of thinking not only of "ends" but of beginnings as well—the "possibility of the new," in Ernst Bloch's phrase—within the seemingly closed, continuous time of nature.[7] In part 1 of the essay, I will consider Balthasar's, Moltmann's, and Landgrebe's critiques of "transcendental eschatology"; in part 2, I will provide a more detailed reading of Kant's text in order to describe his "negative conception" of the philosophy of history.

Twentieth-Century Histories of "Transcendental Eschatology"

In *Prometheus: Studies on the History of German Idealism* (*Prometheus: Studien zur Geschichte des deutschen Idealismus*) (1937), Hans Urs von Balthasar defines transcendental eschatology as the displacement of the relationship between first and last, precedent and consequent. The "final things" become "preconditions"; natural things are no longer the "ends" of history: "Its final things are now no longer (natural [*naturhaft*]) God and worldly things, but the preconditions of its (finite) spiritual being [*Geistseins*]: in the place of 'metaphysical' eschatology, 'transcendental' eschatology enters."[8] For the "ends" to be the "preconditions" (*Voraussetzungen*) of finite existence, Kant must posit a "before" (*Voraus*) anterior to finite existence and an "end" in advance of time. At the very least, this formula requires a rethinking of the connections among temporal, logical, metaphysical, and moral "priority." This new relationship between "precedent" and "consequent" results from the requirement that the individual act on the basis of the highest principle; she must make the transcendent highest principle into an immanent object of her will. Only by making the highest principle an "end" of our action can we hope, Balthasar explains, to become "worthy" (*würdig*) of happiness (104). These preconditions place on the individual a demand that, if fulfilled at any point in the future, will always already have been satisfied, since each of the subject's actions will have been a result of making the highest principle an object of her will. Such a demand thus reveals the tension between the phenomenal order of temporal succession and the moral need to render actual a practical, absolute requirement.

Balthasar traces the relations between immanence and transcendence within what he terms the "limit problem" (*Grenzproblem*) in Kant's conception of the end of all things. He identifies this problem as arising when the *demand* on the person exceeds his sensible capacities. At the moment in which this demand surpasses the capabilities of the temporal order, philosophy comes into confrontation with theology: "With this the limit problem in 'The End of All Things,' the problem of the (immanent) transcending (as object of philosophy) and of (the becoming-immanent) transcendent (as object of theology), achieves its sharpest point" (104). This point of "convergence" between philosophy and theology—the moment at which the strictly transcendent nevertheless becomes the "object" of a practical demand—displays, according to Balthasar, the paradoxical structure of a purely subjective transcendence. As we will see, however, Kant in fact thinks of this limit as immanent to philosophy itself. In Balthasar's reconstruction, the "character of transcendence" becomes a subjective "need" (*Be-dürfnis*), expressing both the "basis of natural necessity" and the superstructure (*Überbau*) of free ability (*Dürfen*).

This brief sketch of Balthasar's description of the paradox of transcendental eschatology reveals several important points. First, for Balthasar, this paradox arises because transcendental eschatology seeks to locate transcendence solely on the side of the subject—a charge echoing Hegel's account, in "Faith and Knowledge," of the sundering of subject and object. This paradoxical structure remains central to Moltmann's later discussion and forms the backdrop for his criticism of transcendental eschatology. The paradox of a purely subjective transcendence is, however, important for an additional reason: It traces the essential structure of the demand or need (*Bedürfnis*) for a convergence between the orders of nature and freedom. This relationship can be understood through Kant's notion of "negative presentation";[9] conceiving of it in this way, however, does not amount to dissolving the conflict between immanence and transcendence but rather locates the emergence of historical time in a demand that exceeds any possible realization in experience. From Balthasar's initial characterization of this paradox, we can turn to Moltmann's more extensive critical treatment of the same problem.

In his *Theology of Hope* (1964), Moltmann adopts Balthasar's conception of "transcendental eschatology," identifying Kant as the modern founder of a transcendental approach that takes up the Greek doctrine of the *logos* and reinterprets it as a principle concerning the *self*. This tradition serves, according to Moltmann, as a pagan response to the Christian conception of God's Being as futural.[10] In his reconstruction, transcendental eschatology starts from the claim that the doctrine of the end of the world is meaningless if interpreted as a predictive thesis concerning events in the world, but significant as an unveiling of the fundamental, unchanging inner nature of the individual as moral being. In this sense, end and origin are identified, and the apocalypse—taken in the sense of the Greek term for *uncovering*—reveals our moral nature.[11] Moltmann criticizes this internalization of eschatology on the grounds that it evacuates meaning from the world of phenomena by locating it in our moral nature and, as a result, "rationalizes" the phenomenal world. Recalling Hegel's criticism in "Faith and Knowledge," Moltmann charges transcendental eschatology with introducing an ineradicable and impermissible duality between noumenal subject and phenomenal object.[12] Furthermore, he claims, to interpret the eschaton as an atemporal principle hollows out any notion of history, because the eschaton would be "equally near and far to all times of history" and would thus be the "transcendental meaning of all time."[13]

Two aspects of Kant's account immediately cast doubt on Moltmann's characterization of transcendental eschatology. First, for Kant, our moral nature consists in a disposition (*Gesinnung*) that is acquired even though not acquired within time. Our disposition is the principle that comes to expression in our actions in the phenomenal world, but it is itself the product of a free choice. Contrary to Moltmann's charge, it is not an ontological ground for practical rationality that would be prior to the free choice of the person: As an original *acquisition*, it is not sundered from the world of action but is itself the preeminent act.[14] Kant's theory of original acquisition, in which our "disposition" is at once the principle behind all our choices and the first product of our free choice, constitutes the core of Kant's intricate account of moral personality and historical time. Attending to its complexity shows that Moltmann's description is a mere caricature of Kant's theory of "beginning" and "end." For Kant, the single unconditioned choice of disposition—the action that escapes the basic condition of all other actions, time itself—serves as a "beginning" for our actions in a sense irreducible either to temporal or logical commencement. This notion of the starting point will be complemented by a similarly tricky concept of an "end" that seems both to be an end *of* time and an end *outside* time.

Second, Moltmann's focus on the individual moral personality neglects the importance of the idea of the world as a totality in Kant's analysis. For Kant, the totality of the world is an idea of reason, something to which we are ineluctably led by our cognitive faculties but of which we can have no determinate knowledge. On Moltmann's analysis, Kant's account implies that the world is devoid of meaning, since the only source of meaning lies in the moral character of rational beings—a character that resides in each rational being's disposition. This criticism overlooks, however, Kant's concern with providing a meaning for the world *as a whole*: it is a regulative, teleological principle that *the world* has a purpose because it contains beings that can freely determine their own ends. At first, Kant's picture might seem susceptible to the Hegelian charge of sundering the free agent from the results of her activity in the world; however, Kant argues that the end of the world, as the end of the totality of everything taking place in time, is significant precisely because it can assist practical reason to act *within* the world and with a view toward the world *as a whole*.[15]

Moltmann might respond by claiming that this defense is insufficient because it does not touch on his central concern: transcendental eschatology's lack of a conception of the future that could secure our hope within history. To the tradition of transcendental eschatology, Moltmann opposes his own conception of eschatology according to which the end is intrinsically bound to a futurity that can never be reduced to an existing present.[16] For Moltmann, the primacy of futurity is distinctive of the Christian concept of eschatology; Kant's writings on eschatology would fail because they do not allow for this open future but instead are bound up with a conception of the apocalypse as the "unveiling" of a noumenal moral disposition. Without a notion of the future as containing a "promise," eschatology cannot provide hope. This complaint reveals, however, Moltmann's misreading of "The End of All Things." In fact, Kant's essay prevents any such "unveiling" of the noumenal self; on the contrary, the function of eschatology in Kant's account is to *block* the notion that the noumenal disposition can be made to appear.[17] We can conceive of this disposition, Kant claims, only as a principle essentially hidden from view. Although the origin and the goal meet, the point of convergence takes place beyond the realm of cognition: We know *that* there is such a point, but we can never determine its coordinates. It is only this asymptotic approach that is "uncovered" by transcendental eschatology.[18] In this sense, the practical value of eschatology lies in its antinomic character: Once we see both the impossibility of any theoretical conception of the end of time and the ineradicability of the idea of this end, we will no longer rush toward any vision of an end. The idea of the end of time will serve as a sort of *katechon*, warding off any direct action toward the apocalypse.[19] The idea of an end of time thus serves— like the moral faculty (*sittliche Anlage*) itself, in Kant's formulation—to interrupt the march of cultural progress, to drag behind its quick step and intensify the gravity of history.[20] Kant's account of the inertial force provided by the idea of an end seems to be diametrically opposed to Moltmann's principle of hope in the future: Whereas Kant locates the practical value of eschatology in its power to check the mad enthusiasms of an overhasty rush to perfection—checking, as he writes, the entrance of a "perverted end" of history—Moltmann claims that hope is required for us to conceive of the future as "open," as containing a possibility for liberation.

In this sense, it might seem that despite the inadequacies of Moltmann's interpretation of Kant, he nevertheless identifies a fundamental disagreement between a "transcendental" and a "futural" form of eschatology. Yet it would be one-sided to locate the idea of the end in Kant as serving only as a *katechon*, for this would overlook the role of hope in Kant's theory. For Kant, as for Moltmann, we must postulate an end of all things in order to answer the question "What may I hope?" This question arises because of the human being's dual status both as cognizing and as *acting* subject.[21] Because she has to act according to her representation of ends, she is confronted with the question of whether the order of nature will be in accordance with what she represents as the *worth* of her actions. In other words, can her "ends"—the ends she sets for herself in the practical realm—also be realized in the world? The question of the end of history arises directly from the question of whether our actions can be said to have a "sense," an "end," within that which actually takes place.

In a 1966 article entitled "The Philosophical Problem of the End of History," Ludwig Landgrebe argues that this question constitutes the central problem for any philosophy of history:

> The question of the end of history [*Geschichte*] is thus none other than the question of the *sense*, of the meaning, which this course of events [*das Geschehen*] has for the expectations that direct our action and which is always an expecting in fear or in hope. That there is such a thing as a philosophy of history as thinking reflection derives from the ineluctability of this question—with which it stands and falls.[22]

Far from representing a confusion between temporal and purposive senses of "end," eschatology, according to Landgrebe, is grounded in the close affinity of purpose with time: For there to be any correspondence between the principle of our will and the results of our actions, the telos of action must be represented as taking place in an end to history itself. Without this idea of a temporal end to history, the very concept of history becomes nonsensical, he argues, because we would be deprived of any connection between the principles of our actions and their results in the world. According to Landgrebe, philosophy has forgotten this question of the end of history and thus has lost any ability to construct a meaningful philosophy of history (182–84). He argues that we must return to Kant to remind ourselves of the connection between the possibility of a philosophy of history and the question of an end of all things.

For Landgrebe, the necessity of this return appears all the more clearly when we consider not only the occlusion of the question of the end of history in contemporary philosophy but also the work of several philosophers who sought to deny the very possibility of a philosophy of history. Landgrebe takes Karl Löwith's *Meaning in History* as an exemplary instance of this error. In Landgrebe's reconstruction, Löwith argues that we cannot "experience or cognize" world history as a "unified process" because this would require a "teleological principle," but only a theology of history, not a philosophy of history, is capable of providing such a principle (187). Löwith diagnoses modern man as having lost any principle to ground the continuity of history: Modern man can neither find it in any kind of linear directedness toward the end of the world nor in the cyclical structure characteristic of ancient thought. Instead of consistently pursuing either of these alternatives, the "modern spirit" is undecided between them and becomes incapable of conceiving of historical continuity at all (188). These two alternatives—the cyclical and the linear—are, for Löwith, the only two possibilities for grounding the continuity of historical time. But here Landgrebe points out that Löwith has forgotten Kant's fundamental insight: If we remind ourselves that the question "What may I hope?" cannot be relinquished by philosophy, we will realize that the alternatives Landgrebe sketches are not exclusive. It is thus Kant who shows us how to escape from the dilemma into which the philosophy of history has fallen in the nineteenth and twentieth centuries (188–89).

For Landgrebe, the answer to this quandary emerges when we recall Kant's solution to the "antinomy of the infinity and finitude of the world" (189). The solution to this antinomy relies on the distinction between a theoretical and a practical principle. We can avoid Löwith's Scylla and Charybdis by reminding ourselves that the idea of an end is not a theoretical principle at all but a "regulative principle of action": It derives from practical reflection on the moral course of events and thus "has in this sense practical reality and is thus an idea that can be legitimately explored philosophically" (190).[23] By removing the idea of an end from the realm of theoretical speculation, Kant has thereby saved the philosophical purchase of this idea and preserved the possibility of a philosophy of history. Landgrebe claims that Kant provides a teleological principle that can "mediate" (*vermitteln*) between "what can be cognized and what can be believed" without falling into the "difficulties of Hegel's anchoring of this mediation in absolute knowledge" (190). Landgrebe thus argues that Kant's "The End of All Things" shows the correct basis on which the philosophy of history must be founded, a basis different from the one that has directed philosophical speculation in the past two hundred years.

Despite providing the solution to Löwith's dilemma, Kant's teleological principle is not sufficient, Landgrebe claims, to establish the conditions for a "continuous happening [*Geschehen*] according to a causal principle." It is incapable of explaining the "experience of history *as* history" (192). In arguing for the inadequacy of Kant's grounding of historical time—and thus the necessity of turning to an alternative basis in Husserl's and Heidegger's analyses of the experience of time—Landgrebe returns to Kant's account of time as the form of inner sense in the Transcendental Aesthetic. Time is the form of "succession" and so has only "*one* dimension, which is representable in the image of a line" (192). Events are thus ordered according to a principle of succession, as "givens" in time (193). But, Landgrebe claims, this conception of time as a line is inappropriate both as a description of our experience of time and as the basis for a philosophy of history: Instead, we need to experience a disappearing "now" in order even to understand the idea of time as a form of succession (195).[24] Kant's error, on Landgrebe's account, is to start from a conception of time as the form of representation of a "representing-thinking subject" and not from the more fundamental experience of time that we experience when we act. For Landgrebe, Kant thus ultimately gives priority to the theoretical over the practical, forgetting his own insight into the primacy of the latter. Thus, for Landgrebe, he cannot account for the object of history—historical time.

But if we take seriously Kant's distinctions not only between the theoretical and the practical but also between the constitutive and the regulative, can we be so certain that the study of history *should* in fact have an *object*? Certainly, on Kant's own conception of objecthood, the possibility for an object, as something that is theoretically knowable, seems to be foreclosed. History, for Kant, insofar as it is dependent on an idea with merely regulative and practical significance, cannot be an object of cognition and thus cannot stricto sensu be an object at all. Landgrebe might, of course, respond that we *do* have an experience of historical time and of history as an object, even if not in Kant's specific sense of the term. It would merely be a weakness of Kant's analysis that he cannot—unlike Husserl or Heidegger—describe this experience of fundamental temporality. Does Kant, then, have an argument against Landgrebe as to why we can in principle have no experience of history, why history can only be glimpsed in the distance between the phenomenal world and our awareness of ourselves as subject to a moral law? In my reading of "The End of All Things," I will maintain that it is precisely the strength of Kant's account *not* to develop a positive theory of historical time, for, according to his analysis, any such theory would falsify the limits Kant sets on cognition. This principle of limitation lies, I will claim, in the experience of the gap between the order of nature and the order of freedom. Thus, the possibility of history, for Kant, will be located in an injunction, a demand for these two orders to be linked—a demand that can never be achieved but also cannot be abandoned. In this sense, Balthasar's claim that transcendental eschatology represents an excessive demand is correct. But the very excessiveness of this demand results from the problem itself: to provide the conditions of the philosophy of history that give priority to the practical.

"The End of All Things"

Kant begins the essay with a reflection on dying, conceived of as the passage of an *individual* from time to eternity. He analyzes the phrase "He goes out of time into eternity" (*"Er gehe* aus der Zeit in die Ewigkeit").[25] We can form no concept of the transition from time to eternity, according to Kant, because to postulate a moment connecting time and eternity would place the two strictly incomparable orders within a single series.[26] Eternity, he claims, cannot simply mean a time without end, since this would imply that the dying person continues *within* time rather than achieving the crucial passage out of it. Kant thus follows Boethius and the Thomist tradition in distinguishing between *sempiternity*, "the perpetual running resulting from the flowing, tireless now," and eternity.[27] The duration of eternity cannot be compared to duration in earthly time; it must be a *duratio noumenon*. In this, Kant also seems to follow Boethius and Aquinas, for whom eternity has a duration that is unlike the duration of objects in time. For them, eternity consists in "the complete possession all at once of interminable life"[28] and has "the infinity of mobile time present to it."[29] Although a relation of simultaneity holds between eternity—conceived of as an infinite present—and everything taking place in time, the *duration* of eternity differs from that of objects in time. However, for Kant, unlike Boethius and Aquinas, *duratio noumenon* cannot be said to be present in each temporal object, not only because such a claim would entail knowledge of things-in-themselves but, more specifically, because it would presume that a *transition* between one and the other was possible: Phenomenal and noumenal orders would be joined in a moment.[30] The image of passing from time to eternity depicts instead an *impossible* moment.

Kant concedes that this idea may not have any "objective reality": There may be nothing conforming to its concept, but the nature of human reason is such that we cannot avoid entertaining it. How then are we to contemplate the idea of an end of time, an end to the very conditions of possible experience—which is to say, an end to the possibility of earthly thought at all? Since time is the form of inner intuition, the passage from time to eternity is the transition from an experience determined by the forms of sensibility to an existence lacking these conditions. This initial reflection on the dying person's passage from time to eternity thus introduces a demand to consider the transition to an order that we can know only negatively as not falling under the conditions of sensibility. There are two aspects of this demand that cannot be cognized. First, eternity itself as an "incomparable magnitude" falls outside sensibility and can be thought only as an idea of reason. Kant writes that we can form only a "negative" concept of the magnitude of this duration: The concept can be determined only by negating predicates that pertain to temporal duration and thus assigning the concept of eternity to an infinite realm outside of the concept of temporal extension. Second, we cannot form the concept of a bridge from time to eternity, as *duratio noumenon*, because to do so would imply a contradiction: As they are incomparable orders, no link from one to the other within a single series is possible. Yet Kant speaks of this passage as the survival, the continued existence, of an individual who, even while temporally existing within the world of phenomena, must transcend the temporal conditions of this world. For the continued existence, the *Fortdauer*, of the person, these two incomparable kinds of duration (*Dauer*) must be linked: Kant marks this exigency rhetorically with a prefix, *fort-*, that points to the original dual character of the duration of the existence of the person. The two orders are not related because they share any intrinsic property but merely because the same person exists within both time and eternity.

"The End of All Things" thus begins with the failure of theoretical cognition to conceive of the survival of the moral individual beyond death. But, as Kant proceeds to show, any reflection on the death of the individual in fact already implies the idea of an end of the world. We come across (*stoßen auf*) the "end of all things" because the end of the conditions of sensibility involves the end of all objects of any possible experience.[31] When I, as individual, contemplate my passage from time to eternity, I am led to the idea of an end of the world, but Kant's point is not the mere platitude that the world will not exist *for* the person who has died. The idea of an end of the world derives from the notion of a noumenal order into which the individual passes. The possibility of the continued existence of a person beyond the boundaries of sensible experience carries with it the idea of an end of the world of phenomena; it is the realization of our noumenally unconditioned existence that causes us to be confronted with the idea of an end to the phenomenal realm as a whole.[32] In this sense, far from eternity's being present to every instant in time, eternity can be conceived of only in the absence of the world, under the condition of the world's occlusion. Kant explains that the idea of an end of the world is beneficial for practical reason because only the judgment of our conscience concerning our moral condition at the present time could allow us to judge our fate in the eternal realm.[33] For this reason, Kant writes, only the "dualistic" conception of eternity, where some are saved and the rest are damned, can do justice to our moral notion that our place in eternity corresponds to the moral character of our actions (330). It is morally beneficial to act "as if" there were another life whose character is determined by our actions in this one. It is the "as if," the mark of a certain fictionality, that is essential for us to resist the temptation to take the possibility of another world as dogma.[34] Although we represent this as the determination of our fate after death by our current conduct, this picture is misleading: The event of death is not simply something that might strike at some time or another, at which point the sum of our conduct would determine our fate in the afterlife. If this were the case, then time and eternity would be joined within a single sequence ordered by a relation of succession. Furthermore, we cannot conclude that eternal life is present within us at all instants of time, since this would also establish a relation, simultaneity, that would bind the two orders.[35] Instead, the "end" of all things accompanies all our actions because, in conceiving of ourselves as free agents, we regard ourselves as acting from a noumenal moral disposition. However, this "accompaniment" cannot be cognized, since cognition happens only within the temporal order; it can merely be "presented negatively." The very fact that in this idea we can encounter the limits of our cognitive faculties points to something within us that exceeds the boundaries of sensibility, something unconditioned.[36]

Kant argues that we have the idea of eternity because we are aware of ourselves as agents in the moral order acting according to final causes. The idea of the end of the world as an entity subject to the conditions of time can arise from action because free activity instantiates an order of purposes that is not determined by succession. He intimates this noncoincidence of orders when he writes that the "end" of all things is, at the same time (*zugleich*), the "beginning" of the continued existence of the person "in the moral order of purposes."[37] Beginning and end coincide here precisely because two different types of causality are involved: The end in the order of efficient causation is the beginning in the order of final causation. This duality of causal principles shows how an end to the world might be possible for Kant. He connects the idea of the end of the world with the notion of a purpose or goal when he answers the question of why people expect an end to the world. This expectation, Kant writes, is grounded in the voice of reason, ". . . because reason tells them that the duration [*Dauer*] of the world has value only insofar as the rational beings within it are in conformity with the final end [*Endzweck*] of its existence; if this were not achieved, creation itself would appear purposeless to them: like a play [*Schauspiel*] that has no end and makes known no rational aim" (330–31). As Peter Fenves has remarked, this analogy between the world and a play establishes a relation of "rational spectatorship."[38] Just as we would judge a play without a conclusion to lack all meaning, so the rational observer of the world would view its existence as senseless without the notion of a conclusion. If the world could not be viewed as a completed totality, then it could display no rational aim.

Kant's claim in this passage draws on the analysis of the concept of the world developed in the *Critique of Pure Reason*. In the Antinomy of Pure Reason, Kant defines our concept of the world as the "mathematical whole of all appearances and the totality of their synthesis"[39]; the very notion of the world is that of an infinite totality. In the First Antinomy, Kant shows that this leads us to a contradiction if we attempt to gain knowledge from it, since we would be compelled to maintain both that the world has a be-ginning—and parallel to this, an end—in time and that it has no such be-ginning (or end). The thought of an infinite totality hence exceeds human understanding and is merely an idea of reason. Thus, we can only have an idea of the world but cannot cognize it. Kant's analogy between the world and a play derives its meaning from his argument that we must have an idea of the world, an idea of an infinite whole; however, he goes further in "The End of All Things" by suggesting the sense in which we can think of an "end" to the world. We are able to think of an infinite totality, albeit only through practical reason, because we have the notion of a moral end or purpose. Since we cannot cognize the end of the world as an event within time without miring ourselves in the contradiction of the First Antinomy, we must locate the real basis for our notion of this end within another order, that of the "final end" to the world. In order for creation to have meaning for the rational beings who are both participants and spectators within the world, this final end must be not merely promised but achieved. The achievement of the final end of the world calls on human beings, as rational agents, to live up to the requirements of that very final end. Only if the conduct of human beings conforms to this end can the world be said to have a purpose and creation to be meaningful. But what is this final end to which human beings should be in conformity?

In section 84 of the *Critique of Judgment*, Kant distinguishes between the "ultimate end" (*letzer Zweck*) and the "final end" (*Endzweck*) of nature: If we think of nature as displaying a purposive structure, where one being exists for the sake of another, then the "ultimate end" of nature must be the natural being for whose sake all other beings within nature exist, whereas the "final end" must be "that end which needs no other as the condition of its possibility."[40] The final end is unconditioned, whereas the ultimate end is merely that for which everything within nature exists, but the ultimate end may, in turn, exist for the sake of something outside nature. This idea of nature as a teleological system is a principle only of reflective and not of determinative judgment, since it is not a condition of possibility for the existence of objects of experience but necessary only for the use of our own power of judgment. Thus, the ultimate and final ends can be known neither through experience nor through a priori determinative principles but can only be thought as regulative ideas guiding our judgments. Kant argues that reason leads us to the idea of nature as a "system of ends," the "ultimate end" of which is "found within the human being" (429). In addition to distinguishing between "ultimate" and "final" ends, he separates ends into those that the system of nature might itself satisfy and those for which nature can be put to use. The first of these would be happiness; the latter, culture (430–32). Only culture, however, is capable of serving as an ultimate end of nature, because the "vocation" of the human being as "titular lord of nature" is only "conditional": It depends on his ability to set an end for himself that would be "independent" of the order of nature, a final end (431). The ultimate end is thus something within nature that will "prepare" the human being to make the final end of the world actual. Culture can serve as this ultimate end because it promotes the ability to choose one's own ends, thereby enabling the rational being to become a final end. The purpose of nature as a system is thus to make way for a final end lying outside its scope: As an unconditioned end, the *Endzweck* cannot occur within nature, yet it may be made real when the rational beings in the world make the moral law their end.

This argument explains Kant's claim that the duration of the world can be seen as meaningful only if the rational beings within it conform to its final end. Human beings, existing in the world of phenomena, are called on to instantiate the final end—to adopt the moral law freely. If human beings were not measured against the standard of the moral law as final end, then the world could not be judged to have any meaning at all. For the world to be meaningful, a relation between rational beings and the supersensible must be posited. As beings subject to the conditions of sensibility, we can never make the final end actual but must instead always think of it as the telos of an infinite process; however, the practical use of this idea requires that we think of our moral disposition as an unchanging condition capturing all of our temporal actions. Through the concept of this disposition, we can think of the world as possessing a final end—as always measured against a freely determined principle that is, for this very reason, unconditioned.

Although we must have the idea of an end to the world, this does not determine what the nature of the end must be. Kant, in fact, writes that the majority opinion is that the world will come to a bad end.[41] Thus, when Kant claims that the rational beings in the world must be in conformity with its final end, he means not that these beings will necessarily measure up to this end but merely that they must always be compared with it. It is always possible—and expected by most—that human beings will fail and that an end "filled with terror" will occur. In the final section of the essay, Kant describes an end occasioned by a particular kind of incongruity between rational beings in the world and the final end of the world: the "counter-natural" or "perverted" (333) end. We can bring such an end about, Kant writes, by misunderstanding the final end. It is in the very act of attempting to impose an end that we comprehend it falsely and thus pervert it, for, Kant argues, human beings cannot grasp hold of the idea of the final end and enact a plan to achieve it but must leave it to providence (*Vorsehung*) (337). Kant chooses Christianity as his example: Christianity is "determined" (*bestimmt*) to be the world religion (339) because its ethical principles are "worthy of love" (337). They are "worthy of love," however, only insofar as they do not command obedience but instead assist in the fulfillment of the dictates of practical rationality. For Kant, Christianity can be a "world religion" only if it leads the rational beings within the world to achieve the final end of the world, to act as free legislators in the kingdom of ends. Thus, as a type of culture, it adopts the role of the ultimate end, but despite this determination, it may nevertheless not be "favored by fate" (339). A historical contingency may intervene to block it from playing its role. This ultimate end threatens to pervert the final end it is supposed to promote. If it were to assume the cloak of authority and command obedience to its principles—as Kant saw occurring in the government of the new Prussian king, Friedrich Wilhelm II—then it would not only no longer be worthy of love but would lose its status as a world religion and be transformed into its opposite. Kant's idea of the end of the world thus includes the possibility that the very thing, Christianity, that had been destined (*bestimmt*) to become a world religion can instead be put to the service of the Antichrist. The Antichrist, in the guise of a domineering Prussian king, may always come to divert nature and, with it, the world from its final end.

The very idea of human history depends on the actions of free subjects: This idea can be misunderstood and thus pervert the end, or it can be conceived in its correlation with the final end of morality. Human actions in the world thus do not merely provide the content of history but determine its form. The possibility of a philosophy of history depends on the capacity of an idea to provide the sense, goal, and end of events. If the course of events is not directed by such an idea, then the long course of human actions loses its orientation and dissolves into senselessness. Since human beings are not merely driven by instinct "like the bees or the beavers" nor capable of putting into practice a plan "like rational world-citizens," the chances for a history directed by the "natural final end" might seem remote. Kant seeks, as he writes in the "Idea for a Universal History," a guiding thread (*Leitfaden*) a priori (18) for the construction of such a history: In "The End of All Things," he locates this *Leitfaden* in the ineradicability of an idea that lies beyond all cognition. Furthermore, the very potential for the idea of an end to turn into its perverse counterpart reminds us of the reason why Moltmann's understanding of transcendental eschatology misconstrues the relation between events within the world and their transcendental grounds. Rather than functioning as a transcendental principle that would secure a world evacuated of all significance, as Moltmann claims, the end of the world depends on what actually occurs. This implies that history does not exist as such but has merely been shown to be possible: There *is* no universal history, but the idea of an end secures the *potential* for history. No historical time is *given* because history can emerge only through the idea of a *duration* that would depart from that of things in the world.

Landgrebe is right, then, to point out that Kant does not provide a specific form for historical time, a principle for the continuity of action. Indeed, no such positive description of historical experience would be possible for Kant. Instead, in acting—and acting not as isolated subjects but through the idea of humanity as a whole—human beings put into practice an idea, a hope, for an end or a sense. Insofar as this idea accompanies our actions, history can emerge as something beyond all experience or constitutive principles. It is in this sense that history arises "negatively" for Kant: It is neither presentable in the time of natural science nor does it have its own phenomenally accessible form of time. Rather, it can be felt only in the demand for a correspondence between the phenomenal world and the claims of practical reason. In "The End of All Things," Kant does not describe the project of bringing about the "end" simply as an infinite task: Instead, it is an end that can reorient the course of events wherever it directs our actions, a principle that can serve both as beginning and as end.

CHAPTER 7

Migrations of the Bohemian

Joshua Wilner

Ces pauvres gueux, pleins de bonadventures,
Ne portent rien que des Choses futures.

—CALLOT ENGRAVING

The messianic is for us a thing of the past, inscribed as such in the Western calendar and memorialized each time we register day, month, and year. What is thus marked is both an advent and an end, the end of messianic expectation, and so the end of the messianic as a thing of the future or, better, the end of the messianic as the form of the future. When I was a child, I was taught that Christians believed the messiah had come and that Jews were still waiting. But is this "still waiting" not the melancholic form of "no longer waiting," the shadow of a hope on which the sun has gone down but that, unable to be relinquished, has becomes its own object? And would this not be the structure of the "weak messianic power . . . given to us, like every generation before us, . . . on which the past has a claim"— the weak messianic power of which Benjamin writes in the "Theses on the Philosophy of History"?[1] What follows is a reading of the fortunes of the bohemian, a figure with a long and wandering past but entering modernity via the straits of its sojourn in mid-nineteenth-century Paris and its involvement in the failed revolutionary hopes of 1848, as bearer of and claimant on this weak messianic power, the telling image of a postmessianic history.

Consult the 1798 edition of the dictionary of the Académie Française and you will read that its entry for "*bohémien*" in no way refers to "those people who live in the part of Germany known as Bohemia" but solely to "a class of "vagabonds who roam the countryside at large, telling fortunes and stealing with craft."[2] By the sixth edition, in 1835, the use of *bohémien* as an equivalent of *Egyptien*—i.e., *Gypsy*—is already designated a "former" usage, something that "se disait autrefois." And by mid-century, Henry Murger can declare "axiomatically" in his introduction to *Scènes de la bohème* (the novel on which Puccini's opera is based) that "Bohemia is the artistic stage of life" and that "it exists and is possible nowhere but in Paris."[3] Indeed, for Murger's Bohemians, it is "a matter of honor to differentiate themselves" from "the classes long given that name."[4]

Of course, if categorical assertions and points of honor are the order of the day, this also tells us that the reterritorialization of nomadic "Bohemia" on Paris's Left Bank was hardly a settled affair. Murger's efforts (and those of the Académie) notwithstanding, the older deterritorialized and deterritorializing usage of *bohème* survives through much of the nineteenth century, even as its identification with the specifically Parisian subculture whose place in the national imaginary Murger's work consecrates is consolidated. Thus, to cite only a few prominent examples, Merimée in *Carmen*, published in 1845, uses *bohémien* in its nomadic sense, as does Baudelaire in his sonnet "Bohémiens en voyage" (translated by Howard as "Gypsies on the Road"), to which we will return. Still later, in 1859, Lizst would entitle his long monograph on Gypsy music *Des Bohémiens et de leur musique en Hongroie*. And the primary definition of "bohème ou bohémiens" in the *Littré* (1872): "Bohemian: Name of vagabond bands without fixed abode or regular trade and often involved in fortunetelling: also called Egyptians and Zingaris."[5]

The paradoxical effects that could result from the interference of these two semantic fields, and something of the potential political charge of that interference, are well illustrated by a passage from Balzac's *Un prince de la Bohème* (first published in 1840 under a different title). For in contrast with Murger (whose introduction clearly contains echos of Balzac), Balzac uses "la Bohème" simultaneously in the service of a nationalist rhetoric and to unsettle it. On the one hand, Bohemia, "which by rights should be called the doctrine of the Boulevard des Italiens,"[6] is given an eminently local habitation and a name. On the other hand, "the word *Bohemia* tells you everything. Bohemia has nothing and lives upon what it has. Hope is its religion" (73),[7] a characterization that evokes both the Bohemians "bearing nothing but future things" who are depicted in the famous Callot engraving (whose legend I reference in the epigraph) and the biblical archetype of

messianic hope whose outlines Baudelaire traces, as we will see, in the Callot.[8] Even more strikingly, "Bohemia" is presented, however sardonically,
as a quintessential revolutionary energy that France harbors, unrecognized
and unexploited, at the heart of its national power: "What an irrational
central power which allows such tremendous energies to run to waste!
There are diplomatists in Bohemia quite capable of overturning Russia's
designs, if they but felt the power of France at their backs" (72–73).[9] Yet
that quintessence is also imagined as so isolated in its distinctness as to be
radically disenfranchised and transplantable, in a way that thoroughly con-
fuses questions of national allegiance: "If the czar would buy Bohemia for a
score of millions and set its population down in Odessa—always supposing
that they consented to leave the asphalt of the boulevards—Odessa would
be Paris within the year" (73).[10]

In Balzac's reading of Paris, *Bohemia* evokes the situation of Restoration youth following the July Revolution of 1830, an event that, in leading
to the establishment of a constitutional monarchy and the installation of
the "bourgeois king," Louis-Philippe, managed to simultaneously rekindle
and repress both France's revolutionary and its aristocratic heritage. It
thus offers ready evidence for Marilyn Brown's argument that "from its
inception, bohemia was a 'picturesque' response to, and sublimation of,
the failure of revolution."[11] What Brown's formulation does not account
for, however, are the figures of internal exile and hypothetical deportation
that give Balzac's characterization of Paris Bohemia its strange force and
that bear the stamp, I have been suggesting, of the older image of Bohemia
as a class of rootless wanderers. Freighted with the weight of disappointed
revolutionary hopes, that older image now begins to summon up still older
messianic archetypes. It also anticipates, as we will see, a later and darker
moment in the succession of abortive revolutionary movements that punc-
tuate the turbulent political history of nineteenth-century France.

2.

Consider, first of all, Marx's corrosive reference in *The Eighteenth Brumaire*—written within months of the publication of Murger's novel in
1851 (though a few years after the novel's periodical appearance, without
the preface from which we have quoted, as a series of stories)—to "the
whole indefinite, disintegrated mass, thrown hither and thither, which the
French term *la bohème*."[12] Marx's characterization (which, along with a related quotation, serves Benjamin as a point of departure for the "Bohemia"
section of "Paris of the Second Empire in Baudelaire") makes short shrift,

of course, of the sentimentalities consecrated by Murger. At the same time, it does so by implicitly drawing on Bohemia's old associations with a drifting, disaggregated mass of population "with dubious means of subsistence and of dubious origin."

As Marx is writing *The Eighteenth Brumaire* in late 1851 and early 1852, immediately following Louis-Napoléon's dissolution of the Second Republic and seizure of dictatorial powers, Baudelaire is sending to Théophile Gautier, in hopes of publication (largely disappointed), a packet of twelve poems, among them a sonnet entitled "La caravane des Bohémiens," later to be published in *Les Fleurs du mal* as "Bohémiens en voyage."[13] And as we will see, recent events, what happened *yesterday*, "hier," are an unspoken, and largely undetected, subtext of the poem. Here is the text of 1857:

La tribu prophétique aux prunelles ardentes
Hier s'est mise en route, emportant ses petits
Sur son dos, ou livrant à leurs fiers appétits
Le trésor toujours prêt des mamelles pendantes.

Les hommes vont à pied sous leurs armes luisantes
Le long des chariots où les leurs sont blottis,
Promenant sur le ciel des yeux appesantis
Par le morne regret des chimères absentes.

Du fond de son réduit sablonneux, le grillon,
Les regardant passer, redouble sa chanson;
Cybèle, qui les aime, augmente ses verdures,

Fait couler le rocher et fleurir le désert
Devant ces voyageurs, pour lesquels est ouvert
L'empire familier des ténèbres futures.

(The prophetical tribe, that ardent eyed people,
Set out last night, carrying their children
On their backs, or yielding to those fierce appetites
The ever ready treasure of pendulous breasts.

The men travel on foot with their gleaming weapons
Alongside the wagons where their kin are huddled,
Surveying the heavens with eyes rendered heavy
By a mournful regret for vanished illusions.

The cricket from the depths of his sandy retreat
Watches them as they pass, and louder grows his song;

Cybele, who loves them, increases her verdure,
Makes the desert blossom, water spurt from the rock

Before these travelers for whom is opened wide
The familiar domain of the future's darkness.)

Translated by William Aggeler

Literary history has long recognized as Baudelaire's more visible point
of departure for an early seventeenth-century etching by Jacques Callot
(Figure 1), the first in a series of four known as "Les Bohémiens." Various
visual elements of Callot's etching figure in Baudelaire's poem: the many
small children being carried on their mothers' backs or nursed; the men
on foot who flank the wagons, bearing arms; the long late-afternoon shadows. And in the legend that I have referenced in the epigraph ("tramps full
of fortunes / Bear nothing but future things"), one recognizes the textual
germ of which Baudelaire's sonnet is the expansion. Thus, the legend's
play on the reputation of Bohemians as vagrant fortunetellers, "diseurs de
bonaventures," is mobilized by Baudelaire from the outset, but also situ-
ated within a context of messianic expectation: "La tribu prophétique aux
prunelles ardentes / Hier s'est mise en route." The latent identification of
Callot's Bohemian caravan with the Jews of Exodus then approaches explic-
itness in the sonnet's penultimate lines: "Cybèle, qui les aime, augmente ses
verdures / Fait couler le rocher et fleurir le désert." In Riffaterre's formulation: "These gypsies become Hebrews in search of a promised Canaan."[14]

Figure 1

For several reasons, however, one should be wary of reaching too quickly for the stability of the biblical paradigm. In Riffaterre's case, for example, it leads directly to the dehistoricizing claim that "at this point the reader is compelled to recognize in the poem a variant of the theme of the Human Caravan trudging through the desert of life towards its ultimate destiny." Such a characterization may match up well with the platitudes of Gautier's own "La caravane" ("La caravane humaine au Sahara du monde")—yet another of Baudelaire's sources. But it seems an ill fit for the idiosyncratic syncretism of "Bohémiens en voyage," with its displacement of Jehovah by Cybele and, by extension, its conflation of the Jews of Exodus with the self-castrated votaries of the goddess's wandering cult.

First of all, and most immediately relevant to the subject of this volume, here, as elsewhere—"Le Voyage" and "Les septs veillards" come immediately to mind—Baudelaire's use of the topos of Jewish wandering is thoroughly mediated by the Christian medieval legend of the Wandering Jew, transmitted to Baudelaire through numerous Romantic sources, most notably Maturin's *Melmoth the Wanderer* and Sue's *Le Juif errant*. The quasi-citations of the biblical books of Exodus and Isaiah are commonplaces and, as such, entirely third-hand. One can debate to what extent its Romantic avatars reproduce or mitigate the anti-Semitic cast of the medieval figure, but the point I wish to focus on here is that the story also arose as the by-product, the unassimilated residue, of the typological negation and incorporation of the Old Testament by the New as its prefiguration: The same devotion to the letter that makes the Jews faithful guardians of the prophecies among the heathen also makes them unable to recognize in Christ's coming the spiritual fulfillment of those prophecies and so condemns them to wander perpetually through or outside history. That Baudelaire was familiar with this doctrine, for which the chain of transmission runs from Paul through Augustine and, in France, Pascal, is suggested by one disturbingly prophetic entry in the late intimate journal, *Mon coeur mis à nu*:

> Belle conspiration à organizer pour l'extermination de la Race Juive.
> Les Juifs, *Bibliothécaires* et témoins de la *Rédemption*.[15]

> (A fine conspiracy to be organized for the extermination of the Jewish Race.
> The Jews, *Librarians* and witnesses of the *Redemption*.)

It is not, I would argue, then, the "Hebrews in search of a promised Canaan," to recall Riffaterre's formulation, so much as this spectral and *postmessianic* figure of the wandering Jew to which Baudelaire assimilates his

Bohemian caravan. That Baudelaire's prophetic tribe is cast out not simply from its home but altogether from the design of biblical history it articulates is of a piece with the substitution of Cybele's maternal concern for Jehovah's providence.

Second, Baudelaire's syncretism also involves the topical dimension of reference whose genealogy we began by tracing. As T. J. Clark recalls, in contrast with artistic figures such as Gautier, who sided with the forces of order in the June Days of 1848, Baudelaire "fought for the rebels . . . with Bohemia"—which Clark characterizes as "the mob of unemployed, criminals and *déclassés* of every sort, the first victims, the first debris of industrialism—which made up one part of the rebel fighting force in June 1848."[16] Whether or not one can sharply distinguish—as Marx did and Clark pointedly does not—between a heterogeneous *lumpenproletariet* and a proletariet conscious of itself as a class united by common interests, in the aftermath of the June insurrection some fourteen thousand of the Parisian poor were transported in government convoys to Algeria.[17] Although Marx in *The Eighteenth Brumaire* portrays this as a summary deportation (which it in effect amounted to),[18] the transported population was in fact lured with promises of agricultural resettlement in favorable conditions on Algerian soil, promises that could assume biblical proportions. Thus, "according to the *Moniteur Universel* [reporting in Paris], these fortunate pioneers would find on arrival 'une terre belle et féconde; ils n'auraient . . . qu'à la frapper du pied pour en faire sortir les moissons.'"[19] The reality that awaited them was, of course, otherwise. In the scornful words of one of the generals in Algeria charged with responding to growing unrest among the *colons*, "à Paris, on leur a promis un eldorado; ici, il trouvent la nature, âpre et brute."[20] I would suggest, then, that "Bohémiens en voyage" also encodes an extended reference to the Algerian transports and that, not unlike *The Eighteenth Brumaire*, it takes the mass deportation as emblematic of the aftermath of the June insurgency.

Further evidence for this possibility may be found in a series of works by Daumier, with whom Baudelaire was in regular contact at this time.[21] Variously known as "The Emigrants" or "The Refugees," these paintings, sketches, and bas-reliefs are generally recognized as responses to the deportations.[22] At least some of them are thought to have been indebted as well to Callot's "Bohémiens" series.[23]

Whether or not Daumier's "Emigrants" and Baudelaire's "Bohémiens en voyage" share a reference to Callot, they offer graphic evidence of a shared political imaginary surrounding the events of 1848. Compare, first of all, the "Emigrants" of 1848–49 (Figure 2) with the oil sketch Daumier

submitted in April 1848 for the official competition "for a painted figure of
the Republic" (Figure 3). Chosen as a finalist, Daumier received a commission
to execute a final version of the painting but never did execute it.[24]

Drawing in part on the iconography of the First Republic, "La République nourrit ses enfants et les instruit" ("The Republic nourishes her
children and instructs them") conflates Rome as nurse of Romulus and
Remus with Rome as Cybele, Mater Magna, and guardian of the republic.
Comparing Daumier's painting with these lines from Baudelaire's early
poem "J'aime le souvenir de ces époques nues," one recognizes the identical conflation:

> Cybèle alors, fertile en produits généreux,
> Ne trouvait point ses fils un poids trop onéreux,
> Mais, louve au coeur gonflé de tendresses communes,
> Abreuvait l'univers à ses tétines brunes
>
> (Cybele then, abundant in her yield,
> Did not regard her sons as burdensome,
> But, tender-hearted she-wolf, graciously
> Suckled the universe at her brown dugs.)

Translated by Richard Howard

Just as "La République" finds its counter-image in "Emigrants," so do
these lines anticipate the downcast figures of "Bohémiens en voyage," the

Figure 2

Figure 3

only other poem by Baudelaire besides "J'aime le souvenir" in which Cybele figures.

   More specifically, these lines anticipate the movement that organizes
the relationship between the sonnet's two quatrains: from the powerfully
regressive, even animalistic, image in the first quatrain of mothers "livrant
à leurs fiers appétits / Le trésor toujours prêt des mamelles pendantes" to
the men of the second quatrain, their eyes weighed down ("appesantis")
with the memory of "chimères absentes" (in which one can read "mères

absentes"), and who trudge *on foot* beside the wagons bearing their huddled "brood," as Howard translates it.

This division, far sharper in Baudelaire than in Callot, initiates an imaginative progression that the sestet then continues. As several commentators have noted, with the sestet the poem moves beyond anything observable in Callot's etching: The cricket and its redoubled song, Cybele and the multiplying signs of her favor, are Baudelaire's imaginative augmentations of his pictorial source at the same time that they involve quotation from or allusion to numerous texts. It is thus significant that with the first of these details, at the sonnet's turn, Baudelaire writes into the scene his own poetic activity via a miniaturized image not unlike the butterfly stamp that Whistler used to sign some of his paintings:

> Du fond de son réduit sablonneux, le grillon,
> Les regardant passer, redouble sa chanson.

The iconic self-figuration looks back to La Fontaine's "La Cigale and la fourmi," but also (more interestingly and strangely) forward to the Sphinx of "Spleen," "assoupi dans le fond d'un Sahara brumeux/ . . . et dont l'humeur farouche/Ne chante qu'aux rayons du soleil qui se couche" ("Drowsed in the depths of a hazy Sahara/ . . . and whose fierce moods/Sing only to the rays of setting suns" [translation by Richard Howard, modified]), an association to which we will return.

The movement of the poem through a zone of heightened specularity then continues in the evocation of Cybele and her favors, since the goddess's regenerative transformation of a barren landscape into one of burgeoning abundance reflects the poem's own reparative imaginative response to the etching's barren surround:

> Cybèle, qui les aime, augmente ses verdures,
>
> Fait couler le rocher et fleurir le désert
> Devant ces voyageurs. . . .

One needn't rely, however, on the comparison with Callot to foreground the workings of this reparative impulse: The Mater Magna is restored on a mythic scale, as a relationship between a people and the earth, the "trésor toujours prêt des mamelles pendantes" that closed the first quatrain and then yielded in the second to "le morne regret des chimères absentes."

Whether, within the imaginative logic of the poem, the manifestations of Cybele's care are to be seen as real—which is to say, miraculous—or imaginary is an open question. But that they materialize "devant ces voyageurs" (*before* these travelers) certainly invites a reading of them as mirages—comforting or tantalizing—always *just* ahead, always *just* out of reach, their appearance a function of the movement of the nomadic band of figures through the landscape of the poem. Such a reading is also in keeping with the way the poem's movement traces a solar arc, its organizing principle that of a day, of *today*. What immediately precedes the time of the poem is yesterday, "hier"; what it approaches in approaching its end is night. That is at least one common reading of "L'empire familier des ténèbres futures"—a reading that would, as John Hollander has suggested, be grounded in Callot's etching if we read its shadows as cast by a sun declining in the west.[25] The specular imagery associated with Cybele that we have been considering would then essentially figure the future as mirage, the function of a logic of optical, specular reflection, the "mirror-stage" of the Lacanian imaginary. It is *thus* figured as mirages, mirages that will vanish with the setting of the sun, that traces of the messianic promise recur within the poem. Just as "Le trésor toujour prêt des mamelles pendantes" prefigures and is subsumed within the subsequent imagery of earthly abundance, so does "le morne regret des chimères absentes" adumbrate its metaleptic transumption by "l'empire familier des ténèbres futures," the assured reascendancy of night, disillusion and, ultimately, death.

At the same time, "l'empire familier des ténèbres futures," the phrase with which "Bohémiens en voyage" rejoins Callot's etching—not only its imagery but also its inscription—should not be understood only, or even primarily, as extending or expanding the aegis of the solar metaphor whose arc we have been tracing. While the funereal majesty of the transumptive conclusion may be read as of a piece with that metaphor, following as surely as night follows day, more profoundly the entry into its "familiar empire" signals a movement beyond the dominion of the solar metaphor altogether and the opening of a relation to the future beyond the future of messianic expectation. Here I return to my suggestion that Baudelaire's "tribu prophétique" is a postmessianic figure, the unassimilated residue of a typological reading of history, a minoritization of millennial and revolutionary hope. The empire of the wandering fortuneteller, who is endowed at most with what we might call, adapting Benjamin, a "weak prophetic power," is not Tomorrow, the Day or Night of final Deliverance, but the day after tomorrow. In the *Investigations*, Wittgenstein writes: "A dog believes his master is at the door. But can he also believe that his master will come the day after tomorrow? . . . Can only those hope who can talk?" He replies: "Only those who have mastered the use of a language. That is to say, the manifestations of hope are modifications of this complicated form of life."[26] To be reminded of this is to be reminded that what separates to-day from tomorrow and the day after tomorrow is not just a span of time, another turn or two of the orbiting earth on its axis, but the intervention in time of the possibilities and limits of language.

CHAPTER 8

Paul Celan's Improper Names

Anna Glazova

Explicit references to Judaism in Paul Celan's poems are rather sparse (with the exception of the poems written in connection with his journey to Jerusalem in 1968). Even though Celan had more than a marginal interest in post-rabbinical Judaism and Jewish mysticism, as his private library attests, hardly any of his texts allude to these contexts directly. This makes it particularly hard to speak about Celan's relation to Jewish texts and rituals. While in Jerusalem, he once characterized his relationship to Judaism as "pneumatic," thus indicating his distance from any dogmatism in his relation to it.[1] Nevertheless, echoes of Jewish religious texts, devoid of manifest markers, are scattered throughout Celan's texts. Sometimes thematized as invocations of rituals, these echoes are more often perceptible on the purely linguistic level. They appear as "foreign bodies" (*Fremdkörper*), to use Celan's metaphor for quotations[2]—i.e., as Hebrew words, usually phonetically transliterated and unmarked as foreign within the German text. Celan's knowledge of Hebrew, limited as it was, affected his texts in these instances semantically, phonetically, or graphically.

It is in general not uncommon for Celan to let a foreign language "invade" his poems and establish a further layer of signification. In a poem entitled "Bei Wein und Verlorenheit" (With wine and lostness), for example, Celan lets French resonate in German, when he lets the word *Neige* (dregs) anticipate *Schnee* (snow) in the following lines, for *neige* means "snow" in French. Unlike other authors, however, who often employ plays on words—most famously, perhaps, James Joyce in his *Finnegans Wake*—Celan's "heterolingual" words aren't meant as jokes. Joyce uses his puns to thematize a correspondence between languages; the words coinciding phonetically or graphically in different languages are, as it were, missed opportunities of a "literal," semantic translation. His detours from translation dictionaries are meant to expose the emptiness of signification; Celan, on the contrary, uses these words to contract and condense meaning. Words like *Neige* communicate that "snow" and "dregs" may be different ways of saying the same thing in a poem. Both words give up their fixed, dictionary meanings to point at something besides their "literal" meaning, at something Celan calls—half hopefully and half desperately—"a singable remnant" (*singbarer Rest*).[3]

As in the example above, where French and German coinhabit Celan's poem, there are recognizable instances of conflation of German and Hebrew in his texts.[4] Using a poem, "Unter die Haut meiner Hände genäht" (Sewn under the skin of my hands), from his book *Atemwende* (Breathturn), I propose to show in my essay that Celan reflects on his readings in Jewish mysticism; more specifically, on two texts he owned and read carefully, as his notes document—namely, Gershom Scholem's book *Die Geheimnisse der Schöpfung* ("Secrets of creation"—his translation of selected passages from the Zohar, the kabbalistic book of creation, with introduction and commentary) and Hugo Bergmann's essay "Die Heiligung des Namens" (Sanctification of the name) from an anthology entitled *Vom Judentum* (On Judaism) and published by the Bar Kochba organization in Prague. In this poem, Celan transfers a sacral linguistic act onto the poetic plane and, with this transformation, comments on language in Jewish mysticism on the one hand and, on the other hand, on language in poetry. Celan's poetic paradigm reveals itself in this poem as peculiarly resonant with the language "theory" of a certain strain of mysticism: Sabbateanism.

It is not an uncommon practice for Celan to start with a direct allusion in a draft and then to remove the reference from the final version. Allusions to Jewish mysticism are no exception; for example, Celan writes a poem entitled "Shechina" (in Jewish mysticism, God's presence in the exiled world after creation and before redemption) but later decides to remove the title before publishing the poem in *Die Niemandsrose*. Celan avoids using this mystical term by name in his poem but the theme associated with it—living in the world of shattered divine presence—remains the poem's main content.[5] The removal of the reference, rather than undermining any of its complexity, makes the invocation of Shechina even more problematic than would have a direct reference. With the removal of this name, Shechina, God's presence, becomes exiled not only from the world but also from the poem: The fate of all creation in Judaism affects the poem's final version literally, no longer merely metaphorically. This gesture is somewhat reminiscent of the kenotic refusal to make any positive statements about God, since none of his qualities can be known to us. Further, this gesture resembles rhetorically the prohibition to pronounce God's name, except that the name Shechina suppressed here is not the Tetragrammaton forbidden in Judaism. The peculiarity of Celan's poetic language is that he avoids explicit references, and his gesture is not entirely foreign to those who avoid calling "the Name" by name. His language, however, operates in the realm of poetry rather than in any sacral context and so renders the unnamed names not only unpronounceable but, moreover, unrecognizable. The very act of naming is, as it were, suspended in this poetry. Those not called stay anonymous.

The name—the name of God but also the proper name in general—in Jewish mysticism begins to interest Celan intensively around the time of *Die Niemandrose* and *Atemwende*. Hugo Bergmann's Zionist agenda was not the point of Celan's attention, but he encountered in Bergmann's essay, "Sanctification of the Name," a description of a linguistic procedure in Judaism that might have influenced his own writing. This procedure consists in treating all words as if they were proper names.[6] Words that oscillate between languages—like the word *Neige*—share the namelike quality of staying the same in translation. Celan attempts in his poems to reach the untranslatability of names. His heterolingual words-names are "legitimate," in the sense that they belong—unlike Joyce's hybrids—to the recognizable vocabulary of standard language use; this, however, makes their floating between languages all the more elusive. As word-names their function is suspended, peculiarly, between signifying and naming.[7] This transitory state of language is characteristic of the word "Ha-Shem," which Bergmann focuses on in his essay:

> "Shem" means "name." It signifies the divine name Yahweh but must be differentiated from it. It stands for what one can express with words, say about God, the potentiality of the divine that remains to be actualized by humans yet. As soon as the man accomplishes within himself the unification, the *Yechud Hashem*, he becomes able to say to God: God, Yahweh.

("Schem" heißt "Name," es bezeichnet den Gottesnamen Jahwe, ist
aber von ihm zu scheiden. Es ist das, was man von Gott mit Worten
bezeichnen, *sagen* kann, die Potenzialität des Göttlichen, die vom Menschen noch zu verwirklichen ist. Wenn dies getan ist, wenn der Mensch
die Einung, den *Jechud Haschem*, in sich vollzogen hat, dann erst kann er
zu Gott: Gott, Jahwe sagen.)[8]

Shem is the name replacing the name of God, *Yahweh*; but *Shem*, "name," is
itself neither exactly a name, since it does not provide an alternative name,
nor exactly a word, since it is not meant universally but only as a surrogate
for one name, *Yahweh*. This "name" is improper rather than proper, and its
linguistic status points at the limit where language gives up its—supposedly stable—referential structure.

The linguistic status of proper names is important for Celan's poetry
from early on. Two poems from *Atemwende* (which are connected with
each other through their imagery), however, thematize not so much proper
names as the power of naming in general. Even though no direct reference
to Jewish mysticism is present in these texts, evocation in place of utterance
of the "name" and "names" here is reminiscent of the replacement of God's
forbidden name with the misnomer *Shem*.

Von Ungeträumten geätzt,
wirft das schlaflos durchwanderte Brotland
den Lebensberg auf.

Aus seiner Krume
knetest du neu unsre Namen,
die ich, ein deinem
gleichendes
Aug an jedem der Finger,
abtaste nach
einer Stelle, durch die ich
mich zu dir heranwachen kann,
die helle
Hungerkerze im Mund.[9]

(BY THE UNDREAMT etched,
the sleeplessly wandered-through breadland
casts up the life mountain.

From its crumb
you knead anew our names,
which I, an eye

similar
to yours on each finger,
probe for
a place, through which I
can wake myself toward you,
the bright
hungercandle in mouth.)[10]

Unter die Haut meiner Hände genäht:
dein mit Händen
getrösteter Name.

Wenn ich den Klumpen Luft
knete, unsere Nahrung,
säuert ihn der
Buchstabenschimmer aus
der wahnwitzig-offenen
Pore.[11]

(Sewn under the skin of my hands:
with hands
comforted, your name.

When I knead
the lump of air, our nourishment,
it is soured by the
letter-shimmer from
the mad-open
pore.)[12]

In an earlier poem entitled "Psalm" and included in *Die Niemandsrose*, Celan uses the image of kneading to invoke a (failed) repeated creation of man: "Niemand knetet uns wieder aus Erde und Lehm, / niemand bespricht unseren Staub. Niemand" (No one kneads us again out of earth and loam / no one evokes our dust. No one).[13] The image of kneading in the two poems cited above may refer to the same narrative of creation of man out of earth and the poems can, along with "Psalm," be read as an inverted praise for this creation. In the two later poems, however, names rather than bodies are the focus of speech. In the time between *Die Niemandsrose* and *Atemwende*, Celan read, along with Bergmann's essay, Scholem's translation of the Zohar, in which Scholem points out that this text (central to the kabbalistic tradition) treats different divine names as sources of power, which Scholem calls "magic,"[14] and which build the cosmos, each on its designated stage of creation. In the two poems of *Atemwende*, Celan binds together name and creation, but what is created, "kneaded" anew, is the names: "knetest du neu unsre Namen" (you knead anew our names). Thus, naming is itself creation. Kneading the names is analogous to kneading bread, except that its "dough" is speaking. The gesture of hands actively "working" on speech rather than following speech is a part of kabbalistic knowledge, too, and builds the core ritualistic procedure in another mystical book, Sefer Yetzirah, which Celan was very unlikely aware of. In this book the ten divine names, each designating a particular sefira from the tree of sefiroth, are assigned to the ten fingers, five on one hand and five on the other. When one prays in accordance with this ritual, one concentrates on this division between names and fingers while holding one's palms facing each other to "polarize" the names and, with their help, to fill one's prayer with mystical strength. One's fingers thus shape one's language with the help of divine names in this ritual. In Celan's poems, name and (kneading) fingers complement each other in speaking, too; what remains unknown, however, is the name and the names and who or what is to be named. There is no form-giving name in these poems about names; the words, unlike the prayers of a kabbalist, rely on no higher power from a higher order of language.

Before I move on to a discussion of names in Celan's poems, I will outline the "polarization" of names as the purifying power in Sefer Yetzirah. This detour will help me to interpret Celan's decision to suppress the name *Shechina* and the kneading of the name in *Atemwende*.

In Sefer Yetzirah, a correspondence between the ten sefiroth (divine vessels, emanations) and the ten fingers is established:[15] The sefiroth are polarized between the left hand and the right hand, and while the unity binding the sefiroth persists, a tension is created, whose focus lies precisely in the middle point between the hands.[16] This focus, the unifying covenant Brit Yachid (ברית יחיד), has the power of circumcision and of purification. This covenant unifies the congregation and purifies one's hands and tongue for prayer.[17] Creating earth with one hand and heaven with the other,[18] YHWH channels the power of separation and unity between sefiroth, and creation separates itself from the primordial chaos (*tohu*).[19] Although cosmos is formed from sefiroth, they—unlike letters that have form and sound, and also unlike digits that become associated with the sefiroth only at a later stage of creation[20]—are formless and expressionless: Sefer Yetzirah speaks of *sefiroth beli-mah* (בלי-מה), *beli-mah* meaning "expressionless" or "ineffable" (literally, "without-what").[21] The word *beli-mah* occurs only once in the Bible and is used in differentiation to chaos (*tohu*): "He stretches out the north over empty space [*tohu*] and hangs the earth on nothing [*beli-mah*]" (Job 26:1).[22] Written as בלם (*balam*), it means "to bridle," and both variants occur simultaneously in Sefer Yetzirah 1:8:

> Ten Sefiroth of Nothingness [בלי-מה]
> Bridle [בלום] your mouth from speaking
> and your heart from thinking
> And if your heart runs
> return to the place.
> It is therefore written,
> "The Chayot running and returning." (Ezekiel 1:24)
> Regarding this a covenant was made.[23]

Beli-mah, the expressionless, both separates and restricts (bridles)—it is the cutting and the covenant, the dividing and the unifying power of circumcision. When one prays and lets one's hands and, with them, one's speech be controlled by the purifying power of the polarized sefiroth, one separates the impurities from one's thoughts and attempts to achieve a higher unity with the divine name. In this ritualistic practice, proper order is brought about by the expressionless, mute power that separates cosmos from chaos and, also, articulate speech from the inarticulate.

About three hundred years after the date of the earliest known manuscript of Sefer Yetzirah, the kabbalistic narrative about creation becomes reformulated in the widely influential interpretation of Isaac Luria, who is still considered by many the most authoritative figure in the history of the Kabbalah. Luria's version of the representation of creation in the oldest kabbalistic book, Sefer Yetzirah, adds a crucial addition to the story of creation of cosmos through God's contraction (or *tsimtsum*, as known from many sources preceding Luria). This addition is the mirroring of the breaking of sefiroth resulting from this contraction. Once these vessels broke, the divine light contained within them spilled and, with it, the universe came into existence. According to Luria, however, the world consists of two types of material: The pure divine light from the broken vessels, and their inferior shards. The fatal breaking of the vessels was a sin and needs to be rectified. The task of every individual is to restore the unity of the vessels by helping God in separating divine sparks trapped in the broken shards (*qellipoth*). The process of this recollection, *tikkun olam* (repairing the world), will continue until it is completed by the Messiah; then the perfection will be restored and the messianic age will begin.[24] Prayer is the key instrument of accomplishing one's part in the universal process of *tikkun*. The language of prayer thus not only purifies the individual who prays but also the world in general. While the movement in *tsimtsum* is that from the perfect order expressed in the divine name to the imperfect state of the world after the fall, the movement in *tikkun* is reversed. In *tikkun*, the world experiences a finalizing shift, or separation, in which the language is perfected. Even the divine word is not yet complete or perfect.

A major event in the history of the Jewish diaspora, now known as the Sabbatean apostasy, occurred around a century after Luria's reformulation of the Kabbalah. Sabbatei Zevi proclaimed himself the Messiah and promised to bring the world to perfection within a few years. Zevi's fame grew largely owing to vigorous support of Nathan of Gaza, a kabbalist scholar, who formulated the Sabbatean prophecy in the course of creating his own, highly idiosyncratic version of the Lurianic system. The effects of the Sabbateanism were immense, in terms both of the messianic hope raised by this prophecy and of the disillusionment after the hopes came to nothing. Here I will single out one aspect of this peculiar variation of the Kabbalah: the Sabbatean "language theory"—i.e., Nathan's thought that language is impure as of yet and needs to be purified through prayer. In his infamous letter of September 1665, enunciating the arrival of the messianic age, Nathan urged believers to pray from then on by meditating solely on the name of God, YHWH (יהוה), rather than on any particular sefira. The reason for this is that with the arrival of the messianic age the name of God will transform and, for the first time, take on its definite form:

> In our days all things will be purified with God's help, the [mystical] lights will spread, [*the sefirah*] *Malkuth* [that is, the Shechina] will be [restored to the mystical state symbolized as] "the crown of her husband." The holy name YHWH will then be read as a double YHYH, and Scripture will be fulfilled [Zech. 14:9] "in that day YHWH shall be one and His name one." For the WH of the Tetragrammaton will be in complete union with YH, and they will never be separated.
>
> *Sevi Sabbatei*, 271[25]

The arrival of the messianic age will not cancel the existence of language as such; yet it will bring about a defining shift in language that will effectively repair the universe. Language needs to be purified and perfected before it can be used as the tool and medium of the universal perfection. Whereas people can help to bring about this finalizing shift, the Messiah alone can accomplish the purifying separation, preparing the ground for the ultimate unity. This is how Nathan describes this function: "The Messiah . . . will tear (Hebrew *para*—a verb which also serves as a technical term, denoting the uncovering of the *glans penis* at circumcision) the 'prepuce' of the *qelippah*" (*Sevi Sabbatei*, 309).

To free the sparks of the divine light from the shards, the Messiah must cut away what is obstructing it from revealing itself. The crude matter of the *qellipoth* needs to be separated cleanly, so that the unity of God and his creation can be restored. The "good" cosmos, in other words, needs to be freed from the "bad," imperfect chaos:

> For the *qellipoth* are called *golem*, that is, a formless mass. For that reason it is said [Gen 1:2], "and the earth was without form (*tohu*) and void"—for there is a building [that is, structure, *kosmos*] and there is formless mass (*tohu*) which is the *qellipoth* and which will be perfected by him [the Messiah]" (*Sevi Sabbatei*, 309).[26]

It follows from Nathan's description of the Messiah's task that language, like all things in the world as of now, is to a certain extent a *golem* language. When the Messiah redeems the language of its imperfections, the power of naming will, for the first time in human experience, gain the creative power that it had in the prelapsarian age in the Garden of Eden. Thus, one of Sabbatei's tasks would be to change the divine name so that the old name, YHWH, would be transformed into YHYH. One could go as far as to say that Sabbatei's messianism failed not at the point when Sabbatei was taken captive and renounced Judaism for Islam but well before that, when he failed to accomplish the task of changing God's name for good. Once Sabbatei (and Nathan after him) pronounced this new name, YHYH, the purifying "cut" on the word YHWH didn't render the old name obsolete and, thus, the mystical procedure was not accomplished.

When Celan leaves the names unpronounced, he does not refer to the Pentateuch. Instead, the names remain unknown to us. They are not antonomastic in the sense that they do not replace the name that needs to be left unpronounceable but still is silently meant. These names remain truly anonymous. Having made this claim, I have to admit that Celan's poem, with its lack of direct allusions, cannot be read as an invocation of religious contexts. The poem can and must also be read independently of its hints toward the power of naming within the realm of Judaism. Celan in his poems about names does, however, repeat the thought common to all kabbalistic texts: that naming is a power needed for creation. Furthermore Celan, like Sabbatei and Nathan, treats language as imperfect and points at the possibility that names, if renewed and reborn, can alleviate the fate of language to remain cut off from its highest function—to build the world out of names. In view of Sabbatei's "theory of language," Celan's poetry speaks on the condition of imperfection, when names are unpronounceable not only because of awe before God's omnipotent name but also because the names have not yet been created. Thus any name given by people today can be spoken only in the *golem* language—the language that follows the laws of creation but does not prescribe such rules. Sabbatei's ambition was to recreate language and thus the world; whether his attempt has contributed to the process of the *tikkun* cannot be decided by us. Celan's poems about the creative power of names do not share this ambition, but they affirm that names do indeed have the power to create. These names, however, are not known to us, not even to the author himself.

In the first poem names are said to be malleable, like a breadcrumb— they can take a different form when kneaded:

BY THE UNDREAMT etched,
the sleeplessly wandered-through breadland
casts up the life mountain.

From its crumb
you knead anew our names.

The bread from which names are formed sustains the life of those who are named. Their names are inseparable from their mortal existence and, like the human body in the biblical narrative, are molded from inanimate substance rather than born. Whereas the crumb is formless—like chaos, or *tohu*, before creation—the name is form-giving. Names, it is said, are being kneaded anew: Thus, the existing names are preliminary, their form is not yet definite. The insight of these lines is that language has a plasticity; Celan elsewhere calls the language of his poems "language in statu nascendi."[27] Perhaps the concluding lines speaking of hunger indicate that the bread cannot be eaten before the names are complete. If so, then the later poem tells of the transformation in names during which the bread becomes edible:

Unter die Haut meiner Hände genäht:
dein mit Händen
getrösteter Name.

Wenn ich den Klumpen Luft
knete, unsere Nahrung,
säuert ihn der

Buchstabenschimmer aus
der wahnwitzig-offenen
Pore.

(Sewn under the skin of my hands:
with hands
comforted, your name.

When I knead
the lump of air, our nourishment,
it is soured by the
letter-shimmer from
the mad-open
pore.)[28]

The name is inscribed, sewn into hands ("genäht") and made closer ("nah" and "näher"); the syllable -*näh*- in *genäht* mirrors *hän*- in *Hände*, as letter after letter cuts deeper into hands, so that the air we breathe can become our bread ("Nahrung"), our *pneumatic* bread, and our proximity (as in *Nah*-rung). The name, inscribed into *two* hands, shimmers through *one* pore: This is the madness of this openness. The name stays one in its division between plasticity and ultimate form. In the movement from *hän* to *näh* to *hän*, the writing turns from left to right to right to left, in which both syllables, neither making a complete word, turn to each other, and counter each other, turn one into another, without becoming one another. These split words speak German circumcised by the direction of writing. This German poem, through this turning of the syllable, speaks Hebrew devoid of Hebrew words and devoid of the Hebrew alphabet. It does preserve, however, the Hebrew alphabet's countermovement, which invokes a Jewish presence in the German text while not speaking Hebrew. The name—possibly a German or a Hebrew name—remains unspoken, suspended between languages. This incomplete, imperfect act of pronouncing the name is the poet's attempt to fulfill language in his poetry. This act—which is a speech act—binds the poet to the tradition while it separates him from ritualistic Judaism. Celan, after all, writes a poem rather than a prayer, and his language is German rather than Hebrew. This imperfect continuation of tradition is his paradoxical attempt to retain his Jewishness while taking leave from Judaism. Yet the fulfillment of this language relies perhaps on something that stays unpronounced in the poem: the divine name that remains silent behind the poet's speech. It is not only unpronounceable as YHWH; it is an unnamed name, not known. It is common to both the New and the Old Testament that God's presence is revealed in the change of name of the one called, starting with the patriarch Abraham. When Sabbatei calls on believers to change God's name, he claims for himself this ability to mystically transform names. Celan's silence about names, his refusal to speak the name *Shechina* in his poem has nothing in common with Sabbatei's heretic act of naming; it does, however, signal his recognition of the power of naming.

Names in Celan's poems remain unnamed. Their anonymity shows that they cannot be called yet, for language is still *in statu nascendi*; in this state, any pronounced names would be preliminary and thus, in the end, false. We can only guess that the uncalled names in the poem would be Hebrew, like all the unnamed names in a later poem from *Lichtzwang*, where they are called "die rückwärtsgesprochenen / Namen, alle" (all the names / spoken backward).[29] These names are recognizable to us only in the direction of writing, backward from the point of view of a German speaker, since Hebrew words are written right to left and not left to right, as in European languages. That the names in the poems above are Hebrew is suggested by the anagrammatic pair *hän-/näh-*. That the inversion of the German alphabet into Hebrew as a token of Celan's "pneumatic Judaism" does indeed take place in the poem is a hypothesis that needs further substantiation. In my view, this substantiation is to be found in the fact that the book contains both a poem with the preliminary title "Shechina" and explicit references to the Lurianic Kabbalah; thus, Jewish mysticism builds at least one layer of signification in *Atemwende*. Further, the two poems I discuss operate with an imagery reminiscent of the biblical narrative of creation and also contain hints of the story of the exile of the divine presence (*Shechina*) in the world but also of the Jewish people in the desert. The plight of hunger in the desert turns into a hungry vigil in the "bread land," where names are being kneaded while their bearers are subjected to a fast. In a time of hunger, the biblical David ate the otherwise forbidden bread of the presence, without any guilt associated with his deviation from the law whereby this bread is reserved for priests. The "air leavened by the name" in "Unter die Haut" can be read as Celan's inverted transformation of the bread of presence into the air, the insubstantial pneumatic "bread." The sourness of bread, its sour-making, is not kosher when one commemorates the exile in the desert: Leavened bread is unclean for Passover. In preparation for Passover, leaven (*chametz*) must be carefully separated from any foods in the kitchen and disposed of. Passover, the celebration of exile but also of freedom, is, both in its rituals and in its content, the holiday of separation: The way to freedom leads through separation of Jews from non-Jews and of Jews from their homes. In remembrance of the Jews who had no time to let their bread rise as they left Egypt, the Jews spend days separating *chametz* from their houses. In Celan's poem, the name, however, the unnamed name, itself becomes *chametz*: It is the impure leaven that makes "unsere Nahrung" (our bread) rise. The name—like leaven raising the bread—fills the air with air. The source of the sourness is the light of the name ("der Buchstabenschimmer"), the dwindled rest of the primordial light and the rest of the divine breath, perhaps, which had started the initial cosmic separation in *tsimtsum* but now perseveres only as a fluorescence of something sour and rotten. The name seems to give shape to the substance that escapes being formed. When the hands move in the gesture of kneading, they shape the air along with the name shaping the language of the poem. If the "I" of this poem is the one who is invoked in "Vom ungeträumten," then "I" shapes the names that have stayed yet unformed. It kneads names as food for those who wander hungry. The sourness of the bread is an inversion of the narrative of the exile from Egypt. Unleavened bread has a longer life and would sustain the wanderers longer; that the name leavens the bread is disastrous for them, since it makes their hunger plight imminent. The name of God is no longer the warranty of salvation in this poem, as it is in the biblical narrative of exile. Rather, it is an anonymous name, not known to the speaker and, like the speaker himself, mortal.

Celan shares with Sabbatei this recognition: Names, like bread, are perishable and, like people, mortal. In Nathan of Gaza's understanding of *tikkun*, the arrival of the messianic age depends on the completion of the initial separation between God and world. In Celan's poem, this separation takes on the character of an indefinite openness: The name, not a divine name, not even properly a name, is not a proper name. The language of the poem is that of an indeterminately postponed approximation to naming. It does not bring about the completion of logos in the perfection of the divine name, and by turning on itself, it suspends itself in the movement of turning. "Our nourishment" (*unsere Nahrung*)—more incisively than the conclusive lines of the earlier "Tenebrae," "Pray, Lord. // We are nigh" (Bete, Herr. // Wir sind nah)[30]—extinguishes hope by fulfilling it in endless approximation.[31] And, again, more incisively than in "Tenebrae," "eyes hang so open and empty" (Augen und Mund stehn so offen und leer):[32] The air—the medium of vision, on the one hand, and of our breath, on the other—fills neither the mouth nor the eyes but the hands. The poet's hands become his eyes and respiratory tracts, *Atemwege*, rendering the poet's body and poetry disturbed, mad (*wahnwitzig*). According to the biblical narrative of creation, the divine breath provided the air that we breathe; now it can be shaped by hands, by food rather than spirit. The *pneuma*, the divine breath, persists only as a means of fermentation of food. Its divine character is lost, or hidden, anonymous like the names not called.

In the poem, the name inscribed into the hands is deprived of Jewish connotations, but this erasure is not merely a lack. It leaves a trace, a tone, a gesture in the air—precisely "nothing of revelation" (das Nichts der Offenbarung), which is constitutive for Celan's pneumatic Judaism.[33] Whereas in the earlier "To one who stood at the door" ("Einem, der vor der Tür stand"),[34] circumcision is explicitly mentioned on the semantic level—"circumcise his/word,/write living nothingness/into his/flesh" (Diesem/beschneide das Wort,/diesem/schreib das lebendige/Nichts ins Gemüt), here it cuts into the structure of the word. The sub-semantic movement and countermovement from letter to letter within a word subverts logos as the essence of language. Between the poet's hands, the poem is suspended in the air stretched between "under the skin" and "pore," in the focus of separating and binding. While the Sabbatean apostasy perforates the divine name, Celan's poetry brings Hebrew into German without calling the language by name. It translates Hebrew as a language written backward, and this translation is not audible. It can only be read on paper. This renders names—if they were to be pronounced aloud—truly unpronounceable, for they could be spoken only in German. Hebrew keeps silent in Celan's poem. Yet precisely owing to this silence, Hebrew becomes communicable in German. Whereas the apostatic Sabbatean statement that God's name is imperfect replaces it with another name spoken in the same imperfect language and thereby undermines the perfection it calls for, Celan's poem brings about the hope for the communicability between languages, which allows for the hope that one day the Babylonian dissemination of languages will be overcome. Celan's poem is messianic precisely because it promises nothing and says nothing about the divinity of the name that remains unnamed and unnameable.

By cutting away the notion of circumcision from its initial ritualistic content and translating it into the language of poetry, Celan attempts to transform this word, *beschneiden*, into a Jewish gesture outside Judaism. This operation is illegitimate from at least two points of view. First, it transgresses the Jewish law that enforces circumcision as the mark of separation from the gentiles. Second, free from this law, circumcision of the word, (*das beschnittene Wort*) separates itself from its previous meaning and thus becomes semantically imprecise, suggestive. Once circumcision is circumcised from its ritualistic meaning, the very meaning of the word becomes illegitimate, as it no longer refers to the mark of Jewishness known to Jews and gentiles alike. What meaning does the circumcised word then acquire? How does this transformation affect the language within the poetic realm? Is this not a retreat into the reductionism of metaphors and tropes that Celan, again and again, attempts to escape? Does "the circumcision of the word" (*das Beschneiden des Wortes*), this genitive metaphor of which he was so traumatically accused,[35] not stand as another symbol ready to be turned into an image, trope, figure of speech, "an object or subject matter" (*ein Objekt oder Sujet*)?[36] Rather than a fixed trope, this transformation of circumcision is intended as a *cut* into rhetorical figures: *Pore*, from πόρος, is a way through the aporia, a passage through the impassibility of tropes. The Jewishness of this procedure is no longer Judaic; it becomes poetic, as much as it is apostatic from the perspective of rabbinic Judaism. Yet the question remains open—and perhaps must necessarily remain open—whether this cut on circumcision does in truth open the language of poetry rather than stand as a mere metaphor for "opening." Can it be that this openness, perhaps just "openness," is nothing but an "as if" and thus just another simile? Does the quotation from the Kabbalah, and be it only on the level of gesture or sub-semantic movement in the text, not necessarily implement scare quotes, "*Hasenöhrchen, Gänsefüßchen*,"[37] to this opening?

These questions bother Jacques Derrida in his Celan studies constantly. His project is to analyze Celan's poems in view of their Jewish references. The circumcision of the word, Jewish hands, and the connection between circumcision and Friedrich Hölderlin's caesura (thus, the connection between the ritualistic procedure and the poetologic term) are recurrent motifs of Jacques Derrida's interpretations of Celan's poetry. Perhaps the most relevant passage is the one related to Celan's poem "Einem, der vor der Tür stand" in *Schibboleth pour Paul Celan* (1986):

> The circumcised word [*parole*] is *above all* written, at once incised and excised in a body, which may be the body of a language and which in any case always binds the body to language: word that is cut into, written because cut into, caesuraed in its origin, with the poem.
>
> The circumcised word is, *next*, readable, starting from *nothing*, but readable, *to be read* to the point of wounding and to the point of bleeding (*Wundgelesene*).
>
> *By the same stroke*, as it were, the circumcised word grants access to the community, to the covenant or alliance, to the partaking of a language, in a language. And in the Jewish language as poetic language, if all poetic language is, like all poets according to the epigraph, Jewish in essence [this is a reference to the epigraph, in which Celan quotes

Marina Tsvetaeva's startling aphorism "All poets are Yids"]; but this essence promises itself only through dis-identification, that expropriation in the nothing of the non-essence of which we have spoken. The Germanic language, like any other, but here with what privilege, must be circumcised by a rabbi, and the rabbi becomes then a poet, reveals the poet in him.[38]

Derrida reads Celan's poem as a circumcision, an opening of language in poetry: This circumcision cannot be Jewish in essence, can be Jewish only in the non- or dis-essence, it cannot declare itself to be Jewish, nor, for that matter, to be non-Jewish, since in that case it would be only by way of a negative identification—i.e., not open. The circumcised word can announce itself only in openness that is neither Jewish nor non-Jewish, indecisive in its decision not to decide. The circumcised word is the expiration of Judaism in any language, and perhaps in Hebrew above all. It is not merely a foreign word in a national language but a word that is not quite a word, a "counterword," to use Celan's term from the *Meridian*—a word that has turned on itself in the *Atemwende*. Yet how is it possible to circumcise a word outside the mystical practice of the Kabbalah? And what gives Derrida the right to insist that this non-Jewish Jewishness is, in fact, *a* Jewishness at all?

Celan's answer to this question lies in letting Hebrew speak through his poems written in German. Even unrecognized as Hebrew words, the Hebraisms in his poems are those "spoken backward" names that cannot be called aloud until the language becomes messianic and true names reveal themselves. Until then, any name remains an antonomasia, a false name standing for the proper name. An episode in Celan's life suggests that he was consciously treating names as antonomasia—i.e., as words standing for names, appellative rather than proper. In a letter exchange with Peter Szondi, Celan asks for Szondi's help in a matter that he considers to be a disguised attack on his poetry in the press. When Celan reads a short story, "Do I Even Exist?" ("Gibt es mich überhaupt?") by a certain R. C. Phelan in the same magazine in which a selection of his poems are published, he interprets the author's name as a distorted version of his own pseudonym, Paul Celan, and the story itself (a narrative about ghostwriting) as an accusation of plagiarism in connection to the Goll affair.[39] In a letter of August 11, 1961, Celan writes:

Even "the best" tend to sublate the Jew—and this is simply a figure of the human, yet undeniably a *figure*—as subject and pervert him as object or "subject matter." . . . It's a fatality that some believe truly and maybe even straightforwardly that the claw can replace the hand.

(Noch von den "Besten" wird der Jude—und das ist ja nichts als
eine Gestalt des Menschlichen, aber immerhin eine *Gestalt*—nur
allzu gerne als Subjekt aufgehoben und zum Objekt bzw. "Sujet"
pervertiert. . . . Das Fatale ist, daß einige allen Ernstes und vielleicht
sogar in aller Einfalt daran glauben, daß die "Klaue" die Hand ersetzen
kann.)[40]

Celan uses "eine Gestalt" as a synonym of a "figure" or "persona" and
describes with this word not so much the individuality of a single person but rather the universal idea of "Menschlichkeit" in an individual.
The characteristic feature of this figure is the hand, in distinction to the
claw (*Klaue*) of those who cover up their anti-Semitism with a fake philo-
Semitic gesture.[41] As *a* figure of the human, the Jew can be recognized by
his handshake (*Händedruck*), which cannot be feigned. When Celan writes
that the poem is not different from the handshake,[42] he must then imply
that his poems reveal a figure of a Jew and that this figure's hands have
a specifically Jewish "imprint" (*Hände-Druck*). In a later letter to Szondi,
from January 15, 1962, the figure (*Gestalt*) of the Jewish hand appears in
a gesture, as Celan eliminates any linguistic, thematic reference to hands
in favor of the immediacy of handwriting. The letter is—atypically for
Celan—typed, not handwritten. Celan adds to the typescript only a few,
though crucial, handwritten corrections, and, most curiously, signs the letter with his name in Hebrew characters:

We have to do with a "certainty." And not with an "alliance." But with
you as a person. Persons are—as you know—no allies. But maybe one
can say about what makes each one a person that it is a *union* [*Bund*]. An
old union. A union—and I must call it thus, after all the experiences of
what has become acute again—a union in spirit rather than in kin [in
place of "in blood," struck out by hand].

Sincerely yours,
Paul Antschel, *false* Paul Celan . . .
וברכה שלום!
פאול צלן[43]

(Es [gestrichen: 'ist'] hat mit jener 'Gewissheit' zu tun. Also nichts mit
dem 'Verbündeten.' [Gestrichen: 'Vielleicht aber'] Sondern mit Ihnen
als Person. Personen sind—Sie wissen es ja—keine Koalisierten. Aber
[gestrichen: 'sie steh'] vielleicht darf man für das, was sie zur Person
macht sagen, dass es ein *Bund* ist. Ein alter. Ein—ich muss es, nach

allen Erfahrungen mit dem wieder akut Gewordenen, *so* nennen –: ein [handschriftlich hinzugefügt: '*blut*- und'] *art*fremder [handschriftlich gestrichen: '*bluts*ferner']. Ein geistiger.

Herzlich Ihr

Paul Antschel, *false* Paul Celan . . .

!וברכה שלום

[44](פאול צלן

Celan writes this in response to the letter by Szondi, in which the latter reports that he has found information about the author of the story, R. C. Phelan, who, it appears, is a real person, an author living in the United States and publishing science-fiction short prose. Celan, if not completely relieved, offers Szondi his trust and friendship and, as a token of them, signs his name in Hebrew (written longhand), after listing both his names, Ancel, transcribed to sound right in German, and his pen name. With this, Celan obviously refers to the anagrammatic play he mistakenly saw in the name R. C. Phelan; but, beyond signing in Hebrew as a gesture of gratitude to Szondi, Celan hides a play on words in his Hebrew signature, which must have remained obscure to the receiver, for Szondi didn't speak Hebrew, as Celan knew. The way the name is spelled in Hebrew deviates from the usual format of transcription of foreign names. Celan transcribes his name without vowels and, thus, signs with a Hebrew "germanism," a word rather than a name. Transcribed in this manner, his last name becomes "telling"—it means "shadow."[45] Through this play on words, Celan, in a way, pictures himself as the character of Phelan's story—as a shadow, a ghost that writes. Celan takes his name away, as he transforms it in his translation from name to word. "Un-calling" his pen name, itself an anagram of his real name, Celan makes it translatable. This name made word, a name-word, gives us, perhaps, an example of "names spoken backward" that can be transformed, kneaded in the poetic language. These names not only move unchanged between languages, like names; they also move, but only in translation, from being proper to appellative. Therefore, words have the potential to turn into names. Unlike Sabbatei Zevi, who replaces God's name to bring the messianic age closer, Celan points at a language in which words and names would coincide. This language would be completely untranslatable, antonomasia would not function in it, and there would be no difference between the word *word* and the word *name*. The entire universe consists, for the Sabbateans, of the divine name fallen apart and needing repair. Celan's poems speak about the possibility of transforming names; this transformation is, however, not a prophecy. The changeability of names, as imagined in these poems, points at the incomplete, imperfect state of language-of-yet. Perfection of language is not prescribed as it is in Sabbateanism; it is, nevertheless, a possibility spoken of, not named.

CHAPTER 9

"When Christianity Is Finally Over": Images of a Messianic Politics in Heine and Benjamin

Peter Fenves

At the beginning of their depiction of Naples, Walter Benjamin and Asja Lacis make the following comment: "Should [Catholicism] disappear from the face of the earth, its last foothold would perhaps not be Rome but Naples."[1] Despite its brevity, this remark establishes the perspective from which they view the city of Naples: the disappearance of Catholicism, if not of the Christian era as a whole. And at the beginning of a section of *Einbahnstraße* (One-way street) entitled "Souvenir" (*Reiseandenken*), which is reminiscent of Hölderlin's "Andenken," also written in remembrance of an encounter with a southern seacoast, Benjamin makes the following remark about Atrani, a small fishing village near Naples: "If one turns around, the church verges like God himself on the sea. Each morning the Christian era breaks on the rock; but between the walls below, the night always falls into the four old Roman quarters" (*GS* 4:121). Taken together, these passages suggest that the spatial limitations of the southern Italian coast correspond to temporal limits of the Christian era. Neither passage reveals anything about what lies beyond this era; but they nevertheless indicate that, for Benjamin and Lacis—to whom *One-Way Street* is dedicated—the bay of Naples is both a spatial and a temporal threshold. As soon as viewers execute an unspecified "turn," one of Atrani's buildings, here called a "church," also takes a turn, for it becomes a trope of "God himself."

In at least one respect it is scarcely surprising that the environment of Naples should elicit reflections on temporal as well as spatial limits. As Benjamin and Lacis emphasize near the beginning of "Neapel" (Naples), the name *Pompeii* functions as a "magic word" (*GS* 4:308) for tour guides. Because tourists are here today, gone tomorrow, they are drawn toward buildings with a similar structure—here today precisely because they disappeared long ago. The experience of transience accords with the mood of melancholia. As Benjamin shows in the major work he wrote during the time in which he travelled to Naples, *Ursprung des deutschen Trauerspiels* (Origin of the German mourning play), melancholia is not always unpleasant. The melancholic takes pleasure in allegory, where images acquire meaning as a result of subjective imposition, only to lose their meaning for the same reason. Travel images function in a similar manner: They acquire meaning because they are supposed to be meaningful, and the discovery of the suppositional character of their meaning requires the acquisition of more images and thus further travel. Benjamin had much to say about allegory around 1925. About the acquisition of travel images he has almost nothing to say—a silence that is perceptible at the opening of "Naples," as he and Lacis, by avoiding this site of ruins, distinguish themselves from the foreigners who are enchanted by the name *Pompeii*. Whatever mood accords with their mode of expression, it is not melancholia, which finds satisfaction in imposing the word "decline" or "decay" on the images it creates for its enjoyment.

And in this way, meager though it may be, Benjamin's work bears comparison with Heinrich Heine's. Uncovering a deeper affinity between these two German Jewish writers, each of whom produced a series of distinct travel images, is by no means an easy affair, even though they were, in fact, related to each other. Heine's mother was a van Geldern, as was the maternal side of Emil Benjamin's line. Walter knew about this illustrious relation; but he seemed to have been rather ashamed of it. In any case, he rarely discusses his distant cousin and in his extant writings says nothing about their common kinship. In the few places where Heine's name appears, his tone is almost always disparaging. To a certain extent, this aversion can be understood in generational terms. Heine was a German Jewish icon whom Emil Benjamin might have held in high regard. His children, by contrast, would have been less inclined to admire the poet of *Buch der Lieder* (The book of songs) than the author of "Heine und die Folge" (Heine and the consequences)—namely, Karl Kraus, who famously attributes the decline of the German language to the kind of journalistic confusion of subject and object that Heine was credited with inventing. Gershom Scholem, who learned of Benjamin's relation to Heine early in their friendship, summarized the effect of this "generation gap" in a diary entry from 1914: "The older I get," the sixteen-year old student writes, "the more distance I take from Heine. . . . I believe we must break with this type of Jewish modernity. Heine is, for us, the monument of a past epoch in our history."[2] The most impressive evidence of Benjamin's aversion to Heine, however, can be found in a remark he once made to Ernst Bloch, who, many years later, passed it on to Hans Mayer: "I must confess something to you, dear Ernst," Benjamin whispered, "I'm *related* to Heine!" To which Bloch added: It was as though he was confessing that one of his cousins was a criminal.[3]

In more formal circumstances, Benjamin simply keeps silent. In 1936, Werner Kraft edited a small collection of Heine's work for Schocken Press. The ostensible purpose was to revive interest in Heine among the generation of German Jews who had grown up under the influence of Kraus; its real purpose, however, was to keep the name of the poet in print, even if the printing press was in Prague, during a time in which the Nazis were in the process of systematically eradicating a once great name from the canon of German culture. In response to Kraft's efforts, Benjamin appears to welcome the volume—but has nothing positive to say in response. On the contrary, he admits that he had never been able to accustom himself to Heine's work and no longer had either the time or the energy to do so, for he is wholly absorbed in a vast project of his own.[4] From the tone of his response, the reader of the letter would have good reason to presume that the project in question was far removed from the work and world of Benjamin's distant cousin. Yet the very name of the project indicates the singular oddity of his remarks to Kraft: "Paris, capital of the nineteenth century." Whatever may be uncertain about Heine's life—and the uncertainty is so great that even sympathetic biographers (Jeffrey Sammons, for example) often complain—there is no doubt that he had a great deal to say about Paris as the capital of nineteenth-century culture. As Benjamin himself emphasizes, Heine produced the only book of lyric poetry, the effects of which are comparable to those produced by Baudelaire's *Fleurs du mal*, the gravitational center of the aforementioned project (*GS* 5:416–17). Nevertheless, Heine is mentioned only in passing in the dozens of files that comprise the *Passagenwerk* (Arcades project).[5]

For Heine, the major representative of the communist cause whom he came to know and admire—even if he also kept a certain distance from

him—was Karl Marx, whose Parisian exile coincided with his own. For
Benjamin, it was Asja Lacis, the Latvian revolutionary and coauthor of
"Naples." An improbable affinity emerges from this grouping. What Marx
saw in Heine, and Heine in Marx, is a common front against "Nazarene"
forms of thought and conduct, which mendaciously distract their propo-
nents from the material conditions of life. "Nazarene" is, of course, one of
Heine's favorite terms, and despite the protean character of his work, one
motif remains constant throughout: its repudiation of Nazarenism, which
generates, among other things, his enthusiasm for Bonaparte's politics and
Goethe's poetry. The same term, with the same valuation, unexpectedly
appears at the conclusion of Benjamin's long essay on Goethe's *Elective
Affinities*, where he makes his final case, as it were, against the language of
Ottilie, who silently starves herself to death at the end of the novel: "Not
this Nazarene being but, rather, the symbol of the star passing over the
lovers is the form of expression appropriate to whatever of the mysterium
in the exact sense inhabits the work" (*GS* 1:200). Whereas Benjamin's essay on *Elective Affinities* thus concludes with a Heine-like repudiation of
a "Nazarene being," the essay he wrote with an eminently non-Nazarene
woman takes this repudiation as its point of departure: the "rich . . . barbarism" (*GS* 2:307) of the Neapolitan population makes them into kindred
opponents of Nazarenism. An elective affinity between Heine-Marx and
Benjamin-Lacis thus emerges: Benjamin begins his tentative affiliation
with communism while traveling with Lacis to Naples, just as Heine's trip
from Munich to Genoa generates an image of historical development that
the mature Marx would later adopt for the purpose of solidifying the theoretical foundation of the communist party.

Apropos the battlefield of Marengo, Heine writes the following in *Die
Reise von München nach Genoa* (The trip from Munich to Genoa): "Every
time has its task, and through the solution of these tasks humanity presses
forward."[6] In the preface to his *Kritik der politischen Ökonomie* (Critique of
political economy), Marx transforms this proposition into the basic credo
of historical materialism: "Humanity poses for itself only such tasks as it
is able to solve."[7] Both of these formulations are doubtless indebted to a
certain professor of philosophy at the University of Berlin; but the rhetoric
of task and solution is Heine's, not Hegel's. And the affinity between Heine
and Benjamin is stronger still, for, although the journey that produced
The Trip from Munich to Genoa was written almost exactly a hundred years
before the one that gave rise to "Naples," they were taken for exactly the
same reason. Both Heine and Benjamin were in the process of trying to
secure an academic position at a German university, and in both cases, as a

consequence of their failure, they were forced to become "freelance writers." Writing about Italy was a way of testing out this unwanted freedom, which in both cases contrasted with the life course of Goethe, who traveled to Italy, of course, but only after he had secured for himself a solid position in the institutional apparatus of a small German state.

As if, finally, all of this were not reason for reflecting on Heine's and Benjamin's images of Italy, which result from a conscious effort to bide their time—a time that would never come—it should be pointed out that both sets of images are immersed in virulent polemics against poets with aristocratic lineages and liberal-egalitarian politics. Heine's polemics are much better known, not least because they are an integral element of a sequel to his account of his trip to Genoa, *The Baths of Lucca*, where he attacks August von Platen for a number of reasons, most infamously because of his homosexuality. Responding to one of Heine's barbs in an earlier series of "Travel Images," von Platen had included a number of anti-Jewish remarks, which caused Heine to launch a full-scale assault on the person and poetry of von Platen.[8] The object of Benjamin's ire was Fritz von Unruh, who had recently published the pacifist-oriented contribution to the literature of travel, *Flügel der Nike, Das Buch einer Reise* (Wings of Nike, the book of a journey). As Benjamin himself notes, his review of von Unruh's novel is an "absolutely barbarous polemic [that] devours the author from skin to bone" (*B* 4:23). Yet, of all the affinities between Benjamin and Heine, none is stranger, and none more closely connected to the enigma of temporal limits, than the reversibility of their relation. To modify Benjamin's arche-image of travel, the relation between Benjamin and Heine is a two-way street. Just as Benjamin dissociates himself from Heine, so Heine wants to keep his distance from Benjamin. The line from von Platen that most enraged Heine describes the author of the *Book of Songs* as a "Pindar from the little tribe of Benjamin."[9]

The dissociation between Heine and Benjamin is almost immediately legible in their respective images of Italy. Whereas Benjamin leaves himself out of Naples, Heine inserts himself into the scenes of his travels. Whereas Benjamin develops a theory of politeness in the course of his southern journey (*GS* 4:402–3), Heine begins his excursion by declaring himself the "most polite person in the world" (*W* 2:237). Whereas Heine rarely describes the places he sees, except insofar as they occasion reflections on his own state of mind, Benjamin practices a kind of *Sachlichkeit*, or "matter-of-factness," that can be called "new" only because his images of Naples represent his first attempt to practice a kind of writing in which "every-

thing factual is already theory" (*GS* 1:278). And—but this only reiterates
the previous point—whereas Benjamin allows the buildings of Naples to
speak for themselves, Heine lets a particularly prominent building in Milan speak to him. Listen, then, to what Heine hears in the middle of night,
as he approached the Milan cathedral: "'You see,' a very strange saint said
to me, a saint who was made in the most recent times from the most recent marble, 'you see, my older colleagues cannot grasp why the Emperor
Napoleon busied himself so assiduously with the building of the cathedral.
But I know very well: he saw that this great house of stone would in any
case be a very useful building and also still serviceable once Christianity is finally over'" (*W* 2:292). Regardless of his intention—and it may be
precisely this—Heine captures an image of dialectical motion. If, in accordance with Hegelian doctrine, every phenomenon develops the elements
of its own destruction, then the cathedral in Milan can be seen to express
the dialectical process *in concreto*. Thus, Heine continues: "I was simply
shocked, when I heard that there are saints in Italy who produce such language, and indeed do so in a plaza where Austrian soldiers march up and
down with caps and satchels" (*W* 2:292). Heine entertains no doubts about
what the stone says, still less that it speaks in his own language. Christianity
will be over someday, and the only question remains: What is to be done in
light of this eschatological insight?

The genius of Napoleon—and this passage marks one of Heine's many
expressions of his Bonapartism—lies in divining an answer: The cathedral
can be designated as "dual use," at once amenable to a decaying religious
ritual and conducive to an incipient political praxis: "Yet," Heine notes, as
he concludes his description of the incident, "the oddball stone was right
to a certain extent; the interior of the cathedral is comfortably cool in the
summer, and cheerful and pleasant and would retain its value even with an
altered vocation [*Bestimmung*]" (*W* 2, 292). What is said of the buildings as
a whole goes for each of its parts, including the speaking stone: Its function will also change "with an altered vocation." Instead of marking a place
for the administration of the mass, it will help organize mass politics, for
this is precisely the role Heine assigns to the intuitive intellect of a Napoleon in the previous set of travel images: "He never conducted individual
intrigues, and his strokes [*Schläge*] always took place by means of his art
of grasping and steering the masses" (*W* 2, 169). It is as though the new
installed work of art, which does not fail to hide its intentions, were in the
process of formulating one of the principal theses of Benjamin's forthcoming "Work of Art in the Age of Its Technical Reproducibility": "At the very
moment in which the criterion of authenticity fails to apply to the produc-

tion of art, the entire social function of art is revolutionized. Its founding in ritual is replaced by its founding in another praxis: namely, its founding in politics" (*GS* 7, 357).

It is no exaggeration to say that the rest of Heine's journey from Munich to Genoa revolves around this nocturnal illumination. Not only is Catholicism over, but so too is Christianity and, a fortiori, the very era of "religion." There is no need here to enter into a discussion of Heine's relation to Saint-Simonianism or even to analyze the dialogue on religion that takes shape in *The City of Lucca*, which appropriately begins with a conversation with a stone. The subsequent chapters of *The Trip from Munich to Genoa* are sufficient in this regard, for they conjure up the image of the coming era, which, thanks to Napoleon's victory at Marengo, is already in the process of succeeding the Christian-religious one: "Every time has its task and through its solution humanity moves forward. . . . Let's praise the French! They cared for the two greatest needs of human society, for good food and civil equality; in the art of cooking and in freedom, they have made the greatest progress, and when all of us, as equal guests, conduct a feast of reconciliation, we will offer our first toast to the French. . . . We are then united, and united we fight against other evils of the world, perhaps in the end against death. . . . Do not smile, late reader. Every era believes its battle is the most important. . . . We want to live and die in the religion of freedom, which perhaps deserves the name 'religion' more than the empty, moribund ghost to which we are still accustomed to attach this name" (*W* 2:295–96). Despite the complexity of this passage, in which "late readers"—not "dear readers," to whom Heine generally speaks—are on the verge of smiling, presumably because they, too, are latecomers in the battle against "religion," the passage effectively announces that Christianity is finished. Only its ghosts survive in the form of imperial regiments, which can doubtless suppress the voice of the people, who are mortal, but—and this is decisive—not that of the buildings, which are not. Only one thing is needed, therefore, beyond the genial agent of non-Nazarene politics: the figure of a "Heinrich Heine," who mediates between the language of stones and that of human beings by removing the prejudice that stones always speak only of our past and therefore of our own passage into skeletal remains.

But all of this depends on one thing: that Heine hear indeed the voice of the stone; that he not be "imagining things," as we say; that this explosive passage from *The Trip from Munich to Genoa* not be understood as a species of personification, in which case it says, in effect, "The stones themselves say nothing, only I do, and if only I do, there is no end to Christianity, and that's, in effect, the end of me, except insofar as I am the lament that I am the very alteration, otherwise known as the 'conversion,' of the I that I am." Melancholia with a vengeance, so to speak, which then finds a means of expression—an inadequate one, to be sure—in a violent verbal assault on a man who dared describe him as a "Pindar from the little tribe of Benjamin." The silence of the stones, the requirement that I speak in their name because their language is utterly foreign to me, that nature has gone mute, and that I am left with only my own dashed hopes, which are raised above those of a dispersed and oppressed people solely by virtue of the sympathetic immersion of my hopes in the people's dispersion and oppression. What is this but, in Benjamin's words, "left-wing melancholia"? And, indeed, in the essay entitled "Left-Wing Melancholia," Benjamin, doubtless influenced by his recent work on Kraus, names Heine as one of its progenitors (*GS* 3:280). The ambiguity, nay, the bipolarity of the passage in question is striking. Everything depends on the answer to the question What did Heine hear at midnight as he approached the Milan cathedral? His own thoughts or those of the stone? Which is to ask: his own subjectivity or that of a *Gegen-stand*? This question is unanswerable—and not only because we cannot recover the past as though it were a modification of the present. In answering it, we would have to be sure that we knew whether we were responding to the light of evidence rather than to the obscurity of the desire contained in the phrase "When Christianity is finally over."

Benjamin can be understood to respond to this question—and nowhere with greater cunning than in his jointly authored essay on Naples. It is as though this entire essay were written with the episode of the Milan cathedral in the background. In another, less famous reflection on the city of Naples, Benjamin may even allude to this episode, or similar ones in Heine's work, when he claims that "ghost stories" arise as soon as an "intellectual-itinerant proletariat" comes into contact with an "entrenched primitive population" (*GS* 3:133). In a review of a book whose title alludes to Heine, *Neapel: Reisebilder und Skizze* (Naples: Travel images and sketches), Benjamin does not tell his own ghost story but, instead, only explains to the readers of *Die literarische Welt* that during his own sojourn in Naples, late at night, after having been momentarily separated from his friends, including Ernst Bloch, he suddenly experienced "what it means to enter into the vicinity of a spell [*Bannkreis*]" (*GS* 3:133). Nothing of this experience is reproduced in the essay he wrote with Lacis, and indeed little is revealed in the aforementioned review. It would not be wrong, however, to think that something of this episode can be discerned in "Naples." In contrast to the "magic word" *Pompeii*, which leads bourgeois tourists away from the city, a "spell" draws impoverished intellectuals into its spectral center. And this is what they learn when they arrive: No one clings more tenaciously to Catholicism than do the people of Naples; but this is not true of its buildings, which are as disengaged from Catholicism as the Florentine stone encountered by Benjamin's distant cousin. This is the cardinal point: The architecture of Naples outlives the rituals to which its people cling. What the architecture of Naples says to Benjamin and Lacis is equivalent to what the stone tells Heine. Churches that were built under a supposedly "Nazarene" regime can be refunctioned once it finally disappears. Such is the nature of Naples in extremis. The use of its buildings can never be fixed once and for all; transience is their permanent condition. It is not lethargy but, rather, the spirit of improvisation that makes it impossible for anything in Naples to be finished until—but this is not said, of course—Catholicism is finally over, and there is absolutely nothing solid, nothing permanent, no stone, and therefore no See of Saint Peter on which to stand. At this paradoxical point of architectural liquefaction, in which incompleteness is itself complete, something akin to the "task of world politics" (*GS* 2:204) emerges. Mount Vesuvius perhaps looms in the background of this, the final sentence of the so-called *Theological-Political Fragment*, which Benjamin may have written in its shadow, as he reflected on some nocturnal conversations with Bloch; in any case, a form of "messianic nature" can be discerned in the improvisational architecture of the ancient neo-polis: "Nature is messianic by virtue of its eternal and total transience. To strive for this transience, including for those strata of human affairs that are nature—this is the task of world politics, whose method must be called nihilism" (*GS* 2:204).

But "Naples" never says anything about the end of Christianity. Whereas *The Trip from Munch to Genoa* is daring in this regard, Benjamin and Lacis are reticent. And this difference corresponds to their respective modes of expression: Whereas Heine makes copious use of the little word "I," especially when he encounters a stone that speaks German, Benjamin and Lacis never once use the word "we." The difference between the I-centered character of Heine's travel images and the absence of "we" in "Naples" can doubtless be understood from the following perspective: While Heine makes himself into the figure of a free, self-sustaining subject in his campaign against a well-entrenched aristocracy, the coauthors of "Naples" make no reference to themselves in their campaign against a weakened bourgeoisie. Nevertheless, it would be a mistake to see the difference between the two travel images solely in these terms: Heine as a supporter of the bourgeoisie, Benjamin-Lacis as champion of the proletariat. For Heine is not an uncritical proponent of the bourgeoisie. On the contrary, Genoa, as the terminus of his journey, is the place from which he most wants to flee, for he cannot abide its famously commercial character. If Munich encompasses the old religion, then Genoa represents the transformation of Christianity into the religion of capital. Heine takes flight from the city of commerce by seeking refuge in its museum, where—so he supposes—something other than money will finally have a chance to speak. As Heine surveys silent portrait after silent portrait, however, the amused "I" of his southward journey turns into a mournful "we" of permanent stasis: "Still worse than the feeling of an eternal dying, of a desolate, yawning annihilation, the thought grips us that we do not even die away as originals but only as copies of human beings who have long since passed away unnoticed, ones who were like us in body and mind, and that after us, once again there will be human beings who look and feel and think like us, and whom death will once again annihilate—an eternal place of repetition, without consolation" (*W* 2:305). The terminus of Heine's journey is thus the thought of the eternal return of the same, in which the museum is no different from the market, where there is no hope in death because everything that appears to be alive is always already dead.

Those who look to art as a refuge in the city described by Benjamin and Lacis also find themselves "ill at ease" (*GS* 4:307). The illness does not, however, stem from anything resembling objective reasons—for example, the world of art cannot be disengaged from that of commerce—but because tourists are afraid of being robbed of their possessions as they search for alluring works of art. The institution of property arises only under the condition that the proprietor can effectively demand that a so-called possession be returned, if someone else happens to possess it. In Naples, this crucial condition is not secured by the policing apparatus of the modern state, with its putative "monopoly on violence," but, instead, by the porous and improvisatory institution of the Camorra, which Benjamin and Lacis soberly describe as the "self-administration of criminality." According to Ernst Bloch, who published an essay entitled "Italy and Porosity" in 1926—*after* Mussolini had acquired full dictatorial powers—Naples represents an Arcadian alternative to the desolate cities of northern Europe, whose bourgeoisie want nothing so much as the chance to shut the doors against the onslaught of the burgeoning proletariat.[10] By contrast, the essay Benjamin and Lacis published a year earlier would not be significantly altered if it adopted as its epigraph the opening line of Erich Mühsam's poem from 1925, which revises the primary image of Goethean desire in light of contemporary political-social conditions: "Kennst Du das Land, wo die Faschisten blühn?" (Are you familiar with the land where the fascists thrive?).[11]

Benjamin and Lacis are exact in their description, even if their description does not exactly correspond to the state of the Camorra around 1925. The power of this secretive gang derives from its ability to uphold the institution of property by means of layered levels of intermediaries: "Whoever is injured does not think of calling the police if he is set on getting back what it is. Through civil or clerical intermediaries, if not by himself, he goes up to a Camorrista. Through him he agrees on a ransom" (*GS* 4:307). This description is not political theory, as the term is generally understood, and it is not precisely a description of facts as they could be reported in a commission on organized crime in southern Italy. Rather, everything factual is already theory. The factual account of the Camorra is in this case a theory of Italian fascism, which could be expanded into the following formula: Fascism systematizes and thus modernizes the fragmentary form of "criminal self-administration" that takes shape among Neapolitan Camorristi. The Camorra is thus an ambiguous phenomenon. Its persistence opposes the monopolizing tendency of the modern state; but at the same time, it represents a disturbing prefiguration of full fascist rule, in which nontransparent layers of intermediaries protect and intensify the acceleration of the "movement." None of this depends on any clichés about "the Italian character." Still less does it depend on a categorical difference between us, the civilized foreigners, and them, the barbaric natives. The "rich . . . barbarism" of the Neapolitan people arises solely from the "heart of the metropolis itself" (*GS* 4:307). And foreigners feel threatened only because they are foreign; that is, they do not know the intermediaries to whom they should appeal when they want to retrieve their possessions. The civic function of retrieving stolen goods, including abducted people, falls to a criminal gang only because it alone can administer the institution of property under current conditions. The greater the threat to this institution—under the assumption that it must be maintained—the greater the likelihood that the layerlike operations of Camorra rule will be modernized into a systematic gang of criminals in which everyone other than its "leader" is potentially a foreigner who, as such, can never be certain that a previously unknown layer of intermediaries has arisen. The difference between "mine" and "thine" is thus protected even as it dissolves into the larger-scale and wholly uncertain distinctions between inside and outside.

If, however, the institution of property were to disappear from the face of the earth, then the Camorra would no longer have its definitive function. Fascism, in turn, would no longer be able to flourish in the land of lemon trees. And this is precisely what happens in "Naples"—not in the city, to be sure, but rather *in the essay*, which begins by envisioning the end of Catholicism and proceeds by bracketing the workings of the Camorra.

Another Naples thus comes into a view—not an Arcadia, to be sure, for none of the squalor is similarly bracketed. The other Naples, which exists perhaps only in the images of the essay, fulfills the promise of its porosity: No doors can be closed, no windows shut. No barriers are fixed, not even the barriers erected by ecclesiastical institutions between days of the week. Never perhaps has a more subtle picture been drawn of the "Sabbath of history," which is here not a time of rest but, rather, a time in which the Sabbath permeates the rest of the week, for there is no authority over time, no temporal authority, that can put a halt to this interpenetration. The porosity of the city is so pervasive that everything Neapolitan permeates everything else, with the result that there can be no firm distinction between "mine" and "thine." It is tempting to say that Benjamin and Lacis, whose joint authorship of "Naples" makes it into the model of communal work, seek to show that the city, left to itself, can make a spontaneous transition to communism, understood as the form of social production in which the means of production are held in common. But there is good reason to avoid this temptation, especially since the essay shows no interest in the means of production, even as it describes the scattered sites of improvised distribution. It would be more accurate, and closer to Benjamin's own political-philosophical itinerary, to say that the other Naples is characterized by a certain form of "nihilism." In a letter to Scholem, Benjamin indicates why he wishes to write an essay on Naples with a Latvian revolutionary whom he recently met: not for the sake recounting his travels but in order to gain a clearer insight into the doctrine of "nihilism," to which his work is dedicated.[12] In light of the resulting essay, this doctrine is clearly less concerned with the question of God's existence, or the institutions through which divine service is rendered, than with the precise status of what Roman law calls *res nullius*, "things that belong to no one."[13] Naples is a place where everything is in the process of turning into "no one's thing."

At the beginning of a series of notes on the category of justice Benjamin provides an abbreviated theory of the origin of property: "To every good, limited as it is by the spatio-temporal order," he writes around 1916, "there accrues a possession-character. But the possession, as something caught in the same finitude, is always unjust. No order of possession, however articulated, can therefore lead to justice."[14] Instead seeking a form of legality that will generate a state of justice, Benjamin directs his attention to what not only eludes possession but, in so doing, thwarts the spatio-emporal condition that gives rise to the institution of possession in general: "Rather, this [the path to justice] lies in the condition of a good that cannot be a possession. This alone is the good through which goods become possessionless."[15] And from 1916 onward, Benjamin's politico-philosophical itinerary can be described, in turn, as the search for this elusive counter-possessive good. One possibility is pure language, which communicates itself rather than a content defined by a speaking subject. Another is pure *Gewalt*, understood as neither precisely "force" nor as "violence" but as the "holding sway" (*walten*) that cannot itself be "held" or "stored" but only enacted and therein exhausted. Still another possibility—drawn from a more materialist vocabulary—is glass architecture, about which Benjamin makes the following enigmatic comment in "Poverty and Experience": "The things of glass have no 'aura.' Glass is in general the enemy of secrets. It is also the enemy of possession" (*GS* 2:217). And something similar can be said of Neapolitan architecture: Its porosity obviously makes it the enemy of secrets; less obviously, it is the enemy of possession as well. Minus the layers through which the Camorra retain power over the city, Naples is the nucleus not so much of communism as "no one–ism."

Nevertheless, Naples is not *altogether* porous. There is, after all, a limit to the "pervasiveness" or "interpenetration" (*Durchdringen*) that otherwise characterizes the city. This limit appears only in the last paragraph of the coauthored essay, which is eschatological in more than one sense: "The language of gesture reaches further than anywhere else in Italy. Its conversation is impenetrable [*undurchdringlich*] to anyone from the outside. Ears, nose, eyes, breast, and shoulders are signaling stations that are drawn together by the fingers. This apportionment returns in their delicately specialized eroticism. Helping gestures and impatient touches strike the foreigner with a regularity that precludes chance. Yes, he would be betrayed and sold off (*verraten und verkauft*), but the Neapolitan, being of good nature, sends him forth. Sends him a few miles further to Mori. 'Vedere Napoli e poi Mori,' he says, using an old pun. 'See Naples and die,' says the German after him" (*GS* 4:316). Benjamin and Lacis do not specify "the German" to whom they refer; but it could be—beyond the generic tourist, rushing off to Pompeii—both Goethe and Heine. The version of the saying Goethe records in his *Italienische Reise* (Italian journey) demonstrates the hyper-indescribability of the landscape by removing the copula in the description of its indescribable magnificence. The limit to descriptive language is not matched, however, by any limit to the power of translation, as Goethe effortlessly renders the Italian saying in German: "About the setting of the city and its splendors, which have so often been described and praised, no word. 'Vedi Napoli e poi muori,' they say here. See Naples and die!"[16] For Heine, writing in French to an Italian princess, there is as little reason for translating the saying into another language as there is for undertaking the perilous journey to see what would in any case be indescribable: "I was on the point of going to Naples, and I thought of asking you for some letters of introduction in that city. But on the eve of my departure I learned that cholera had also struck Naples and was still ravaging the city. Only fools would go to meet useless danger, and consequently I very wisely remain in Provence. I do not want to *veder Napoli et poi morir*."[17]

The "after-sayings" of the two Germans complement each other: Whereas Goethe is so fully absorbed in the object that he cannot even complete his description of its indescribability, Heine presents himself as the paradigmatically rational subject, who would not exchange his life for a vision, regardless of its splendors. Benjamin and Lacis, for their part, align themselves with neither the subject nor the object but are, instead, concerned with an ever so slight difference in language, which, as such, belongs to neither the object nor the subject. The saying, as spoken by Neapolitans, differs from the "after-saying" of travelers, including their illustrious predecessors, who gloriously or nervously impute an extra letter to the name *Mori*. Reducing the word by a single letter—whether it be *u* or *r*—the coauthors of "Naples" practice redemptive philology. The proper word, *Mori*, is restored to the saying, and this word, now recognized as a name, does not mean "death" but, rather, designates a space outside of the economy of human trafficking. If *Pompeii* is a "magic word" that lures tourists into the site of ruins, *Mori* is its salvific counterpart, which foreigners understand as "death." The impenetrability of Neapolitan gesture, combined with the "good nature" of its people, guarantees that the porosity of the city is not yet fully saturated by the forces that, for the time being, stand at the disposal of the Camorra. In the absence of this "good nature," however, there is only a single, highly fragile guarantor: "the language of gesture."

PART III

Negating the Messiah

CHAPTER 10

The Crisis of the Messianic Claim: Scholem, Benjamin, Baudelaire

Oleg Gelikman

> Whoever wishes to know what the situation of a "redeemed humanity" might actually be, what conditions are required for the development of such a situation, and when this development can be expected to occur, poses questions to which there are no answers. He might just as well seek to know the color of ultraviolet rays.
>
> —WALTER BENJAMIN, "Paralipomena to *On the Concept of History*"

Post-theological invocations of the messianic have an alarming tendency to turn on themselves whenever their central concept comes to the fore. In the second thesis of "On the Concept of History," Walter Benjamin assigned a messianic power to each historical generation, but qualified this power as "weak"; reflecting on the messiah's entry into history, Kafka wrote of his arriving not on the last day, but on the very last; in his writings on the messianic, Jacques Derrida would not allow "messianicity" to appear unaccompanied by the cautionary "without messianism" or an equivalent disclaimer; etc.[1] These invocations revoke the messianic at the same time as they invoke it. Disrupted by a strange stutter, they proceed while paying tribute to some inherent impossibility, but proceed nonetheless.

The twists and turns of these formulations repulse readability with considerable ferocity. The immediate effect of such formidable and no doubt deliberate obstructions is to make determining the function of the negative within the discourse of the messianic into a condition of the further possibility of this discourse. More radically, these forbidding gestures require one to verify in what sense these voices allow—themselves and others—to entertain a discourse *on* or *of* the messianic at all. This requirement is no ordinary hermeneutic constraint, if only because in exposing the instability of the messianic, these invocations of the messianic themselves are obviously afflicted by the same instability: Why does Benjamin claim that the force is "weak"? Is the delay Kafka builds into messiah's arrival simply a matter of imitating Haggadic teachings? Is Derrida's "without messianism" meant to be a surgically precise subtraction of the undesirable content or an ongoing purge, a permanent complication in the code of vigilance?

Answering any one of these questions hermeneutically is a necessary if daunting task. However, if given in isolation, each answer leads away from the necessity insuring the recurrence of this *type* of question across these otherwise distinct appeals. By leading away, hermeneutics postpones reflection on *the political crisis the messianic claim brings forth* in every iteration. This crisis can be defined as follows: For reasons that are epistemic rather than confessional, no modern conception of historicity can be defined without explicit or implicit recourse to messianism; but no responsible recourse to messianism can ignore the unbound violence—i.e., violence to oneself and others guided only by criteria immanent to the exercise of this violence—contained in any version of eschatology. Consequently, throwing messanism into crisis is simply a matter of responsibility to what one can know. But emerging from this crisis is a practical matter and a difficult one, for, if one is to remain consistent, one must renegotiate the promise of renewal contained in the messianicity of our historiography with the appropriation of, or submission to, divine violence that, within any version of the messianic, serves as the exclusive means of transcending the intolerable given. Because the problem centers on the transmutation or reinvention of divine violence, either self- or other-directed, the crisis of the messianic claim is political; it arrives because the world, for reasons sufficiently extreme to prompt recourse to narratives of salvation, has become uninhabitable. In what follows, my goal is to examine instances of this crisis both in the apophatic aspects (what do they reveal about modernity as a form of collective self-consciousness?) and pragmatic implications (how does a given version of the messianic perform the task of renegotiation, or, to use Scholem's coinage, "neutralization" of messianism? what specific modes of speech, action, or conceptualization does it put forth as the primary means of the "extraction" of the messianic from theology? etc.). To this end, I will consider, in addition to the work of Gershom Scholem, the texts by Charles Baudelaire and Walter Benjamin. In placing these texts side by side, I intend primarily to examine the morphology of the messianic rather than to construct a genealogy. Because the neutralization of messianism remains far from complete, the genealogies of the transmuted messianisms will have to wait for some barely imaginable future.[2]

The Neutralization of Messianism: The Price of the Idea and the Crisis of the Claim

On the day the Temple was destroyed the Messiah was born.

BABYLONIAN TALMUD

For Scholem, the messianic idea is closely connected with the experience of failure. This must be understood in a double sense, referring both to the genesis of the messianic idea and to its structure.

STÉPHANE MOSÈS, *The Angel of History*

It is common to define Scholem's achievement in historiographic terms. This tendency survives even in those assessments that dissent with this view (as it does, for instance, in David Biale's interpretation of Scholem's work as "counter-history"). However, since the recent publication of the diaries Scholem kept in his youth, the existence of the speculative foundation for Scholem's thinking can no longer be placed in doubt.[3] This discovery puts the historiographic interpretation of Scholem under considerable strain.

Gershom Scholem's relation to esoteric Judaism could never be one of restoration or reclaiming. The muted quality of the apologetic element in Scholem's studies of Jewish mysticism points to a key element in his critical construction of Jewish thinking. Not surprisingly, the philological study of historical sources led Scholem to see Jewish mysticism as a product of exile and dispersion. Accordingly, he viewed messianism in a dual light: as an assertion of spiritual independence and as a means of making tolerable the exclusion of Jews from political and economic life of their host countries. Less predictable in Scholem's engagement with Judaism is his notion that the idea of the messiah was a vehicle of the repeated self-destruction of Jewish people. For instance, the fear that in time the messianic past will exact a terrible toll infiltrates Scholem's relation to the reconstituted Hebrew, as evidenced by the following lines from a letter to Franz Rosenzweig:

One believes that language has been secularized, that its apocalyptic thorn has been pulled out. . . . If we transmit to our children the language that has been transmitted to us, if we—the generation of transition—resuscitate the language of ancient books so that it can reveal itself anew to them, must then not the religious violence of this

language one day break out against those who speak it? And on the day
this eruption occurs, which generation will suffer its effects?[4]

It is considerations such as these that led Scholem to speak of the neutralization of messianism as the present task of Jewish history, and, in
the course of his long career, time and again to look for models of such
neutralization both within and without the sphere of Jewish thinking
proper.

Scholem's pairing of messianism with neutralization displays an instability similar to the one at work in Benjamin, Kafka, and Derrida. More
important, Scholem's example shows why these suspensions or implosions
are necessary, systematic, and unavoidable; they manifest the awareness
that, insofar as the reappearance of Jewish thinking in the twentieth century is concerned, one can negate messianism without effacing the spiritual identity of Jewish thought no more than one can endorse messianism
without renewing its destructive tendency. On the last page of "Toward an
Understanding of the Messianic Idea in Judaism," Scholem formulates the
vocation of the negative within the discourse of the messianic with utmost
clarity. This vocation is to think the weakness of messianism together with
its greatness, or, to anticipate Scholem's metaphors in the quotation below,
the "horizons" of hope together with the "abysses" of destruction. If the
emergence of Jewish thinking is to evade the history of destruction that
scarred it, the reconstitution of the messianic must be understood as the
phenomenon of the universal history:

> One word more, by way of conclusion, should be said about a point
> which, to my mind, has generally received too little attention in discus-
> sions of the Messianic idea. What I have in mind is the price demanded
> by Messianism, the price which the Jewish people had to pay out of
> its own substance for this idea which it handed over to the world. The
> magnitude of the Messianic idea corresponds to the endless powerless-
> ness in Jewish history during all the centuries of exile. . . . For the
> Messianic idea is not only consolation and hope. Every attempt to
> realize it tears open abysses which lead each of its manifestations *ad
> absurdum*. . . . One may say, perhaps, the Messianic idea is the real
> anti-existentialist idea. Precisely understood, there is nothing concrete
> which can be accomplished by the unredeemed. This makes for the
> greatness of Messianism, but also for its constitutional weakness.[5]

For Scholem, the Messianic idea defines the political rather than solely the
historical situation of the Jewish people. It programs the duality of their
political being:

On the one hand, messianism delivered the gift of universal history to non-Jews, thereby inscribing the resultant political theologies in a filial relationship they were bound to erase in the movement of auto-foundation. On Scholem's view, the sovereignty of the Jewish neighbor emerges in the persecution of messianism by the messianic means—a truly monstrous figure of transmitted and reassimilated messianicity.[6] The gift of messianism, the bite of its "apocalyptic thorn," offers no immunity. Quite to the contrary, it exposes the giver to the uncontainable wrath of the recipient, to the cannibalization by the endless history that the Jewish sacred texts helped to frame via the network of donation—i.e., figural interpretation, translation, and hostile re-creation.

On the other hand, messianism represents the political element of Jewish life in its difference from others. According to Scholem, the politics of Jewish life is singular because dominated by the deadlock between the restorative-rational and utopian-anarchic version of messianism, between nostalgia for the harmony of Creation and ecstatic enunciation of Redemption. To the extent that Scholem desired to release Jewish thinking from the very history that he was bringing to light, his recovery of messianism cannot be taken to proceed along the restorative or utopian track.[7] With this in mind, it becomes clear that in speaking of the price of messianism, Scholem is alerting his reader to the dangers contained in the alternative between the restorative and the utopian construction of messianism. Scholem's strictures must not be mistaken for an indirect advocacy of the rationalization of messianism (along the lines of Maimonides, or Zionism, or some inexplicated conjecture we may be tempted to attribute to Scholem in the attempt to shield ourselves from the destructive intent of his view). Nor can one understand Scholem to be rejecting messianism as a symptom of weakness pure and simple; his whole point seems to be that, in virtue of the messianic structure of history, such rejections are bound to be ineffectual, and therefore self-blinding.[8] Rather, Scholem issues a twofold demand: first, that the recovery of messianism take care not to reproduce the historical structure of its object (i.e., the alternative between the restorative and the utopian construal of messianism); and, second, that it acknowledge the dangers that this history and this structure bring to life whenever they are unrecognized, but also when they are.

This precarious constellation of tensions between the doctrinal body and the political being of the Jews calls for an engagement that Scholem calls "neutralization."[9] Neither a determinate negation nor a tactical appropriation of messianism, "neutralization" nominates the "messianic" as a mediating term in an unbreachable relation between the singularity of Jewish self-consciousness and the universal history. Accordingly, "neutraliza-tion" belongs to neither of these realms but manifests a critical, if esoteric, tendency in Scholem's thinking that so far has been approached under the names of "counter-history" (Biale), "political theology" (Jacobson), and "religious anarchism" (Scholem's own designation).

At the end of "Toward an Understanding of the Messianic Idea in Ju-daism," this tendency surfaces in Scholem's express desire to protect the newborn Jewish state by pointing out the complicity between messianic anarchism and self-destruction: "Whether Jewish history will be able to endure this entry into the concrete realm without perishing in the crisis of the messianic claim which has virtually been conjured up—that is the question which out of his great and dangerous past the Jew of this age poses to his present and his future" (36). The "neutralization" of messian-ism, therefore, does not name a critique or elimination of the messianic commitments but recognizes the "crisis of the messianic claim" as the trau-matic, precarious encounter between the messianic past and the actuality of state-building. Neutralization acts as the safeguard against the catastrophic passing of one into the other and thus demands a greater sensitivity to the range of the messianic effects than so far has been achieved.

Because of Scholem's insistence on the filial connection between Jew-ish messianism and its geopolitical offspring (which may count early Christianity, Reformation movements, the rationalist Enlightenment, Romanticism), it would be shortsighted to imagine that the mastery of the messianic can be or ever was a purely Jewish affair.[10] As a first step, this mastery requires a neutralization of universal history on a par with Scho-lem's neutralization of Jewish messianism, and especially at the strategic junctures that, generalizing Scholem's usage, I'd like to designate as the "crisis of the messianic claim."

To verify that such a crisis began to afflict the concept of universal his-tory already in the middle of the nineteenth century, in the section that fol-lows I turn to a text that, while standing outside Scholem's immediate hori-zon, deploys the strategy of neutralization with a singular force—Charles Baudelaire's posthumous "La Fin du monde." If in Scholem the crisis of the messianic claim erupts because of the connection between messianism and the state, in Baudelaire it is motivated by the response to the onset of modernity. I will argue that "La fin du monde" brings about a collapse of the apocalyptic interpretation of history and initiates movement toward chronicle as an alternative historiography of modernity. Outlined and abandoned in Baudelaire, this intervention into the messianic-theological unconscious of modernity reappears in the work of Walter Benjamin, Baudelaire's most famous reader and—perhaps—an implicit addressee of Scholem's strictures. In bringing together Scholem's "religious anarchism," Baudelaire's final conception of modernity, and Benjamin's historiography, I aim to stage an encounter between different versions of the neutralization of messianism and thereby to gain a better understanding of the stakes and fortunes of the crisis of the messianic claim.

"Le ridicule d'un prophète": Charles Baudelaire's *"La Fin du monde"*

Let's just imagine the last human being sitting on the arid desert of the decaying planet earth—

FRIEDRICH NIETZSCHE, *Unpublished Writings*

For the prophet, life and the world, social events and cosmic events, have a unitary and pre-determined meaning.

MAX WEBER, *Economy and Society*

The mystery of Baudelaire's prominence in the twentieth century cannot be solved by means of reference to his poetic achievement or the good fortune he had with readers. It wouldn't be a mystery at all if not for the fact that Baudelaire's works retained immediacy and critical relevance despite multiple waves of canonization.[11] These began to submerge and overwhelm his own sense of cultural identity already in his later years. When he found out that *Le Parnasse contemporain* branded itself as the "Baudelaire school," he only shrugged his shoulders. One work by a future contributor to *Le Parnasse*, however, did catch the poet's eye. Somehow, a short prose piece about the future reached his hands in manuscript. He summarized its content as follows: "The world is going to end. Humankind is decrepit. A future Barnum shows to the degraded men of his time an artificially conserved female beauty of the ages past. 'Oh, wow,' they say, 'could humans be as good-looking as this?'"[12] Assessing this end-of-days fantasy, Baudelaire opined: "an ingenious notion, but not absolutely correct one" (une conception ingénieuse, mais non absolument juste) (831). History, however, managed to overlook Baudelaire's reservations. In 1875, eight years after the poet's death, the prose poem appeared in print as Stéphane Mallarmé's "Le Phénomène futur."

Baudelaire's bemused reaction to "Le Phénomène futur," and the fact that he felt the need to articulate his reaction on paper, can be taken as signs of his intensified concern with the historiography of modernity in the last phase of his writing. This concern amounts to pursuing the following question: If modernity is a historical condition defined by constant destruction of its own past, what kind of being—artistic, moral, and political—will live to withstand this orgy of renewal? By what political, moral, aesthetic means will this being teach itself to inhabit the uninhabitable?

Baudelaire's obsessive preoccupation with death and apocalypse can be seen as a direct consequence of his understanding of modernity as a period of accelerated obsolescence.[13] The chronological interpretation of modernity drove his theoretical thinking from the revolutionary Romanticism of the 1840s to the arch modernism of the Second Empire period, but neither of these configurations succeeded in yielding the enduring answer he was looking for. In his last writings, Baudelaire returns to the problem of the historiography of modernity with renewed vigor. At the center of the final configuration of his thought, one finds a programmatic text of uncertain provenance—"La Fin du monde." It opens with a line that Baudelaire used as a synopsis for Mallarmé's "Le Phénomène futur": "The world is going to end" (Le monde va finir).

Discovered after Baudelaire's death, "La Fin du monde" was first published in 1887. A florid meditation on the world's last days, Baudelaire's report on the catastrophe terminates in what seems to be his final profession of dandyism: "As for myself, who sometimes feel within me a prophet's absurdity, I know I shall never find therein a doctor's charity." (Quant à moi qui sens quelquefois en moi le ridicule d'un prophète, je sais que je n'y trouverai jamais la charité d'un médecin [*OC* 1:667].)

A highly polished piece of writing, this fragment has no precise place in Baudelaire's corpus. Even in calling it "La Fin du monde," we do no more than follow the decision of the editors. We don't know what Baudelaire would have called it, or how he would have used it. It may be a beginning of the novel he was planning, or a prose poem. It also could have been destined for *Fusées*, a collection of aphorisms and reflections where it is now placed.[14] There is some evidence to support each these conjectures but not enough to help us choose between them.

Since it quickly became common to present Baudelaire's late output as a product of dementia, this fragment attracted few readers. Rhetorical and discursive, it appeared to pose no hermeneutic problems. As a result, it was mobilized to solve one: The vehemence of its rhetoric made "La Fin du monde" serve as conclusive evidence of Baudelaire's descent into virulent misanthropy, recantation of the revolutionary legacy of 1848, capitulation to the spirit of reaction, or just syphilis-induced delirium. All these views agree in construing this prose fragment as a sign of the end, a point of arrival, a testimony to the exhaustion of Baudelaire's creative genius, and thus of his historical significance.[15]

There is one notable exception to this rule. In his "Baudelaire: Poet or Prophet?" Lloyd Austin approaches the fragment in a different perspective.[16] He invokes "La Fin du monde" in order to highlight the limitations of Baudelaire the thinker in comparison with the intuitive reach of Baudelaire the poet. Accordingly, he conjectures that Baudelaire must have rejected this piece of writing, and then goes on to endorse this rejection.[17] Austin's reading culminates in the following paraphrase:

> In "La Fin du monde," Baudelaire drapes around him the prophet's mantle and foretells nothing less than the end of the world. For him, the world is going to end, not with a bang, as once again seems not beyond the bounds of possibility, nor with a whimper, as Eliot declared in *The Hollow Men*, but in a rather more sinister way still, by the "debasement of the heart of man."
>
> *Poetic Principles and Practice*, 4

It is certainly true that Baudelaire drapes the prophet's mantle around himself. But does this gesture suffice to brand him a generic doomsayer? At the very least, we should test the assumption that what Baudelaire calls "le ridicule d'un prophète" is the same thing as prophecy pure and simple. Nor can we be absolutely sure that Baudelaire is indeed "foretelling the end of the world," since the fragment's second sentence speaks of the world's continuing to exist: "The only reason why it [i.e., the world] could go on is the fact that it exists." (La seule raison pour laquelle il pourrait durer, c'est qu'il existe [*OC* 1:665].)

"La Fin du monde" bears close resemblance to the so-called intertestamental apocalypses distinguished by their anthological compilation of signs stemming from heterogeneous cultural traditions, objectified representation of history as irrevocable decline, and the overripe style that earns them the label of "decadent." In the analysis that follows, I will try to demonstrate that, while picking up on these stylistic cues, Lloyd Austin misses that Baudelaire's exaggerated fidelity to apocalyptic rhetoric is a means of undercutting the apocalyptic construction of history. Further, this deadpan mockery, this "ridicule d'un prophète," does not dispense with the idea of historical record-keeping altogether. In the movement parallel to Scholem's treatment of messianism, the Baudelaire of "La Fin du monde" works to neutralize the teleological history of modernity and then goes on to outline a different form of historicity (the one to which later on I will refer as the "absolute" or "intransitive modernity"). Below I will single out three key points of this conceptual trajectory:

    1. "The world is going to end. The only reason why it could go on is the fact that it exists. How weak this reason is compared with all those heralding the opposite, and especially this one: what is there left for the world to do from now on under heaven?" (Le monde va finir. La seule raison pour laquelle il pourrait durer, c'est qu'il existe. Que cette raison est faible, comparée à toutes celles qui annoncent le contraire, particulière- ment à celle-ci : qu'est-ce que le monde a désormais à faire sous le ciel? [*OC* 1:665].) "The world is going to end." Baudelaire gives no exposition to this formula. It is assumed it requires none; it represents the discourse so ingrained, so present, that one needs not to rehearse it; a quotation will do. But this end is only the beginning. In "La Fin du monde," the end holds no promise: The categorical prognosis of the world's end remains incon- sequential. In the two sentences that follow, Baudelaire considers the pos- sibility that because it already exists, the world will not end, and he gives an impression that, even if this reason is weaker than those announcing the end, it may be the strongest by his measure.

    For Baudelaire, the drying up of the strong reasons for history—"What is there to do on this earth from now on?" (qu'est-ce que le monde a désor- mais à faire sous le ciel?)—does not bring history to a halt. It is not the end of history. It is only the end of the understanding of history as a realiza- tion of strong reasons—i.e., as actualization of the Idea in time as a living totality, or Spirit. The end of the world is a transcendental illusion (in the sense Kant uses the term in *Critique of Pure Reason*). It is born not of any "evidence" but of the ethical interpretation of history that concludes that, because the reasons for actions are becoming detached from substantive ethical life, collapse is imminent through mutual destruction of rational agents. But, as far as Baudelaire can see, the end won't come. Instead, at the end of its ethical phase, the civilization that emerged in the European pen- insula will face not a climactic reckoning of right and wrong—the triumph of judgment its prophets dreamed about, in other words, some version of Judgment Day—but the failure of ending.

    Contrary to appearances, the opening of "La Fin du monde" does not foretell the end of the world but retreats from its own prophecy. Baudelaire proclaimed the end only to mock the puerile death wish such formulas ful- fill. To provoke the reader, he dangles the apocalyptic bait in front of her. But entrapment is not all there is to "La Fin du monde." As the argument of this work unfolds, it becomes evident that he set out to demonstrate the inability of eschatology to comprehend the experience of modernity and to flag the incapacity of modernity to model itself on a non-eschatological pattern. Therefore, instead of anchoring the text in apocalyptic discourse, Baudelaire's "La Fin du monde" turns against it and strives to loosen the hold of apocalypse on our historical imagination. How does this about-face take place? To begin with, Baudelaire's opening substitutes for the idea of history as a temporal flow toward Judgment Day *an ambiguous scene of the encounter* between the strong reasons announcing the end of the world and the weak reasons that support the notion that it will continue to exist without them.

The significance of this substitution lies in the fact that it inscribes modernity in a register that is neither apocalyptic nor temporal. Understood as an encounter and conflict of reasons, modernity thereby becomes a qualitatively different concept. It is no longer a pattern of development or a chronological period. As Baudelaire's following sentence suggests, it stands for the tentativeness of material existence, and thus, perhaps, for weakness itself:

2. "For even supposing it kept on existing materially, would it be an existence worthy of the name and of the historical dictionary?" (Car, en supposant qu'il continuât à exister matériellement, serait-ce une existence digne de ce nom et du dictionnaire historique? [*OC* 1:665].) While urging us to imagine the world persisting for weak reasons, Baudelaire airs a suspicion that this incoming geopolitical structure—the nonapocalyptic, endlessly ending existence—may not be appropriately named the "world," nor would it comfortably fit into the annals of history, the "dictionnaire historique." (If one is to continue to refer to this fragment as "The End of the World," one has to keep in mind that, simply put, there is no world in it to end. So while the poetics of the text is apocalyptic, its rhetoric is consistently antiphrastic. Hence, the insufficiency of the standard view exemplified in Austin).

The paragraphs that follow flesh out Baudelaire's vision of modernity as a duration in which the exuberant positivity of political and economic phenomena overwhelm the cunning of ethical reason. His expository technique is to set up a system of antitheses between anterior history and the notion of modernity he is in the process of elaborating. Accordingly, in the long quotation that follows, we will see Baudelaire contrasting one world with another—the material world of persistence (i.e., modernity) with the historical world of accomplishment; the world where the death of God was still a meaningful proposition with the one where empathy with the divine is a compulsion that has no grip on collective experience; a world of positive historical development with the one projected by Baudelaire's perennial interlocutors, the French utopian socialists Pierre-Joseph Proudhon and Charles Fourier; the world in which revolutions could still be inherited with the one in which the forces that made past revolutions possible are no longer operative. This paragraph, I suggest, should be read as a funerary oration over the corpse of a messianic Romanticism that Baudelaire could never stop holding on to. Now, with the "vengeful ogre" of humanity in the offing, he finally masters the courage to let go. Not without parallel to Marx, Baudelaire here intuits that capitalism is the permanent revolution, a meta-revolution he could not yet conceptualize during the barricade days of 1848. Hence, the rhetorical sweep and gleefully demonic vehemence of Baudelaire's tone:

> A further example and further victims of the inexorable moral laws, we shall perish by what we thought we should live by. Machinery will have Americanized us so much, Progress will have so completely atrophied within us the spiritual part of our being, that nothing in the blood-thirsty, sacrilegious or antinatural dreams of Utopians will be comparable to its positive results. I ask any thinking man to show me what remains of life. Of religion I think it is useless to speak or to seek its remains, since still taking the trouble to deny God is the only scandal in such matters. Property had virtually disappeared with the abolition of the Law of Primogeniture; but the time will come when humanity, like an avenging ogre, will wrest their last morsel from those who think they are the legitimate heirs of the revolutions.[18]

The mechanics of modernity as such endless, posthistorical world is simultaneously self-consuming and self-perpetuating. Legal institutions, shared beliefs, political programs, and ethical dispositions hang in balance between self-destruction and self-affirmation. As a result, nothing ends, while the illusion of ending is constantly engendered. In light of Baudelaire's final conceptual breakthrough, the institutions of modernity, his terra incognita, cannot become historical because they consume themselves too fast; existence and extinction energize one another in a pattern of subsistence that neither utopian naturalism nor theological spiritualism can fully comprehend. In fact, Baudelaire argues that the only real scandal is epistemological—that is, that we continue to frame the historiography of this "absolute modernity" in terms of organic ripening of conditions or eschatological expectation of the end. Baudelaire, on the other hand, reaches for a different descriptive model. In his description, the enactment of ethical programs and moral dispositions—the forces Baudelaire names "inexorables lois morales"—has the effect of suspending the mediations of community, thereby creating an omnipresent political immediacy or "generalized animality." We should not rush to identify this condition with Hobbes's "state of nature," though it bears a family resemblance to it. In Baudelaire as in Hobbes, "state of nature" is a matter of interruption, not prehistory; for both thinkers, "animality" is a product of history's breakdown, not its foundation. But this is where the resemblance between the two ends. Baudelaire's new animality inherits the Leviathans that are ill-suited to control it, driving them to more and more insidious forms of domination. It is here, in what would have seemed a demented exaggeration at the time, that Baudelaire managed to prophesy the horrors of the century that followed his: "Need I say that what little politics remain will have to struggle painfully to survive amid the grip of the general animality, and that in order to maintain and create a semblance of order, the rulers will be forced to have recourse to measures that would make our present-day humanity shudder, hardened as it is?" (Ai-je besoin de dire que le peu qui restera de politique se débattra péniblement dans les étreintes de l'animalité générale, et que les gouvernants seront forcés, pour se maintenir et pour créer un fantôme d'ordre, de recourir à des moyens qui feraient frissonner notre humanité actuelle, pourtant si endurcie? [*OC* 1:666].) In the state of absolute modernity, politics, rather than nature, history, or religion, is the only remaining source of order. Furthermore, this "residual" politics changes the meaning of politics as well, for it is driven neither by claims to emancipation nor by preservation of right. It is an arena where the warring parties contest the power to impose and maintain the fictions of order ("fantômes d'ordre").

3. In the course of "La Fin du monde," Baudelaire deploys apocalyptic discourse only to expose its inadequacy. One could argue that this "mockery" amounts to a systematic undoing of three interrelated facets of the apocalyptic discourse. First, he suspends the notion of history as a hermeneutic Whole connecting Creation and Salvation; second, he undoes the vision of each historical present as objectively progressing toward a predetermined end, "the day of the Lord"; third, he break with eschatology that frames the individual experience of historical presents with the promise of salvation. In shorthand, one could say that Baudelaire substitutes synchrony for diachrony, while subtracting prolepsis as the kernel of the subjective experience of history. As a result, modernity is no longer a stage in the objectified historical becoming of humanity (say, a journey from rude nature toward eternal peace) but an internal limit that humanity's becoming can never stop approaching. For obvious reasons, this concep-

tion of modernity has to be separated from chronological ones, including Baudelaire's own; this is also why I call it "absolute" or "intransitive," for this modernity functions as an asymptote to the curve of becoming, rather than as a point or a segment on the line. My conclusion is that Baudelaire's extraction of modernity from apocalypse yearns for the mathematical tropes he can only intuit. As we now know, it will take a wholly different style of thought, and a new century, to effect this shift from the theological to mathematical tropology of becoming.[19]

But Baudelaire's most forceful gesture takes place when he declares that this new geopolitical constitution is not just a wild conjecture or dandy's latest pipedream. Instead, he suggests that absolute modernity could have already arrived: "These times are perhaps very near; indeed, who knows if they have not come already, and if the coarsening of our senses is the only obstacle preventing us from appraising the environment in which we live!" (Ces temps sont peut-être bien proches; qui sait même s'ils ne sont pas venus, et si l'épaississement de notre nature n'est pas le seul obstacle qui nous empêche d'apprécier le milieu dans lequel nous respirons! [*OC* 1:667].) The event of absolute modernity may have occurred already, which means that both the utopian interpretation of history and the dream of its apocalyptic interruption are kept alive only by our blindness to this event. The end-of-days catastrophe we project into the future may in truth be a distorted echo of the past we continue to disavow.

Neither an apocalyptic prophecy nor a revolutionary critique, "La Fin du monde" is a theory of modernity as a world-constituting power. It rehearses Baudelaire's last concept of history according to which existence becomes animalistic, and hence, fully political. This is not biopolitics; it is zoo politics on the planetary scale. The latter amounts to the following conjecture: The realization of modernity does not bring history to an end but inaugurates a historical duration in which each day becomes an event of confrontation between weak and strong reasons, or between persistence and accomplishment. Because oversaturated by history, modernity cannot unfold progressively. The growth of competing planetary forces locks them in spectacular battle for survival, a battle that impedes a realization of any single tendency. The escalation of struggle for power inhibits the intelligibility of the total process, eroding the hermeneutics of the Whole. We are left with a weak earth where all depend on all and where sovereignty is at once a memory, a dream, and a fiction of order.

The relentless critical advance of "La Fin du monde" is designed to drive the reader to the following exhortation: "What does one do in a world like this?" At the end of the fragment, Baudelaire supplies the following answer:

> As for myself, who sometimes feel within me a prophet's absurdity, I
> know I shall never find therein a doctor's charity. Lost in this awful
> world, jostled by the crowds, I am like a weary man whose eye can see
> behind him, in the depths of bygone years, nothing but disillusionment
> and bitterness, and before him nothing but a storm containing noth-
> ing new, neither instruction nor suffering. On the evening when such a
> man has stolen from fate a few hours of pleasure, lulled by his diges-
> tion, oblivious—as far as possible—of the past, content with the pres-
> ent and resigned to the future, intoxicated by his self-possession and
> his dandyism, proud of not having sunk so low as the passersby, he says
> to himself while contemplating the smoke from his cigar: What does it
> matter whither all these minds are going?
>
> I think I have strayed into what the professionals would call an intro-
> duction. Nonetheless, I will leave these pages—because I want to date
> my ~~rage~~. sadness[20]

Does the world go up in smoke, then? Can historical existence be dis-
sociated from temporal consciousness—the dissociation hinted at in
Baudelaire's denial of originary power to the past ("que désabusement et
amertume") or the future ("rien de neuf")? Is pursuit of private pleasures,
consciousness of one's superiority and resignation to the opaque, impenetrable future all that is left?

Unlike what Nietzsche argues in "The Use and Abuse of History," in
Baudelaire's conception the excess of history does not render the Euro-
peans unnatural. Rather, it makes them into beings that are political and
theatrical. Counting epochs in a world like this will do only as a nostalgic exercise; absolute modernity disallows the experience of belonging as
such, including the experience of belonging to oneself; perhaps this is why
Baudelaire's dandy never finds out whether it is rage or sadness that speak
through him.

Nonetheless, Baudelaire's narrator does not surrender completely to
modernity's paralyzing exuberance: "Cependant, je laisserais ces pages—
parce que je veux dater." He opts to record his analysis and thus to date
the impossibility of experience. In sharp contrast with the apocalyptical
stance, he is aiming to rebuild the sense of the world day by day rather
than to grasp the entirety of history as an ideal pattern. Defining itself as
an introduction, "La Fin du monde" closes with a promise of other dates

and other acts of dating—i.e., further attempts to inhabit modernity as a Living Present. On this score, Baudelaire's engagement with Belgium in *Pauvre Belgique!* still has much to tell us. Perhaps this is why the late poet placed in this work the reference to Mallarmé's prose poem with which I began.

Rather than a reactionary attack on modernity, "La Fin du monde" is an exercise in constructing a concept of modernity no longer anchored in theological commitments; it is an hors-d'oeuvre that introduces modernity as the pièce de résistance. Its conceptual strategy can be characterized as neutralization of the theological element in the historiography of modernity in the service of a quasi-mathematical concept of historicity. It produces, but only in bare outline, a figure of the *chronicler* as the one who accumulates dates rather than experiences—the final incarnation of Baudelaire's dandy. In the concluding section of the essay, I suggest that the writings of Walter Benjamin resume the interrupted work of "La Fin du monde."

"Paradise and Pandemonium": Walter Benjamin's Heliotropic Sequels to "La Fin du monde"

Si la religion disparaissait du monde, c'est dans le cœur de l'athée qu'on la retrouverait.

BAUDELAIRE

The recurrent tensions in the discourse of the messianic that I have been highlighting so far—starting with the imploding invocations of the messianic in Benjamin, Kafka, and Derrida; pointing to Scholem's neutralization of messianism; reconstructing Baudelaire's theory of absolute modernity—constitute a network of gestures whose affinity with each other comes from being involved in what may be designated as the recall of the messianic. This recall is triple. It retrieves, neutralizes, and redeploys the historical messianism that it recalls. Instead of appropriating messianism as a definitive image of the expired past, this recall gathers the critical force alienated in the past intentions that messianic phenomena represent. The recall of the messianic enacts a reappropriation of the critical moment that the historical messianisms always threaten to extinguish. Therefore, in addition to all the resistances that it enacts vis-à-vis theological memories and traditions, the byzantine evasiveness of the messianic discourse also harbors a concept of criticism no longer oriented by the values of tradition or memory. The resurgence of the figure of the chronicler within Benjamin's concept of critique as redemptive act furnishes us with salient indications of the powers and the limits of the strategy of recall.

Benjamin's idea of redemption is strongly anti-utopian.[21] In a late addition to "On the Concept of History," Benjamin implies that even Marx—to say nothing of Friedrich Engels or Gregory Plekhanov—failed to grasp completely the true significance of the idea of classless society: "In the idea of classless society, Marx secularized the idea of messianic time. And that was a good thing. It was only when the Social Democrats elevated this idea to an 'ideal' that the trouble began" (*SW* 4:401; *GW* 1.3:1231). Developing this somewhat belated gibe against the social-democratic view of history into a full-scale critique of utopianism, Benjamin goes on to deny that "classless society" could be understood as anything other than a formal indication of messianism:

> Whoever wishes to know what the situation of a "redeemed humanity" (*erlöste Menschheit*) might actually be, what conditions are required for the development of such a situation, and when this development can be expected to occur, poses questions to which there are no answers. He might just as well seek to know the color of ultraviolet rays.
>
> *SW* 4:402; *GS* 1.3:1232

These questions are unanswerable; they are also the wrong questions to ask. Deploying time as an empty form of becoming, these social-democratic questions frame action as waiting—i.e., as inaction. They thereby cede in advance whatever the critical potential that the concept of a "redeemed humanity" may contain at the moment. In correlation to time as an empty form of experience, these questions unearth *phusis*—i.e., the maturation and growth of the ideal inscribed in the order of things. In its turn, the idea of time as a delay in the auto-manifestation of *phusis* effectively forfeits the authority of thought in favor of mythic creationism.

In Benjamin's severe judgment, instead of capitalizing on the reappearance of the messianic in the idea of classless society, the social democrats framed it as a myth, obfuscating the political chance contained in Marx's coinage. Benjamin's own *recall* of the messianic, therefore, will invert the scene of the *reappearance* of historical messianism in Marx and its transformation into the myth of modern time by his social-democratic heirs. To the stance of the social-democratic prophet, Benjamin will oppose the figure of the chronicler. He sketches it in the third paragraph ("thesis") of "On the Concept of History":

> The chronicler who narrates events without distinguishing between
> major and minor ones acts in accord with the following truth: noth-
> ing that has ever happened should be considered as lost to history. Of
> course, only a redeemed mankind is granted the fullness of its past—
> which is to say, only for a redeemed mankind has its past become
> citable in all its moments. Each moment it has lived becomes a *citation à
> l'ordre du jour*. And that day is Judgment Day.[22]

This fragment is cut in half by the caesura contrasting the perspective of
the chronicler with that of the prophet: While the prophet proceeds as if
the fullness of the past has *already* become available to deciphering, the
chronicler inquires into experience while suspending the purely historical norms responsible for distinguishing "major" events from the "minor"
ones. To become a prophet is to reject the notion that only a redeemed
humanity has the total possession of its past. By means of a prognostic attitude, the prophet arrogates omniscience, which no historical existence can
claim. For the prophet, every day is the last day; the chronicler approaches
every day as the first.

   In Benjamin's dialectical canon, Karl Kraus represents the most extreme
possibility of the chronicle. Why? It is largely a matter of the aggressive
and concrete style in which *Die Fackel* related the actualities of the moment.
But Kraus's virtuoso use of language is not all Benjamin has in mind.

   The chronicler, Benjamin told us, has neither the image of redemption nor the fullness of the past to guide him. Nonetheless, he refuses to
abandon the idea of redemption in the universe that cast out its creator.
The notion that redemption is written in ultraviolet ink plunges the alle-
gorist into the "cesspool" of melancholic contemplation. The chronicler,
by contrast, remains resistant to it.[23] He is impermeable to the debilitating
irony that connects the persistence of paradise to its unavailability, because he refuses to accept this unavailability as fatal. Instead of reading it
as a theological limit of creaturely condition, he assaults the sphere of the
events ("was sich jemals ereignet hat") as nonetheless available to historical
inscription. Because this inscription cannot proceed in the restorative or
prophetic mode, the chronicler represents a demonic element. He knows
that his demand for absolute transparency of creation has no chance of being fulfilled. Rejecting the hand and the word of God, he opts to read the
book of creation as a dialectic of redemption (*Rettung*) written in ultraviolet ink. The figure of the chronicler marks the moment when modernity
reengages the chthonic, polymorphic forces that its historians relegate to
comfortably distant prehistory.

At the point where the chronicler acts like a demon, Benjamin places Karl Kraus: "He provides an unprecedented, ambiguous, genuinely demonic spectacle of the accuser eternally calling for justice [*Recht*], the public prosecutor who becomes a Michael Kolhaas because no justice [*Justiz*] can satisfy his accusation and none of his accusations satisfy him. His linguistic and ethical quibbling is not a form of self-righteousness" (*SW* 2:194; *GS* 2:624–25). In addition to indicating the subterranean connection between Kraus and Kleist, Benjamin also objects to construing Kraus's work as philological quibbling of the self-appointed representative of the "last men." Benjamin continues: "The fact that this man is one of the very few who have a vision of freedom, but can further it only by assuming the role of chief prosecutor—all this presents his powerful dialectic in a pure form" (*SW* 2:194–95, translation modified; *GS* 2:625).

The demonic condition of the chronicler is evident in his acting as the nightmarish public prosecutor dissatisfied with his own accusations, uninterested in admissions of guilt or in the execution of criminal justice. Yet this condition is not the self-perpetuating mirroring of decay and paralysis, the vocation of melancholia's angels. On the contrary, the demonic excesses of the chronicler represent a moment when the messianic element (which Benjamin discreetly positions here as "a vision of freedom") erupts into presence.[24] Kraus thereby becomes a record of "powerful dialectic," a dialectic whose power is capable of turning the demon against himself.

This transfiguration of the demonic appears all the more enigmatic because Benjamin portrays the demonic as an absolute persistence in one's being, a stubborn ontic attachment repelling any form of consolation or contact. Mere intensification of the demonic along the lines of "Soyons réalistes, demandons l'impossible" does not break the enchanted circle of theology. If the demonic is to become, as Benjamin says, a "powerful dialectic," then it must undergo an immanent dissociation into antithetical elements. What could be the site or the place of this passage from the theological to the messianic version of the demonic? Benjamin finds this type of redemptive dissociation at work in Kraus's public reading of Jacques Offenbach's operetta *La Vie parisienne*: "The miraculous thing about it was that it was brought about by the man who had devoted his life work to *Die Fackel*, with its world of pandemonium and paradise, whose inhabitants have now paired and have plunged into a rotund dance of Offenbach's characters around them" (*SW* 2:110; *GS* 4:1:516).

In taking the stage, Kraus also becomes the stage on which the creatures populating the insular universe of *Die Fackel* are thrown into the hands of Offenbach's bohemians. The reading, then, is not at all a recitation but a

dance that takes the originals involved beyond the domain circumscribed
by the contrast between a faithful rendition and a free one:

> So the events on stage stand completely outside the stubborn alterna-
> tive of productive and *reproductive* performance [*Leistung*] that applies
> only to the more or less vain or servile tricks [*Manöver*] of virtuo-
> sos. . . . Kraus is no more a "virtuoso" as a lecturer than he is a "master
> of language" as an author. . . . But the fact is that he does not voice
> Offenbach's words; rather, he speaks from inside Offenbach [*Aber
> er spricht ja in Warheit nicht Offenbach; er spricht aus ihm hinaus*]. And
> every now and then he casts a breathtaking, half-blank, half-glinting
> procurer's glance at the crowd before him, inviting them to an unholy
> wedding with the masked figures in which they fail to recognize them-
> selves, and invoking here too the evil privilege of the demon: the right
> to ambiguity.
>
> > *SW* 2:110–11, translation modified; *GS* 4.1:516

By releasing his language into Offenbach's works, Kraus takes a demonic
possession of their author, delivering his lines from his inside or insides:
"er spricht aus ihm hinaus." The triumph of this demonic possession is celebrated in the sovereign gaze with which Kraus surveys the crowd caught
between complacent agreement with the satirical intent and an inability to
recognize themselves as the objects of satire. Contrary to appearances, the
demonic ambiguity does not control the ambiguity it releases, just as Kraus
cannot be identified completely with the persona of the demon he assumes.
The demonic *performance* dissociates the demonic into the dance of the
possessive and messianic powers that grant the participants in the spectacle a place in the paradise and pandemonium where difference between
originals and copies, past and present, the performer and the audience is
reconfigured into a transient pattern of communicability:

> Offenbach's works here [i.e., in Kraus's performance] undergo a mortal
> crisis. They contract, shed all superfluous trappings, venture the risky
> passage through this life and reemerge at the end, redeemed [*gerettet*]
> and more real than before. . . . At times they are transformed into a
> curtain; and like a fairground showman whose wild gestures accompany
> the entire performance, Karl Kraus tears this curtain aside, exposing
> the contents of their and our own chamber of horrors to our gaze.
>
> > *SW* 2:111; *GS* 4.1:516

In the messianic medium of Kraus's performance, Offenbach's works attain
the relational being that they had not possessed before. Instead of acting

as a script or a veil, they become a curtain concealing a spectacle. This spectacle, a medium in which the distinction between horrors described and horrors remembered falls away, signifies the pinnacle of demonic possession. But the demon has already been replaced by the fairground performer whose vocation is to interrupt:

> At this point Kraus—intentionally, rightly—explodes the framework of the entire evening. Anarchically, he turns directly to the audience during an interval in a brief speech that applies to Berlin the refrain we just heard: "I bring out the worst in each town." And in so doing he affects his listeners directly, in the same way he does with the texts he reads—that is to say, he assaults them unexpectedly, destructively, disrupting the prepared "mood," attacking the audience where they least anticipate it. In this respect he can only be compared to a puppeteer.
>
> *SW* 2:111; *GS* 4.1:517

Kraus's "attack" on the audience during the intermission collapses the power of the demonic established by the mimetic communion of the spectacle; the demonic is revealed as a mask rather than as Kraus's true being, a power that he is capable of using as well as it is capable of using him. While acting demonic, Kraus exposed the demon as a mask and emerged in the authentic position omnipresent in his language—a fairground performer, a puppeteer, an angelic amalgam of the child and the man-eater that will reappear as Benjamin's final judgment on Kraus.[25]

As long as confined to the insular universe of *Die Fackel*, Kraus's language could only seem demonic. By entering into contact with Offenbach, he retrieves the messianic element that lays buried in the absolute demand for justice that the demon directs at creation. This element appears as music. In Kraus's performance, "anarchy, the only international constitution that is moral and worthy of man, becomes the true music of these operettas. The voice of Kraus speaks [*sagt*], rather than sings, this inner music" (*SW* 2:111–12; *GS* 4.1:517). The true music, the messianic rhythm, can only be spoken. It appears only in performance—i.e., in the refusal to be defeated by the full knowledge of its transience. Just as Offenbach's words revealed the true nature of Kraus's demon, Kraus's performance returned the favor by setting Offenbach's text to the true music that always speaks in history—anarchy as the messianic ground of the moral dignity of mankind.

By revealing the chronicler as a performer rather than a historian of the present, Benjamin's description of Kraus's performance completes his idea of the chronicle as a messianic passage or transit. The chronicler, far from representing a demonic contrast to the prophet, displays the mastery of the demonic. Rather than offering images of redemption, the chronicler lets the relational powers of performance emerge as the messianic element that shatters his demonic stance. The chronicler does not represent experiences but reenacts them. In place of events, he places the event of experience as the medium of his uninterruptible performance. His performance is without a script. Like Kant's aesthetic ideas, such performances are diagrams that animate the concepts they put into play and thus endow them with a concrete yet inorganic living body. Wherever they take place, such performances are all the more powerful for being transient, since they embody an otherwise impossible renunciation of stubborn, creaturely attachment to one's natural being and the way of the world.

Like the narrator in Baudelaire's "La Fin du monde," the chronicler in Kraus does not rest content with collecting experiences. *Die Fackel* is not a museum of sensibility but a stage or projection room where experiences are performed. By reenacting the difference between text and history, existence and persistence, demonic and prophetic as a living spectacle (rather than as evidence of the apocalyptic decline), the chronicler awakens absolute modernity to its political essence: "History knows nothing of the image of bad infinity contained in the image of the two wrestlers locked in eternal combat. The true politician reckons only in dates" ("One Way Street," *SW* 1:470, translation modified; *GS* 4.1:122).

Neither a doctor nor a prophet, the chronicler whose figure traverses Baudelaire, Kraus, and Benjamin laments, vituperates, mocks; he is a dialectical assemblage of gestures, masks, and tics. More important, his performance puts in play the messianic-theological difference that neither theologies nor messianisms of the Enlightenment can sustain. In the tradition of this difference, the chronicler represents the appropriation of the political constitution of modernity, whereas the prophet marks a moment when this opportunity is wasted.

In Benjamin's final work, "On the Concept of History," the powerful dialectic glimpsed in Kraus returns, this time in order to position the materialist writer in relation to the revolutionary struggle. Thesis Seven sounds a decisive repudiation of melancholic acedia as unwitting sympathy with the victors in the historical fight for domination: "There is no better way of characterizing the method with which historical materialism has broken with. It is a process of empathy. Its origin is the indolence of the heart, that *acedia* which despairs of appropriating the genuine historical image as it briefly flashes up. . . . The nature of this sadness becomes clearer if we ask: With whom does historicism actually sympathize? The answer is inevitable: with the victor" (*SW* 4:391; *GS* 1.2:696). But empathy with the defeated is not the solution Benjamin is looking for. He knew only too well that placing the writer in proletarian conditions is ineffectual, for it tends to yield bohemians or ideological fellow travelers, not proletarian writers. Therefore, the task of the historical materialist must not be to join the victors in the process of revolution. Rather, it is to make sure that in this victory the following set of qualities does not disappear: "But these things ["spiritual and refined" as opposed to mere survival], which are present in class struggle, are not present as a vision of spoils that fall to the victor [i.e., the proletariat]. They are alive in this struggle as confidence, courage, humor, cunning and fortitude, and have effects that reach far back into the past" (*SW* 4:390; *GS* 1.2:694). The historical materialist does not passively await the coming revolutionary possession of cultural heritage; rather, he intervenes in the process of its appropriation for the sake of the demonic qualities without which revolutionary struggle will turn out to be defective. The qualities listed by Benjamin—courage, humor, cunning and fortitude—mark the return of Kraus's chronicler who mobilizes the chthonic forces in the service of a "powerful dialectic." Accordingly, the ultimate object of the "revolutionary thinker" is not the victory of the proletariat but stubborn, demonic advocacy of revolutionary chance: "In reality, there is not a moment that would not carry with it its revolutionary chance—provided only that it is defined in a specific way, namely as the chance for a completely new resolution of a completely new problem [*Aufgabe*]" (*SW* 4:402; *GS* 1.3:1231). Such advocacy is guided by the concept of universal history as a heliotropic movement of messianic-theological difference: "As flowers turn toward the sun, what has been strives to turn—by dint of secret heliotropism—toward the sun which is the rising in the sky of history" (*SW* 4:390; *GS* 1.2:694–95). This sun is the "paradise and pandemonium" glimpsed in Kraus's performance.

The convolutions of the discourse of the messianic offer a surprisingly robust concept of modernity. The history of modernity they record is, rather than progression or regression, the repetition of the crisis of the messianic claim. The neutralization of the messianic is the logic guiding these crises; the chronicle figures as their most legible form. These crises offer as bewildering a spectacle as Scholem reading messianism, Baudelaire reading apocalypse, or Kraus reading Offenbach—a dance of destruction and origination set to the true music of history. This music speaks the separability of history and persistence, of the messianic and theology. The notion of absolute modernity revealed in Baudelaire is therefore best understood as a rhythm rather than a development. In Benjamin's conception, criticism bids for the power held out and withdrawn by this rhythm in every moment of historical existence. This is one concept of criticism harbored in the interminable crisis of the messianic claim.

CHAPTER 11

Messiahs and Principles

Paul North

An old argument erupts between Franz Kafka and his fiancée, Felice Bauer: He uses the word "bis" where she uses the word "wenn," and in this fact seems to lurk a criticism of Kafka's grasp of German, though one that Kafka often levels at himself and his friends. "Bis" for Felice is a calculation of time up to but not including a limit, a uniform stretch before a deadline, similar to what is said in the English preposition "until." Kafka, in contrast, thinks "bis" can mean "when" in the sense of "as soon as," the limit that has to be reached in order to trigger an event, or the event that marks the limit. Toward the end of September 1917, Kafka writes his friend Felix Weltsch in Prague with a "library request."[1] "You know our old 'bis'-dispute," he writes. It has arisen again and he has finally understood what she means; "bis" can be used, according to Felice, only to mean "solange bis"—an action valid for a time to a terminus. His asking Weltsch to look this up in Grimm's dictionary may be motivated, however, not so much by lexicographic curiosity or *Rechthaberei*; the dispute may have another meaning and his request another purpose. If rightly settled, the dispute could help illuminate Kafka's position toward Felice. He has what he calls a "Doppelstellung," a double position with respect to her. Kafka is two kinds of dog, "an earth-hound and a hellhound" ("ein[] Erd- und Höllenhund").[2] Although he explains this description no further, we could assume that, if Kafka is right about "bis," by proving this linguistic possibility he will have been her loyal friend, faithful protector, and companion. If he is wrong, he will have attacked her, out of his own mean nature.

The question is whether there is any significance to this dispute beyond the personal or psychological. Goodness knows Kafka is prone to overreaction, especially where Felice is concerned. Reappearing as it does during the final death throes of the five-year relationship that ended for good within a month of the renewed "bis" strife, one might suspect that it is, in fact, a displacement of more fundamental differences than the difference between "until" and "as soon as." From a psychological point of view this may indeed be the case. But Kafka's position toward Felice is not simply psychological; there stands between them not only love or abuse (although both are in evidence, and often indistinguishable). Vis-à-vis Felice, Kafka's is also an intellectual as well as an ethical position, and these are the aspects that appear in his self-designation as "earth-dog" and "hell-hound." The twin positions good and evil, and quotidian and mythological (or even theological), remind us of the dualisms that Kafka in his writings of the winter of 1917–18 names, dissects, and tries to reduce to original ambiguities. Good and evil, creation and redemption, language and meaning, being and having—these theological doublets, and several others, traverse his notebooks and fall under his scalpel. Here the cut runs directly through the word "bis," scoring a line between Kafka and Felice, and perhaps also between Prague and Berlin, and all the differences that implies, a line certainly between happiness and mourning, and most peculiarly, between time and— . . . no time, non-time, or simply not time. Many other things could have led him to question his "position" toward his fiancée. Why focus on "bis"? A worry about this word and in turn also a worry about language led him to a German authority, Grimm's dictionary—one that sublates the Prague–Berlin difference, referring to a monumental German, Romantic origin—to resolve the matter. Perhaps Kafka worries that, of the two of them, he speaks the more fallen language, one that ur-Germans struggle to understand.[3] Perhaps Kafka's own speech has fallen so far that it has become an idiolect. Not so: Weltsch confirms that he too hears "bis" this way.[4] Perhaps Kafka is worried about communication: Prague German and Berlin German do not coincide in some respects.[5] Or, he worries that the German he aspires to speak and write is internally riven—that there is no one German language but that within its supposed analyticity, unity, and uniformity lies a monstrous multiplicity. Perhaps the German he has been speaking and writing is not German or is not only German.[6] This reading is supported by the many moments in diaries and letters in which Kafka frets aloud that "his" language betrays him, not to mention by the talk he gave on the Yiddish language. Around the time of the "bis" fight, the motif of betrayal by language appears once again in a letter to Brod, where Kafka corrects oddities in Brod's translation of Janáček's *Jenufa*. Of Brod's language he writes sardonically: "Is that not the German that we still have in our ears from our un-German mothers?"[7] Betraying these mothers by speaking properly, this is what is on his mind; but it is first and foremost a linguistic betrayal, not a libidinal one—one or more potential dissonances with and against the mother's tongue.

But it is also not purely or merely linguistic. "No mortal pulls off this veil, until [*bis*] I myself lift it."[8] This quote from Schiller is one of the examples Weltsch adduces from Grimm in his response to Kafka. Another, "lend it to me *bis* we meet again," Kafka cites in his next letter as the only example from Grimm that proves "as soon as" is a possible meaning of "bis."[9] Weltsch writes, in turn, that he doesn't think this sentence proves anything of the sort.[10] One could take this evidence as a point of departure for a Kafkan theory of the internal rivenness of languages. A specter of a secondary confusion of tongues, a post-Babel chatter arises within a purportedly single language, such that even a master dictionary does not guarantee communication among its speakers. And without communication, how could a marriage work out?

There must be more to this. What does it mean, we should also ask, to take "until" for "as soon as"? Or instead or in addition, what does it mean to admit a perhaps otherwise illicit indistinction between the two? At the very least, this "bis" has a different object of concern: Instead of focusing on the time up to a point, instead of dwelling on the meantime in which one awaits the coming of a limit (even if one is not actively waiting, but rather distracted, living), it focuses on the transformative instant in which the meantime gets converted into something else. "Lend it to me *until* we meet." With this F. Bauer would set the temporal extent of a contract, at the end of which the meeting would be unimportant. "Lend it to me *as soon as* we meet." With this F. Kafka would intend the change that the meeting would bring, which would invalidate or render superfluous what came before. An engagement is a good example of this sort of contract, and this sort of double meaning, bind, or bond. It is a kind of loan, a loan of one's social standing, a loan of one's libidinal forces, but most important, a loan of the future, until . . . one marries, or absolves the loan and dissolves the relation. What linguists call the "terminative function" is in question in Felice's "bis." Hers is calendrical, a measuring out of a space of time. Franz's is messianic. As soon as its object arrives, the calendar is voided and another—or none—must begin.

The Chosen Language

When he finally arrives, what language will the messiah speak? An obvious although not also uninteresting answer is "Hebrew," or "Greek." This answer implies that a messiah, his being and meaning, is carried, somehow, in the specificity of the language in which his coming will have been announced. His arrival is predetermined by texts written long ago and which themselves most likely were quotations and translations from the language of prophecies or previous scriptures, evoking, in turn, a first word, spoken, one assumes, in the superlative language of God, now silent.[11] This answer—conjuring up a great chain of languages—also refers, lest we forget, to the language in which a messiah continues to be received long after revelation or after his departure, and, too, after the departure or death of any and all originary languages, in pidgins and jargons, argots and slang, not to forget the language of the unconscious, the language of dreams. The messiah must continue to be announced in each new language, and in every semi- and para-language, until the moment comes—lest we forget him and his name. And yet, this necessity is not without an accompanying fear. Without access to the ur-language, it is feared, one will not be able to receive the messiah properly, as soon as (*bis*) he comes, or, for that matter, get an accurate picture of him beforehand, until (*bis*) he should come. The ongoing reception of the original Greek or Hebrew, in which the messiah repeatedly reoriginates as *meshiach* and *christos*, takes place in at least two ways: philologically, by those who resurrect "dead" languages, and pistologically, through a translation, which despite its tacit claim to speak in place of the original keeps the corpse of the old tongue nearby, in order to draw on its authority.[12] The original remains nearby, not only so that it may authorize the translation again and again but also, when needed, to impugn its probity. Hebrew, Greek—and Aramaic—for instance, insult the English of the New Revised Standard Version (the barbs take the form of footnotes in scholarly and religious editions), and despite its injuries, the translation thrives off these attacks. They are the marks of a superior power that the translation can never overcome. In this way, translated scripture displaces questions of authority and probity onto the original, leaving a purer, if also weaker, but therefore also more trustworthy text—to be trusted insofar as it continually denies its perfection. Far from problematic, this pistological displacement makes up the denial structure of scriptural authority and probity. Behind or beyond the language of any scripture there is always another higher language. A holy text establishes its trustworthiness on the basis of a dead language that it resurrects as the inaccessible living flesh of its dry bones. Its power as scripture depends on its ability to open graves. An inkling about this process seems to have plagued Luther when he was writing *De Libertate Cristiana*; he argues repeatedly that the Word, which he says is the true object of faith, is separate and higher than words.[13] He intuits here—ergo his repetitive assertions—that trust in words precedes belief in the Word and that the Word is but the excuse by which words proceed to animate themselves.

Insisting that a messiah will speak again in the tongue in which he was once invoked or in which he himself once spoke brings on other complications as well. Should Jesus have spoken, when he sermonized or counseled, Hebrew or Aramaic? What relation do these languages and their external and internal dissonances have to the Greek in which they were first, at least in part, translated and immortalized? In the case of multiple Jewish messiologies, one of many dissonances occurs between the languages and dialects of commentary and the language of scripture. This is to say that, empirically speaking, original languages have also tended to depend on others, both centuries later and right from the start, in ways that require careful analysis and interpretation in each specific case.

It is perhaps inevitable that we speak of "Judaism" and "Christianity" in this context, but it is also unsatisfying, since the status of language within the shifting histories and differing self-definitions that these single names disguise and distort itself shifts and alters. Let us say for the sake of argument that we believe the generalization and cliché that the one, Judaism, is driven, in its passion for exclusivity, by a demand to preserve the force and position of the original language, despite history, and that the other, Christianity, is driven, in its passion for universal acceptance, by the need to abandon the original over and over again, to translate, expanding outward geolinguistically but also at the same time without closing itself off to as yet unspoken languages. If this were true, each delimited tradition would still, nevertheless, derive the authority for its particular claim about language (infinite untranslatability, infinite translatability) from an original word that had dictated to them the status of language, and it would be forced to return again and again to affirm its command of that tongue. Yet this word would have to have been spoken in a language that was neither translatable nor untranslatable, one with no extension in time, one that vanishes just beyond the limits of the holy tongue or infinitely translated tongues and that would authorize unequivocally and forever both the law of perpetual translation and the law of eternal untranslatability. One candidate for this most permissive of languages is silence, understood in a particular way, *not* as the absence of language.

Regardless of these complications, which a positivist theory of philology or a coherent theological hermeneutics could, if only for appearance's sake, neutralize, when it comes to the messiah and the messianic arrival, all words are canceled. Who is to say that the messiah will speak the language in which he was described or that he spoke once so long ago? Who is to say we or he will recognize what he does as speaking? Who is to say that he will have this name, or any name? The language of the first coming, we would have to concede, may not be the same as the second; redemptive language may not equal creative language—indeed, it had better not. If it did, it would not produce a redemption but a re-creation. It is a commonplace of theology that each time finite beings try to circumscribe creation, the freedom of the creator is unfairly attacked. Why don't we say the same thing about the messiah? Is not the freedom of the messiah imperiled when we limit him in messianic words, predictions, and predications? Whenever we identify him as speaking or responding to this or that language, do we not impose on him a demand that he be and remain intelligible according to pitifully finite criteria? The desire for a messiah who speaks our language is easy to understand. A messiah whom we do not understand is repulsive. How would "our" messiah fail to speak to us, about us, in the language of our desires, confirming at a minimum some one prior statement about him? And this is just the problem.

The problem shows messianic statements in crisis, insofar as at a minimum they predict that their claims, whatever their content, will remain meaningful and intelligible until the end—until after the end. The messiah's messianicity is in this way in advance always subordinated to the amessianicity of one understanding of language. We do not say: When (bis)—"as soon as"—the end comes, the proper language will be determined. On the contrary, any statement about a messiah implies that it is equal to the coming messiah and higher, dominant over, determinant of his being and his language or whatever language he inaugurates. What we say about messiahs usurps the messianic privilege and power to speak a different language or to speak this one differently. Any messiah that we speak about is diminished in the process. And yet, a language in which a messiah is evoked—Hebrew, Greek, English—sets its compass by the messianic language that it, legitimately or illegitimately, claims to anticipate and to interpret. Revelatory speech anticipates redemptive speech, calls out to it, worriedly modeling itself on what it hopes it will say. In effect, statements about messiahs in whatever language are translations avant la lettre from an unknown and unknowable language, which may in fact turn out to be unlike anything we now call "language." This is what gives messianic statements their great semblance of power as well as, to be frank, their tendency to be ridiculed and denied. Statements about messiahs deny all the evidence of worldly language's fallibility, ephemerality, indeterminacy. Messianic statements themselves are already spoken by the messiah, or one who assumes his position—the statements are the messiah, for us, now, canceling time and the progress of misunderstanding, anticipating and supplanting a figure that wants to be determined neither positively nor negatively by them.[14]

The Chosen Mode

Within a single language, among the strategies and sets of marks and relations it calls its own, a similar problem arises. This is particularly the case in those languages that recognize the mode of statement or principle as its highest form. It is sometimes thought that this mode provides the answer to the most intractable problem of languages. The statement, and even more so the principle, is supposed to belong to a universal code beyond the babel of tongues, with its supposed universal translatability. If any mode of language could reach the messiah before he reaches us, a principle could. "All men are mortal" arrogates for itself the post-temporal position of a redeemer who can finally claim, without doubt and without contradiction, a clear view of this profane hypothesis as true.

In the (perhaps) special case of statements about messiahs and in principles of messianic behavior, the problem persists. Statement and principle reach out to a meaning or an event about which they have no right to assert anything.[15] A statement is like a little messiah. Insofar as it has meaning—that is, insofar as the statement is understood and its sense preserved until such time as it should prove true, it will have made a messianic arrival, arriving much earlier in the messiah's place. Moreover, when we say that "there is no messiah," messianism is already at work. What becomes interesting in this case is the intransigence of the messianism of statements. It continues to operate where it is flatly denied. What is the source of this messianism's special resistance? One obvious place to look is the syntagma that forms the basis of both statements. If we could show that the syntagma "there is" operated as a species of prediction or, dare we say it, as prophecy, we could know that it was the source of the problem. It is true: the existential marker "there" in English encourages us to think of ourselves as awaiting fulfillment of our speech in a state of affairs that is fundamentally different from it, separated from language in a being or a situation whose existence it asserts but with which it does not fully coincide. There is a messiah / the messiah is over there. The existential marker "there" may derive from the locative "there"; and yet, in departing from its spatializing origin, it does not sever all semantic ties. One could ask why English does not derive the existential marker from "here." Perhaps a linguistic accident, it also conveys a habit about existential claims in this language. The syntagma of existence, "there is," insofar as it has been conceived of as something like a gesture toward something distant or something beyond—beyond language, beyond the fleeting present—may be messianic in this way: It awaits confirmation in the arrival of the thing, which never is here but is always coming from "over there," a thing until whose advent (*bis*) and in whose name the truth status of the statement remains in suspension, albeit in a fairly delimited way.

According to the messianicity internal to "there is," which springs, we could guess, from the metaphysical assumption of a difference between the statement and the thing stated, the statement "there is no messiah" does not cease to announce an arrival, to predict its fulfillment in a coming thing or event, as the event of a not-coming. It doesn't really "not come." It comes as a nothing. And as is common with the statement form, the thing awaited (nothing) arrives first in language, in advance of itself. Arriving ahead of it, the statement is neither what creates nor even what discovers the arriving thing. Instead, it subordinates itself completely to the coming and draws all its authority from the deferred arrival. A minor and deficient pointer toward an arrival, a subpar prearrival in language. Despite its deficiency (it is not yet the thing), it does have its own effects. For one thing, in both syntagmas, "there is" / "there is no," time is conceptualized as the medium both of arriving things and of things that definitively do not arrive. Time arises from this way of speaking as a course, a movement. As such, time is conceived as underlying and synthesizing statement and the stated. "There is a messiah," like its negative counterpart, "there is no . . . ," implies that time "is there" to support the theory of language that silently determines this understanding of meaning.

No messiah is the messiah of anti-messianism. Awaiting something, awaiting nothing: Both project, on the basis of the concept of arrival, a sense that the period until the phenomenal arrival is consistent with itself. Both "there is" and "there is no" first and foremost assume a continuous time underlying the shift from language to event. This is not to say that atheism and monotheism are the same, or that this rather coarse manner of asserting a belief or a fact—"there is x"—is their only recourse. It does seem, however, at a minimum, in moments where they rely on principles (and not, say, purely on faith), that atheism and monotheism share an inability to rid themselves of a messianic moment that should arrive to confirm their truths, finish their sentences, and prove time to be ultimately what "there is" for us. And yet we cannot say "there is time," for fear of losing ourselves in a vortex.

There are many reasons for wanting to deny elements of the messianic equation, or indeed to deny the whole thing—historical reasons, natural-scientific reasons, moral and political reasons, and religious reasons, too, of course. And yet negating a messiah's existence leaves untouched, or so it seems, a messianism that is more pernicious if only because more deeply concealed. Negating a messiah's existence does not release us from the grip of the messianism internal to the statement or principle form. A messiah lives on in "there is none" to the extent that, although the existence of the messiah may be challenged, our concept of time remains, strengthened even by our use of the same linguistic gesture to attack it. If, therefore, the arrival of a messiah cannot be canceled and a messiah idea cannot be destroyed by any statement, the whole equation begins to take on a tyrannical and fateful character. How can one be rid of it if one cannot consciously turn against it? What can one say, how can one speak, and so forth?

A messiah who did not arrive would be hard to recognize. A messiah who might be coming but whose coming did not take the form of an arrival and whose path or route did not take the form of time would not return in the way all messiahs, even negative ones, do—to satisfy the terms of a contract drawn up and signed in the deepest history, a contract about the meaning of time. Not long after the "bis"-controversy, Kafka writes this in his notebook: *The decisive instant*[16] [Der entscheidende Augenblick] *of human development arrives when we let our concept of time drop away everlastingly.*[17]

Statements about messiahs assure us that we live in the middle of the contractual period, under the rule of "our concept of time," and not at either extreme. Messianic subjects can be relatively sure their responsibility for the order of things is minimal, living under a law whose revered legislators are dead and whose all-powerful judge has not yet opened the trial.[18] Non-messiah and messiah constitute time in this way, as a deferral of judgment. And messianic statements and principles participate in, or rather enact again each time, this deferral. This is why messiahs must arrive or be about to arrive and cannot just come or be coming. Already arrived, not arriving, is their mode of appearance. That they are predetermined to reach exactly to us and be meant for us and us for them is the reciprocal guarantee that our actions in the meantime have meaning, that they are both means to the messianic end (or at least not obstacles) and also merely the mean between distant extremes, while we wait for all we have stated is the case to be confirmed. The connection between irresponsibility and meaning will have to be investigated elsewhere. At the center of this reasoning, however, lies a discrepancy. When historical messiahs arrive, once believers have sold their belongings and dressed themselves for a new life, disappointment almost always follows. The messiah proves not to be the messiah or goes away again to return at the *right* right time. For beings accustomed to meantime,[19] to mean-ing and a measure of irresponsibility with regard to fundamental decisions, his departure or failure to appear must also be something of a relief. Still, this does not diminish the central part that the arrival plays in messianisms. Even if believers are spared the arrival once again, preserving for an hour, a week, a century "our concept of time," the concept of arrival still operates. "There is" / "there is no" messiah means in fact, since both of these will have had to arrive in advance, that neither statement is messianic or anti-messianic—enough.

Kafka's Messiahs

"Meantime," time that uniformly metes out its contents and reduces extremes to means, is hinted at in the note: *The decisive instant* [Der entscheidende Augenblick] *of human development arrives when* [wenn] *we let our concept of time drop away everlastingly* (immerwährend).[20] If the decisive instant, whatever its content or effect, arrives only when time will have been "let fall," then time should be conceived of as what produces an unwillingness to decide, a resistance to anything decisive. The indecisive meantime, as Kafka notes here, is not a property of a metaphysical entity "time" but rather the effect of a concept that we do not possess but that possesses us, and a quality of experience that holding onto the concept produces. Theologically, time is the curse of the fallen. Here it is time that undergoes a fall. Fallenness must fall. Masquerading as us and as the central determinant of "life," the time concept, although it appears to lead us to it, in fact stands between us and the arrival of a decisive instant, the messianic arrival.[21] Time is the very obstacle to the messiah, and with this the proper order is inverted. One is accustomed to thinking: As soon as—*bis*—the decisive moment arrives, things will change. This is what "decisive" means. It applies to the contents of time, but not to time's structure. In contrast to *kairotic* time, the "right time" at some point within a course of time, in this Kafkan dictum it is time that will have to be "let fall" if the decisive moment is to arrive at all. This other fall that overcomes the fall without stepping over it into eternity must occur in a scarcely imaginable, nontemporal moment. Indeed, we are asked to produce this fall "everlastingly" (*immerwährend*), a word intimately bound to "our concept of time." Time must be suspended for all time; and this makes sense, for if we allow it to slip back for even an instant, all is ruined. When the indecisive meantime is cut off once and for all, only then is one receptive to a decisive instant. Again, it is not some substrate "time" that Kafka—unlike Kierkegaard, several of whose books he read for the first time over the winter[22]—attacks here but the grim force with which the concept of time has a hold on us. When this same winter Kafka mentions "our time concept" again, it is to teach us just how far postponing judgment until the end of time is already a sentence executed on us. *Only our concept of time allows us to name it the last judgment, in fact it is martial law.*[23] In fact, one could suggest, without distorting Kafka's thought too much, that the punishment meted out perpetually by the final court is time itself.

In two of the notes Kafka wrote in notebooks in the fall of 1917, he mentions messiahs, and in these notes he navigates the straits of messianism and the cataracts of messianic anti-messianism by means of what are at first glance rather obscure formulations. In the notes he tells us, or tries to, how to rid ourselves of messianism without its returning secretly in another form and without our preserving time as meantime. The solution is not to negate it but to support it more strongly, albeit in a different way. In the notes he also offers a clue about how to accomplish the paradoxical requirement to "let" our time concept "fall" everlastingly. Both passages begin with the syntagma *the messiah will come*, which itself is a version of a messianic statement or principle. "The messiah will come" is in effect an analogue of the syntagma "there is a/no messiah," but it also announces the deferral hidden in the existential syntagma. In *the messiah will come* the existence of the messiah is asserted, and at the same time the disjunction between statement and fulfillment is legible in the tense of the verb.

On November 31 and then around December 5, 1917, Kafka wrote these two notes, each beginning "the messiah will come," in one of the small notebooks he carried with him during his stay at his sister's small rented farm northwest of Prague.[24] The dates are irrelevant . . . or almost. The year was thick with events personal and historical: end of the five-year S-and-M game with Felice, lung hemorrhage and diagnosis of tubercu-

losis, first attempt to learn Hebrew, intensification of the war before its
end, escalation of violence in the Czech struggle for independence, and,
on November 2, the Balfour Declaration, news of which rippled quickly
through Europe. By mid-November the text of the declaration had appeared in many of the journals that Kafka regularly read. These self- and
world-changing moments notwithstanding, during his stay in the country
Kafka withdrew to a great degree from the obsessions that characterized
his life in Prague. Most surprisingly, the diary entries slowed to a trickle
and in November stopped for two years. His letters focused on daily life in
Zürau, often lingering over interactions with animals. When he discussed
his illness or the final breakdown of his engagement, it was usually under
pressure from Brod, and in these moments his responses fill with sarcasm,
as though he were being forced to write on a topic he preferred to avoid.
Any writing activity he hides completely from his friends. "Since . . . I am
not writing at all" (Da . . . ich ja gar nicht schreibe) begins a paragraph to
Brod in a letter from the end of November.[25]

The messiah will come when . . . Both passages, written—or, as Kafka
would have it, "not at all written"—several days apart, begin with this
clause, and with this clause they also depart from one another. The difference does not only lie in that the first relies on "bis" to communicate its
temporal claims and that the second relies on "wenn," although this is also
important. But it is as though, after Kafka wrote the first passage, something in the writing bothered or embarrassed him and he had to all but
retract it, or the important part of it, in the second. The first note begins
with the line *The messiah will come* as soon as [bis] *the most unrestrained individualism of faith is possible, no one annihilates this possibility, no one tolerates its
annihilation, and so the graves open up.*[26] A theological-political treatise that
began with this assertion might go on to argue, in an extreme interpretation of Luther, that the "sola" in "sola fides" was all that mattered, that the
route to God could never be walked by a group, that the only purpose of a
collective of faith, therefore, was to give solace to individuals, to commis-
erate about the difficulty of the solitary journey each one had to make. And
yet it is not hard to see, speaking logically or historically, how a community
of faith could indeed be founded on the most radically individual relationship to God without in the least impinging on the commonality of the
content and institutions of belief. Ideas of God, believer, scripture, ritual,
faith, and most of all "the individual" can easily be shared; no reason they
can't even be normative; indeed, they must be in order for a practitioner
to be conceivable as an individual. What Kafka calls for, in contrast to the
individual according to the norm, is a multiplicity of norms, an individual-

ity of the idea, of the institution, and of the institution of the individual. More than an echo of Kierkegaard can be heard here.[27]

Even those who share belief in the same object—assuming this could be ascertained—will, *as soon as* [bis] *the messiah comes*, by the force of this requirement for plurality, not believe in the same way. "To believe" will not mean the same thing for all or maybe for any of them, when he comes. *The messiah will come as soon as the most unrestrained individualism of belief is possible.* The opening sentence in the first messiah note, although it takes the form of a prediction, promotes at the same time a loosening of theological determinations, calling for, at the most extreme, complete indifference with regard to the content and form of faith. Messianic conditions are imposed here, to be sure. The messiah will come not just anytime or to just anyone, and the messiah "is" as a "will be" (will have this or that quality, or will exist, in a manner recognizable as existing). Yet, so indifferent must the faithful become toward the form and content of faith that even the dead, who have no reason any longer for faith in anything, awaken to join them. In effect, the line argues that, in order for the messiah to come, faith has to be so emptied of content that it can include the absolutely faithless as full participants in its rewards. This faith looks nothing like faith. The messiah comes on the condition that faith become infinitely plural, and thus in any one case indeterminate, and in some cases indistinguishable from disbelief, in effect subtracting faith from the messianic equation. Each individual has *a* faith, but this means that faith in general is virtually meaningless. As a consequence, the parochialism of the messiah—our belief that he will arrive to us and for us and for us alone—has to be revised. Arrival can be the messiah's mode of appearance only insofar as he also arrives for those to whom he was not promised, for an indiscriminate collective to whose rainbow of faiths and meanings of faith would seem to correspond, as a result, various messiahs.

A plural messiah corresponds to an amalgam of faiths and not-faiths, and it also thus includes a not-messiah, or several of them. Before one takes Kafka at his word and begins to derive the consequences of this peculiar prediction, however, one should also take into account the second passage, written six days later. It imposes another heavy restriction that cuts into the plurality of faith and nonfaith that the first passage seems to assert. The *apokatastasis pantón* that Kafka supports on November 31, however far it goes beyond what Peter said in his speech at Solomon's portico,[28] will be revised on December 4 or 5.

The messiah will come only when he will no longer be needed.[29] The opening of the second messiah note signals a shift in Kafka's thinking about how

to talk about messiahs. It would be worthwhile to investigate not only this
shift but also others in and across these passages, as well as the intention to
make or allow shifts, insofar as it may be one of the strategies governing the
"gar nicht Schreiben" of Kafka's winter *auf dem Land*.[30] Displacements of
perspective, argument, logic, tone, and intention occur within and across
many of the passages so that, in any instance, it becomes risky to bet that
resemblances between them can secure their meaning. A case in point: Between November 31 and December 5 or thereabouts, a different messiah
arrives. It may well be that the first insight into a new messianicity disappointed Kafka, the plural messiah of a diaspora of faiths, so that the second
comes to correct or improve on it. It is most probably the case that both
passages, in the final judgment, didn't satisfy him, since he copied neither
into the fair copy of the small writings that he, wholly uncharacteristically,
prepared for publication, writing them out in a clean hand on small cards
and then preparing a typescript or having one prepared.

The second passage is the more famous of the two. *The messiah will
come only when* (wenn) *he will no longer be needed, he will come only after his
arrival, he will not come on the last day, but* (only/first, erst) *on the very last.*
On reading this one might ask: Has Kafka gone over to Felice's side? It
looks as though he has rejected the productive ambiguity, not to mention
the tension with and within the mother tongue, that "bis" implied for him,
settling instead for the less equivocal "wenn." Are his days as a "hellhound"
over? Has Kafka come to heel? Rather, he turns his teeth on himself. In the
second passage one type of faith is subtracted from the infinite spectrum
of faiths and messiahs evoked in the first. Any faith that reflects a human
need is not to be considered messianic. According to this Feuerbach-style
principle, a messiah could not resurrect the dead, at least insofar as the
dead want to be alive or we want them to be; he cannot alleviate suffering,
cannot restore the monarch to the throne or the people to their proper
geography. He cannot even prove to believers that their belief has been
justified, cannot fulfill the final and most primordial need underlying any
act of faith: the belief that it would have been right to believe. Faith is first
and foremost an unfounded decision for faith and, one might also say, a
decision in bad faith.

In this light, the two notes with their two principles of messiahs appear
to contradict each another. The first messiah will have fulfilled everyone's
need, everyone's faith, at the same time fulfilling the faith in faith, even if
the act is irrevocably plural. Plurality is singular; there is only one plural,
no matter how many are included. Where its messiah will fulfill everyone's
needs and desires, the second messiah will fulfill no one's. At a minimum

it will not have confirmed the underlying faith in faith, which constitutes faith's own secret need.[31]

The shift from "bis" to "wenn" in this fragment may be accidental; it may mean little or nothing. And then again, if "bis" is the marker by which Kafka differentiates between Felice's mundane understanding of an "engagement" and his messianic one, if "bis" for Kafka can cease meaning the "meantime" and designate the "decisive moment," then the replacement of "bis" with "wenn" here could well indicate a step back from this emphasis, although not necessarily a return to Felice's position of waiting. Something in the "as soon as" may have ceased to satisfy Kafka.

Perhaps this is a good juncture to interject a doubt, a tiny gesture of a lack of faith in Kafka's procedures. We could ask how any statement of principle—*the messiah will come when*—could expect to govern a messiah if he is the one who on his arrival suspends the law that has been in effect in the meantime, even when he does so by, against all expectations, fulfilling it perfectly, as Maimonides, for one, believed. Isn't this mode of language—the principle—a reflection of our desire for the certainty, authority, and permanence that we await? A faux authority, then, trumped up to look like authority that speaks, when it actually speaks, in ambiguous silence. Principles substitute for the true authority, and they also diminish it. A messiah who was subject to a law, any law, but also and especially to a law of messianicity that said a messiah was a messiah under this or that condition or by this or that name would be as unmessianic as anyone who lived in the meantime. This logic is troubling. A messiah subject to a principle would be forever awaiting himself. In order to remain the messiah, *the messiah will come when*—to borrow Kafka's legalistic formulation, the condition, the principle—*the messiah will come when* the principle of his arrival and when principles and "Law" no longer apply, when "will" no longer will be in force.

It is highly peculiar that Kafka would write—not at all write—in this way, in categorical statements of fact or principles written with the calm stroke of certainty and a light of clarity that could never be mistaken for hesitation or cloudiness. This is not the same Kafka of the parables, or so it seems. Little in their tone or form indicates that these passages pose problems of interpretation. In the first passage he deduces an absolute diversity of belief. In the second he infers the superfluity of the messiah's arrival with respect to human need and proclaims it as though it applied to everyone, in all instances, for all time.

A more famous letter to Felice—one of the last to her, not long after the renewal of the "bis" controversy—bears out our suspicion that Kafka

was conscious of a turn in his writing, a turn toward something like principles. About a month before noting down the messiah principles, Kafka
makes a confession: If he tested his life and work against his "ultimate goal"
(*Endziel*), it is clear that he does not and will not in the future act as though
his life corresponded to "a highest court" (*einem höchsten Gericht*). In other
words, he does not and will not live messianically. Rather, he has undertaken and will continue to undertake an operation he calls "Zurückführen,"
leading back, returning, reducing, retracing, on behalf of the "entire human and animal communities," their ideals and their commitments, drawing them back to the "simple precepts" (*einfache Vorschriften*) out of which
they sprang.[32] The language of law can be heard in this word, *Vorschriften*,
and something more, or less, than law. One hears the less codified provi-
sions and prescriptions that precede written law and fill in where it doesn't
reach. One hears the oral Torah that supplements and expands the written. To return—*zurückführen*—human and animal preferences (*Vorlieben*),
wishes (*Wünsche*), and ethical ideals (*sittliche Ideale*) to their origins in fundamental unwritten principles: This, he says, is his amessianic work. Then,
after outlining this program, he repudiates once again any hopes that it
will have a higher meaning. He has said that his life and his life's work will
never correspond to a "highest court"; instead it is beholden to a "human
court." And so the aim of Kafka's *Zurückführen* is not critical—he is not
proofing the foundations of human knowledge in order that the human
court be justified by purified, criticized transcendental principles. His aim
is rather to deceive the court: *Betrug*. "Und dieses," Kafka writes Felice of
the human court in which such basic principles of preferences, wishes, and
ideals are adjudicated, "and this I will moreover defraud, though without
fraud" (*und dieses will ich überdies betrügen, allerdings ohne Betrug*).[33] He plans
to reduce the manifold of human and animal behavior, psychology, and
ethics—almost the entirety of the scope of a practical philosophy—to its
precepts, not in order to better defend animals and humans in this court
but to defraud the court, even, he writes puzzlingly, if defrauding the court
will occur without deception. And to be sure, in a truly human court, without a higher instance, all decisions would be fraudulent, insofar as they
presented themselves as justified without justification. To betray such a
court is no fraudulent act, since the court betrays itself continually. Fraud
is rather the strongest, and perhaps also the first true, fidelity to the basic
lack of principles of a truly human court.

   A principle is: a Sentence that ranks before other sentences and other
truths and authorizes some or all of them on the basis of its status alone.
It would seem, then, that the two are highly compatible, principles and

messiahs: Both arrive "before" everything else, before themselves, even. Writing down a principle, like evoking the messiah, means taking dictation from a prior or even an a priori source. And yet the enunciation of a principle is not its fulfillment as truth or as practice, just as the evocation of a messiah is not his arrival or his correspondence to our prayers. Sentences about arrivals, even if they repeat predictions made first in the deepest past, do not bring about arrivals; instead, they feed off the detainment of the messiah in an indeterminate place. In effect, then, principles belong to the meantime and are just as incompatible with its end. To state as a principle that the messiah will arrive reproduces time as meantime and wards off any break, through a legal claim made on a figure who categorically refuses such claims. A messiah always returns as a stateless exile to confront the horror and unwelcoming violence of the law, which is by definition always against him, even and especially any law of messiahs.

If we add a line to the second messiah passage in Kafka's notes of 1917, some of these difficulties begin to be abrogated. *The messiah will come only when he will no longer be needed—*. Here Kafka adds: *He will only come after his arrival, he will not come on the last day, but* [only] *on the very last. . . .* Yet the distinction on which the final statement about the messiah's arrival hangs, the distinction between last and very last, *letzt* and *allerletzte*, seems as determined to frustrate our understanding as to satisfy it.

Maimonides' Messianic Share

In the fall and winter of 1917–18, Kafka was preoccupied with theological questions. So were his intellectual friends and interlocutors. In September, Max Brod had argued in the strongest terms in an article in *Neue Rundschau*, which Kafka read, that Zionism should not be degraded "to a mere political thing" (*zu einem bloßen Politikum*). It is essentially "a religious thing" (*ein Religiosum*),[34] where religion means an "immediate experience of the one and only God" (*unmittelbares Erleben des einigen Gottes*).[35] In a letter to Felix Weltsch the day before he noted down the first messianic principle, Kafka indicated his own interest in theological matters. Kafka intended to read Augustine's *Confessions*, at least in part to find out what kind of heresy Pelagianism was.[36] The letter also includes a barely veiled criticism of Weltsch's interest in religion: "That you turn to the religious surprises you?" Kafka chides. "You originally built your ethics without a foundation—the only thing I believe with certainty that I know about it—, and now you notice, perhaps, that it has a fundament. Would that be so strange?"[37] Kafka's criticism, that religion was left unthought in Weltsch's ethical theory, follows an earlier comment in a letter of November 15 in which Kafka alludes to Weltsch's "divergence [*Auseinandergehen*] from Max or even from me" on the subject of "belief and grace" (*Glaube und Gnade*).[38] In the letter of November 30 he also mentions, beyond Augustine, a figure we meet nowhere else in Kafka's correspondence or diaries: Moses Maimonides.[39] Kafka recommends that Weltsch read Solomon Maimon's autobiography, which contains, he makes a point to mention, "a digest of Maimonides' teaching."[40] Maimonides, it should be said, is, if not the first, then certainly the strictest and most infamous instituter of a messianism that operates solely by principles, or almost.

Like Kafka, Maimonides writes down messiah principles more than once, though the instances are farther apart in time and more similar to each other. Let us concentrate on his first statement of a messiah principle, since it is accompanied by the most thorough justification for the use of principles. It appears in his famous "Thirteen Principles of the Jewish Faith," which are set into his commentary on the Mishnah, completed in 1168. As with most of Maimonides' philosophizing, the principles appear in a commentary on a sacred text. The line on which he comments, the line that gives rise to the need for principles of faith and a messiah principle in particular, is the first mishnah of the tenth chapter of tractate Sanhedrin: "All Israel have a share in the world to come."[41] This announcement, although qualified later, does not immediately give any conditions for receiving the messianic share. It does not say which if any beliefs are required of one in order to be counted a member of Israel. Maimonides' introduction and the principles in it are thus a response to this problem.[42] The sentence "all Israel have a share in the world to come," he complains, has been an excuse for all sorts of faulty reasoning and wild imaginings. In fact, the words of the sages about the world to come opened by the messiah have been liable to three types of misunderstanding. The uneducated take the sages literally and see in their words only things that are familiar to them. When the rabbis say, "The land of Israel will one day produce cakes ready baked, and garments of fine silk," these believers prepare for a world in which they will eat and dress well.[43] The more educated take these words literally too but, instead of believing, they ridicule them as fantasies. A third class knows that the wise speak in parables and riddles and guess that there is a more general import to the sages' words, although without long study they cannot specify exactly what it is.

Maimonides adds to this a fourth class: Those who rely on principles. Justification for this turn he finds in the Mishnaic saying "In the world to come there will be no eating and no drinking, and no washing and no anointing and no marriage; but only the righteous sitting with crowns on their heads enjoying the splendor of the Shechinah."[44] All images, even the ones that depict the relation between the redeemed and God, are to be interpreted as parables, which means their image character must be taken away and replaced with an abstract meaning. "By their remark, 'enjoying the splendor of the Shechinah,' the sages do not mean a sensual enjoyment; the sages mean that those souls will reap bliss in what they comprehend of the creator."[45] Redemption consists in intellectual comprehension, and for this reason only principles, as rules of thought, can point the way to it. "I have thought fit to speak here concerning many principles belonging to fundamental articles of faith which are of very great importance."[46] In Maimonides' hands, principles of faith—*usul*, in the Judeo-Arabic in which he wrote, derived from a botanical metaphor, "roots," or, in the Hebrew into which it was almost immediately translated, *ikkarim*—supplant other mechanisms by which the religious group is constituted and preserved against disintegration or attack. To put it formulaically, Maimonidean "roots" substitute rational for mythic or historical criteria for the constitution and continuation of the collective. Physical proximity or historical continuity with God is replaced, in the principle form, with intellectual presence. The world to come is so far beyond art and imagination, one can relate to it only through a rule. Maimonides quotes Berachot 34b: "The world to come no eye hath seen save God."[47] In this way Maimonides' simplified "roots" are constructed to contain and preserve what cannot be seen until the otherwise unimaginable messiah arrives. All Israel have a share in the world to come—and the messiah himself will distribute this share on judgment day, or the day after; what we do know is that it cannot be received beforehand. And yet, a sharing out of the messianic share, accomplished in advance of the messiah's advent, takes place in and through principles. In what amounts to a theological earthquake, old marks and signs suddenly become insufficient. Israel receives its messianic share from the messiah, but the giving of a political share in Israel is accomplished by intellectual assent to fundamental principles well in advance. "When all these principles of faith are in the safe keeping of man, and his conviction of them is well established, he then enters 'into the general body of Israel.'"[48] The *ikkarim* prearrive the messiah and pass judgment in his stead.

Although they come at the end of the list of principles, after the assertions that God exists, is one, prior, sublimely large, immaterial, and so forth, the twelfth and the thirteenth principles, the messiah principle and the principle of the raised dead, are in effect first principles, principles of all the others. This makes sense, because *ikkarim* are by nature messianic, as much a force for the Jew in the meantime, across the span of history, as they are signposts for the end; they have a meantime function and an end-time significance, keeping minds turned toward the arrival. To see the stark difference principles made, a contrast is helpful. One alternative to principles was martyrdom, when unity through covenant, ritual, narrative, and political sovereignty were weakened or absent. In place of any of these, Maimonides introduces faith. He writes in the twelfth principle: "The days of the Messiah. This involves the belief and firm faith in his coming, and that we should not find him slow in coming. 'Though he tarry, wait for him (Hab. 11. 3).'"[49] And he goes on: "We must have faith in him, honoring and loving him."[50] What the object of this faith is, we cannot see or say. What we can say is, simply, despite appearances, that he will arrive, that he is his arrival. "There is a messiah," *the messiah will come when . . .* "though he tarry, await him," and before this: You, accept these principles. Before the content of the principle, the principle form. And so there are two messianisms at work in Maimonides' formulation, at least two. The usual messianism of scripture or of the ecclesia or of the psychological act of faith is supplemented by a messianism of principles, which becomes the medium in which faith is enjoined. Here principles become independent conditions of a messianic share, and they assume authority for it. At the same time, as with faith, their authority is sent out for confirmation in the messianic event of which we can make no image. Principles act as suspensions of and substitutes for all other modes of receiving the messiah in advance of his coming—sensual images, halakhic stories, attitudes, wishes, faith.

He tarries: If he did not, we would have image, content, existence; we would have his body. Principle is the messiah's linguistic body. A consequence of this reasoning may be the following: There will arrive, when he arrives, in addition to a messiah or the Messiah, another thing besides him or it, fulfilling the messianic dimension of the general principle of messianisms as such—the requirement to suspend content, image, story. What a messiah is, his being, the subject of the principle, arrives only with the messiah, or indeed afterward. Existence precedes essence, arrival precedes existence, and indeterminacy precedes arrival, including a special indeterminacy of principles. Maimonides' most radical postponement of the image, meaning, and content of the messiah in actuality makes it difficult if not impossible to know precisely when the messiah will have arrived. What will have arrived when he has arrived? That is what we cannot ever say in advance. And for this reason, corresponding to the two messianisms there are in the Maimonidean principle two principles. The exoteric principle says, "Wait for the messiah and a share will be yours"; the esoteric principle, the meaning of principles, as it were, says, "Wait and see what such a thing as a messiah might look like." And furthermore, "Wait and see what this sentence might mean." And wait and see what language it will be in, and what language is. Does it still count as waiting when the object is taken away, or when we cannot articulate it to ourselves? Does it still count as a principle when its sense is unconfirmable? Such an arrival does not so much divide sinners from the saved as show once and for all what the messiah or "a" messiah is. And the right language and the right rhetorical mode arrives with him—after him—as well. In its most rigorous formulation, if it is purged of all utopian, fantastical, imagistic, human, or anti-human content, when it is made into an empty ordinance, principle, or *Vorschrift* governing universal Jewish life (or any life), the messianic, as by law contentless, imageless, and without any predetermination—once the last haggadic element has been expelled (if we assume, of course, that it can be)—the messianic can no longer be imagined as an arrival, along with its conceptual corollaries: destiny, destination, predestination, and a coordinate system by which the reward can be triangulated. In its strictest formulation (to which Maimonides does not always adhere),[51] the Maimonidean messiah principle removes all criteria for judging that what arrives will have been what was promised, hoped for, called to, or legislated in the principle and that risks proving that the promise, hope, evocation, or legislation—let alone principle—are or were not appropriate.

In light of this kenosis of the messiah (and not the kenosis on behalf of him), we could write down another principle, or something of the sort, derivative of Maimonides, quoting him but also going somewhat against his faith in principles: Messianism will not have made sense until after the messiah will have appeared. The sense of his appearance—which is not an arrival, since it does not fulfill a need, meet an appointment, indicate the "for whom"—will arrive after him, once we have had time to experience whatever it is that he is. Only then do we become able to articulate what he may be or become for us. The concept of "messiah," the promise that fulfillment will correspond to promise, the promise that promising makes sense, with meantime its way and means—these are fragments or figments, awaiting completion or proof to justify them. And so, if it is a principle, it is a wishful principle and a wish for a principle, nameable here and now only in a fantasy of perfect clarity that Maimonides requires and with the same stroke prohibits. Parable, Maimonides calls it, and rightly. But the *Commentary on the Mishnah* avoids revealing here the more precarious implications of his rationalizing. In order to say definitively that haggadic legends or dreams about the messianic age are unreliable, Maimonides assumes, of course, a meaning, an image, a signified: enough of a content to decide that this or that image, and image per se, does not correspond to what the messiah will be or will have been. He will not, for example, be well dressed. It is foolish to think so. According to the most thoroughgoing logic of the messianic parable, however, one cannot prohibit what one cannot specify, imagine, delineate, or name. He may just as well be a dandy as a pauper, a fish or a fowl, gendered or ungendered, salvific or destructive, or neither, or both. We could ask, then, with Kafka in mind, how Maimonides can be sure that we must wait for what, by his own strict reasoning, can have no content. One surprising consequence of this reasoning is the following. An empty messiah leaves open the possibility that the messiah is already among us.

What we mean when we say messiah, *was der Messias heisst*, is undetermined—and so we wait, in some sense, without knowing whether waiting is the right activity or whether what we are doing is in fact the right kind of waiting. By banning images, Maimonides tries to avoid the weakness of a messiah dependent on the human imagination. As a consequence, he stumbles onto the harrowing idea of a messianicity whose content is deferred. This may be a clue to reading the second part of Kafka's reflection on time. *The decisive instant of human development arrives when we let our concept of time drop away everlastingly* goes on like this: *That is why revolutionary intellectual movements are right when they declare everything before them null and void, since nothing has happened yet.*[52] Nothing has happened: This nothing includes all prior messianisms and messianic principles within its sweep.

When, on or around December 5, Kafka writes, though it doesn't count as *schreiben* in any of the usual senses—record, produce, transcribe, inscribe, synthesize, communicate—that the messiah *will come only* [erst] *after his arrival*, Kafka betrays a promise made in Maimonides' intellectualized messianic principle. Kafka betrays the messianic essence of principles, leaving the messiah to come as pure contents, which determine, only after they appear, the shape of any messianism that could have preceded them. This is the more radical ramification of Borges's comment that Kafka invented his precursors. He comes amessianically—which is to say, without an arrival, rejecting all claims that he correspond to what should have preceded him. He may, he may not; it is irrelevant. From the perspective of this messiah, formal differences (for instance, past and future) are themselves restrictions on the future, and so, in contrast, a messiah of contents—whose uncontainable elements "stick out" of whatever form or law, just as perhaps Odradek's elements stick out from its being, affirming it—rejects even the hope for absolute alterity. His difference may or may not be absolute. He

comes after the desire for him has petered out or at its very height, after
his own arrival, which may well mean before, beyond the constraints of any
prediction or principle, including the constraints of "our concept of time."
An after-messiah (but by no means a post-messiah) disregards principles
and their intention; we are saved, if we are saved, not from our needs but
from time, in his very indifference to it.

This is something like what Walter Benjamin will formulate in 1921
in his "Theological-Political Fragment." Nothing has happened; this is
what messiah means and does. Nothing has happened, but especially not
any messianism. For Benjamin, everything happens with and through, "after" (*bis?*) him, in a extratemporal sense. A history attracts itself to him ex
post facto, a history that receives an unprecedented shape only through
him. "Only the messiah himself consummates all historical happening—
namely, in the sense that he alone redeems [*erlöst*], consummates [*vollendet*],
creates [*schaft*] its relation to the messianic." (Erst der Messias selbst vollendet alles historische Geschehen, und zwar in dem Sinne, dass er dessen
Beziehung auf das Messianische selbst erst erlöst, vollendet, schaft.)[53] The
messiah is the one only after whom there could exist something like messianism, and also time.[54]

To distinguish these two amessianic messianisms will be critical for us,
going forward, if we want to come to terms with the future we keep inheriting from deconstruction, the future's future, if we want to know how to
behave, what attitude to take toward a broken, postponed futurity—even
if it is no coherent attitude—sometime before we stumble into it, again. A
few suggestive remarks will have to suffice for now. Where Benjamin speaks
of future history as an act of consummation, creation, and redemption,
a retrospective, selective, and at least partially fictional teleology, Kafka
speaks of an arrival after the arrival, a nonarrival, which loosens us from
the magnetic pull of "before" and "after." It is not that he arrives late, so
that we are forced to wait a little longer and eat our meal cold, but that this
messiah does not come in the form that has been awaited. His coming is
not arriving, but it is also not an ever repeated deferral of arrival, which, to
make sense, would have to keep the idea of an arrival once and for all alive.
In this they are united, Kafka and Benjamin: The messiah is more important for his being here and now than for his perpetual to-come. Benjamin's
messiah is form-giving, his backward glance producing a course of history as if there had been a traditional messianic trajectory. Kafka's messiah
is form-dissolving or he simply does not recognize such a thing as form.
Where Benjamin seeks to disentangle the messiah from any determinism
by giving all the determining power to him, the post hoc power to shape

the past, to consummate "what never was," Kafka envisions a messiah who does not determine anything, an undetermining messiah, not determined as messianic in this or that way in advance, and so, one who is in advance of all messianisms (unmessianic, unexpected, unfulfilling) whether of principle, of history-shaping, of absolute alterity—one who is already here in the undone, incomplete, chaotic, vague, or cloudy. Benjamin reverses the stream of messianic causality, while Kafka dams it up. What Borges says in this light is partly wrong, or perhaps self-serving. Kafka may invent his precursors, but this is just Kafka the writer, who, in Borges's estimation, is a messiah in the way that Benjamin describes one. The messiahs that Kafka envisions do not operate in this way. Kafka's messiahs are against time, against history as formed experience, against consumations, even retrospective ones. It is not the shape of time but the seeming trivialities that find no place in any form, on whose behalf time needs to be not simply reversed or put out of joint but suspended as a category.

At last, the last last—we should come to terms with, by which I mean find words for, the way Kafka thinks about last things, given his rebuke of all conceivable messianisms as principles-in-advance, which may be related, we should add, to his almost pure aversion to narrative endings. What he writes about "lasts" on December 4 and 5, 1917, is intuitively profound but conceptually inscrutable. About it we must know at least one thing, otherwise we are lost. We must know, or at a minimum be able to come to know, the difference between a last day and a last day of all, if this is how we should render in English the crucial distinction between "am letzten Tag" and "am allerletzten." *He will not come on the last day, but* [only] *on the very last . . .* This is, we should confess, his last explicit word on the subject of messiahs.

We do not have to bring up mathematics—and indeed Kafka did not —to see that at least one of the possible differences implied in the disjunction "last"/"very last" is the difference between a run-of-the-mill limit and an absolute limit. Without direct reference to mathematics, nevertheless, points, lines or "ways," infinities, and limits or borders crop up repeatedly in the scraps. We can talk about these figures the way Kafka did, without paraphrasing them in the vocabulary of a supposedly more precise discipline. Just as, for mathematics, the concept of a point is nonsense outside a geometric context, and just as for philosophy the concept of beginning is nonsense outside a temporal context (see Aristotle's critique in the *Physics* of Plato's description of time in the *Timaeus*), the concept of last is nonsense outside an infinite context, or at least one that appears infinite, such as life. Parroting Kierkegaard, Kafka warns that *the fact that our task is ex-*

actly as big as our life gives it the appearance of infinity.[55] Life appears to the living to have no limit, and indeed the limit is more elusive than any other part of life. Death is, in every case—in the case of mine or yours, theirs, past deaths and future deaths—the semblance of death that is fully a part of life.[56] To put it otherwise, death is after death. Everything that could belong to another side is in fact a part of this one.

Think the last, just try. A series admits only before and after, and never, we should say, a before without an after. "Before what?" you would ask. And once the limit is passed it is no longer last, but the first of another series with its own last, or lack of one. Lasts inaugurate ever broader series in a neverending *scala ultimatae.* To think a limit that is only last and not also first is what we have to try to think—yet no lifetime, it seems, will suffice to produce this thought, since it is not a matter of time or intelligence but an *alogon*, an absurdity that steals intelligence away. When we say we are thinking the last, we are always thinking the second to last.

Thus the last is always before something, penultimate, and so a general description of "last things" can perhaps be posited. Only when a limit has proven itself to have not been the last limit can it be said to be a limit. Being last and saying "last" do not coincide; "last" starts it up, again. On the very last day we always again celebrate that something has not ended completely; saying "last" shows confidence that the final last is imminent but not yet upon us. Termination is interminable—and when time cannot propose an end to itself, or a proper mode of transit into eternity, it begins to lose its determinacy as well. If the final limit, what all finite, partial, temporary lasts, echoes of the absolute terminus, imitate is indeterminate, finitude begins to look as if it had no final determination. This is also to say that there will be no day when all these minor and particular limits meet their great limit. As an ontological feature, limit is unbounded; as a concept, it is indeterminate. A "last day" formally participates in a "last of all"—it instantiates it but in a degraded fashion, and each "last day" refers to a "last of all days," in which the idea of a limit of a series would meet its ultimate shape. If the last day of all has no shape, how can we separate anything from anything?

This is also to say that "last" is always a transition. The calendrical series of days, modeled on the natural-number series, implies transitions, although it does not represent them pictorially. However we make pictures or imagine the transitions between time units, on the last day of all this feature of time does not occur; no more transitions; the very last is a medium or mode in which transition makes no sense. And so the change from time to eternity can look like anything *except a transition.* That is to say, the metaphor for it is no longer locomotion, and thus also not change. In a typical Kafkan turn, we are lead to believe that this does not mean the end of eternity—not at all. It means, simply, that the way to eternity is not a way. If eternity cannot be accessed, made present, entered, transitted to, represented with metaphors of motion, then metaphors of nonmotion may be the proper mode of presentation, or at least this is one of Kafka's wagers. Eternity presents itself to those who refuse change. Paradise appears when we stop striving. The messiah does not come, if coming is a means to arrival; we must consider that he was, instead, never away. Under these conditions, looking for a difference between a last and a last of all, seeking the difference that makes the ultimate ultimate, distances us from him again and re-ups the quest.

One solution to these dilemmas that Kafka entertains in the scraps and notes from that winter is the following. He does not try to do away with eternity or the other world. It serves a purpose as a fantasy, for one thing. The fantasy that transit, change, development, "coming" and "arrival" and all that they imply, foresight, planning, promises, contracts, law, generation and generations, are possible is a motivation for much human activity, and as such it is also a justification for living a certain way, and *no human being can live an unjustified life* (kein Mensch kann ein ungerechtfertigtes Leben leben).[57] If one can put the drive for justification aside for a moment, however, one can be transported—to where one already is. If human action implies a messianic continuum of lasts leading to and drawing on a final last in which the meaning of "last" is once and for all determined, then a kind of impassivity and inaction, a resolute refusal of ending, may be the same thing as a messiah who has released us from the need for justification. Whenever things look unjustified, in other words, the messiah may be there.

CHAPTER 12

Messianic Not

Werner Hamacher

If the Messiah—as is said—"comes," then he not only changes the relations between humans, between humans and things, between each individual thing and itself, but he thereby also changes the relations of space and of time. If the Messiah "comes," he changes the relation called "coming."

If the time *until* the "arrival" of the Messiah is represented as a linear extension from the past into the future, then no longer may the messianic time itself be the time of this representation; it may no longer be the linear movement from an earlier to a later; nor may it be the inverse movement from the future into the present and the past. Without being able to know before its "arrival" how this messianic time is shaped—or whether it is "shaped" at all—one must nevertheless assume, even now, that within it all coordinates of familiar time may be displaced in such a way that what was future may now be past, what was past may be present, what was present may be another present or other than the present. Absolutely nothing can exclude the possibility that there are more than three dimensions in this time—at least a fourth, in which these three relate to, are loosened from, and transform their relationship with one another. And since this fourth dimension for that *other* time must already be conceded now, the time of this now also cannot be thought without that *other* time and thus cannot be thought without what is perhaps something other than time—and therefore other than *is*.

This consideration is a mere requirement of the structure of messianicity—that everything be other and also that the becoming-other not remain what it is. That the time of the Messiah could be a time *other* and otherwise structured than the time *before* his arrival requires no dogmatic pronouncement and depends on no legitimation by a historical religion or sanction by any accredited belief—whether synagogal or ecclesiastical, orthodox or heretical. If the time of the Messiah were only a future epoch—of concord, of justice, of happiness—if it could be reached by the advancement on a time line or by a leap in this time sequence, then this messianic time would be only the continuation of the movement of time leading out of a missed or discarded past into a desired or feared future. Then absolutely nothing about the temporal schema with which we are familiar—if, indeed, we are familiar with it—would change, and the messianic change could only insert itself *into* this woeful schema, this schema of woe, which is that of time, without effecting even the least change in this schema, not to speak of an overturning transformation. The representation of messianic time, which is essentially the representation of a messianic *future* and of the *arrival* of the messianic realm, this representation of one who *comes*, of a coming time and a coming other—of another world or another sense—amounts to nothing other than the domestication of this other in the house of time. It amounts to such a domestication even and precisely when the end of time is made into the goal of time and when the beginning of an *aeternitas* or *sempiternitas* is supposed to confirm the reign of time and to secure its house. Even when the end of time is thought to be, for its own part, temporal—as the time of the end, the time of ending, and the time of finitude—time remains within the horizon of its three-dimensionality, its terminability and fulfillability; in short, it remains thought within the framework of its possible self-sufficiency as (a modifiable and, in the modes of past, present, and future, modified) presence—and remains *un*thought as a time open to the *other*, the messianic time, to this *other* that must be able to be *no* time.

With the question of the Messiah arises, first and foremost, the question of the structure of time and its temporalization—not only of the remaining, coming, and passing *in* time but of the remaining, coming, and passing of time *itself*—and thus the question of the modal categories of the possibility, actuality, and necessity of a transformation that figures in the concept of time, and of a transformation of time *itself*, a transformation of the transformation that is time. The question of the Messiah concerns above all a modification that goes beyond the modes of possible, actual, and necessary being captured by the categories; it concerns the form, the formation, and the transformation of the transcategorial "being" named in the categorial modalities. This question asks: *Is* the Messiah? And more precisely it asks: In what *sense* can it be said of the Messiah that he *is*, even if it can in each case be said of him only that he *comes* and that he *will be*? For the discourse of messianic time is that of another time, which brings with it not merely another future but another futurity, not only another present but another presence, and which brings with it another time, another temporality—and, perhaps, something other than temporality. Since what is called "Messiah" must be thought as the disruption of the homogenous continuum of time, it must be thought both as a discontinuation and as a start of time—as the coming of another coming of time, the future of another future of time, temporality as alteration itself.

In a footnote to "Nudity" (Nudité), the preface to his book *La pensée dérobée*, Jean-Luc Nancy makes a remark in which—for the first time, it seems, in his writings—he touches on the problem of messianicity. I will refrain from commenting here on Nancy's remarks on the concept of messianicity in Benjamin, Derrida, and Agamben, because I believe that these remarks rest on misunderstandings that are less important than the misunderstanding that Nancy correctly attacks. I will confine myself to a brief—perhaps too brief—commentary on the single sentence in which the footnote addresses the problem just outlined. It follows the sentence "There is the to-come of a naked coming" (Il y a l'à-venir d'un venir nu) and reads, "If it is a matter, for us, of 'deconstructing Christianity'—the task of a work in progress—then, after the Messiah, no kind of messiah comes, and another coming comes, *or, rather*, a beyond of coming in general." (S'il s'agit, pour nous, de 'déconstruire le christianisme'—programme d'un travail en cours—, alors après le Messie ne vient aucune espèce de messie, et vient une autre venue, ou bien un au-delà de la venue en general.)[1]

"Or, rather" (*Ou bien*). It is almost superfluous to point out that the contention that, after the Messiah, no further Messiah will come accords very badly with the canonical texts of Christianity, which most decidedly announce the return of the Messiah, a second coming, obviously "another coming" (*une autre venue*) in another sense than what Nancy announces. It may be just as superfluous to insist that every "deconstruction of Christianity"—a task that certainly belongs among the most urgent undertaken since Kant and, who knows, perhaps since Paul and perhaps even since Jeremiah—also has to consider the messianism of Judaism and the near-absence of messianic perspectives in Islam: the not-yet and the never of a messianic occurrence in both of the other monotheisms. On the other hand, it is not superfluous to remark that Nancy's decisive formula, "and another coming comes, or, rather, a beyond of coming in general" (et vient une autre venue, ou bien un au-delà de la venue en general), represents an aporia and a challenge to the thinking of coming, of the Coming, of the future. An other coming, in particular a second, is still a coming; the coming of a "beyond coming in general" may of course be the coming of something other than coming, but also this other would still have to come—it would be in extremis, the coming of a not-coming. As such, it would offer the aporia—the path-lessness, the un-adventality or nonoccurrence (*Unankünftigkeit*)—of coming; it would be bare coming-to-presence (*An-wesen*), approaching-to-presence (*Heran-wesen*), without presentness (*Anwesenheit*) and without a stable, lasting, substantial presence (*Präsenz*). That coming-beyond-coming would be, in Nancy's words, "naked occurrence" (*survenance nu*)—a "survival" (*survenance*) that most likely translates Heidegger's term *Überkommnis* (overcoming) from *Identity and Difference* and designates in each context both the taking place of transmission and the unexpected, unprepared entrance of an event that breaks with the continuum of time and its arrival from the future.[2] *Überkommnis* (overcoming), "occurrence" (*survenance*) is the over-adventality (*Überankünftigkeit*) without a stay and thus the nakedness of a coming beyond every coming of the determinate or even determinable, anticipated or anticipatable, projected or projectable. Considered as an overcoming (*Überkommnis*), the future would be *simultaneously* un-advental and over-advental, and this impossible simultaneity (of the *un* and the *over* within the *ad* of advent)—we could thus add—would be the decisive, the critical trait both of the future and of time in general, a trait opening as a fissure in time, a rupture of its coming and becoming.

One can comment somewhat more discursively on this aporetic coming—to which Nancy refers only in this one Heideggerian formula of the coming of a beyond-coming—in the following manner: If the future is to be thought in its pure movement, if it is to be thought as itself, and thus as mere coming without the arrival (*Ankunft*) of any sort of present, and thus thought without any determination through this present, then it must be thought as come-able—as the mere possibility of coming or as the possibility that is itself nothing other than coming, the coming of the coming without term or determination. If, however, the coming itself is merely coming, then it is in no sense already there; it is not an actual, in some way empirical or sensory coming, nor does it accord with a transcendental schema that would constitute its coming-to-be. It rather voids the sense of its ever being present and dissolves the structure that grants the actuality of its being coming; indeed, it can never—so long as it, as coming, is referred to as coming—and at no time (namely, in no coming) *be* a coming. It is not we who wait; the coming itself waits for the coming. It is the already-there of the still-never-having-been-there and of the never-ever-being-there.

The mere possibility, then—the capability (*Vermögen*), the inclination (*Mögen*), and the power—of coming turns out to resist itself and its self as its naked *im*possibility—the inability (*Unvermögen*), the structural incapacity, the powerlessness to come. If, however, the future, as the letting-come of time, is the becoming possible of time; and if it, as mere allowing, is the restraining from coming and thereby its not-becoming-possible, then the categories of being-possible, being-actual, and being-necessary—the primitive transcendental concepts of the understanding and the formative schemata of our thinking—can no longer have any validity. The structure of the future is *ana-categorial*. Future means: the coming, while coming, does not arrive; its nonarrival comes. Only thus does it remain the future, mere time. Time is not the river in which events move but what flows away from itself and backs up against itself: the parting of waters, the incessant divide, self-discontinuation—not one single time is it the same river, and thus it is not a river at all. Time *is*, transitively, its not-being—its in-transition—and thus both the attestation and the contestation of its *not*, a *not* against the nothing in each of its moments, each of its dimensions or *ekstases*, in its coming as in its remaining and its parting, a future beyond any future. Time is structurally futural; but its futurity does not belong to the three modalities of time and being, it is not a being-future that adds to their being-present and their being-past but remains a fourth "time" of a fourth, nonmodal and nonmodalizable "being," or un-being.

If, however, the *An* stripped of its essence—of its coming—is the future as bare time, and if this *An* of the future allows absolutely no decision concerning whether it is the *An* of a coming or of a not-coming, then the more formal—the more naked—structure of the *An* is that of the coming-*or*-not, the leap that opens with the "or" and, within it, the "or" as opening (*Öffnung*), as disclosure (*Eröffnung*) of the open and as the revelation (*Offenlegung*) of the realm in which something might occur. *Or*—that is the "naked coming" (*venue nue*), the *sit venio verbo, venudité* of time, thus of the future, thus of sense, thus of being. *Or*, that is to say, time-*or*-none is the *or*igin of temporalization, the fourth dimension of time, which in every here and now displaces just this here and just this now, and which thereby also displaces the structure of times that are organized by past, present, and future. Precisely this time, this fourth, may—and it alone should—be called *messianic time*. Every time and every dimension of it must, however, in a singular way be shot through with it, with this future and with its pending *An:* The past also comes out of this future, also the present, if it comes and over-comes us.

With this fourth, this un- and over-time, that transforms any conceivable time, the categories of possible and of actual being are transformed as well: Possibility would no longer precede actuality, the possibility of the present would not lie in the past, the possibility of the future would not lie in the present—possibility would not be *essentia* as *exigentia existentiae* (Leibniz); there would exist no relation of progression between *essentia* and *existentia*, none between possibility and actuality, none between an already given and its future, be it extension, continuation, explication or decay, diminution, or destruction of this future. Essence would be subsequent to existence; possibility would offer itself only with actuality, the future only with the present. The notion of the arrival of the Messiah is thereby transformed. If the Messiah transforms time, then the time of the Messiah—the time in which or as which the Messiah appears—is no time we know. The future of the Messiah may then already be a past; then the Messiah may be in every now, here, there; the now and here might then be a never and nowhere. If the Messiah is only whoever, or whatever, it is that opens and transposes the temporal order, then he, she, or it may always also not yet still come; then it is inadmissible—indeed, against the *sense* of the Messiah—to speak of its advent or its future; then it is mistaken and misleading to speak of an *à-venir* at all without at the same time conceding that this *à-venir* must be capable of having a completely different sense from that of a future present and from that of a region accessible in the crossing of the temporal order into the future. The continualism of the ideology of progress, as Benjamin knew, is a fundamentally anti-messianic conformism, above all because it conforms to the transcendental form of intuition of mechanical time. But only that time is messianic that dissolves its transcendental form and with it every form.

The Messiah, the Coming One par excellence, does not come, and if he comes, then only in such a manner that he goes—for only one who goes can come. He does not come, and if he comes (*kommt*), then only in such a manner that he does not arrive (*ankommt*) and that his non-coming arrives with him. If, however, he were to arrive, then the *An* of his coming (*Kommen*) would mark the impossibility of precisely this coming and the un-advent itself; then it would be more than a coming, an excess beyond coming, from which coming would be left behind. It would be *over-*

coming (*Überkommnis*), *survenance*, but not as a—merely psychologically conceived—surprise (*Überraschung*) but as *ex-venance* and *é-venance*, as e-vading (*Ent-kommen* and *Ent-Kommnis*). It would be the *ex tempore* of time and of its advent. The coming-to-presence (*An-wesen*) of messianic time can emerge only out of its non-essence (*Un-wesen*), and if it is truly coming-to-presence (*An-wesen*), then only as the *An-* of this *Un-wesen*.

No Messiah, only that would be a Messiah.

In the Messiah, no *who* would come and still less a *what*; in him would barely come, bared, manifest and open to it*self*, the *that* of this coming— and this *that* in its doubling as *that* or *not that*. That something yet still comes always means that it may also not come. In the Jewish tradition, this doubling is thought as the duality of the dying Mashiach ben Joseph and of the victorious Mashiach ben David. In the Christian tradition, this doubling is concentrated in the one person of the dying Christ and Christ resurrected from death, of the once and once again coming Christ. Both pairs of Messiahs, the one presumably the double of the other, are integrated into a dual and diachronic scheme of power and impotence, triumph and defeat, death and survival, which respects the ordering of chronological succession and its repetition and reversal. The Judeo-Christian paradigm certainly does not introduce this chronological order, its splitting and reversal for the first time, but it installs them as a historiographical schema that even today dominates historical belief well beyond the realm of Judeo-Christian civilizations. The resources of messianicity are not, however, exhausted with the messianic pair of doubles; for, while the ordered succession of times is thought within it, the coming-forth of time, its temporalization, and the displacement of time arising therefrom are not.

The idea of the Messiah—that is, the idea of a future from which any temporal order springs forth, the idea of a time that is constitutive and at once deconstitutive of any possible structure of time—this idea of a messianic time is first exhausted, used up and clarified, in the thought of a Messiah that is not one at all. The Messiah cannot be one of the two Judaic or Christian Messiahs; he cannot be the two Messiahs one *after* another (or else he would follow a temporal order that would be displaced by his coming); he cannot be one *through* the other without reducing this other to a mere tool; he must be the one Messiah *of* the other; he must be the *that* of a *not-that*, the existence of an in-existence and thus the *not* in and against a nothing; he must be the leap of a not-nothing.

Only that future that comes as its not-coming can be the bare future itself. Only that Messiah who saves nothing and saves the nothing of the Messiah would be truly a Messiah. He would be the savior of the unsavable. His current name should therefore be understood as a normalizing abbreviation of the all too heteroclite and stuttering "Me-Messiah."

Thus far my—admittedly hyperbolic, admittedly extra-vagant—commentary on Jean-Luc Nancy's remark about the structure of messianicity and the transformations that are necessary in the course of a "deconstruction of Christianity." This "deconstruction," one should add, must be not only a theoretical but a historical alteration and, precisely for this reason, first and foremost a change in the understanding of historical time, in the understanding and the experience of "temporality," of the "shape" and the "essence" of time, and must therefore above all concern the structure of coming, of the future, of the messianic. Nancy sees it as linked to a Judeo-Christian inheritance; I do not doubt this heritage but do doubt that the structure of messianicity is thoroughly determined by it. The thought of messianicity is the thought of a wish—or the wish of a thought—that holds itself open to the future and to a future of futures, thereby first allowing temporal orders to establish themselves. It is in advance of every accredited religious system, of every imaginable religion demanding belief or even obedience, and beyond every such religion, beyond every belonging to a confession. It is, even if Christian communities maintain the opposite, not Christian, and, even if the prophets first used this name—in an initially wholly different sense, as we know—it is not Jewish. It does not allow itself to be confined to any civilization, for it precedes and goes beyond each one. It cannot be civilized, legitimated, or delegitimated. It is the dimension—or *ekstasis*—of a furious or desperate expectation, of a furor toward the other and against the other, which is always dampened into compromise formations by religions and societies and thus ducked or icily rejected and ostracized. Messianicity is the *n*existential structure—the ex-structure—of being-there as the transcendence into being-out, being-open, and being-otherwise-than-being. It is not Christianity that deconstructs Christianity but the un-Christianizable messianicity, the amessianicity within it, its own outside. We are, now, perhaps at the point—it may be a very long point, a fermata—in history at which the tensions of the structure of messianicity come, slowly or quickly, to an explosion. What we explore, if we think clearly and with a minimum of protective devices about these tensions within the "bare coming" (*venue nue*) between the messianicity and the amessianicity of what is to come, is part, only a small but not a negligible part, of this fermata of the explosion.

One more remark for further clarification on the margin. In the analysis of the structure of time one must consider more closely that the bare future—the sheer *An* and *Heran* of its movement—has hitherto been thought as a "coming-toward-us" (like an arrow) and has thereby been assumed to be one that is directed to us, determined for us, due to us, and therefore cognizable and recognizable by us. We—or rather the I constitutive of time—are represented as the target of an arrow. (In his *Theological-Political Fragment*, Benjamin speaks of such an arrow and of its relationship to the messianic realm—but not without complicating its direction with that of another, contrary arrow.) The arrow of the future is represented as coming upon us from *in front*. The concepts of time throughout modernity are governed by a veritable obsession with the pre-, the ahead- and the in-front-of-us, with pre-sentation and prolepsis in Kant, with production in Hegel and Marx, pro-tention in Husserl, the "going-forward into the future" in Heidegger, with the pro-ject and the anti-cipation. But the future that lies ahead for us remains an obstructive, an obsessive, and a sedimented time; it remains the time of a predetermined, controllable, supervisable place, a topo-logical time: the time *for* us and *before* us, presenting itself, in principle, to our sight and foresight, an exclusively theoretical and ideational time without any other extension than that of a line directed toward the point of a constitutive ego. It remains the time of control, of self-domination, self-regulation, and self-policing, the economic and eco- and ego-technological time, since it is the time that approaches *frontally* or comes *frontally* toward us as the place of its determination. It is a directed time, a time of intention, in which the self comes back to itself. This coming time (*Zukunft*) is essentially a time coming-back (*Zurückkunft*). It is the ur-time of subjectivity as it develops itself in time—a time under the repetition compulsion of the self. But just this compulsion to think time as coming-to, as coming-back to the place of its origin and therefore its destination, indeed to think of it as coming at all, can be read as the index of another possibility—namely, the possibility that it misses or lacks precisely this intention. It may, this future, also go past us; it may pass by us, pass over or through us, without *concerning* us—unremarked and ungrasped, since not constituted by our consciousness.

In every *An*, if it remains without essence, as it must, something moves past us, a *lateral* future, a peripheral possibility, that we have not even *not* chosen. As what is detached from *us* as its point of destination, this infinitely lateral future is the still barer future, the one disrobed of any subjectivity. Only this is, in the literal sense of the word, parousia, a *para*-ousia, not that of the frontal but of the lateral *An-wesen*, of a future not on one but on different sides, a future that is spatial—and spatial to the extreme. For time is not spatial if it collects, bundles, and concentrates many times into one point, line, circle, or sphere; it is spatial only if, multilateral and multi-

*trans*lateral, *for* each and *in* every sense peripheral, it does not relate space-time *to* us concentrically and if it does not contract it *around* us in order to sublate and preserve it in the concept—the concentration of relations par excellence. Time has as yet been thought only as relation, in particular as an in-itself negative relation, and always as *our* relation *to ourselves*—as self-affection and thereby as the constitution of a self. It is still conceived of as such a relation when it is thought as contingency, for contingency—the possibility to be otherwise or even not to be at all—is, since it is capable of becoming actuality, already essentialized and solidified into the truth of *our* essence. But what is in question is exactly the relationship to us in which time consists—and the un-relatedness (namely, un-adventality) without which it would not be time. If it is un-advental exclusively in its frontal relationship to us, then its *An*-character is thought only restrictively: Then it is the arrow that is delayed and pauses in flight, or the arrow that is followed by a myriad of others each of which—up until the last—is absorbed by us and whose delays scan the meter of our lives. However, the "*An* without *Wesen*" of time does not follow any direction whose start and endpoint would lie in us; it must always be able to take place going past us, without regard for us, without return to us, without even a merely thought or (transcendentally) imagined relation to us, and thus in extremis as an "*An* without space" and as an "*An* without *An*." This *correlative* possibility of an *irrelational* time and of a future of futures that is not oriented toward us and that does not have its *origo* in us—one may ask whether one *can* still think it, but one *must* think it in the attempt to think bare time and a future stripped of all teleological determinations.

If messianicity is sheer futurity, and if futurity is stripped of the protective figure of the *before*-us and the *to*-us, then the Messiah must also be able to come from the past; he must also be able to be there now and here, and he—bare time—must be able to pass us by any time: not only before our eyes and over our heads but behind our backs and under our feet, right and left, however we turn ourselves, without our having the chance to direct our attention, our consciousness, our capacity for cognition and recognition to him—yet still within the space of this possibility, according to the possibilities of space. With this, the concept of coming, of arriving, and of the future has already just as fully forfeited its formative power as the corresponding concepts of passing away and of remaining. If the coming of messianic time, the coming of time itself, is stripped of its frontal presentation, then the entire rhetoric of coming must be given up. The future can no longer be called what-is-to-come and can no longer be grasped as what-is-to-come if it is bare future and thus denuded of the placing-before (*Vor*-stellung), *pro*-tention, and *pro*-duction of its coming.

The Messiah, if he comes, does not *come*.

If, however, messianicity, in a further step that is already implied by the dissolution of the figure of the *pre*- or *pro*-, is also stripped of the apotropaic schema of the around-and-about-us and of the laterality of space-time and thus emancipated from the possibility of a relationship to us, then the coming and passing time is no longer restricted to the concentric space of the capacity for consciousness; then it is the absolutely *non-advental*, the inappropriably *exvental*, the directionless and orientationless time, time without origin and goal, without determination and sense. Heidegger's question in the last sentence of *Being and Time*—whether time manifests itself as the horizon of being and therefore as the horizon of the meaning of being—loses its pertinence, since it holds onto the phenomenality of time, although time does not form a phenomenon. Time surpasses any pro-jection, any before, and with it any sense and orientation; it withdraws from that region "wherein the comprehensibility of something resides."[3] A time without *our* comprehension—only this would be bare time, stripped of *us* and of our question of sense and our sense-horizon; it would be a-horizontal time, and thus it alone would be time itself: no horizon of understood or even merely understandable being. A "future" without form and one that peels away all forms ever adopted by it and all possibilities of form; only this, which *is* not "the future," would have a future; only this, which *has* no "time," would be on time.

The Messiah of this time would be one neither of a productive or pro-tentional nor of a passive or receptive consciousness with its formal idealities; it would be, in truth, a dehabilitated and debilitated Messiah and indeed—who knows?—a *débile*, a moronic one.

Only if we still think this incapacitated and powerless Messiah can we—if this can still be called *can*—think a future and a messianic time without bounds, a Messiah even of the incomprehensible and unthinkable. It would be a Messiah out of the infinity of a directionless outside-of-one-another or out of the oppositionless inside of a crack in self-affection that would precede the self and would not exist for it.

It would be the Messiah of a not-a-Messiah—a Messiah for the *not* of a Messiah, for the *not* of a for.

Corollaries

1. The use that we make of inherited concepts answers to what tradition hands over, but it shows just as much that we use them because we need them. We are given to them just as much as they are given over to us. That they mark a lack in our abilities becomes apparent—and sometimes painfully apparent—whenever we use them. Such is the case with all concepts reaching beyond any given totality—for example, that of the future and that of the Messiah.

The concept of the Messiah, if indeed it satisfies the requirements for a concept in the strong sense at all, is just as little the prisoner of a determinate historical culture, philosophy, or religion as are other concepts of the same extension—the good, for example, or the just. As the least objectivized, least representable, and least thinkable about which we cannot avoid thinking; as that toward which our wishes and even our wishes for wishes are directed, the messianic is not a determinate figure within an already determined horizon. It can be reduced neither to any type of concrete representative content nor to a form or the form of a relation. But, although it is beyond all determinate forms and entities, there is still something in a movement connected with the movement of what we call "future." It may be a sound, a glance, a gesture, a nuance, or a nothing—the deobjectivizing attraction that is exercised by it has always already been at work whenever we name it and attempt to import it into a system of representation. In this attraction, in this pull and withdrawal, "we" stand. "We" are used by what we cannot use in it. That is to say, however: "We" are held up, held afar, and held back by it. But it means also and "at the same time" that we have been abandoned by it, let loose, relinquished to "ourselves." And therefore it means: We are held *in* this letting-loose and used *as* the unusables. The structure of messianic time is the structure of *our* time; the structure of messianic existence is that of *our* existence. We are, if not the Messiah, nonetheless messianic; we are determined by the notbeing-there, the imminence of a possible coming and of a just-as-possible *not* of this coming—we, the messianically undetermined, we the unusable, we whose *un* may be usable and whose usability remains determined by this *un*. We, the freed from the we.

The concept of the Messiah is certainly a concept of tradition. But it is one of a tradition that has turned itself toward the future and in this future toward the uncertainty over whether it will arrive or will not arrive. This possibility of a *not* of the future, this possibility of its impossibility belongs—even if it is pushed to the side again and again, even if it is denied and reproached—to the experience of what is to come. If its coming does not hold back within its not-coming, it is not future. Only he or it is the Messiah that "saves" the not of his or its coming. The not, retreating from coming and allowing to come, is messianic. The concept (or, rather, since it does not capture and does not contain what it means, the name) of the messianic can be of use only if the *not* is also used in it, if the *not* of its tradition and of its traditional, its "historical" usage—if its uselessness is used.

Philosophers and theologians have used only the usable of messianism, its salvational and illusionistic qualities; the point is, however, to support and further its un-usability. For this, it is not sufficient to avoid the name of the Messiah; nor does it suffice to furnish it with an altered meaning—to re-semanticize it—and to subject it to a new usage. The point is to use the *not* of its usefulness and to expose the messianic to precisely that *epoché* out of which alone it could become a coming even beyond coming. Therefore, once again: The point is to further the unusability of the future. We need it.

2. A note of Kafka's that is by now obscurely famous may be read in the sense of an *epoché* of the messianic: "The Messiah will only come when he is no longer necessary, he will only come after his arrival, he will not come on the last day, but on the very last."[4] He who comes a day after his arrival comes twice—and, of course, so that he comes as the one who has already arrived (and thus is superfluous, not necessary, and not usable) or as the one who comes *after* himself, thus when he *himself* has not yet come, and comes once again and as the one who himself does not come (whose coming is therefore not necessary and not usable). According to Kafka's definition, the Messiah is the one who comes as the one-who-does-not-come and in whom the not-coming comes. His concept is not unusable, but he is the concept of the unusable who could make everything usable—but usable only through the addition of a *not* (of a *not*-necessary coming, of a coming *after* its arrival). Kafka's triple definition culminates in the difference between the "last" and the "very last" day, in a difference that lies only in the nuance of an intensification. Within it, the last is still in itself beyond itself: mere *transcendens* not beyond the end but of ending itself—the utmost end as unending *transcendens*—therefore a mere "but," a differentiating, nuancing, sharpening of the *eschaton* towards a *ex-eschaton*.

3. The danger of every encounter with the future consists in not meeting its terms. One may want to disregard or reject it, claiming "No Future!"; one may acknowledge it with reservation, claiming with Paul's formula

hōs mē, tamquam non, "as if not."[5] The first claim, a formalism, remains bound to what it denies; the second indulges in aestheticism by reducing the "not" to a mere semblance.

4. Concepts are tractanda, not propaganda. The maxims for their use could be: Use concepts in such a way that they are not determined only for all but for no one as well—forget not the no one.

Whoever uses them in such a way that the unusable will also become clear has a chance to loosen concepts—and not only them—from their tradition. He shows that they must have never belonged to this tradition with every fiber of their being. He de-traditionalizes, de-necessitates.

5. "It is in names that we think":[6] It may be that Hegel was right in this statement, but he can have been right only because he did not express it in a name but in a sentence. Thus, it would be more correct to say: It is in sentences that we think. And to add that the semantics of names can be defined and redefined only through syntagmatic combinations that, for their part, never join into a nominal unity. Since syntagmatic combinations are, however, always insufficient, sympragmatic ones are never given *in toto*, and syncategoremata—let us say, "or"—can mark empty syntagmata or empty sympragmata, we must presumably say: It is in ana-tagmata and ana-pragmata that we think. So much to the *name* "Messiah."

6. If I speak of the "fourth," nonetheless uncountable dimension of time, I think first of all not of Heidegger's *Es gibt* (it happens) which was designated in *Time and Being* (1962) as a fourth dimension but of the "no fifth" in a note by Paul Celan in *Counter-Light* [*Gegenlicht*]: "Four seasons of the year, and no fifth, to decide for one out of them." (*Vier Jahreszeiten, und keine fünfte, um sich für eine von ihnen zu entscheiden.*)[7]

In this fifth, which *does not exist,* decisions would be made. In the world of the four seasons one would have therefore to say, "There is no 'there is,'" (*Es gibt kein "Es gibt"*), and to ask oneself whether this sentence is translatable into "It—that does not happen—happens" (*Es, das es nicht gibt, gibt*). If it were so, then the giving would give itself only in and out of its holding back, the coming would come out of its not, and both would be minimal conditions of the future as of the basic structure of time. Celan's "no fifth" season and Heidegger's "fourth dimension" of time and space would be *neighboring* attempts to think time not as a linear order of homogenous now-points but out of a $+ (-n)$ *beyond* them.

7. On method: Do not forget the no one.

INTRODUCTION: SAVING HOPE, THE WAGER OF MESSIANISM
Anna Glazova and Paul North

1. Some well-known recent books that announce or promote an end
to secularity and a "return" to or of religion in society in general, and in
the human and social sciences in particular, are Charles Taylor, *A Secular
Age* (Harvard, 2007); Michel Henry, *I Am the Truth: Toward a Philosophy of
Christianity* (Stanford, 2003); and Luc Ferry, *Man Made God: The Meaning
of Life* (University of Chicago, 2002). A sampling of critical analyses of the
processes and idea of secularization include: Michael Allen Gillespie, *The
Theological Origins of Modernity* (University of Chicago, 2008); Talal Asad,
Formations of the Secular: Christianity, Islam, Modernity (Stanford, 2003);
Marcel Gauchet, *The Disenchantment of the World: A Political History of Religion*
(Princeton University Press, 1997). Works by Jean-Luc Marion fall by and
large into a border-zone between theology proper and phenomenological
revisions of theological categories. To the latter class belong *Visible et le révélé*
(Cerf, 2005), *De surcroît: études sur les phénomènes saturés* (Presses universitaires
de France, 2001), and *Étant donné: Essai d'une phénoménologie de la donation*
(Presses universitaires de France, 1997). These have been translated as *Visible and the Revealed* (Fordham, 2008), *Being Given: Toward a Phenomenology
of Givenness* (Stanford, 2002), and *In Excess: Studies of Saturated Phenomena*
(Fordham, 2004). Two books may be considered the mothers of all critiques
of secularity: Carl Schmitt, *Political Theology* (1921; University of Chicago,
2006), and Karl Löwith, *Meaning in History: The Theological Implications of the
Philosophy of History* (University of Chicago, 1949).

2. Uncovering motifs, concepts, images, and motivations traditionally associated with religion or theology persisting in purportedly secular
thought has a rather long tradition. Marx's critique of Feuerbach is one of
the earliest in post-Kantian thought, Heidegger's critique of ontotheology
one of the most far-reaching. Resuscitation of the messianic theologoumenon in particular has a fairly limited genealogy. Epimessianic writing
first fans out in the twentieth century. One strand revitalizes eschatological
themes identified as Jewish and loosely responds to political Zionism: Franz

Rosenzweig, Der *Stern der Erlösung* (J. Kauffmann, 1921); Walter Benjamin, "Theological-Political Fragment" (probably 1922–23), *Ursprung des deutschen Trauerspiels* (Rowohlt, 1928), "Franz Kafka: On the Tenth Anniversary of His Death" (1934), and "Historical-Philosophical Theses" (1940); Jacob Taubes's dissertation, *Abendländisches Eschatologie* (A. Francke, 1947); certain fragments in Theodor Adorno's *Minima Moralia: Reflexionen aus dem beschädigten Leben* (Suhrkamp, 1951); Gershom Scholem's 1959 and now infamous and much-cited lecture "Toward an Understanding of the Messianic Idea in Judaism" (in *The Messianic Idea in Judaism*, Schocken, 1971). Transformations of the concept of "futurity" among thinkers identified as "Jewish" can be found in Pierre Bouretz's *Witness for the Future: Philosophy and Messianism* (Johns Hopkins, 2010). Another strand of epimessianic writing attempts to revitalize Paul of Tarsus as the savior of theory. Some texts in this genre that focus on or include messianism are Daniel Boyarin, *A Radical Jew: Paul and the Politics of Identity* (University of California, 1994); Alain Badiou, *St. Paul: The Foundation of Universalism* (Stanford, 2003); Jacob Taubes, *The Political Theology of Paul* (Stanford, 2004); Giorgio Agamben, *The Time That Remains: A Commentary on the Letter to the Romans* (Stanford, 2005). Jacques Derrida's *Specters of Marx* (Routledge, 1994) and "Marx & Sons," published in translation in *Ghostly Demarcations* (Verso, 1999) do not fall directly along any of these strands.

    3. Much of the analysis of the "turn" or "return" has been carried out by Hent de Vries, first and most directly in *Philosophy and the Turn to Religion* (Johns Hopkins 1999), which was preceded by *Theologie in Pianissimo*, a study of theological figures in Adorno and Levinas (Peeters, 1989), translated into English as *Minimal Theologies: Critiques of Secular Reason in Adorno and Levinas* (Johns Hopkins, 2005). De Vries's study of the renewed theophilosophy, *Religion and Violence: Philosophical Perspectives from Kant to Derrida* (Johns Hopkins, 2002), was published amid a stream of anthologies edited by him on the topic of the "return": *Post-Theism: Reframing the Judeo-Christian Tradition* (Peeters, 2000, with Henri A. Krop and Arie L. Molendijk), *Religion and Media* (Stanford, 2001, with Samuel Weber), *Political Theologies: Public Religions in a Post-Secular World* (Fordham, 2006, with Lawrence E. Sullivan), and *Religion beyond a Concept* (Fordham, 2008). Along this trajectory one notes a turn in de Vries's focus. At first he seems to be responding to the reappraisals of philosophemes traditionally considered religious, but later he seems to be reevaluating religion itself. A good introduction to the "turn" in French philosophy is the collection *Phenomenology and the Theological Turn* (Fordham, 2000). In it there are important contributions by Dominique Janicaud, Jean-François Courtine, Jean-Louis Chrétien, Michel Henry, Jean-Luc Marion, and Paul Ricouer.

4. A name not on this list is Franz Rosenzweig. In his major book, *The Star of Redemption* (1921), he certainly sees the relationship between the existent human being, God, and world fulfill itself along a messianic trajectory. Yet the project proposes a strengthening of what Rosenzweig himself continues to call "theology" rather than the transplantation of its motifs or structures outside it.

5. Taylor's book focuses on the effects of the rejection of faith. There are, however, scattered hints of a messianism underlying Taylor's whole project. What he calls "the realm of anticipatory confidence" is not without its similarities to messianic faith (551). His underlying messianism becomes especially pressing in the chapter "The Dark Abyss of Time" (322–51). Here Taylor dramatizes the need for a renewal of faith against the backdrop of the nineteenth-century shift toward understanding time as infinite duration, whose image is an abyss. It is specifically then the loss of belief in an eschaton that motivates the return to faith.

6. Kant suggests this much in the preface to *The Critique of Pure Reason:* "Our age is the genuine age of criticism, to which everything must succumb. Religion through its holiness and legislation through its majesty commonly seek to exempt themselves from it. But in this way they excite a just suspicion against themselves, and cannot lay claim to that unfeigned respect that reason grants only to that which has been able to withstand its free and public examination" (100–1).

7. Feuerbach, in *The Essence of Christianity* (1841).

8. In his "Theses on Feuerbach," Marx objects: "Feuerbach . . . does not see that the 'religious sentiment' is itself a social product, and that the abstract individual which he analyses belongs to a particular form of society" (in *German Ideology*, 571).

9. In *The German Ideology*, Marx writes: "In all previous revolutions the mode of activity always remained unchanged and it was only a question of a different distribution of this activity, a new distribution of labour to other persons, whilst the communist revolution is directed against the hitherto existing mode of activity, does away with labour, and abolishes the rule of all classes with the classes themselves, because it is carried through by the class which no longer counts as a class in society" (60).

10. This is how Kant explains the necessity of the eschatological thought: "But why do human beings expect *an end* of the world *at all*? And if this is conceded to them, why must it be a terrible end (for the greatest part of the human race)? . . . The ground of the first point appears to lie in the fact that reason says to them that the duration of the world has worth only insofar as the rational beings in it conform to the final end of their existence; if, however, this is not supposed to be achieved, then creation itself appears

purposeless to them, like a play having no resolution and affording no cognition of any rational aim. The latter point is grounded on our opinion about
the corrupt nature of the human race, which corruption is great to the point
of hopelessness; this makes for an end, and indeed a terrible one, the only
end (for the greatest part of humanity) that accords with highest wisdom and
justice, employing any respectable standard" ("The End of All Things," in
Religion and Rational Theology, p. 224–25).

   11. Toward the end of the chapter "The World as Will" in his *The World
as Will and Representation*, Schopenhauer states that the will comes to a
standstill once all desires leave the individual: "It is fortunate enough when
something to desire and to strive for still remains, so that the game may be
kept up of the constant transition from desire to satisfaction, and from that to
a fresh desire, the rapid course of which is called happiness, the slow course
sorrow, and so that this game may not come to a standstill, showing itself as a
fearful, life-destroying boredom, a lifeless longing without a definite object, a
deadening languor" (164–65). At the end of his study, however, he comes to
the conclusion that "we have to banish the dark impression of nothingness."
Instead, he asks us not only to embrace nothingness but to will it: "We freely
acknowledge that what remains after the complete abolition of the will is,
for all who are still full of the will, assuredly nothing. But also conversely, to
those in whom the will has turned and denied itself, this very real world of
ours with all its suns and galaxies—is nothing" (411–12).

   12. In his book *Das Prinzip Hoffnung*, Ernst Bloch, whose thinking was
informed by Marx, describes human history as thoroughly determined by
hope. From "anticipatory passions" to rational and less rational utopian
schemes, from philosophical concepts such as "possibility" to the Marxian
injunction to "change the world," the forms of hope that drive European history are catalogued by Bloch. The book, an attempt to describe every single
form of hope in every single form of human activity in every epoch, in fact
leaves little hope. In its encyclopedism it appears as the most thoroughgoing
determinism, and so may in fact lead the reader toward despair. In essence
Bloch thinks a totality of hope. Addressing the suggestion that an earthly
utopia might not last, he writes: "As is unfortunately only too evident, what
is intendable as such presence, as such manifested identity does not yet lie
anywhere in a Becomeness, but it lies irrefutably in the intention towards
it, in the intention which is never demolished, and lies unmistakably in the
historical and world process itself . . . This most hoped-for thing of all in
hope, called highest good, also represents the region of final purpose in which
every solid positing of a purpose in man's struggle for liberation participates.
The All in the identifying sense is the Absolute of that which people basically want"
(1:315–16).

13. Peter Fenves's *The Messianic Reduction: Walter Benjamin and the Shape of Time* (Stanford, 2010) traces Benjamin's early transformations of Husserlian phenomenology and Kantian theoretical and practical philosophy. He transforms them, to put it very generally, by reorienting them within a nonteleological historicity, which Fenves, citing Benjamin, calls plastic time.

14. See the remark on this crucial distinction in *Specters of Marx*, p. 37: "It is there that differ*a*nce, if it remains irreducible, irreducibly required by the spacing of any promise and by the future-to-come that comes to open it, does not mean only (as some people have too often believed and naively) deferral, lateness, delay, postponement. In the incoercible difference the here-now unfurls. Without lateness, without delay, but without presence, it is the precipitation of an absolute singularity, singular because differing, precisely [*justement*], and always other, binding itself necessarily to the form of the instant, in *imminence and in urgency:* even if it moves toward what remains to come, there is the *pledge* [*gage*] (promise, engagement, injunction and response to injunction, and so forth). The pledge is given here and now, even before, perhaps, a decision confirms it. It thus responds without delay to the demand of justice. The latter by definition is impatient, uncompromising, and unconditional. . . . No difference without alterity, no alterity without singularity, no singularity without here-now."

15. Derrida, *Specters of Marx*, 81.

16. Benjamin, *Kritische Gesamtausgabe*, 19:18.

1. OF THEORY, AESTHETICS, AND POLITICS: CONFIGURING
THE MESSIANIC IN EARLY TWENTIETH-CENTURY EUROPE
Lisa Marie Anderson

This essay previously appeared, in slightly different form, as Lisa Marie Anderson, "Of Theory, Aesthetics, and Politics: Configuring the Messianic in Early Twentieth-Century Europe," *Postscripts: The Journal of Sacred Texts and Contemporary Worlds* 3, nos. 2–3 (2007): 223–37. Reprinted with permission of Equinox Publishing. © Equinox Publishing Ltd 2007. Some of the material is also discussed in Lisa Marie Anderson, *German Expressionism and the Messianism of a Generation* (New York: Editions Rodopi, 2011).

1. Mark Lilla, *The Stillborn God*, 9–10. See also John Gray, *Black Mass*, 2007. Since 2004, at least three international scholarly conferences on messianism have produced collections on the subject: Wayne Cristaudo and Wendy Baker, eds., *Messianism, Apocalypse, Redemption: 20th-Century German Thought* (Hindmarsh: Australian Theological Forum, 2006); Thomas Crombez and Katrien Vloeberghs, eds., *On the Outlook: Figures of the Messianic*

(Cambridge: Cambridge Scholars Press, 2007); Vivian Liska, Bernd Witte and Karl Solibakke, eds., *Messianism and Politics. Kabbalah, Benjamin, Agamben* (Würzburg: Königshausen und Neumann, 2008). This is in addition to a vast number of recent journal articles on messianism, particularly in area studies disciplines.

2. Wassily Kandinsky, *Über das Geistige in der Kunst*, 43. Unless otherwise indicated in a note or in the bibliography, translations in this essay are my own.

3. Ernst Bloch, *Geist der Utopie*, 151.

4. Richard Blunck, *Der Impuls des Expressionismus*, 7.

5. Kurt Pinthus, ed., *Menschheitsdämmerung*, 14.

6. This poem has been read as "a poignant case in point" of the Expressionists' "aestheticization of politics." Rainer Rumold, *The Janus Face*, 23.

7. Hugo Zehder, "Zeit, Theater und Dichter," 3.

8. Ernst Toller, 2:51.

9. Georg Kaiser, 4:548–49.

10 Kurt Hiller, "Überlegungen zur Eschatologie und Methodologie des Aktivismus," 195.

11. Ludwig Rubiner, "Die Änderung der Welt," 65.

12. Rudolf Leonhard, "Literarischer Aktivismus," 137.

13. Hiller, "Überlegungen," 195, 210.

14. Sigmund Freud, *The Standard Edition of the Complete Psychological Works*, ed. James Strachey (London: Hogart, 1955), 18:99. The psychology that Freud identifies in group members gathered around a messiah-figure corresponds to many of the criticisms leveled at the Expressionists: "the dwindling of the conscious individual personality, the focusing of thoughts and feelings into a common direction, the predominance of the affective side of the mind and of unconscious psychical life, the tendency to the immediate carrying out of intentions as they emerge" (18:122).

15. Max Weber, *Gesamtausgabe*, 1:17, 101, 105.

16. Theodor W. Adorno, *Gesammelte Schriften*, 2:244.

17. Bloch, *Geist der Utopie*, 260.

18. Adorno, *Gesammelte Schriften*, 2:244. Bloch's concern with messianism, like his relationship to Expressionism, certainly transcends *The Spirit of Utopia*, as evidenced, for example, by *Thomas Münzer, Theologian of the Revolution* (1921), in which Bloch seeks to establish the relevance of a sixteenth-century millenarian movement for the socialist revolutions of the twentieth century.

19. Georg Lukács, *Dostojewski*, 111–12, 156–57, 182, 189.

20. See Michael Löwy, "Ernst Bloch and Georg Lukács Meet in Heidelberg," 291.

21. Georg Lukács, "Bolshevism as a Moral Problem," 420–21.

22. Georg Lukács, "Expressionism: Its Significance and Decline," 78.

23. Ernst Bloch, "Discussing Expressionism," trans. Rodney Livingstone, *Aesthetics and Politics* (London: Verso, 2007), 22–23.

24. Georg Lukács, "Realism in the Balance," p. 55.

25. Jacques Derrida, "Faith and Knowledge," 17. This portion of Derrida's text is written almost entirely in italics. All italicized words in quotations in this essay appear as such in the original.

26. Jacques Derrida, "Marx & Sons," 248.

27. Derrida, "Faith and Knowledge," 17.

28. For Benjamin as a critic of Expressionism, though in a very different vein from that of Lukács, see Rumold, *Janus Face*, 110–17.

29. Walter Benjamin, *Gesammelte Schriften*, 2:149.

30. Richard Wolin, *Walter Benjamin*, 21, 26.

31. Benjamin, *Gesammelte Schriften*, 1:701, 703–4. The final translation is Harry Zohn's. See Walter Benjamin, *Selected Writings*, 4:397.

32. Wolin, *Walter Benjamin*, p. 6. Michael P. Steinberg, "Walter Benjamin Writes the Essays 'Critique of Violence' and 'The Task of the Translator,'" 403.

33. See Wolin, *Walter Benjamin*, 49.

34. Jacques Derrida, *Specters of Marx*, 181.

35. Derrida, "Marx & Sons," 249–50.

36. See Fredric Jameson, "Marx's Purloined Letter," 33, 60–62. See also Werner Hamacher's contribution to the same volume, "Lingua Amissa," 169.

37. Derrida, "Marx & Sons," 254.

38. Lukács, "Expressionism," 87, 112.

39. Richard Samuel and R. Hinton Thomas, *Expressionism in German Life, Literature, and the Theatre*, p. 184.

40. Steinberg, "Walter Benjamin," 403.

2. ON THE PRICE OF MESSIANISM: THE INTELLECTUAL RIFT BETWEEN GERSHOM SCHOLEM AND JACOB TAUBES
Thomas Macho

This essay was originally published as "Der intellektuelle Bruch zwischen Gershom Scholem und Jacob Taubes: Zur Frage nach dem Preis des Messianismus," in *Abendländische Eschatologie: Ad Jacob Taubes*, edited by Richard Faber, Eveline Goodman-Thau, and Thomas Macho, 531–43.

1. See Gershom Scholem, *A Life in Letters*, 363.

2. Ibid., 468.

3. See Thomas Sparr, introduction to Gershom Scholem: *Briefe II*, xxvn1. In the English edition, this preface is missing.

4. Aleida Assmann, Jan Assmann, and Wolf-Daniel Hartwich, introduction to Jacob Taubes: *From Cult to Culture—Fragments towards a Critique of Historical Reason*, ed. Charlotte Elisheva Fonrobert and Amir Engel, xxiv.

5. Scholem, *A Life in Letters*, 468.

6. Ibid., 426 (translation modified). In a similar thank-you letter to Peter Szondi (not included in the English edition), Scholem underlines the idealization of "lack of ceremony" with the following words: "Anniversaries belong, as unfortunately the Talmud does not say, to the things that are immeasurable. The prayer book includes the relevant points."

7. Scholem, *A Life in Letters*, 431; and *Briefe II*, 214–18 (not included in the English edition).

8. Scholem, *The Messianic Idea in Judaism*, 1.

9. The original German title is *Das anstößige Volk*, by Jochanan Bloch (Heidelberg: Schneider, 1964).

10. Helmut Gollwitzer, "Das anstößige Volk: On Jochanan Bloch's Eponymous Book," 367.

11. See Scholem, *Briefe II*, 153–54 and 292–93 (not included in the English edition). See also Gershom Scholem, *Über einige Grundbegriffe des Judentums*, 168–70.

12. Jacob Taubes, "The Price of Messianism," in *From Cult to Culture*, 4.

13. On this question see also Gunnar Heinsohn, *Warum Auschwitz? Hitlers Plan und die Ratlosigkeit der Nachwelt*, 164–72.

14. Taubes, *The Price of Messianism*, 5.

15. Ibid.

16. Taubes, "The Iron Cage and the Exodus from It, or the Dispute over Marcion, Then and Now," in *From Cult to Culture*, 146.

17. Taubes, *The Price of Messianism*, 5–6.

18. Taubes, "Der liebe Gott steckt im Detail. Gershom G. Scholem und die messianische Verheißung," 1.

19. Taubes, *The Price of Messianism*, 8.

20. Scholem, *The Messianic Idea in Judaism*, 35.

21. Taubes, *The Price of Messianism*, 9.

22. Scholem, *The Messianic Idea in Judaism*, 10.

23. Ibid., 35.

24. Jacob Taubes, *Occidental Eschatology*, 16.

25. Taubes, *The Price of Messianism*, 8–9.

26. The original German title is *Messianismus, zionistisch oder marxistisch?* By Jacob Taubes. Copy from the estate of Arthur A. Cohen, Beinecke Library of Yale University (prepared by Evelyn Adunka, Vienna), 2.

27. Ibid. See also Jacob Taubes, "Walter Benjamin—ein moderner Marcionit? Scholems Benjamin-Interpretation religionsgeschichtlich überprüft," 138.

28. Taubes, *Occidental Eschatology*, 19.

29. Taubes, "Walter Benjamin—ein moderner Marcionit?" p. 139. See also Jacob Taubes, "Messianismus, zionistisch oder marxistisch?" 2.

30. Scholem, *The Messianic Idea in Judaism*, 35.

31. Taubes, "Walter Benjamin—ein moderner Marcionit?" 143.

32. See, Taubes, *Die Politische Theologie des Paulus*, 97–106.

33. Walter Benjamin, "Theologisch-politisches Fragment," *Gesammelte Schriften*, Bd. 2.1, p. 203. See also, Jacob Taubes, "Walter Benjamin—ein moderner Marcionit?" 140, 142. On the discussion surrounding Benjamin's *Fragment*, see also Sigrid Weigel, *Entstellte Ähnlichkeit: Walter Benjamins theoretische Schreibweise* (Frankfurt/Main: Fischer, 1997), 71–75.

34. Taubes, *Die Politische Theologie des Paulus*, 22.

35. Taubes, *Messianismus, zionistisch oder marxistisch?* 4.

36. Jacob Taubes, *Gespräche mit Peter Sloterdijk*, 50–51.

37. Quoted by Friedrich Niewöhner in "Der wahre Glaube ist verborgen: Ein schwieriger Prophet: Gershom Scholem zwischen Kabbala und Zionismus," *Frankfurter Allgemeine Zeitung*, no. 278 (November 29, 1997).

38. Taubes, *Gespräche mit Peter Sloterdijk*, 51.

39. Ibid., 134–36

40. Harold Bloom, *Kafka-Freud-Scholem: Drei Essays*, 72 (my translation).

41. Taubes, *Messianismus, zionistisch oder marxistisch?* 11–12.

42. See Odo Marquard, "Lob des Polytheismus. Über Monomythie und Polymythie," 91–116. See Taubes, "On the Current State of Polytheism," *From Cult to Culture*, 302–14.

43. See Jacob Taubes, *Ad Carl Schmitt: Gegenstrebige Fügung [Ad Carl Schmitt: Contrary Submission]* (Berlin: Merve, 1987): 27–29. See also Scholem, *A Life in Letters*, 468.

44. Taubes, *Der liebe Gott steckt im Detail*, 1.

3. IMPURE INHERITANCES: SPECTRAL MATERIALITY IN DERRIDA AND MARX
Nicole Pepperell

I would like to thank Duncan Law, who collaborated on the earlier conference presentation on *Specters of Marx* from which this paper grew: Nicole Pepperell and Duncan Law, "Handling Value: Grasping the Fetish in Marx's *Capital*," Derrida Today International Conference, Macquarie University, Sydney, Australia, 2008. I would also like to thank Robert Briggs, who has been involved with this paper from its first origins in an online academic discussion, and who has encouraged me to develop the argument in full. Earlier versions of the analysis presented here have been published in "Handling Value: Notes on Derrida's Inheritance of Marx," *Derrida Today* 2, no. 2 (2009): 222–33; "When Is It Safe to Go on Reading *Capital?*" in *The Devil's Party: Marx, Theory, and Philosophy*, ed. Tom Bunyard (London: Centre for Cultural Studies, Goldsmiths University of London, 2009), 11–21; and "The Exorcism of Exorcism: The Enchantment of Materiality in Derrida and Marx," *Ctrl-Z: new media philosophy* (May 2013).

1. Derrida, Jacques, *Specters of Marx: The State of the Debt, the Work of Mourning, and the New International*, trans. Peggy Kamuf (New York: Routledge, 1994).

2. Derrida distinguishes his concept of the messianic from Benjamin's, but the argument about selective inheritance holds an affinity with Benjamin's notions of the ways in which the present forms nondeterministic "constellations" with particular pasts in which the present recognizes its own concerns; Derrida, *Specters*, 180–81n2; Benjamin, *Illuminations*, trans. Harry Zohn, ed. Hannah Arendt (London: Pimlico, 1999).

3. Derrida, *Specters*, 113–15.

4. Although I am using "fetishism" here for consistency with Derrida's interpretation of the passage in terms of ideology critique, Marx's term is actually "fetish character." The original term makes it clearer that Marx is trying to pick out not a subjective process or something ideologically projected onto the commodity but rather a distinctive character that the commodity actually possesses. For a good discussion of the important difference between "fetishism" and "fetish character" as ways of rendering the rhetorical sense of Marx's passage, see Sutherland, Keston, "Marx in Jargon," *World Picture* 1 (2008). http://www.worldpicturejournal.com/WP_1.1/KSutherland.pdf.

5. Marx, Karl, *Capital: A Critique of Political Economy*, trans. Ben Fowkes (London: Penguin Classics, 1990), 1:164–65.

6. Derrida, *Specters*, 156, 165.

7. Ibid., 157–58.

8. Ibid., 158.

9. Derrida seems to miss the sarcastic tone of these claims that commodities cannot speak, walk, exercise will, etc., and therefore takes the passages as unintentionally paradoxical or contradictory. The perspectives being voiced in the early chapters of *Capital* are intended as ironic enactments of political economic perspectives whose definitions act as though labor-power does not exist: These positions are the targets of Marx's critique, not positions that he advocates. He explicitly reveals the ironic character of these early definitions in chapter 4 of *Capital*, when he introduces labor-power as a category, but

the earlier chapters foreshadow this by constant use of jarring examples and sarcastic asides that undermine the definitions currently on display. Derrida notices some of this foreshadowing but interprets it as evidence that Marx is self-contradictory, and therefore overlooks the joke. Werner Hamacher follows Derrida in making this mistake in "Lingua Amissa" (212). For a more detailed analysis of the importance of this and other ironic gestures in *Capital*, see my "Capitalism: Some Disassembly Required," in *Communization and Its Discontents: Contestation, Critique and Contemporary Struggles*, ed. Benjamin Noys (London: Autonomedia/Minor Compositions, 2011): 105–30. For other interpretations of *Capital*'s literary structure that recognize the ironic character of such passages, see Wheen, *Marx's "Das Kapital,"* and Dominick LaCapra, *Rethinking Intellectual History.*

10. Derrida, *Specters*, 159.

11. Marx, *Capital*, 165, cited in Derrida, *Specters*, 166.

12. Marx, *Capital*, 165.

13. Derrida, *Specters*, 5

14. Stanley Edgar Hyman, *The Tangled Bank: Darwin, Marx, and Freud as Imaginative Writers;* Thomas Keenan, *Fables of Responsibility: Aberrations and Predicaments in Ethics and Politics;* Dominick LaCapra, *Rethinking;* John Evan Seery, *Political Returns: Irony in Politics and Theory, from Plato to the Antinuclear Movement;* Wylie Sypher, "Aesthetic of Revolution: The Marxist Melodrama"; Edmund Wilson, *To the Finland Station: A Study in the Writing and Acting of History;* Robert Paul Wolff, *Moneybags Must Be So Lucky: On the Literary Structure of Capital.*

15. Seery, *Political Returns*, 1990; LaCapra, *Rethinking*, 1983.

16. Seery, *Political Returns*, 243.

17. Ibid., 253.

18. LaCapra, *Rethinking*, 332.

19. Marx, Capital, 125, citing *A Contribution to the Critique of Political Economy*, 27.

20. Keenan, *Fables*, 105–6.

21. Marx, *Capital*, 125.

22. Ibid., 126–31. Keenan comments on the way the text seems to "backtrack," covering the same ground several times in the course of the chapter, leading to an ironic framing of the earlier sections in the commodity-fetishism passage; Keenan, Fables, 113, 117–18, 121, 128, and 133.

23. Marx, *Capital*, 127.

24. For a more extended analysis of Marx's relationship to Hegel, see Nicole Pepperell, "The Bond of Fragmentation: on Marx, Hegel, and the social determination of the material world," *Borderlands* 10, no. 1 (2011), http://www.borderlands.net.au/vol10no1_2011/pepperell_bond.

25. Georg Wilhelm Friedrich Hegel, *The Phenomenology of Mind*, trans. J. B. Baillie (New York: Dover, 2003).

26. Hegel, *Phenomenology*, 64–66.

27. Marx, *Capital*, 163.

28. Ibid., 163.

29. Keenan, *Fables*, 128.

30. Marx, *Capital*, 163–64.

4. AGAMBEN AND THE MESSIANIC: THE SLIGHTEST OF DIFFERENCES
David Ferris

1. Walter Benjamin, "In der Sonne," in *Gesammelte Schriften*, ed. Rolf Tiedemann and Hermann Schweppenhäuser (Frankfurt am Main: Suhrkamp, 1991), 4.1:419 (this edition of *Gesammelte Schriften* will hereafter be referred to as *GS*, and the corresponding English edition, *Selected Writings*, as *SW*). This remark reappears in Benjamin's Kafka essay of 1934 as follows: "The Messiah, about whom a great rabbi said that he will not wish to change the world by force but will merely make a slight adjustment in it" (*GS* 2:432, *SW* 2:811). This parable first appears in print in Ernst Bloch's "Die glückliche Hand," in *Spuren* (1930; Frankfrut am Main: Suhrkamp, 1985), 1: 201–2. However, in a letter (1934) to Benjamin, Gershom Scholem states that "the great Rabbi with the profound dictum on the messianic Kingdom who appears in the Bloch is none other than *I* myself. . . . It was one of my first ideas on the Kabbalah" (*The Correspondence of Walter Benjamin*, ed. and trans. Manfred R. Jacobson and Evelyn M. Jacobson (Chicago: University of Chicago Press, 1994), 446. Agamben will also refer to this story in his account of the messianic; see "The Messiah and Sovereign: The Problem of Law in Walter Benjamin," in Potentialities (Stanford: Stanford University Press, 1999), 174, and *The Coming Community*, trans. Michael Hardt (Minneapolis: University of Minnesota Press, 1993), 53.

2. Here, messianism is the name for "determinate figures and forms of the Messiah" which, Derrida continues, accredit "one tradition among others and a notion of an elected people, of a literal language, a given fundamentalism." "The Villanova Roundtable," in *Deconstruction in a Nutshell: A Conversation with Jacques Derrida*, ed. John Caputo (New York: Fordham University Press, 1996), 23. This text will be subsequently referred to as "Roundtable."

3. See "The Origin of the Work of Art," in *Poetry, Language, Thought* (New York: Harper and Row, 1971), and the essay "Aletheia," in *Early Greek Thinking* (New York: Harper and Row, 1975).

4. An earlier essay on Benjamin and the Messianic predates this prominence. In Agamben's essay "Benjamin and the Demonic: Happiness and His-

torical Redemption" (1982), he makes no large political, ethical, or juridical claim on its behalf at this time. "Benjamin and the Demonic," *Potentialities*, ed. and trans. Daniel Heller-Roazen (Stanford: Stanford University Press, 1999), 138–59. Rather, Agamben undertakes a correction of Scholem's account of Benjamin's messianism. See in particular 144–48.

5. On Derrida's remarks concerning Benjamin's weak messianism, see *Specters of Marx: The State of the Debt, the Work of Mourning, and the New International*, trans. Peggy Kamuf (Stanford: Stanford University Press, 1994), esp. 277n2, and the interview "For a Justice to Come An Interview with Jacques Derrida," in the *Brussels Tribune*, February 19, 2004, 6–7, http://www.brusselstribunal.org/pdf/Derrida_EN.pdf.

6. Derrida's remark on horizon and limit is as follows: "One of the reasons I am keeping such a distance from all these horizons—from the Kantian regulative idea or from the messianic advent, for example, at least in their conventional interpretation—is that they are, precisely, *horizons*. As its Greek name suggests, a horizon is both the opening and the limit that defines either an infinite progress or a waiting and awaiting." Derrida, "Force of Law," in *Acts of Religion*, ed. Gil Anidjar (New York: Routledge, 2001), 55.

7. Agamben, "The Messiah and the Sovereign: The Problem of Law in Walter Benjamin," in *Potentialities* (Stanford: Stanford University Press, 1999), 162. This essay will be subsequently referred to as "Messiah."

8. Giorgio Agamben, "Il messia e il sovrana. Il problema della legge in W. Benjamin," in *Anima e Paura. Studi in onore di Michele Ranchetti*, ed. Bruna Bocchini Camaiani and Anna Scattigno (Macerata: Quodlibet, 1998), 12. This essay will be subsequently referred to as "Il messia."

9. The thesis is repeated in 1995, without any strategic hesitancy, as "the Messiah is the figure in which religion confronts the problem of the law, in which religion and the law come to a decisive day of reckoning." *Means without End: Notes on Politics*, trans. Vincenzo Binetti and Cesare Casarino (Minneapolis: University of Minnesota Press, 2000), 135.

10. Curiously, this foreshadowing manner of interpretation is precisely what Agamben takes Scholem to task for in the latter's reading of Benjamin in the chapter "Walter Benjamin and the Demonic: Happiness and Historical Redemption," *Potentialities* (Stanford: Stanford University Press, 1999), 138–59.

11. Walter Benjamin, "On the Concept of History," *SW* 4:391.

12. The effect of this paradox is quite different from the tension that Peter Fenves discusses in his account of a "messianic reduction" in Benjamin's response, in his early work, to Husserl's phenomenology, and does so precisely because of a historical directionality that remains as a consequence of Agamben's understanding of time. See Fenves, *The Messianic Reduction: Walter*

Benjamin and the Shape of Time (Stanford: Stanford University Press, 2001), esp. 73–78.

13. *Geltung ohne Bedeutung:* This phrase, which will also resonate through Agamben's treatment of law in *Homo Sacer*, encapsulates Agamben's reading of how Scholem responds to Benjamin's request that Scholem explain a remark he had made about a draft of Benjamin's Kafka essay. In this exchange Benjamin seeks an explanation for what Scholem calls "the Nothing of Revelation." In the translation of this correspondence, Scholem writes: "You ask what I understand by the 'nothing of revelation'? I understand by it a state in which revelation appears to be without meaning, in which it still asserts itself, in which it has *validity* but *no significance.* A state in which the wealth of meaning [*Reichtum der Bedeutung*] is lost and what is in the process of appearing (for revelation is such a process) still does not disappear, even though it is reduced to the zero point of its own content, so to speak." Gershom Scholem to Walter Benjamin, September 20, 1934, *Correspondence*, 142). What Scholem actually writes is important to recall here lest the translation appear to authorize Agamben's condensation of Scholem's response: "Ich verstehe darunter einen Stand, in dem sie bedeutungsleer erscheint, in dem sie zwar noch sich behauptet, in dem sie *gilt*, aber nicht *bedeutet.*" Walter Benjamin, Gershom Scholem: *Briefwechsel*, ed. G. Scholem (Frankfurt am Main: Suhrkamp, 1980), 175. A more exact rendering would be: "I understand by the 'nothingness of revelation' a state in which revelation appears devoid of meaning, in which revelation still truly asserts itself, in which revelation has value, but does not signify." It is this sentence that Agamben condenses into the phrase "Being in force without significance." However, in the original published version of this essay, unlike the English translation, Agamben emphasizes this phrase in German before glossing it in Italian: "*Geltung ohne Bedeutung*, vigenza senza significato: questa è, per Scholem, la corretta definizione dello stato della legge nel romanzo kafkiano." "Il messia," 18. At no point does Scholem condense his explanation into this eminently quotable phrase—and neither does the Italian translation also referred to by Agamben. The Italian translation of Scholem's "in dem es *gilt*, aber nicht *bedeutet*" is as follows: "in cui *vige*, ma non *significa.*" Walter Benjamin e Gershom Scholem: Teologia e utopia. Carteggio, 1933–1940 (Torino: Einaudi, 1987), 163. Beyond the question of how much Agamben is willing to rephrase the texts he cites as well as present this rephrasing in the original language as if it were an authorized version (rather than perhaps stating, "Scholem appears to say"), there is the more crucial question of what Agamben does with a rephrasing in which he transforms a verb into a noun and, in so doing, produces a meaning that is not exactly authorized by Scholem's emphasis or usage. Furthermore, by giving this phrase in German, Agamben makes it look as if Scholem had said it

in the sense Agamben wishes to claim. In Agamben's hands, "es gilt" becomes substantiated as "Geltung" and then becomes "vigenza" in his Italian rendition, a transformation that moves closer and closer to a verb, *vigere*, whose narrower usage in a legal context reflects an overdetermination of Scholem's and Benjamin's correspondence with respect to the legal thesis Agamben pursues. As the immediate context of Scholem's words makes clear, his emphasis is on an appearing that persists even after its content has disappeared. What continues to appear is a validity that survives the loss of an object to refer to. Agamben equates this appearance with the exercise of Schmitt's "state of exception" and, in so doing, would affirm his initial thesis—namely, that the messianic is in fact not just the correct definition of the state of law in Kafka's novels but is *the* correct definition of the foundation of the law in general ("*The Messiah is, in other words, the figure through which religion confronts the problem of the Law, decisively reckoning with it*"). This definition rests on the slightest of differences, but it does so only because that slightness presupposes that there is, in effect, no difference between "validity" and "being in force," between Scholem's "in dem sie gilt" and Agamben's *Geltung*, not to mention between *Geltung* and "vigenza." To be able to presuppose that there is no such difference requires that there must be within every system of thought, within the claimed *sovereignty* of every state, community, law, religion, a point of absolute difference, an exception so strong that two utterly different intents cannot be distinguished. Agamben refers to such a point as a paradox: "One of the paradoxes of the state of exception lies in the fact that in the state of exception, it is impossible to distinguish transgression of the law from execution of the law, such that what violates a rule and what conforms to it coincide without any remainder (a person who goes for a walk during the curfew is not transgressing the law any more than the soldier who kills him is executing it)" *Homo Sacer*, 57. Where there is no law, there can be no transgression or execution of the law. This state does not, however, preclude that the law that has been suspended does not sustain itself as that suspension. This is the Schmittian paradox that Agamben relies on over and over again and not only with respect to the juridical-political context analyzed by Schmitt. It is also the paradox that his reading and positioning of Scholem in relation to Benjamin is interested in sustaining. The state of exception represented by "being in force without significance" becomes a state of expectation, an expectation variously figured by Agamben as "missing time," "time that remains," "messianic time," and nowhere more insistently present than in Agamben's tendency to establish the slightest of differences alluded to in the Scholem–Benjamin story of the Hassidim and the messianic kingdom.

14. The importance of such genuineness to Agamben is reinforced in *Homo Sacer* when Agamben cites his own remarks from the earlier essay "The

Messiah and the Sovereign." In *The Time That Remains: A Commentary on the Letter to the Romans* (Stanford: Stanford University Press, 2005), Agamben refers both to Paul's and to Benjamin's texts as "the two fundamental messianic texts of our tradition" (147). This work will be subsequently referred to as *Time*.

15. Compare "The Messiah and the Sovereign": "Only in this context do Benjamin's Theses acquire their proper meaning" ("Messiah," 172).

16. Dominick LaCapra has accurately and succinctly described the necessity of this index in Agamben's writing as "a compulsively repetitive return to, or even presupposition of, the paradox or aporia to which one moves as does the moth to the flame" ("Approaching Limit Events: Siting Agamben," 143). La Capra's attention to Agamben's compulsions affords a refreshing basis to counter a style of writing whose aphoristic, elliptical character obscures a tendency toward prophecy and pronouncement as a mode of discursive engagement. Concerning this aporia, in *State of Exception*, first published in 2003, Agamben describes what follows the state of exception in these words: "What is found after the law is not a more proper and original use value that precedes the law, but a new use that is born only after it" (64). Getting to this different use value for the law does however depend on fulfilling the aporetic so that a new use can be claimed on the basis of such a fulfillment.

17. See *The Coming Community*, 54. The original Italian edition of this work is published in 1990, two years before he would again claim Benjamin's slightest of differences in "The Messiah and the Sovereign" and ten years before the Italian publication of *The Time That Remains* in 2000.

18. Agamben, *Means without End*, 135–36.

19. Agamben's indexing of the messianic as future promise on the basis of a distinction between messianism and the messianic reiterates the distinction that Derrida had employed strategically in the roundtable discussion referred to earlier in this essay but also in his *Specters of Marx*, first published in French in 1993. Derrida's language also creeps into Agamben's account here when he adds that it is through such messianism that the Church has frozen "the messianic event" (*Means*, 135).

20. Martin Heidegger, *Nietzsche* (New York: Harper, 1991), 1:154.

21. Nietzsche, *Werke*, ed. Karl Schlechta (Frankfurt am Main: Ullstein, 1955), 3:634.

22. In a 2004 interview with Ulrich Rauff, Agamben admits the importance of Nietzsche but immediately displaces that influence into a paraphrase of Benjamin: "Oh, Nietzsche was important for me also. But I stand rather more with Benjamin, who said, the eternal return is like the punishment of detention, the sentence in school in which one had to copy the same sentence a thousand times." *German Law Journal* 5, no. 5: 614.

23. This is not the only work in which the messianic and nihilism are associated by Agamben. In *The Time that Remains* Agamben writes that "every nihilism implied an as if" (37), a remark that assumes that every nihilism implies another nihilism similar but not the same, that is, slightly different. Agamben also characterizes this understanding as Nietzschean. Later in this same work, in which the existence of two senses of time is at stake (as well as host of other terms that will be parsed according to the slightest of differences), Agamben will make Nietzsche into the return of Paul ("Nietzsche, in cloaking himself in the garments of the Antimessiah. is actually only reciting a script written by Paul" [112]), or, more precisely, into the script Agamben presents as Paul.

24. Gianni Vattimo, "Nihilism: Active and Reactive," 15–22.

25. Derrida states in 1994 that any claim on behalf of messianicity as a fundamental ontology is a question still be resolved: "The problem remains—and this is really a problem for me, an enigma—whether the religions, say, for instance, the religions of the Book, are but specific examples of this general structure of messianicity" ("Roundtable," 23). While Agamben will not use this language ("fundamental ontology") his claim for a genuine messianic tradition has simply transposed this language into a fundamental messianicity as the condition of existing.

26. "For a Justice to Come: An Interview with Jacques Derrida," *Brussels Tribune*, February 19, 2004, 6–7; http://www.brusselstribunal.org/pdf/Derrida_EN.pdf.

5. MESSIANIC LANGUAGE AND THE IDEA OF PROSE: BENJAMIN AND AGAMBEN
Vivian Liska

A shorter version of this text was published as "Messianic Language and the Idea of Prose: Benjamin and Agamben." *Bamidbar. Journal for Jewish Thought and Philosophy*, 2/2012, 44–57.

1. Franz Kafka, *Nachgelassene Schriften und Fragmente*, ed. Jost Schillemeit (Frankfurt am Main: S. Fischer, 1992), 2:141.

2. Walter Benjamin, "The Storyteller," *Selected Writings*, ed. Michael W. Jennings, 4 vols. (Cambridge, Mass.: Belknap/Harvard: 2003), 3:155.

3. Giorgio Agamben, *Potentialities*, ed. and trans. Daniel Heller-Roazen (Stanford: Stanford University Press, 1999), 171.

4. Giorgio Agamben, "Language and History. Linguistic and Historical Categories in Benjamin's Thought," in *Potentialities*, 48–62; *Walter Benjamin: Tempo storia linguaggio*, ed. Lucio Belloi and Lorenzina Lotti (Roma: Reuniti, 1983), 65–82.

5. Agamben, *Potentialities*, 56; Hans-Georg Gadamer, *Truth and Method*, trans. Joel Winsheimer and Donald G. Marshall (New York: Continuum,

1993), 458; Gadamer, *Wahrheit und Methode* (Tübingen: J. C. B. Mohr, 1960), 523–34.

   6. Agamben, *Potentialities*, 57.

   7. Benjamin, *Selected Writings*, 4:402. *Gesammelte Schriften*, ed. Rolf Tiedemann and Hermann Schweppenhäuser (Frankfurt am Main: Suhrkamp, 1991), 1:3:1232.

   8. Benjamin, "The Storyteller," *Selected Writings*, 3:143–66; "Der Erzähler," *Gesammelte Schriften*, 2.2:438–65.

   9. Benjamin, *Selected Writings*, 4:405–6. "Die messianische Welt ist die Welt allseitiger und integraler Aktualität. Erst in ihr gibt es eine Universalgeschichte. Was sich heute so bezeichnet, kann immer nur eine Sorte von Esperanto sein. Es kann ihr nichts entsprechen, eh die Verwirrung, die vom Turmbau zu Babel herrührt, geschlichtet ist. Sie setzt die Sprache voraus, in die jeder Text einer lebenden oder toten ungeschmälert zu übersetzen ist. Oder besser, sie ist diese Sprache selbst. Aber nicht als geschriebene, sondern vielmehr als die festlich begangene. Dieses Fest ist gereinigt von jeder Feier. Es kennt keine Festgesänge. Seine Sprache ist integrale Prosa, die die Fesseln der Schrift gesprengt hat und von allen Menschen verstanden wird wie die Sprache der Vögel von Sonntagskindern." Benjamin, *Gesammelte Schriften*, 1.3:1239.

   10. Benjamin, *Selected Writings*, 4:404; *Gesammelte Schriften*, 1:31235.

   11. Benjamin, *Selected Writings*, 4:406; *Gesammelte Schriften*, 1:3:1238. For further versions, see *Gesammelte Schriften*, 1:31234, 1235.

   12. See also Irving Wohlfarth, "Krise der Erzählung, Krise der Erzähltheorie. Überlegungen zu Lukacs, Benjamin und Jauss," in Erzählung und Erzählforschung im 20. Jahrhundert, ed. R. Klopfer and G. Janetzke-Dillner (Stuttgart: Kohlhammer, 1981), 269–88.

   13. Benjamin, *Selected Writings*, 1:62–74; *Gesammelte Schriften*, 2.1:140–57.

   14. Benjamin, *Selected Writings*, 1:253–66; *Gesammelte Schriften*, 4.1:9–21.

   15. Benjamin, *Selected Writings*, 1:116–200; *Gesammelte Schriften*, 1.2:7–123.

   16. Benjamin, *Selected Writings*, 4:406; *Gesammelte Schriften*, 1.3:1238.

   17. Benjamin, *Selected Writings*, 3:152 (translation modified); *Gesammelte Schriften*, 2.2:451.

   18. Benjamin, *Selected Writings*, v3:152; *Gesammelte Schriften*, 2.2:451.

   19. "The Storyteller," Benjamin, *Selected Writings*, 3:154. "Wenn nämlich . . . die Geschichtsschreibung die schöpferische Indifferenz der verschiedenen epischen Formen darstellt (wie die große Prosa die schöpferische Indifferenz zwischen verschiedenen Massen des Verses), so schließt deren

älteste Form, das Epos, kraft einer Art von Indifferenz die Erzählung und den Roman ein. Benjamin, Gesammelte Schriften." 2.2:453.

20. Benjamin, *Selected Writings*, 1:174. *Gesammelte Schriften*, 1.1:101.

21. Benjamin, *Selected Writings*, 1:174. *Gesammelte Schriften*, 1.2:102.

22. Benjamin, *Selected Writings*, 3:162. *Gesammelte Schriften*, 2.2:464.

23. In the storyteller essay, Benjamin quotes these terms from Georg Lukàcs's *Theory of the Novel*: "From this [struggle against the power of time] arise the genuinely epic experiences of time: hope and memory," *Selected Writings*, 3:155; *Gesammelte Schriften*, 2.2:454.

24. Giorgio Agamben, "Idea of Prose," in *Idea of Prose*, trans. Michael Sullivan and Sam Whitsitt (Albany: State University of New York, 1995), 39–41.

25. Agamben, *Idea of Prose*, 39.

26. Ibid.

27. Benjamin, *Selected Writings*, 1: 340–41; *Gesammelte Schriften*, 1.1:181.

28. Agamben, *Idea of Prose*, 27.

29. Agamben, *Language and Death*, trans. Michael Hardt and Karen Pinkus (Minneapolis: University of Minnesota Press, 1991), xi; Agamben, *Il Linguaggio e la morte* (Turin: Einaudi, 1982), 3; Martin Heidegger, *On the Essence of Language: The Metaphysics of Language and the Essencing of the Word; Concerning Herder's Treatise on the Origin of Language* (Albany: SUNY Press, 2004); *Unterwegs zur Sprache* (Pfullingen, 1967).

30. Agamben, *Language and Death*, 86.

31. Agamben, *Potentialities*, 59.

32. Agamben, *Idea of Prose*, 37 (translation modified).

33. Franz Kafka, *Nachgelassene Schriften und Fragmente*, 2:141.

34. Ibid. Excerpt translated by Martin Chalmers.

6. THE DEMAND FOR AN END: KANT AND THE NEGATIVE CONCEPTION OF HISTORY
Catharine Diehl

1. Immanuel Kant, "Das Ende aller Dinge," in *Gesammelte Schriften*, 8: 327–39. All subsequent references to Kant's works will be to this edition; except for references to the *Critique of Pure Reason*, which will be cited using the conventional A/B pagination, they will be indicated by *AA* followed by volume and page number. For a brief discussion of the political context of Kant's essay, see the introduction to "The End of All Things," in *Religion and Rational Theology*, ed. Allen Wood and George di Giovanni, 219–20. Friedrich William II ascended to the Prussian throne in 1786 and passed a censorship edict in 1788. Kant came into conflict with the new king's censors between 1792 and 1794 and was finally banned from writing on religious subjects in October 1794. Emil Arnoldt has argued that "The End of All Things" was

the crucial text leading to this ban. See his "Beiträge zu dem Material der Geschichte von Kants Leben und Schriftstellertätigkeit in bezug auf seine 'Religionslehre' und seinen Konflikt mit der preussischen Regierung," in his *Gesammelte Schriften*, 4:105–46. After Friedrich Wilhelm II's death in 1797, Kant returned to writing on religious questions. In his 1798 treatise *The Conflict of the Faculties* (*AA* 7: 1–116), Kant reflected on the controversy and argued that he was released from his promise by the emperor's death. I would like here to acknowledge my profound debt and gratitude to B. Madison Mount for his immeasurable help in the writing and editing of this essay.

2. For Kant's distinction between cognizing (*erkennen*) and thinking (*denken*) an object, see the *Critique of Pure Reason*, B xxvii, n. 1. In the sentence directly after this footnote, Kant first distinguishes between objects of experience (appearances) and things in themselves. As Peter Cornehl points out in *Die Zukunft der Versöhnung*, theoretical knowledge of the end time would not only violate critical strictures but would also have disastrous consequences for morality: "Cognition of the eschata would make true morality impossible. It would bring about the perversion of the relationship between duty and inclination, happiness and morality. . . . Kant thus sees, as Lessing already did before him, the great danger of eschatology: where otherworldly vengeance is conceived of as driving our present actions, as motivating our moral decisions, it must necessarily corrupt the morality that, on the contrary, it was supposed to make possible in the first place" (75).

3. The texts discussed in this essay are Hans Urs von Balthasar, *Prometheus: Studien zur Geschichte des deutschen Idealismus*; Ludwig Landgrebe, "Das philosophische Problem des Endes der Geschichte," in *Kritik und Metaphysik: Festschrift für Heinz Heimsoeth*, 182–201; and Jürgen Moltmann, *Theologie der Hoffnung*. Another important discussion can be found in Jacob Taubes, *Occidental Eschatology*. "The End of All Things" is one of only two pieces by Kant mentioned by Benedict XVI in his encyclical *Spe Salvi* (November 30, 2007), *Acta Apostolicae Sedis* 99 (2007): 985–1027. In §19 of *Spe Salvi*, Benedict writes that Kant presents a "changed picture" of the role of Christianity in the "rule of God," as compared with Kant's 1792 text "The Victory of the Good Principle over the Evil Principle, and the Founding of a Religion of Good on Earth," the third chapter of *Religion within the Boundaries of Reason Alone* (*AA* 6: 93–147). Benedict notes that, in comparison with his earlier claims, Kant in the 1794 essay considers "the possibility that, in addition to the natural, a perverted [*widernatürliches*] end of all things could take place" (*Spe Salvi*, §19; cf. "The End of All Things," *AA* 8:333).

4. See, e.g., Peter Fenves, *A Peculiar Fate: Metaphysics and World-History in Kant*. Fenves does briefly consider "The End of All Things" in his more recent book, *Late Kant: Towards Another Law of the Earth*, 143–50. As

Landgrebe remarks in his "Die Geschichte im Denken Kants," in *Phänome-nologie und Geschichte* (cited above, note 3), 46–64 at 46, comparatively little attention is paid to Kant's philosophy of history. Despite several recent prominent works on this topic, the literature remains scarce. For evidence of this, see the bibliographies in *The Cambridge Companion to Kant*, 449–70 at 469–70, and *The Cambridge Companion to Kant and Modern Philosophy*, 665–707 at 703–4. Discussions of Kant's philosophy of history have instead focused on his 1784 text "Idea for a Universal History in a Cosmopolitan Sense" (*AA* 8: 15–32). Paul Guyer's exclusive focus on the third proposition of the "Idea" in his influential chapter "Nature, Freedom, and Happiness: The Third Proposition of Kant's 'Idea for a Universal History'" in his *Kant on Freedom, Law, and Happiness*, 372–407, shows the extent to which the "Idea" dominates this discussion.

5. Helmut Holzhey provides a hint of such a connection in his essay "'Das Ende aller Dinge': Immanuel Kant über apokalyptische Diskurse," in *Erwartung eines Endes: Apokalyptik und Geschichte*: "In comparison with the individual memento mori, eschatological thought lacks a human subject that could set itself in a relationship to its end. But this thinking makes an advance that is supposed to allow the subject of moral self-determination to situ-ate himself historically in the tension, insoluble for him, between the homo phaenomenon and the homo noumenon" (34). Cornehl also argues that "The End of All Things" represents a new stage in Kant's thinking about the phi-losophy of history because Kant admits here that the idea of infinite progress described in his 1784 text is insufficient for human hope. As Cornehl quotes from Odo Marquard in *Die Zukunft der Versöhnung* (cited above, note 1), 77, "'Infinite Progress' is the euphemism for hopelessness" [*"Unendlicher Progreß" ist der Euphemismus für Aussichtslosigkeit*].

6. While Landgrebe does not claim that Kant's conception of an end is "atemporal" or merely "internal" rather than connected to a time of ac-tion, he does agree with Balthasar and Moltmann that "Kant's concept of time does not make available to us the possibility of grasping the time of history and history itself as the teleological unity of a process." Landgrebe, *Kritik*, 192.

7. Quoted in Landgrebe, *Kritik*, 201.

8. Balthasar, *Prometheus*, 92.

9. *AA* 5:274.

10. Quoting Ernst Bloch, Moltmann writes that the God of Christianity has the "future as the determination of his being" [*Futurum als Seinsbeschaffen-heit*]. *Theology*, 12.

11. "Within the frame of transcendental eschatology, the question of the future and the goal of revelation is answered with a reflection: The whereto

is the whence, the goal is identical with the origin of revelation." Moltmann, *Theology*, 39.

12. In Hegel's account, religion retreats from the realm of sensibility in order to avoid the danger of objectification by the understanding. The result of this retreat is both a subjective one-sidedness in the "philosophy of reflection"—under which he classifies Kant, Jacobi, and Fichte—and the introduction of an absolute division between the objective, as finite and in accordance with the understanding, and the subjective, as the site for a never fully actualized infinity. Moltmann quotes Hegel's early discussion of "the philosophy of reflection" from the preface to "Faith and Knowledge" (1802): "Religion builds its temples and altars in the heart of the individual. In sighs and prayers he seeks for the God whom he denies to himself in intuition, because of the risk that the intellect will cognize what is intuited as a mere thing, reducing the sacred grove to mere timber. Of course, the inner must be externalized; intention must become effective in action; immediate religious sentiment must be expressed in external gesture; and faith, though it flees from the objectivity of cognition, must become objective to itself in thoughts, concepts, and words. But the intellect scrupulously distinguishes the objective from the subjective, and the objective is what is accounted worthless and null. The struggle of subjective beauty must be directed precisely to this end: to defend itself properly against the necessity through which the subjective becomes objective." G.W.F. Hegel, *Faith and Knowledge*, 57, cited in Moltmann, *Theology*, 42. Although Hegel does not explicitly name "The End of All Things," Moltmann points out (42n1) that Hegel borrows much of his terminology from Kant's formulations in this essay. Compare, for instance, Kant's lines: "Here we have to do (or are playing) merely with ideas created by reason itself, whose objects (if they have any) lie wholly beyond our field of vision." *AA* 8:332.

13. Moltmann, *Theology*, 33 and 41.

14. For a discussion of this principle, see *Religion within the Boundaries of Reason Alone* (*AA* 6:25): "Moreover, to have the one or the other disposition by nature as an innate characteristic does not mean here that the disposition has not been earned by the human being who harbors it, i.e. that he is not its author, but means rather that it has not been earned in time (that he has been the one way or the other *always, from his youth on*). The disposition, i.e. the first subjective ground of the adoption of the maxims, can only be a single one, and it applies to the entire use of freedom universally."

15. In his "'For reason . . . also has its mysteries': Immortality, Religion, and 'The End of All Things,'" in *Kant's Philosophy of Religion Reconsidered*, Anthony Perovich emphasizes that the practical value of the idea of an end

of the world lies in its effects on our actions *within* the world. According to Perovich, a "future life that is outside time" offers the "prospect of an unchangeable moral state along with our subjection to the manner of eternal existence which is consequent on that ultimate moral condition. In this view, all ethical development must occur in the present, while the revelations of conscience about that development help us to anticipate the character of the timeless future and to respond accordingly" (169). While Perovich is certainly correct to point to the effect of the idea of an unchangeable moral disposition on our actions within the world, it is unclear what sort of "anticipation" according to the "revelations of conscience" he is considering. Perovich also neglects to develop the implications of the peculiar temporal structure of a "future . . . outside time" that requires all development to happen "in the present." These formulations do show, however, the complexities into which one is drawn in attempting to relate temporal and eternal characteristics. As we will see, no such coordination is ultimately possible.

16. For a contrasting account of the status of the future in Kant's philosophy, see Taubes, *Occidental Eschatology*: "Therefore, Copernican man gets no closer to his true nature by closing the gap between the world and the heavenly archetype [*oberen Urbild*]. Because the space between heaven and earth has become meaning-less, Copernican man seeks to revolutionize the world according to an ideal that can become reality in the course of time. The ideal is no longer the Platonic idea which dwells on high, but is to be found in the future" (137).

17. Balthasar recognizes that the "transcendental begins" with a revelation of the *boundaries* of cognition: "For this self-cognition of the thoroughgoing inner limitation of essence [*Wesensdurchgrenztheit*] is to such extent an inner limitation and thus to a correspondingly little extent a shining revelation of spirit that 'I do not even . . . know what the word *spirit* means'" (*Prometheus*, 93).

18. Balthasar similarly describes the "end of all things" as a final point that does not itself appear, a "vanishing point" (*Prometheus*, 94) that represents the "precisely uncanny paradox" (99).

19. The idea of a *katechon* as world-historical force operating against an encroaching, barbarian eschaton is popularized by Carl Schmitt in *The Nomos of the Earth*, 59–62. For the original biblical reference, see 2 Thess. 2:6–7.

20. Kant compares the moral faculty (*sittliche Anlage*) to Horace's *poena pede claudo* and writes that it "catches" and "trips up" the hurrying progress of culture "as one may hope under a wise ruler of the world" (*AA* 8:332). Kant's language here echoes that of his 1784 text "What Is Enlightenment?,"

where he describes a "peculiar, unexpected course [*Gang*] in human affairs"—
namely, that "in great things" (*im Großen*), where "nearly everything is
paradoxical," "a greater degree of civil freedom appears to be beneficial to
the freedom of spirit but creates unbridgeable limits to it" (*AA:* 8:41).

21. In the Canon of Pure Reason, Kant identifies this question as one of
the three questions of interest to reason. While the first question, "What
can I know?" is theoretical, and the second, "What should I do?" is practical,
the third interweaves the theoretical with the practical by concluding from
how something should be what it will be. It is "simultaneously practical and
theoretical, so that the practical leads like a clue to a reply to the theoretical
question and, in its highest form, the speculative question. For all *hope* concerns happiness, and with respect to the practical and the moral law it is the
very same as what knowledge and the natural law is with regard to theoretical cognition of things. The former finally comes down to the inference that
something *is* (which determines the ultimate final end) *because something ought
to happen*; the latter, that something *is* (which acts as the supreme cause) *because something does happen*" (A805–6/B833–34). (The translation of the first
Critique used throughout, with occasional modifications, is *Critique of Pure
Reason*, ed. Paul Guyer and Allen W. Wood in this quotation, boldface has
been changed to italics.) As an answer to this question, the idea of an end of
history thus provides the possibility for a practical principle to *appear*—albeit
indirectly and, as I will argue, negatively—within the world.

22. Landgrebe, *Kritik*, 183.

23. See Landgrebe, *Kritik*, 191: "The alternative Löwith offers between
an eschatological, linear process and a circular concept is not acceptable for
the modern spirit not because it wishes to choose neither of the two but
because both fall in the same way into the dialectic that Kant developed in
the first Antinomy. For if the end and the endlessness of the world are representations to which no object of possible experience corresponds in either
case, then it is entirely the same whether endlessness is represented as such
in the sense of a line or in the sense of an eternally circular process coming
back into itself. In this sense, Löwith's alternatives remain on pre-Critical
terrain and are for this reason inappropriate for answering the question of the
conditions of possibility in which a historical process can be represented as a
continuous order of events."

24. Although Landgrebe charges Kant with retaining Aristotle's conception of time as a line and thus with failing to account for the "disappearing
now," it was Aristotle himself who developed the concept of such a "now."
In *Physics* 4.10.218a9–21, Aristotle describes the now that is always destined
to "cease to be" (ἐφθάρθαι); see *The Complete Works of Aristotle*, ed. Jonathan
Barnes (1984), 1:370. While Landgrebe claims that the philosophy of time—

with the sole exception of Augustine—has neglected this "disappearing present" (*Kritik*, 193), it is in fact of central importance to the tradition. My thanks to Werner Hamacher for alerting me to the importance of this "now" in Aristotle and in Hegel.

25. *AA* 8:327.

26. *AA* 8:334.

27. Boethius, *De sancta trinitate* 4.244–45, translated in *Boethius: The Theological Tractates and The Consolation of Philosophy*, 22.

28. Boethius, *Philosophiae consolatio* 5.6.4, translated in *Boethius: The Theological Tractates and The Consolation of Philosophy*, 422.

29. Boethius, *Philosophiae consolatio* 5.6.8, translated in *Boethius: The Theological Tractates and The Consolation of Philosophy*, 424. See also Plotinus, *Enneads* 3.7.3, and Thomas Aquinas, *Summa Theologica*, 1a, q. 10, art. 1. For a sympathetic discussion of the concept of eternity, see Eleonore Stump and Norman Kretzmann, "Eternity," *Journal of Philosophy* 78 (1981): 429–58.

30. For Kant's discussion of this, see the following comment in the *Opus Postumum*: "The transition from one state to another is an alteration in the way in which the thing exists, since in one point in time it namely is no longer but in the following is still not, and an act of two successive points of time constitutes the common border. The transition always demands, however, a time; for two moments [*Augenblicke*] cannot immediately follow one another and this time always presupposes a degree of growth" (*AA* 21:637).

31. *AA* 8:327.

32. In *Kants Schrift: Das Ende aller Dinge*, Hansjörg Alfred Salmony makes this connection between the existence of the individual person and the entirety of the phenomenal world in a particularly perspicuous manner: "The human being, as a perceiving and cognizing being, is perpetually bound to the sensible world, enclosed within it as in a prison whose walls are insurmountably high" (19).

33. *AA* 8:330.

34. See Hans Vaihinger, *Die Philosophie des Als Ob: System der theoretischen, praktischen und religiösen Fiktionen der Menschheit auf Grund eines idealistischen Positivismus.* Vaihinger proposes a theory of the function of certain judgments, which he terms "fictions," in human reason. In an appendix dealing with Kant's use of the "as if," Vaihinger considers the "as if" in "The End of All Things" and claims that it is a fiction: "Consequently: that idea, those ideas are only the products of our own reason and we can therefore say along with Kant: we *are playing merely with ideas created by reason itself*—in short, they are fictions in our sense" (682). What saves reason from turning the idea

of the end of the world into a dogma is the recollection that this idea is nothing more than a product of reason itself.

35. While this position appears to be ruled out by Kant's published text, he does seem to maintain something like it in his unpublished notes on the text: "If time and eternity (as duration) are merely considered according to their magnitude and not according to their quality, then it is an absurd division of all worldly durations into time and eternity, for time also belongs to eternity. Therefore, they must be classified by their different quality. That the human being passes out of time into eternity is a contradictory expression, for he was in eternity when he was in time. That must therefore have been a duration without time—it is the alpha and omega, because the beginning and the end of each thing is simultaneous with God, in other words, only succession drops out of duration, magnitude remains" (*AA* 23:151). Kant seems to prohibit the division between time and eternity according to magnitude but to permit it according to what he calls *quality*—that is, simultaneity or succession. Eternity, according to this view, is simultaneous with the "beginning" and "end" of every thing but bears no relations of succession. This would, then, make Kant's views resemble those of Aquinas and Boethius. Nevertheless, in the published text, there is no sign that Kant holds that the relation of simultaneity can obtain between the *duratio noumenon* and moments in time. This seems also to follow from Kant's critical strictures, since, after all, simultaneity would itself be a relation and we can have cognition of it only for the objects of experience.

36. For a development of this concept, see the "General Remark on the Exposition of Aesthetic Reflective Judgment," the section that follows the exposition of the sublime in the Critique of the Aesthetic Power of Judgment in the third *Critique*, in which Kant describes the failure of the imagination to present the infinite within sensibility, writing: "For the imagination, although it certainly finds nothing beyond the sensible to which it can attach itself, nevertheless feels itself to be unbounded precisely because of this elimination of the limits of sensibility; and that separation is thus a presentation of the infinite, which for that very reason can never be anything other than a merely negative presentation, which nevertheless expands the soul" (*AA* 5:274). See Immanuel Kant, *Critique of the Power of Judgment*, trans. Paul Guyer and Eric Matthews.

37. *AA* 8:327.
38. See Fenves, *Late Kant*, 145.
39. A418/B446.
40. *AA* 5:434.
41. *AA* 8:331.

7. MIGRATIONS OF THE BOHEMIAN
Joshua Wilner

1. "Dann ist uns wie jedem Geschlecht, das vor uns war, eine *schwache* messianische Kraft mitgegeben, an welche die Vergangenheit Anspruch hat." Benjamin, "Über den Begriff der Geschichte." *Gesammelte Schriften*, 1:694.

2. Académie française, *Dictionnaire de l'Académie française* (1798), s.v. "bohémien": "Ces mots ne sont point mis ici pour signifier les peuples de cette partie de l'Allemagne qu'on appelle *Bohème*; mais seulement pour désigner une sorte de vagabonds qui courent le pays, disant la bonne aventure, et dérobant avec adresse."

3. "Nous répéterons en forme d'axiome: La Bohème, c'est le stage de la vie artistique. . . . La Bohème n'existe et n'est possible qu'à Paris." Murger, *Scènes de la Bohème*, vi.

4. "Ce nom de bohêmes, donné longtemps à des classes d'avec lesquelles tiennent à honneur de se différencier celles dont nous avons essayé de retracer les moeurs et le langage." Murger, *Scènes de la Bohème*, vi.

5. Émile Littré, *Dictionnaire de la langue française* (1872–77), s.v. "bohème ou bohémien, ienne": "bohème ou bohémien: Nom de bandes vagabondes, sans domicile fixe, sans métier régulier, et se mêlant souvent de dire la bonne aventure: on leur donne aussi le nom d'Égyptiens et de Zingaris."

6. "La Bohème, qu'il faudrait appeler la Doctrine du boulevard des Italiens." Honoré de Balzac, *A Prince of Bohemia*, 72; *Un prince de Bohème*, 808.

7. "Ce mot de Bohème vous dit tout. La Bohème n'a rien et vit de ce qu'elle a. L'Espérance est sa religion." Balzac, *Un prince de Bohème*, 809.

8. In contrast with Baudelaire, however, who directly identifies his Bohemians as "the prophetic tribe" and draws on Old Testament sources, Balzac's immediate reference is to the Pauline triad of Hope, Faith, and Charity: "Hope is its religion; faith (in oneself) its creed; and Charity is supposed to be its budget" (*A Prince of Bohemia*, 73). ("L'Espérance est sa religion, la Foi en soi-même est son code, la Charité passe pour être son budget" [*Un prince de Bohème*, 809].) The Christianizing trope, however ironic, is of a piece of course with the recasting of the Bohemian as a quintessentially French type.

9. "Quel absurde pouvoir laisse ainsi se perdre des forces immenses? Il se trouve dans la Bohême des diplomates capables de renverser les projets de la Russie, s'ils se sentaient appuyés par la puissance de la France." Balzac, *A Prince of Bohemia*, 72–73; *Un prince de Bohème*, 808–9.

10. "Si l'empereur de Russie achetait la Bohême moyennant une vingtaine de millions, en admettant qu'elle voulût quitter l'asphalte des boulevards, et qu'il la déportât à Odessa dans un an, Odessa serait Paris." Balzac, *A Prince of Bohemia*, 73; *Un prince de Bohème* 809.

11. Marilyn Brown, *Gypsies and Other Bohemians*, 8. In characterizing Bohemia as a "picturesque response to . . . the failure of revolution," Brown is particularly concerned to argue that Clark "exaggerates the case for [Bohemia's] political radicalism." The instability of Bohemia's political location is, I would argue, internal to the trope. What remains constant in this instability is *some* defining relation to millennial expectation.

12. Marx, *The Eighteenth Brumaire of Louis Bonaparte*, 149. The passage as a whole warrants citation, both for its derisive verve and for its identification of *la bohème* with the lumpenproletariet: "On the pretext of founding a benevolent society, the lumpenproletariet of Paris had been organised into secret sections, each section being led by Bonapartist agents, with a Bonapartist general at the head of the whole. Alongside decayed *roués* of dubious means of subsistence and of dubious origin, alongside ruined and adventurous offshoots of the bourgeoisie, were vagabonds, discharged soldiers, discharged jailbirds, escaped galley slaves, rogues, mountebanks, *lazzaroni*, pickpockets, tricksters, gamblers, *maquereaux*, brothel keepers, porters, *literati*, organ-grinders, rag-pickers, knife grinders, tinkers, beggars—in short, the whole indefinite, disintegrated mass, thrown hither and thither, which the French term *la bohème*." (148–49). ("Unter dem Vorwande, eine Wohltätigkeitsgesellschaft zu stiften, war das Pariser Lumpenproletariat in geheime Sektionen organisiert worden, jede Sektion von einem bonapartistischen Agenten geleitet, an der Spitze ein bonapartistischer General. Neben zerrütteten Roués mit Subsistenzmitteln und von zweideutiger Herkunft, neben verkommenen und abenteuernden Ablegern der Bourgeoisie Vagabunden, entlassene Soldaten, entlassene Zuchthaussträflinge, entlaufene Galeerensklaven, Gauner, Gaukler, Lazzaroni, Taschendiebe, Taschenspieler, Spieler, Maquereaus, Bordellhalter, Lastträger, Literaten, Orgeldreher, Lumpensammler, Scherenschleifer, Kesselflicker, Bettler, kurz, die ganze unbestimmte, aufgelöste, hin- und hergeworfene Masse, die die Franzosen *la bohème* nennen." *Der Achzehnte Brumaire des Louis Bonaparte*, 160–61.)

13. Charles Baudelaire, *Oeuvres complètes*, 1:864 (editorial note).

14. Michael Riffaterre, "The Stylistic Approach to Literary History," 42.

15. Baudelaire, *Oeuvre complètes*, 1:706.

16. T. J. Clark, *Image of the People*, 33.

17. "The Commission [*des colonies agricoles*] selected 4,568 households, representing 13,972 people. . . . Some sixteen convoys left Paris between 8 October and 11 December 1848. . . . Almost immediately those who could afford to leave set off back to France or fled to the relative safety of Algiers or Oran. By the time the final convoy arrived, only 12,666 of the original 13,972 remained on the army lists." Michael J. Heffernan, "The Parisian Poor and

the Colonization of Algeria During the Second Republic," 389–93. Marx (see below) put the number at 15,000.

18. "More than 3,000 insurgents were butchered after the victory, and 15,000 were transported without trial." Marx, *The Eighteenth Brumaire of Louis Bonaparte*, 100. ("Über 3.000 Insurgenten wurden niedergemetzelt nach dem Siege, 15.000 ohne Urteil transportiert." *Der Achzehnte Brumaire des Louis Bonaparte*, 122.)

19. "They would only have to strike the earth with their feet to bring forth harvests." 389.

20. "In Paris, they were promised an Eldorado; here, they find nature, bitter and raw." Heffernen, "The Parisian Poor and the Colonization of Algeria During the Second Republic," 396.

21. "Baudelaire me mène chez Daumier." Poulet-Massis in a memorandum, January 14, 1852; cited by Robert Fohr, *Daumier sculpteur et peintre*, 57.

22. For example, Jean Adhémar, *Honoré Daumier*, 39; and Bruce Laughton, *Honoré Daumier*, 28.

23. See Brown, *Gypsies and Other Bohemians*, 59–60.

24. K. E. Maison, *Honoré Daumier: Catalogue raisonné of the paintings, watercolours, and drawings*, 2, 29.

25. John Hollander, *The Gazer's Spirit*, 179.

26. Ludwig Wittgenstein, *Philosophical Investigations*, 184.

8. PAUL CELAN'S IMPROPER NAMES
Anna Glazova

1. Cf. Paul Celan's letter to Norbert Koch: "The experience that we must see things differently today, perceive them differently, speak differently, among other things. That the poem today, more indispensable than ever, is a pneumatic concern." ("Die Erfahrung u.a., dass wir heute anders sehen, anders wahrnehmen, anders sprechen müssen. Dass das Gedicht, unabdingbarer als bisher, eine pneumatische Angelegenheit ist—und nicht nur das." Paul Celan, *"Mikrolithen sinds, Steinchen": Die Prosa aus dem Nachlaß*, 338). See also Celan's interview with Israeli radio Kol Yisrael: "Certainly, the Jewish things can be thematized, but this is merely one aspect. I believe that themes alone don't suffice for a definition of everything Jewish. Jewish things are also, so to speak, a pneumatic concern." ("Selbstverständlich hat das Jüdische einen thematischen Aspekt. Aber ich glaube, daß das Thematische allein nicht ausreicht, um das Jüdische zu definieren. Jüdisches ist sozusagen auch eine *pneumatische* Angelegenheit." John Felstiner, *Paul Celan: Eine Biographie*, 339–40). Celan's "pneumatic Judaism" is a non-rabbinical Judaism that is not confined to a monotheist religion. Further, this term can be understood as a reference to the Greco-Judaic tradition and to Philo of Alexandria in par-

ticular, with whose ideas Celan was somewhat familiar through Ernst Bloch's *Das Prinzip Hoffnung* (The Principle of Hope). Rochelle Tobias interprets this expression as a possible link to Paul of Tarsus. Lydia Koelle documents Celan's complicated relation to Judaism extensively in her book-length study, in which she discusses, among other things, Celan's "pneumatic Judaism." All translations are mine unless otherwise noted.

2. Celan, *Meridian*, 156.

3. Celan, *Gesammelte Werke*, 2:36.

4. Elizabeth Petuchowski, in her essay "A New Approach to Paul Celan's 'Argumentum e Silentio,'" is one of the first scholars to discuss the role of intersections between different languages in Celan's poetry. Werner Hamacher analyzes a particular instance of a Hebrew reference in Celan's "Aus dem Moorboden" (From the bog soil) in his essay "Häm" (Heme), 173–97.

5. Celan's decision to omit the name of one of the divine vessels, Shechina, in the final version creates an uncertainty for the reader who is familiar with the Lurianic imagery of these broken vessels. (I will discuss this piece of Jewish mysticism later in my paper.) This confusion has become manifest in Celan scholarship. Before the volume of drafts and early versions of *Die Niemandsrose* (*The No-One's-Rose*) (including early versions of the collection) had been published, scholars had differing opinions as to whether Celan was, indeed, alluding to the story of the sefiroth. Dietlind Meinecke suggested this connection in her study, *On Paul Celan*, published early, in 1970; Shira Wolosky rejected this reading in favor of a reading less affirmative in its implications ("Mystical Language and Mystical Silence in Paul Celan's 'Dein Hinübersein,'" in *Argumentum e silentio*, 364–77). Allusions to the breaking of the vessels might be at stake in this poem, Wolosky thinks, but, by translating Jewish mysticism into history, as she claims Celan does, he blasphemes against the very notion of the eternity of creation. Thus, for her, Celan's reference to Shechina, even if Celan intended it in the poem, problematizes rather than affirms the mystical tradition. It's worthy to note, however, that Shechina (at least since Isaak Luria's interpretation of the sefiroth) stands precisely for the temporal, exiled existence of God. Once history becomes fulfilled in the messianic age, the temporal character of Shechina will yield to its atemporal essence as the unity of people and God. Hassidism, moreover, is an active and a social—not merely a historical—project of bringing the essence of Shechina into everyday life. Mysticism in Judaism (unlike the Christian mysticism Wolosky refers to in the same breath in her essay) is, thus, not so much an atemporal ideation as an ethical and practical agenda.

6. This is the central motif of Hugo Bergmann's essay. Further, Lydia Koelle formulates this insight as inherent to Celan's poetry: "Hebraisms in

Celan's poems aren't 'words,' they are used as names to which meaning and history adhere and coagulate; they are proper names with proper life histories transposed into a new context." ("Die Hebraismen in Celans Gedichten sind keine 'Wörter,' sie werden wie Namen gebraucht, an denen Sinn und Geschichte haften und sich verdichten, sie sind Eigenworte mit Eigenleben, die in einen neuen Kontext verpflanzt werden.") Koelle, *Paul Celans pneumatisches Judentum.* 110.

    7. When Rolf Bücher analyzes one of the poems I discuss in this essay, "Von Ungeträumten geätzt" (By the undreamt etched), he finds an inner contradiction in Celan's use of names as words and words as names. For Bücher, this makes Celan's language contradictory, for "the word as 'name' turns out to be fundamentally polyvalent" (das Wort als 'Name' [erweist sich] als prinzipiell polyvalent). Bücher, "Experienced Speaking," in *Argumentum e Silentio*, 107. In my view, Celan treats naming and speaking not so much to set them in contradiction to each other as to point at a transitory state of the language we use.

    8. Bergmann, "Die Heiligung des Namens," 38 (italics in the original).

    9. Celan, *Gesammelte Werke*, 2:12.

    10. Joris, *Breathturn*, 67.

    11. Celan, *Gesammelte Werke*, 2:49.

    12. Hamburger, *Poems*, 247 (translation modified).

    13. Celan, *Gesammelte Werke*, 1:225; Celan, *Selections*, 78 (translation by Cid Corman).

    14. Sholem, *Geheimnisse*, 42.

    15. My source here and in the following is Aryeh Kaplan's commentary on Sefer Yetzirah.

    16. Kaplan, 32–37.

    17. The division of ten sefiroth into two parts corresponds to Abraham's covenant, in which ten halves of five sacrificial animals create the purifying tension in the middle (Kaplan 34–35; Genesis 15:9). Ancient Greek rituals of purification, likewise, involved cutting sacrificial animals in two; an object placed between the halves was purified. Cf., e.g., the following passage: "Each spring the Macedonian army reassembled, it was marched between the two halves of a sacrificed dog, which created what has been called an 'absorptive zone' for all its impurities" (Robert Parker, *Miasma*, 22). Parker further notes that this purification ritual has a Near Eastern analogue.

    18. Isaiah 48:13.

    19. Before creation, the earth was "unformed and void" (*tohu va-vohu*), Genesis 1:2.

    20. In this sense, the cosmos of *sefiroth* is somewhat different from the Pythagorean cosmos whose primordial elements are digits.

21. Kaplan, 25.

22. Whereas the Septuagint provides in this verse οὐδέν for *tohu*, and οὐδενός for *beli-mah*, both sharing the same stem (as in ουσια), the Vulgate translates *tohu* as *vacuum*, and *beli-mah* as *nihilum*.

23. Kaplan, 66 (Kaplan's translation).

24. My very brief description of the Lurianic Kabbalah is based on Gershom Scholem's *Die Jüdische Mystik in ihren Hauptströmungen* (Major trends in Jewish mysticism) (Frankfurt am Main: Suhrkamp, 1957).

25. The square brackets are Scholem's. Scholem's translation of Nathan's letter is based on Jacob Sasportas, Sisath Nobel Sevi (Jerusalem, 1954).

26. Scholem quotes from: *Be Iqvoth Mashiah*, a collection of texts from the beginnings of the Sabbatean faith, selected from the writings of R. Abraham Benjamin Nathan b. Elisha Hayyim Ashkenazi, known as Nathan of Gaza, edited by Gerschom Sholem and published in 1944.

27. Celan, *Meridian*, 104.

28. Celan, *Gesammelte Werke*, 2:49; Hamburger, *Poems*, 247 (translation modified).

29. Celan, *Gesammelte Werke*, 2:312.

30. Celan, *Gesammelte Werke*, 1:163; Celan, *Selections*, 62 (translation by Cid Corman).

31. Stéphane Mosès finds that the termination of all messianic hope is at stake in Benjamin's "Über einige Motive bei Baudelaire" (On some motifs in Baudelaire): The invisibility of stars in modern cities due to the electric lights makes constellations hopelessly invisible. With reference to Jewish messianism, Mosès interprets stars as Benjamin's image for "sparks of hope" ("Funken der Hoffnung") (Walter Benjamin, "Über den Begriff der Geschichte," *Gesammelte Schriften*, 1: 694)—i.e., as the sparks of the divine light caught in the world and needing to be recollected in order for the messianic age to arrive. One could add to Mosès's interpretation that the invisibility of constellations, hopeless as it is for city dwellers, does not eliminate stars by mere destructive force; instead, the starlight is absorbed by the weaker light of street lanterns—dispersed rather than hopelessly lost in tenebrae, in darkness.

32. Celan, *Gesammelte Werke*, 163; Celan, *Selections*, 62 (translation by Cid Corman).

33. Gerschom Sholem uses this expression in a letter to Walter Benjamin in reference to Kafka. Stéphane Mosès in his analysis of "Die Posaunenstelle" (The trumpet place) uses this quotation as pertaining to Celan's poetry.

34. Celan, *Gesammelte Werke*, 1:242.

35. The long and tormenting story of Celan's being falsely accused of plagiarism and other literary crimes is documented in the volume *Die Goll-Affäre*, edited by Barbara Weidemann.

36. Celan and Szondi, *Briefwechsel*, 40.

37. Celan, *Meridian*, 12.

38. Jacques Derrida, *Shibboleth*, 63 (the note in square brackets is mine).

39. Claire Goll accused Celan of plagiarizing the poems of her husband, Ivan Goll, as well as her translations of them. The affair grew into a scandal in the press and was extremely traumatic for Celan. Szondi and many others supported Celan in his attempts to defend himself, but they could not alleviate his anxiety.

40. Celan and Szondi, *Briefwechsel*, 40.

41. This image returns in Celan's letter (January 21, 1962) to Adorno. There "the claw" (*die Klaue*) appears as the token of concealed anti-Semitism. *Goll-Affäre*, ed. Weidemann, 552.

42. Celan, *Gesammelte Werke*, 3:177.

43. The last two lines are a greeting in Hebrew and a Hebrew transcription of Celan's name.

44. Celan and Szondi, *Briefwechsel*, 48.

45. I thank Chana Kronfeld for bringing this to my attention. The proper Hebrew transcription would be צלאן.

9. "WHEN CHRISTIANITY IS FINALLY OVER": IMAGES OF A MESSIANIC POLITICS IN HEINE AND BENJAMIN
Peter Fenves

1. Walter Benjamin, *Gesammelte Schriften* (hereafter, *GS*), 4:307. All translations are my own. I would like to thank Samuel Weber, Julia Ng, and Anna Glazova for illuminating comments and suggestions on this essay.

2. Gershom Scholem, *Tagebücher, nebst Aufsätzen und Entwürfen bis 1923*, 1:253; for his knowledge of Benjamin's relation to Heine, see *Walter Benjamin—die Geschichte einer Freundschaft*, 18.

3. Hans Mayer, *Der Weg Heinrich Heines*, 114–15.

4. See Walter Benjamin, *Gesammelte Briefe* (hereafter, *B*), 5:236–37.

5. Benjamin mentions Heine a few times in the *Arcades Project*. Perhaps the most notable is the following quotation from Baudelaire, the first from *L'art romantique:* "his literature [referring to Heine] could be called 'materialist sentimentalism'" (*GS* 5:307). The second appears in a passage recounting something Baudelaire once said: "Jules Janini 1865 criticized Heine for being melancholic in the *Indépendance Belge*, to which Baudelaire replied: 'Baudelaire maintained that melancholia is the source of all sincere poetry'" (*GS* 5:315). The only place in his extent writings where Benjamin mentions Heine's travel writings appears in the article on Jews in German Culture, where they are associated with Ludwig Börne's form of art criticism (*GS* 2:811–12).

6. Heinrich Heine, *Werke*, 2:291; hereafter, *W.*

7. Karl Marx, *Zur Kritik der politischen Ökonomie* (1859), in Karl Marx and Friedrich Engels, *Werke*, 13:9.

8. Benjamin does not follow Heine in this regard; on the contrary, according to Scholem, he considered himself "related" to von Platen; see Scholem, *Walter Benjamin*, 83.

9. See the informative discussion of the Heine-von Platen controversy in Hans Mayer, *Aussenseiter*, 207–23.

10. Ernst Bloch, *Literarische Aufsätze*, 235–79.

11. Erich Mühsam, *Gedichte*, 1:404. For an analysis of this poem in the broad context of German travel to Italy, see Richard Block, *The Spell of Italy: Vocation, Magic, and the Attraction of Goethe*, 197–99.

12. See Benjamin, *Gesammelte Briefe*, 3:466–67.

13. For the lineaments of the doctrine of *res nullius* in private law (divine law has its own doctrine), see Justinian, *Institutes*, 2.1:15–16.

14. Walter Benjamin, "Notes toward a Work on the Category of Justice," which was preserved in Scholem, *Tagebücher*, 1:401. An extensive discussion of these "Notes" can be found in my *Messianic Reduction: Walter Benjamin and the Shape of Time*, 187–207.

15. Scholem, *Tagebücher*, 1:401.

16. Johann Wolfgang von Goethe, *Werke*, 31:23.

17. Heinrich Heine, *Briefe*, 2:142 (October 30, 1836).

10. THE CRISIS OF THE MESSIANIC CLAIM: SCHOLEM, BENJAMIN, BAUDELAIRE
Oleg Gelikman

1. The full text of Benjamin's fragment runs as follows: "The past carries with itself a secret index by which it is referred to redemption. Doesn't a breath of the air that pervaded earlier days caress us as well? In the voices we hear, isn't there an echo of now silent ones? Don't the women we court have sisters they no longer recognize? If so, then there is a secret agreement between past generations and the present one. Then our coming was expected on earth. Then, like every generation that preceded us, we have been endowed with a weak messianic power, a power on which the past has a claim. Such a claim cannot be settled cheaply. The historical materialist is aware of this" (*Selected Writings*, 4:390; *Gesammelte Schriften*, 1.2:693–94). Henceforth, all references to Benjamin will appear in the text, first citing the *Selected Writings* as *SW* and then the German original as *GS*. Kafka's remark occurs in his Octavo notebooks following the date of December 4, 1917, in *Nachgelassene Schriften und Fragmente II*, 55; translated in *The Blue Octavo Notebooks*, 28.

Derrida's suspensions of messianism pervade *Specters of Marx* and the later "Marx and Sons." To my mind, his most revealing statement on the necessity of these multiple contractions occurs at the very end of "Force of Law," a text that predates *Specters*. After pointing to the disturbing proximity of Benjamin's "Critique of Violence" to the critique of the state and political representation in Carl Schmitt and Heidegger, Derrida admits that "this text, like many others by Benjamin, is still too Heidegerrian, too messianico-Marxist or archeo-eschatological for me" (*Acts of Religion*, 298).

2. A more contemporary version of the crisis of the messianic claim can be detected in the recent reappearance of the idea of communism in the works of Alain Badiou, Slavoj Žižek, and Boris Groys. The popular press greeted this project with accusations of reckless or anachronistic advocacy of revolutionary violence (see John Gray, "The Violent Visions of Slavoj Žižek," and Alan Johnson, "The New Communism: Resurrecting the Utopian Delusion"). This type of standoff risks once again concealing the deadlock between violence and salvation internal to the messianic claim, deferring the task of neutralization even further. On a more hopeful note, for the anticipatory neutralizations of messianism, one could consult Andrey Platonov's *The Foundation Pit* and Michel Houellebecq's *The Possibility of an Island*.

3. Gershom Scholem's early diaries were published in two volumes as *Tagebücher nebst Aufsätzen und Entwürfen bis 1923*. A selection from the diaries recently appeared in English translation as *Lamentations of Youth: The Diaries of Gershom Scholem, 1913–1919*. For a preliminary analysis of the speculative dimension of the diaries, see Michael Löwy, "Messianism in the Early Work of Gershom Scholem." Willi Goetschel provided an overview of Scholem's work in light of the diaries in "Scholem's Diaries, Letters, and New Literature on His Work: Review Essay," *Germanic Review* 72 (1997). A decisive reappraisal of Scholem's legacy has been initiated by David Biale in *Gershom Scholem: Kabbalah and Counter-History* and has been resumed by Paul Mendes-Flohr in *Gershom Scholem: The Man and His Work*. This reappraisal is complicated by Scholem's alleged prohibition on accentuating the Romantic exorbitance of his early thought (Löwy, 178n2); see also Joseph Dan, "Scholem's View of Jewish Messianism," and Eric Jacobson, *Metaphysics of the Profane: The Political Theology of Walter Benjamin and Gershom Scholem*.

4. "Confession on the Subject of Our Language," reprinted as an appendix to Jacques Derrida, "The Eyes of Language," *Acts of Religion*, 226. Derrida's texts collected in this volume, especially "The Eyes of Language: The Abyss and the Volcano" and "Interpretations at War: Kant, the Jew, the German," constitute a rich background to the problem of messianism. For a careful examination of Derrida's version of messianism, see Dana Hollander,

Exemplarity and Chosenness: Rosenzweig and Derrida on the Nation of Philosophy; for a contrasting view, cf. Martin Kavka, *Jewish Messianism and the History of Philosophy,* 93–221.

5. Gershom Scholem, "Toward an Understanding of the Messianic Idea in Judaism," *The Messianic Idea in Judaism,* 35.

6. From this standpoint, the practice of forced conversion of Jews in the third and fourth centuries becomes discernible as an early index of the logic binding messianic filiations to persecution. In his biography of Augustine, James J. O'Donnell indicates that persecution was a necessary byproduct of the singularity attributed to the Jews already by the early Christians: "The Jews were unique in the Christian taxonomy Augustine inherited and propounded in that they worshipped the correct God, but worshipped him incorrectly, or rather incompletely. Their fault was entirely moral: they had the scriptures, they had seen Jesus, they worshipped the correct god, but they had not put two and two together, and so they would be damned" (*Augustine,* 188). The Jew is not the enemy of the early Christian but his obscene double, a dark precursor and obstinate survivor—in sum, an intolerable presence. Judophilia and Judophobia are thus two faces of the same coin: "His [St. Augustine's] manner of patronizing [Jews] was not directly toxic, but in his own time, forced conversions, which he condemned in principle, would be harbingers of future persecution" (88). Indirectly toxic patronage, it is suggested, kills just as well, and perhaps even better, than simple hatred. For a counterargument, see Paula Fredriksen, *Augustine and the Jews: A Christian Defense of Jews and Judaism.* See also Daniel Boyrain, "The Christian Invention of Judaism," *Religion: Beyond a Concept,* 150–78.

7. In this regard, Giorgio Agamben's critique of Scholem's assessment of messianism offers an interesting counterpoint (see, for instance, "The Messiah and the Sovereign," *Potentialities,* 166–67).

8. Scholem's conception of messanism is that of an irreversible geopolitical contagion (hence, his fascination of Sabbatai Zevi's conversion to Islam, the "crypto-Jewish" Turkish sect of the Döonmeh, and other figures of messianic contamination). His notes on the restored Hebrew in the letter to Franz Rosenzweig have a definite flavor of the sorcerer's apprentice contemplating the genie he has let out of the bottle. The same apprehension returns, now in the form of a straight assertion of historical filiation, in the following claim on the origins of Enlightenment historiography: "In probing into the roots of this new conception of the Messianic ideal as man's infinite progress and perfectibility, we find, surprisingly, that they stem from Kabbalah" ("The Messianic Idea in Kabbalism," *The Messianic Idea in Judaism,* 37). For Scholem, there can be no abolition of messianism, as it is the medium of contemporary historiographic consciousness. Rather than suppressing its

presence in the interest of secularization, or collapsing the difference between the messianic and the theological (the strategy of fundamentalism), Scholem imagines a different modulation of the messanic-theological difference—i.e., a different style of messianic maintenance.

9. Scholem uses the term "neutralization" in his essay "Neutralization of the Messianic Element in Early Hassidism," *The Messianic Idea in Judaism*, 176–203. But the concern with neutralization is never too far from Scholem's mind and reappears in more or less explicit forms across his writings. For instance, an auto-citation: He closes one of his later essays by citing the passage from "Toward an Understanding of the Messianic Idea" that I quoted above. This passage travels through Scholem's writing like an old letter that he keeps sending to his readers but that always comes back unopened.

10. Scholem's references to his idea of universal history as a messianic filiation are at once numerous and elusive. For instance, describing the relation of Nathan of Gaza to Shabbetei Zevi, he remarks: "To borrow a metaphor from an earlier messianic movement, Nathan of Gaza was at once the John the Baptist and the Paul of the new Messiah" (cited in Michael Löwy, "The Modern Intellectual and His Heretical Ancestor: Gershom Scholem and Nathan of Gaza," 105); see also Scholem's positing of a genetic relationship between the idea of progress as historical development and Lurianic Kabbalah (cited in note 8).

11. The critical debate that greeted Jean-Paul Sartre's *Baudelaire* is a good example of this phenomenon.

12. "Le monde va finir. L'humanité est décrépite. Un Barnum de l'avenir montre aux hommes dégradés de son temps une belle femme des anciens âges artificiellement conservée. 'Eh! Quoi! Disent-ils, l'humanité a pu être aussi belle que cela?,'" *Oeuvres complètes, Bibliothèque de la Pléiade*, 2:831. In the main text, references to this edition will appear as *OC*.

13. For an illuminating discussion of epochal thinking as metaphysical and historiographic phenomenon, see Vincent Descombes, *The Barometer of Modern Reason*, 95–125. Earlier in the book, Descombes favorably contrasts Baudelaire's descriptive sense of modernity as the epoch of reason with rigid opposition between instrumental and communicative reason in Habermas (63–64).

14. In a letter to Arsène Houssaye, written in December 1861, Baudelaire gives a list of poems in prose that includes "La Fin du monde" (*Correspondance*, 2:197). The title "La fin du monde" also recurs in the lists of projected "Romans et Nouvelles" (*OC* 1:366–70, 588–99). The editors of the Pleiade edition placed the passage as the last section of *Fusées* (OC 1:665–67).

15. The presentation of "La Fin du monde" in *Baudelaire par Baudelaire* is revealing of this tendency to bury Baudelaire before he dies: "As the paralysis

and death approaches, [Baudelaire] suffers constant loss of energy" (À mesure que s'approche la paralysie et la mort, une constant déperdition d'énergie l'affecte), 81–84.

16. Lloyd Austin, *Poetic Principles and Practice: Occasional Papers on Baudelaire, Mallarmé, and Valéry*, 1–18.

17. "If it was finally excluded by Baudelaire, this was probably because of its fundamentally expository and ratiocinative character. . . . But whether we accept or reject these [i.e., Baudelaire's] views, we may not feel that to have read them constitutes an aesthetic experience. Our reaction depends on our endorsement or our rejection of the opinions put forward. The appeal is primarily to our reason, rather than to our aesthetic sense. This may well be what caused Baudelaire to exclude this text from the *Petits poémes en prose*." Austin, *Poetic Principles and Practice*, 6.

18. "Nouvel exemple et nouvelles victimes des inexorables lois morales, nous périrons par où nous avons cru vivre. La mécanique nous aura tellement américanisés, le progrès aura si bien atrophié en nous toute la partie spirituelle, que rien parmi les rêveries sanguinaires, sacrilèges, ou anti-naturelles des utopistes ne pourra être comparé à ses résultats positifs. Je demande à tout homme qui pense de me montrer ce qui subsiste de la vie. De la religion, je crois inutile d'en parler et d'en chercher les restes, puisque se donner encore la peine de nier Dieu est le seul scandale en pareilles matières. La propriété avait disparu virtuellement avec la suppression du droit d'aînesse; mais le temps viendra où l'humanité, comme un ogre vengeur, arrachera leur dernier morceau à ceux qui croiront avoir hérité légitimement des revolutions." *OC* 2:665–66.

19. I am referring to the use of differential calculus made by Hermann Cohen, Franz Rosenzweig, and Walter Benjamin in the neo-Kantian tradition, and by Gilles Deleuze in the Bergsonian one. It is not without significance that Gershom Scholem's first vocation was mathematics, and, Peter Fenves has shown, Scholem in 1916–1918 served as the principal conduit for mathematical ideas for Walter Benjamin. For more on this subject, see chapter 4 of Deleuze's *Difference and Repetition*; Reinier Munlt, "God Reveals Himself in Reason: On Hermann Cohen's Analogy between Logik and Religion"; and especially Peter D. Fenves, *The Messianic Reduction: Walter Benjamin and the Shape of Time*, 106–24, 170–86.

20. "Quant à moi qui sens quelquefois en moi le ridicule d'un prophète, je sais que je n'y trouverai jamais la charité d'un médecin. Perdu dans ce vilain monde, coudoyé par les foules, je suis comme un homme lassé dont l'œil ne voit en arrière, dans les années profondes, que désabusement et amertume, et devant lui qu'un orage où rien de neuf n'est contenu, ni enseignement, ni douleur. Le soir où cet homme a volé à la destinée quelques heures de plaisir,

bercé dans sa digestion, oublieux—autant que possible—du passé, content
du présent et résigné à l'avenir, enivré de son sang-froid et de son dandysme,
fier de n'être pas aussi bas que ceux qui passent, il se dit en contemplant la
fumée de son cigare: Que m'importe où vont ces consciences?

> Je crois que j'ai dérivé dans ce que les gens de métier appellent un hors-
> d'œuvre. Cependant, je laisserais ces pages—parce que je veux dater ma
> colère. Tristesse. (*OC* 1:667)

21. In "From Rupture to Shipwreck," Pierre Missac points to the considerable tension between "large-scale" *Erlösung* and small-scale *Rettung*
in Benjamin's usage (211, 215–16). He also admits that one can do little to
resolve or relieve that tension; to maintain it, I will place the German original
in parenthesis whenever Benjamin invokes "redemption."

22. "Der Chronist, welcher die Ereignisse hererzählt, ohne große und
kleine zu unterscheiden, trägt damit der Wahrheit Rechnung, daß nichts was
sich jemals ereignet hat, für die Geschichte verloren zu geben ist. Freilich fällt
erst der erlösten Menschheit ihre Vergangenheit vollauf zu. Das will sagen:
erst der erlösten Menschheit ist ihre Vergangenheit in jedem ihrer Momente
zitierbar geworden. Jeder ihrer gelebten Augenblicke wird zu einer *citation à
l'ordre du jour*—welcher Tag eben der jüngste ist." *SW* 4:390; *GS* 1.2:694.

23. The metaphor of the cesspool appears in the following highly revealing passage in Benjamin's *Ursprung*: "Fate is the elemental force of nature in
the historical event, which itself is not purely nature because even the creaturely condition [*Schöpfungstand*] still reflects the sun of grace. But mirrored
in the cesspool of Adamic debt [*Verschuldung*]" (1.1.308). This architectonic
of worldliness prefigures the heliotropism of redemption in "On the Concept
of History" that I will invoke in the conclusion to this essay. For a commentary on this passage, see Rainer Nägele, *Theater, Theory, Speculation: Walter
Benjamin and the Scenes of Modernity*, 178–79.

24. Here as elsewhere, Benjamin's Kraus designates "a strange interplay between reactionary theory and revolutionary practice" (*SW* 2:438). Deciphering
the logic of revolutionary practice that appears in this "strange interplay" and
actualizing the dialectic of the chronicle constitute the objective that presided
over Benjamin's intense preoccupation with Kraus between 1916 and 1932.

25. This judgment appears in the conclusion to "Karl Kraus": "Neither
purity nor sacrifice mastered the demon; but where origin [*Ursprung*] and
destruction come together, his reign is over. Like a creature sprung from
the child and the cannibal, his conqueror stands before him: not a new man
[*Mensch*]—a monster [*Unmensch*], a new angel" (*SW* 2:457; *GS* 2.1:367).
Ursprung is the most loaded theoretical word in Benjamin's vocabulary. The
cannibal represents the satirist's attitude (*GS* 2:3:1095); according to one

etymology, *satura* is stuffing; the satirist stuffs himself with the entrails of his victims; to eviscerate is his vocation. We must also keep in mind that in Benjamin, the child does not serve as an image of nonviolence but lives a form of creative destruction complementary to that of the satirist (see *SW* 2:101).

11. MESSIAHS AND PRINCIPLES
Paul North

1. Franz Kafka, *Briefe: April 1914–1917*, 327.

2. Ibid., 328.

3. The argument that "bis" meaning "as soon as" was an idiosyncrasy of Kafka's or of Prague German is refuted by Lawson. In fact, this sense is a standing possibility for the word since Middle High German. "Kafka's Use of *bis*," 169.

4. Kafka, *Briefe: April 1914–1917*, 756.

5. In his biography of Kafka's youth, Wagenbach famously describes the "general linguistic situation of Prague" and Kafka's uncomfortable place in it (83–92).

6. The interplay of "Jewish" languages bubbling within Kafka's "German" writing is captured in its complexity by David Suchoff in *Kafka's Jewish Languages: The Hidden Openness of the Tradition*. One of the many strengths of the study is Suchoff's almost complete openness to the multiplicity of currents and versions that make up a Jewish tradition, if indeed, in the light of Suchoff's analysis, it can still be called a tradition.

7. Kafka, *Briefe: April 1914–1917*, 343.

8. Ibid., 748.

9. Ibid., 345.

10. Ibid., 764.

11. Hovering near these reflections is the specter of Zionism, with its messianic, linguistic, and territorial hopes and modes. Kafka's relationship to the forms of Zionism at play in Prague and in his reading throughout his life are illuminated by Iris Bruce in her study *Kafka and Cultural Zionism: Dates in Palestine*. She presents, among many other facets of this vexed relationship, Kafka's anything but ambivalent reaction to the Eleventh Zionist Conference in 1913 (he calls it "ewiges Geschrei," 74–77), his relationship to Max Brod's Buberian insistence that an intensification of "Jewishness" is the first step to renewed Jewish life (see the section on Brod's novel *Die Jüdinnen*, 30–33), his attraction to Talmudism, Hassidic ecstatic ritual, and haggadic narrative (chapter 4 "Forms of Cultural Renewal," 85–112), and the pragmatic projects for the betterment of Jewish life in Europe in which he took part (chapter 5, "Kafka's Cultural Zionism," 113–37).

12. One can look at this in reverse as well. Jorge Luis Borges, in "The Homeric Versions," defends reading translations without knowledge of the original, in the case of certain works of literature. Translations are, in the special case of Homer, for example, higher than the original, because in the text of Homer that we read one cannot tell what in the text was determined by the originality of the author and what was determined by the requirements of the language (or, he might have added, the editors). Borges, 69–74. This ambiguity is multiplied when one does not know Greek, leading to a variety of rich, divergent, and equally valid versions. Borges's is one of the few nontheological theories of translation one can find.

13. One worry is that worldly words may be nothing more than works. Another worry is that God allows such a variety and quantity of words—scripture—to be produced in his name. "You may ask: 'What then is the Word of God and how shall it be used, since there are so many words of God?'" Luther, 55.

14. I will only mention here what is perhaps the earliest identification of a negative theology in Kafka, Hans-Joachim Schoeps's pamphlet "Theologische Motive in der Dichtung Franz Kafkas" (1951). As in his earlier book on Kafka and the tragic, as well as in his correspondence with Max Brod, who championed Schoeps as the savior of Kafka's theological spirit, here Schoeps insists, referring to the two novels *The Trial* and *The Castle*, that "whoever reads these two books, which at base are written in a modern hieroglyphic script, senses more or less clearly that he is dealing with the original scripture of a negative religion." Brod and Schoeps, *Im Streit um Kafka und das Judentum*, 232. In his assessment the unreadable script is, nevertheless, perfectly legible as the writing of God.

15. "It belongs to the essence of this law, in temporal and spatial respects, to be postponed." This is how Joseph Vogl, in analyzing the parabolic "Before the Law," characterizes the contrary to a messianic principle (158). The law of experience, no matter how much we look for it, comes only at the end, to give, always too late, the key to our experience. A principle, in contrast, is a fake or fraudulent law that reaches out for a content it cannot in fact govern. For a description of the mising law of interpretation in and for Kafka's texts, see Vogl, *Ort der Gewalt: Kafkas Literarische Ethik*, especially the first section of chapter 3, "Das Gesetz der Auslegung," 149–69.

16. A Kierkegaardian reading of the decisive instant is given by Ritchie Robertson, who understands it as the act of a person: "The certainty is that a decision is required of us in every instant" (*Kafka*, 207). It is very important to separate a decisive instant from a deciding person, since the deciding person acts in time (in Robertson's terms, deciding every instant), whereas Kafka

is asking us to abandon the time concept, or to let it leave us. A decisive instant severs us from time, opening up a nontime of events.

17. Kafka, *Nachgelassene Schriften und Fragmente* (hereafter *NS*), 2:34. In the final version of this passage, written on a notecard, Kafka excises the words "when we let our concept of time fall," leaving: *The decisive instant of human development is everlasting.* This edit eliminates a conceptual error in the first version, the paradoxical but still misleading implication that the end of time could happen at a specific time (*NS* 2:114). And then he marks the final version for deletion as well. In the earliest version he has also struck this line: *Human history is the second between two steps of a wanderer.* In the composition of this passage, the series of progressive deletions may indicate Kafka's advancing idea of how, or whether, we can critique the time concept. First, we give it an image that diminishes it—human history is but a second. Second, we give the paradoxical conditions for its elimination. Third, we eliminate the last hint that there is a proper time for critique. And finally we eliminate the whole project.

18. Marcel Gauchet calls this "organizing submission through dispossession" (*The Disenchantment of the World*, 13), a goal that can be accomplished only under "the reign of the absolute past" (23). Gauchet's political understanding of messianic time does not repudiate, but also does not require, the thinking suggested by Jakob Taubes, what Taubes calls the "inner logic of the messianic." "Inner" here means psychological; Taubes is interested in the "high price to the human soul" that living messianically entails (10). Gauchet in contrast is interested in the specifically political price—namely, the suppression of politics—which in Taubes's psychological account of messianic time is not important.

19. Charles Taylor, evoking Bernard Williams, writes of "the secular age" that in it "time is homogenized," since all extraordinary or legendary events are demoted to "what happened around here yesterday" (*A Secular Age*, 271). That is to say, without heroes and gods, and without faith, time becomes a medium for nothing much happening. In fact there is a dialectic at work in Taylor's account of "modernity." Time seems to telescope to a narrow, local, unmiraculous few boring days only after European heroes and gods betook themselves to some inaccessible temporal remove. To Taylor, homogenized time is the time of unfaith, but we should admit that it is also the only time in which faith makes sense. In short, the everyday is a messianic mode. Homogenized time corresponds to the wait for something to happen at last, and secularism is the condition, as it always was, for the coming of the divine.

20. The genre of these smallest of Kafkan texts is indeterminate, in two dimensions at least. It changes over the course of the composition, from something like Pascal's *pensées* in the notebooks—written down in the order

of occurrence—to the *Zettel*, the notecards where the thoughts are selected, edited slightly, and rewritten. The genre also changes between passages, although not every passage is a different genre from every other. That is, they are not uniformly one genre or another, and nor are they uniformly a plurality of genres. Some could be called moral sentences; some, interpretations; some, antinomies, and so forth. Moreover, to define them by their form, to make them, willy-nilly, into objects for literary knowledge not only collapses their differences but ignores the peculiar internal play within any note's vocabulary, syntax, and intention. More important even than the internal self-legislation of the form of each are the relations between the contents of different notes. A topic or argument, an image or gesture, may be taken up again and again. Seen as a whole, they constitute a sometimes chaotic polylogue of multiple perspectives in several idioms, and so it may indeed be a grave misunderstanding—perhaps the only one we can identify without the threat of error—to understand their form generically. The interconnectedness of the fragments is the main evidence, to my mind, that "aphorism" is a misnomer for them. Still, an elegant argument for placing them in a largely German aphoristic tradition is made by Richard Gray, in *Constructive Destruction: Kafka's Aphorisms: Literary Tradition and Literary Transformation*. The justification for seeing Kafka as an aphorist is given especially in chapter 3 (119–71).

21. Something like this, although perhaps not so clearly articulated, animates the theological treatise of another friend of Kafka's. Written around the same time and read by Kafka before it was sent to the printers in 1919, Felix Weltsch's *Gnade und Freiheit* does not mention messiahs as such; instead it concentrates on the opposition announced in the title, which contains, in another form, a similar tension between determinism and freedom that at least partially drives Kafka to attack the messiah complex. Weltsch thinks that the idea of grace cancels the possibility of freedom, and so he proposes that the telos of history does not already have being and that "the absolute" undergoes real becoming in time (143).

22. A partial narrative of Kafka's Kierkegaard reading can be found in Ritchie Robertson's *Kafka: Judaism, Politics, Literature*, 191–195. The association of Kafka with Kierkegaard, whether through his readings or through analogy, began very early, first with Brod, who encouraged, or rather insisted that Kafka read the theologian, and then with Brod's protegé, Schoeps, who, in a characteristically cavalier manner, writes Brod in 1929: "All of those for whom the figure of Kierkegaard means something, should not pass by their contemporary Kafka." Brod and Schoeps, *Streit*, 36. After this the key verdicts on the relationship are given in Brian Edwards, "Kafka and Kierkegaard: A Reassessment" (1966); Claude David, "Die Geschichte Abrahams:

Zu Kafkas Auseinandersetzung mit Kierkegaard" (1980); Wolfgang Lange, "Über Kafkas Kierkegaard Lektüre und einige damit zusammenhängende Gegenstände" (1986); and Helga Miethe, *Søren Kierkegaards Wirkung auf Franz Kafka* (2006).

23. Kafka, *NS* 2:54.

24. In a book Kafka would read later, around 1920, Max Brod reminds readers that there are two messiahs in ancient Judaism, one the son of Joseph who dies in battle, the other the son of David, the perfected messiah. One battles earthly misfortune, the other returns at the end of days and cancels time (*Paganism, Christianity, Judaism*, 43). Brod considers the former a moral messiah and the latter an immoral one, insofar as the day-to-day work of battling misfortune is what improves this life. His point of contrast is Hermann Cohen's Kantian idea of an infinite moral task. An infinite approximation remains infinitely distant, he argues (41).

25. Kafka, *Briefe: April 1914–1917*, 368. Earlier, on October 7 or 8, he writes Brod: "My will doesn't really push me toward writing. If I could save myself by digging holes like the fieldmouse, I would dig holes" (Kafka, *Briefe: April 1914–1917*, 343). Perforating the field with holes is not a bad image for the kind of writing Kafka soon begins to do.

26. Kafka, *NS* 2:55.

27. And yet . . . there is no "test" of faith for this plurality, insofar as a test is a door through which only a few can pass. The narrative that Kierkegaard applies to Abraham, a noble knight of faith who survives an ordeal, however ironic the tale may be, cannot apply here. Max Brod falsely assimilates Kafka's work to Kierkegaard's Abrahamic ideal when he says that Kafka is "a poet of the test of faith, of the test in faith." "Kafkas Glauben und Lehre," 5.

28. Acts 3:17f.

29. Kafka, *NS* 2:56–57.

30. The shift between fragments is not in any way, however, a "development." Max Brod calls Kafka's change in attitude toward "religion" and "faith" across his three novels a "development." *Franz Kafkas Glauben und Lehre*, 36–55.

31. To Ritchie Robertson this condition, the subtraction of need from the messianic equation, is the same as the condition set in the previous remark on the infinite plurality of faith (231). In the context of a discussion of the figure K. in *das Schloss*, Robertson also reminds us about Kafka's reading in Jewish history, which contained many descriptions of messianisms and messianic events (228–35).

32. Kafka, *Briefe: April 1914–1917*, 333.

33. Ibid.

34. Brod, "Die jüdische Kolonisation in Palästina," 1267.

35. Ibid., 1268.

36. Kafka, *Briefe: April 1914–1917*, 371. Kafka's interest in Pelagianism is intriguing, especially in light of his extreme interpretation of the messiah equation. Perhaps Kafka, having read Pascal during the summer and planning to read Augustine soon (he actually read Kierkegaard later that winter), wondered if an alternative, Pelagian line, without a doctrine of original sin, would have been victorious in the medieval church, whether a non-messianic temporality might have taken hold in Europe. That is to say, without original sin, would there have been clocks?

37. Kafka, *Briefe: April 1914–1917*, 372.

38. Ibid., 367.

39. From his reading of Graetz's *Popular History of the Jews* and Fromer's *The Organism of Judaism*, Kafka would have already been familiar with the range of Maimonides' thought and his meaning for later Judaisms. See Suchoff, 11 and 214n30–32.

40. Kafka, *Briefe: April 1914–1917*, 371.

41. Abelson, "Maimonides on the Jewish Creed," 28.

42. Hyman, *The Tangled Bank*, 122.

43. Abelson, "Maimonides on the Jewish Creed," 43.

44. Ibid., 39.

45. Ibid., 39.

46. Ibid., 29.

47. Ibid., 40.

48. Ibid., 57.

49. Ibid., 55.

50. Ibid., 56.

51. Maimonides insists later that the messiah will be a king in the line of David who will vanquish the foreign nations.

52. Kafka, *NS* 2:34.

53. Benjamin, *GS* 2.1:203.

54. A related consequence to be drawn from this Benjaminian line is the following, by Werner Hamacher. "The messianic is nothing other than profanization [die Profanierung]" (182). At the very moment when the world should be suspended and drawn into the holy, it is instead thrown back into history.

55. *Daß unsere Aufgabe genau so groß ist wie unser Leben, gibt ihr einen Schein von Unendlichkeit.* Kafka, *NS* 2:71. Kierkegaard in *Fear and Trembling*, which Kafka was reading in the first months of 1918, puts it this way: "As soon as the generation worries only about its own task, which is its highest duty,

it cannot become weary, since the task is always enough for a human life" (Kierkegaard, *Furcht und Zittern*, 114. Translated by me from the edition that Kafka read). Kafka focuses on the apparent infinity of life, the sense, right or wrong but still inevitable, that one never arrives at its limit. Kierkegaard's emphasis is on the task of faith and the automatism with which life, as co-extensive with the task, leads one to the limit—and beyond. Thus Johannes de Silentio boasts: "I can make the big trampoline-leap by which I transit into infinity" (Kierkegaard, *Furcht und Zittern*, 35). Kafka offers a sort of response, when he writes of Kierkegaard's Abraham that *he decides to emigrate, with it* [his concern for the future (Vorsorglichkeit)], *into eternity. Whatever it is, the entrance door or the exit door: It is too narrow—he cannot get his furniture cart through* (*NS* 2:104).

56. Several of the notes and scraps identify death as the highest possible illusion. A cluster of them can be found at *NS* 2:100–1.

57. Kafka, *NS* 2:99.

12. MESSIANIC NOT
Werner Hamacher

The present translation is based on the revised version of the second part of a text that was translated into French by Francis Guibal and Guy Petitdeman under the title "Ou, séance, touche de Nancy, ici (3)," presented in January 2002, at the Collège International de Philosophie and published two years later in the volume *Sens en tous sens—Autours des travaux de Jean-Luc Nancy* (Paris: Galilée, 2004).

The reflections formulated here on the structure of the future and of messianicity follow on "*Lingua amissa*," in *Ghostly Demarcations*, ed. Michael Sprinkker (London and New York: Verso, 1999), and "*Jetzt*—Benjamin zur historischen Zeit," in *Benjamin Studien* (Amsterdam: Rodopi, 2002), and have since been continued in "Das Theologisch-politisches Fragment," in *Benjamin-Handbuch*, ed. Burckhard Lindner (Stuttgart: Metzler Verlag, 2006), "Ungerufen," in *Neue Rundschau* 2007/2 (Frankfurt: S. Fischer Verlag), and "The Relation / The Aphora," in the *New Centennial Revue* 8, no. 3 (2008).

1. Jean-Luc Nancy, La pensée dérobée (Paris: Galilée, 2001), 14. [Trans-lator's note: Translations have been modified throughout.]

2. [Translator's note: In her translation of *Identity and Difference*, Joan Stambaugh renders *Überkommnis* as "coming-over" and provides "over-whelming" as an alternative in a footnote (64). I have instead translated the term as "over-coming" to emphasize the excess or over-abundance of com-ing. See Martin Heidegger, Identity and Difference, trans. Joan Stambaugh (Chicago: University of Chicago, 1969).]

3. Martin Heidegger, *Being and Time*, 142.

4. Franz Kafka, *The Blue Octavo Notebooks*, 28.

5. 1 Corinthians 7:29–31.

6. G. W. F. Hegel, *Hegel's Philosophy of Mind*, §462, 199.

7. Paul Celan, "Du mußt versuchen, auch den Schweigenden zu hören," *Briefe an Diet Kloos-Barendregt*, 89.

Abelson, J. "Maimonides on the Jewish Creed." *The Jewish Quarterly Review* 19, no. 1 (1906): 24–58.

Adorno, Theodor W. *Gesammelte Schriften.* Edited by Rolf Tiedemann. 20 vols. Frankfurt am Main: Suhrkamp, 1970–80.

———. *Minima Moralia: Reflexionen aus dem beschädigten Leben.* Frankfurt am Main: Suhrkamp, 1951.

Adhémar, Jean. *Honoré Daumier.* Paris: P. Tisné, 1954.

Agamben, Giorgio. *The Coming Community.* Translated by Michael Hardt. Minneapolis: University of Minnesota Press, 1993.

———. *Homo Sacer: Sovereign Power and Bare Life.* Translated by Daniel Heller-Roazen. Stanford: Stanford University Press, 1998.

———. *Idea of Prose.* Translated by Michael Sullivan and Sam Whitsitt. Albany: State University of New York Press, 1995.

———. "An Interview with Ulrich Rauff." *German Law Journal* 5.5 (2004): 609–14.

———. *Language and Death.* Translated by Michael Hardt and Karen Pinkus. Minneapolis: University of Minnesota Press, 1991.

———. *Il Linguaggio e la morte.* Turin: Einaudi, 1982.

———. *Means without End: Notes on Politics.* Translated by Vincenzo Binetti and Cesare Casarino. Minneapolis: University of Minnesota Press, 2000.

———. "Il messia e il sovrana: Il problema della legge in W. Benjamin." In *Anima e Paura: Studi in onore di Michele Ranchetti,* edited by Bruna Bocchini Camaiani and Anna Scattigno. Macerata: Quodlibet, 1998. 11–22.

———. *Potentialities.* Edited and translated by Daniel Heller-Roazen. Stanford: Stanford University Press, 1999.

———. *State of Exception.* Translated by Kevin Attell. Chicago: University of Chicago Press, 2005.

———. *The Time That Remains: A Commentary on the Letter to the Romans.* Stanford: Stanford University Press, 2005.

———. *Walter Benjamin: Tempo storia linguaggio.* Edited by Lucio Belloi and Lorenzina Lotti. Roma: Reuniti, 1983.

Aquinas, Thomas. *See* Thomas Aquinas.

Aristotle. *Complete Works: The Revised Oxford Translation.* Edited by Jonathan Barnes. 2 vols. Princeton: Princeton University Press, 1984.

Arnoldt, Emil. *Beiträge zu dem Material der Geschichte von Kants Leben und Schriftstellertätigkeit in Bezug auf seine 'Religionslehre' und seine Konflikt mit der preussischen Regierung.* Edited by Otto Schöndörffer. Berlin: B. Cassirer, 1909.

Asad, Talal. *Formations of the Secular: Christianity, Islam, Modernity.* Stanford: Stanford University Press, 2003.

Assmann, Aleida, Jan Assmann, and Wolf-Daniel Hartwich. Introduction to *Jacob Taubes: From Cult to Culture—Fragments towards a Critique of Historical Reason.* Edited by Charlotte Elisheva Fonrobert and Amir Engel. Stanford: Stanford University Press, 2010. xviii–xlix.

Austin, Lloyd. *Poetic Principles and Practice: Occasional Papers on Baudelaire, Mallarmé, and Valéry.* Cambridge: Cambridge University Press, 1987.

Badiou, Alain. *St. Paul: The Foundation of Universalism.* Stanford: Stanford University Press, 2003.

Balthasar, Hans Urs von. *Prometheus: Studien zur Geschichte des deutschen Idealismus.* Heidelberg: Kerle, 1947.

Balzac, Honoré de. *Un Prince de la Bohème: La comédie humaine.* Edited by Pierre-Georges Castex. Vol. 7. Paris: Gallimard, 1977.

———. "A Prince of Bohemia." In *The Unconscious Mummers (Les comédiens sans le savoir) and Other Short Stories.* Translated by Ellen Marriage. London: Dent, 1897.

Baudelaire, Charles. *Correspondance.* 2 vols. Bibliothèque de la Pléiade. Paris: Gallimard, 1973.

———. *Les Fleurs du Mal: The Complete Text of "The Flowers of Evil."* Translated by Richard Howard. Boston: D. R. Godine, 1982.

———. *The Flowers of Evil.* Translated by William Aggeler. Fresno, Calif.: Academy Library Guild, 1954.

———. *Œuvres complètes.* 19 vols. Paris: L. Conard, 1923–52.

———. *Œuvres complètes.* Bibliothèque de la Pléiade. 2 vols. Paris: Gallimard, 1975.

———. *Oeuvres complètes.* Edited by Claude Pichois. Paris: Gallimard, 1985–87.

Benedict XVI. *Spe Salvi.* In *Acta Apostolicae Sedis* 99 (2007): 985–1027.

Benjamin, Walter. *The Correspondence of Walter Benjamin, 1910–1940.* Edited and translated by Manfred R. Jacobson and Evelyn M. Jacobson. Chicago: University of Chicago Press, 1994.

———. *Gesammelte Briefe.* Edited by Christoph Gödde and Henri Lonitz. Frankfurt am Main: Suhrkamp, 1995–present.

———. *Gesammelte Schriften.* Edited by Rolf Tiedemann and Hermann Schweppenhäuser. Frankfurt am Main: Suhrkamp, 1991.

———. *Illuminations.* Edited by Hannah Arendt. Translated by Harry Zohn. London: Pimlico, 1999.

———. *Selected Writings.* Edited by Michael W. Jennings. 4 vols. Cambridge, Mass.: Harvard University Press, 2003.

Bergmann, Hugo. "Die Heiligung des Namens." In *Vom Judentum: Ein Sammelbuch: Verein Jüdischer Hochschüler Bar Kochba in Prag,* 32–44. Leipzig: Kurt Wolff, 1914.

Biale, David. *Gershom Scholem: Kabbalah and Counter-History.* Cambridge, Mass: Harvard University Press, 1979.

Block, Richard. *The Spell of Italy: Vocation, Magic, and the Attraction of Goethe.* Detroit: Wayne State University Press, 2006.

Bloch, Ernst. "Discussing Expressionism." Translated by Rodney Livingstone. In *Aesthetics and Politics,* 16–27. London: Verso, 2007.

———. *Geist der Utopie: Bearbeitete Neuauflage der zweiten Fassung von 1923.* Frankfurt am Main: Suhrkamp, 1964.

———. "Die glückliche Hand." In *Spuren.* Frankfurt am Main: Suhrkamp, 1985. 198–202.

———. *Literarische Aufsätze.* Frankfurt am Main: Suhrkamp, 1965.

———. *The Principle of Hope.* 3 vols. Cambridge, Mass.: MIT Press, 1986.

———. *Das Prinzip Hoffnung.* Frankfurt am Main: Suhrkamp, 1982.

Bloch, Jochanan. *Das anstößige Volk.* Heidelberg: Schneider, 1964.

Bloom, Harold. *Kafka–Freud–Scholem: Drei Essays.* Basel and Frankfurt am Main: Stroemfeld, Roter Stern, 1990.

Blunck, Richard. *Der Impuls des Expressionismus.* Hamburg: A. Harms, 1921.

Boethius. *The Theological Tractates and The Consolation of Philosophy.* Edited by H. F. Stewart, E. K. Rand, and S. J. Tester. Cambridge, Mass.: Harvard University Press, 1973.

Borges, Jorge Luis. "The Homeric Versions." In *Selected Non-Fictions.* New York: Penguin, 1999. 69–74.

Bouretz, Pierre. *Witness for the Future: Philosophy and Messianism.* Baltimore: Johns Hopkins University Press, 2010.

Boyarin, Daniel. "The Christian Invention of Judaism." In *Religion: Beyond a Concept,* edited by Hent de Vries, 150–78. New York: Fordham University Press, 2008.

———. *A Radical Jew: Paul and the Politics of Identity.* Berkeley: University of California Press, 1994.

Brod, Max. "Die jüdische Kolonisation in Palästina." *Die Neue Rundschau: XXVII.* Jahrgang der freien Bühne. Berlin: S. Fischer, 1917. 2:1267–76.

——. *Franz Kafkas Glauben und Lehre.* Frankfurt am Main: Fischer, 1966.

——. *Paganism, Christianity, Judaism.* University, Al.: University of Alabama Press, 1970.

Brod, Max, and Hans-Joachim Schoeps. *Im Streit um Kafka und das Judentum.* Edited by Julius H. Schoeps. Königstein: Athenäum, 1985.

Bruce, Iris. *Kafka and Cultural Zionism: Dates in Palestine.* Madison: University of Wisconsin Press, 2007.

Brown, Marilyn R. *Gypsies and Other Bohemians: The Myth of the Artist in Nineteenth-Century France.* Ann Arbor, Mich.: UMI Research, 1985

Bücher, Rolf. *Argumentum e Silentio.* Edited by Amy D. Colin. Berlin and New York: de Gruyter, 1987. 99–113.

Celan, Paul. *Breathturn* [Atemwende]. Translated by Pierre Joris. Los Angeles: Sun and Moon Press, 1995.

——. "Du mußt versuchen, auch den Schweigenden zu hören." In *Briefe an Diet Kloos-Barendregt*, edited by Paul Sars. Frankfurt am Main: Suhrkamp, 2002.

——. *Gesammelte Werke in sieben Bänden.* Frankfurt am Main: Suhrkamp, 2000.

——. *Der Meridian: Endfassung, Vorstufen, Materialien.* Tübinger Ausgabe. Frankfurt am Main: Suhrkamp, 1999.

——. *"Mikrolithen sinds, Steinchen": Die Prosa aus dem Nachlaß.* Edited by Bertrand Badiou and Barbara Wiedemann. Frankfurt am Main: Suhrkamp, 2005.

——. *Poems of Paul Celan.* Translated by Michael Hamburger. New York: Persea, 1995.

——. *Selections.* Translated by Pierre Joris. Berkeley: University of California Press, 2005.

Celan, Paul, and Peter Szondi. *Briefwechsel.* Edited by Christoph König. Frankfurt am Main: Suhrkamp, 2005.

Chrétien, Jean-Louis, et al. *Phenomenology and the Theological Turn.* New York: Fordham University Press, 2000.

Clark, T. J. *Image of the People: Gustave Courbet and the Second French Republic, 1848–1851.* Greenwich, Conn.: New York Graphic Society, 1973.

Cornehl, Peter. *Die Zukunft der Versöhnung: Eschatologie und Emanzipation in der Aufklärung, bei Hegel und in der Hegeleschen Schule.* Göttingen: Vandenhoeck und Ruprecht, 1971.

Cristaudo, Wayne, and Wendy Baker, eds. *Messianism, Apocalypse, Redemption: Twentieth Century German Thought.* Hindmarsh: Australian Theological Forum, 2006.

Crombez, Thomas, and Katrien Vloeberghs, eds. *On the Outlook: Figures of the Messianic.* Cambridge: Cambridge Scholars Press, 2007.

Dan, Joseph. "Scholem's View of Jewish Messianism." *Modern Judaism* 12, no. 2 (1992), 117–28.

David, Claude. "Die Geschichte Abrahams: Zu Kafkas Auseinandersetzung mit Kierkegaard." In *Bild und Gedanke: Festschrift für Gerhart Baumann zum 60. Geburtstag,* edited by Günther Schnitzler, Gerhard Neumann, and Jürgen Schröder. München: Fink, 1980.

Deleuze, Gilles. *Difference and Repetition.* New York: Columbia University Press, 1994.

Derrida, Jacques. *Acts of Religion.* Edited by Gil Anidjar. New York: Routledge, 2001.

———. "Faith and Knowledge: The Two Sources of 'Religion' at the Limits of Reason Alone." Translated by Samuel Weber. In *Religion,* edited by Derrida and Gianni Vattimo, 1–78. Stanford: Stanford University Press, 1996.

———. "Marx & Sons." Translated by G. M. Goshgarian. In *Ghostly Demarcations. A Symposium on Jacques Derrida's Specters of Marx.* edited by Michael Sprinker, 213–69. London: Verso, 2008.

———. *Schibboleth pour Paul Celan.* Paris: Galilée, 1986.

———. "Shibboleth: For Paul Celan." In *Word Traces: Readings of Paul Celan,* edited by Aris Fioretos, translated by Joshua Wilner, 3–74. Baltimore: Johns Hopkins University Press, 1994.

———. *Specters of Marx: The State of the Debt, the Work of Mourning, and the New International.* Translated by Peggy Kamuf. New York: Routledge, 1994.

———. "The Villanova Roundtable." In *Deconstruction in a Nutshell: A Conversation with Jacques Derrida,* edited by John Caputo, 2–31. New York: Fordham University Press, 1996.

Descombes, Vincent. *The Barometer of Modern Reason.* Oxford: Oxford University Press, 1993.

de Vries, Hent. *Minimal Theologies: Critiques of Secular Reason in Adorno and Levinas.* Baltimore: Johns Hopkins University Press, 2005.

———. *Philosophy and the Turn to Religion.* Baltimore: Johns Hopkins University Press, 1999.

———. *Religion and Violence: Philosophical Perspectives from Kant to Derrida.* Baltimore: Johns Hopkins University Press, 2002.

———, ed. *Religion beyond a Concept.* New York: Fordham University Press, 2008.

de Vries, Hent, and Samuel Weber, eds. *Religion and Media.* Stanford: Stanford University Press, 2001.

Douzinas, Costas, and Slavoj Žižek, Eds. *The Idea of Communism.* London: Verso, 2010.

Edwards, Brian F. M. "Kafka and Kierkegaard: A Reassessment." *German Life and Letters* 20, (1966–67): 218–25.

Faber, Richard, Eveline Goodman-Thau, and Thomas Macho, eds. *Abendländische Eschatologie: Ad Jacob Taubes.* Würzburg: Königshausen und Neumann, 2001.

Felstiner, John. *Paul Celan: Eine Biographie.* Translated by Holger Fliessbach. München: Beck, 1997.

Fenves, Peter. *Late Kant: Towards Another Law of the Earth.* London: Routledge, 2003.

———. *Messianic Reduction: Walter Benjamin and the Shape of Time.* Stanford: Stanford University Press, 2011.

———. *A Peculiar Fate: Metaphysics and World-History in Kant.* Ithaca: Cornell University Press, 1991.

Ferry, Luc. *Man Made God: The Meaning of Life.* Chicago: University of Chicago Press, 2002.

Feurbach, Ludwig. *The Essence of Christianity.* Translated by George Elliot. 1841. Cambridge: Cambridge University Press, 2011.

Fohr, Robert. *Daumier sculpteur et peintre.* Paris: A. Biro, 1999.

Fredriksen, Paula. *Augustine and the Jews: A Christian Defense of Jews and Judaism.* New York: Doubleday, 2008.

Freud, Sigmund. *The Standard Edition of the Complete Psychological Works.* Edited by James Strachey. London: Hogarth, 1955.

Gadamer, Hans-Georg. *Truth and Method.* Translated by Joel Winsheimer and Donald G. Marshall. New York: Continuum, 1993.

———. *Wahrheit und Methode.* Tübingen: J. C. B. Mohr, 1960.

Gauchet, Marcel. *The Disenchantment of the World: A Political History of Religion.* Princeton: Princeton University Press, 1997.

Gillespie, Michael Allen. *The Theological Origins of Modernity.* Chicago: University of Chicago Press, 2008.

Goethe, Johann Wolfgang von. *Werke.* Edited under the commission of Archduchess Sophie von Sachsen. Weimar: Böhlau, 1890.

Goetschel, Willi. "Scholem's Diaries, Letters, and New Literature on His Work: Review Essay." *Germanic Review* 72 (1997), 77–92.

Gollwitzer, Helmut. "Das anstößige Volk: On Jochanan Bloch's Eponymous Book." *Kirche in der Zeit: Evangelische Kirchenzeitung* (1966): 367.

Gray, John. *Black Mass: Apocalyptic Religion and the Death of Utopia.* New York: Farrar, Straus and Giroux, 2007.

———. "The Violent Visions of Slavoj Žižek." *New York Review of Books* 59, no. 12 (July 12, 2012).

Gray, Richard T. *Constructive Destruction. Kafka's Aphorisms: Literary Tradition and Literary Transformation.* Tübingen: Max Niemeyer, 1987.

Groys, Boris. *The Communist Postscript.* Translated by Thomas H. Ford. London: Verso, 2010.

Guyer, Paul, ed. *The Cambridge Companion to Kant.* Cambridge: Cambridge University Press, 1992.

———. *The Cambridge Companion to Kant and Modern Philosophy.* Cambridge: Cambridge University Press, 2006.

———. "Nature, Freedom, and Happiness: The Third Proposition of Kant's 'Idea for a Universal History.'" *Kant on Freedom, Law, and Happiness.* Cambridge: Cambridge University Press, 2002. 372–407.

Hamacher, Werner. "Häm." In *Jüdisches Denken in einer Welt ohne Gott: Festschrift für Stéphane Mosès.* Berlin: Vorwerk, 2000. 173–97.

———. "Lingua Amissa: The Messianism of Commodity-Language and Derrida's *Specters of Marx.*" Translated by Kelly Barry. In *Ghostly Demarcations: A Symposium on Jacques Derrida's Specters of Marx,* edited by Michael Sprinker, 168–212. London: Verso, 2008.

———. "*Das Theologisch-politische Fragment.*" In *Benjamin Handbook: Leben—Werk—Wirkung,* edited by Burkhardt Lindner. Stuttgart: Metzler, 2006. 175–92.

Heffernan, Michael. J. "The Parisian Poor and the Colonization of Algeria during the Second Republic." *French History* 3, no. 4 (January 1989): 377–403.

Hegel, G. W. F. *Faith and Knowledge.* Edited and translated by Walter Cerf and H. S. Harris. Albany: State University of New York Press, 1977.

———. *G. W. F. Hegel's Philosophy of Mind.* Edited and translated by William Wallace and A. V. Miller. Oxford: Oxford University Press, 2007.

———. *The Phenomenology of Mind.* Translated by J. B. Baillie. New York: Dover, 2003.

Heidegger, Martin. "Aletheia." *Early Greek Thinking.* New York: Harper and Row, 1975.

———. *Being and Time.* Translated by Joan Stambaugh. Albany: State University of New York Press, 1996.

———. *Identity and Difference.* Translated by Joan Stambaugh. Chicago: University of Chicago Press, 1969.

———. *Nietzsche.* New York: Harper, 1991.

———. "The Origin of the Work of Art." In *Poetry, Language, Thought,* translated by Albert Hofstadter. New York: Harper and Row, 1971. 15–88.

Heine, Heinrich. *Briefe.* Edited by Friedrich Hirth. Mainz: Florian Kufferberg, 1950.

———. *Werke.* Edited by Wolfgang Preisendanz. Frankfurt am Main: Insel, 1968.

Heinsohn, Gunnar. *Warum Auschwitz? Hitlers Plan und die Ratlosigkeit der Nachwelt.* Reinbeck bei Hamburg: Rowohlt aktuell, 1995.

Henry, Michel. *I Am the Truth: Toward a Philosophy of Christianity.* Stanford: Stanford University Press, 2003.

Hiller, Kurt. "Überlegungen zur Eschatologie und Methodologie des Aktivismus." *Das Ziel. Jahrbücher für geistige Politik* 3 (1919): 195–217.

Hollander, Dana. *Exemplarity and Chosenness: Rosenzweig and Derrida on the Nation of Philosophy.* Stanford: Stanford University Press, 2008.

Hollander, John. *The Gazer's Spirit : Poems Speaking to Silent Works of Art.* Chicago: University of Chicago Press, 1995.

Holzhey, Helmut. "'Das Ende aller Dinge': Immanuel Kant über apokalyptische Diskurse." In *Erwartung eines Endes: Apokalyptik und Geschichte,* edited by Helmut Holzhey and Georg Kohler. Zürich: Pano, 2001. 21–34.

Houellebecq, Michel. *The Possibility of an Island.* Translated by Gavin Bowd. New York: Knopf, 2006.

Hyman, Stanley Edgar. *The Tangled Bank: Darwin, Marx, and Freud as Imaginative Writers.* New York: Atheneum, 1974.

Jacobson, Eric. *Metaphysics of the Profane: The Political Theology of Walter Benjamin and Gershom Scholem.* New York: Columbia University Press, 2003.

Jameson, Fredric. "Marx's Purloined Letter." *Ghostly Demarcations: A Symposium on Jacques Derrida's Specters of Marx,* edited by Michael Sprinker. London: Verso, 2008. 26–67.

Johnson, Alan. "The New Communism: Resurrecting the Utopian Delusion." *World Affairs* (May–June 2012). http://www.worldaffairsjournal.org/article/new-communism-resurrecting-utopian-delusion.

Justinian. *Institutes.* Edited and translated by Peter Birks and Grant McLeod. Ithaca, N.Y.: Cornell University Press, 1987.

Kafka, Franz. *Briefe, April 1914–1917.* Edited by Hans-Gerd Koch. Frankfurt am Main: S. Fischer, 2005.

———. *The Blue Octavo Notebooks.* Translated by Ernst Kaiser and Eithne Wilkins. Cambridge, Mass.: Exact Change, 1991.

———. *Nachgelassene Schriften und Fragmente.* Edited by Jost Schillemeit. Frankfurt am Main: S. Fischer, 1992.

Kaiser, Georg. *Werke.* Edited by Walther Huder. 6 vols. Frankfurt: Propyläen, 1971.

Kandinsky, Wassily. *Über das Geistige in der Kunst.* Bern: Benteli-Verlag, 1959.

Kant, Immanuel. *Critique of the Power of Judgment.* Translated by Paul Guyer and Eric Matthews. Cambridge: Cambridge University Press, 2000.

———. Critique of Pure Reason. Edited by Paul Guyer and Allen W. Wood. Cambridge: Cambridge University Press, 1998.

———. "Das Ende aller Dinge." *Von den Träumen der Vernunft. Kleinere Schriften.* Wiesbaden: Fourier Verlag, 1979. 393–413.

———. *Kants Gesammelte Schriften.* Edited by Königliche Preußische (later Deutsche) Akademie der Wissenschaften zu Berlin. Berlin: de Gruyter, 1902–present.

———. *Religion and Rational Theology.* Edited by Allen Wood and George di Giovanni. Cambridge: Cambridge University Press, 1996.

Kaplan, Aryeh. *See* Sefer Yetzirah.

Kavka, Martin. *Jewish Messianism and the History of Philosophy.* Cambridge: Cambridge University Press, 2004.

Keenan, Thomas. *Fables of Responsibility: Aberrations and Predicaments in Ethics and Politics.* Stanford: Stanford University Press, 1997.

Kierkegaard, Søren. *Furcht und Zittern: Wiederholen.* Translated by H.C. Ketels. In *Gesammelte Werke,* edited by H. Gottsched. Jena: Diederichs, 1909.

Koelle, Lydia. *Paul Celans pneumatisches Judentum.* Mainz: Matthias Grünewald Verlag, 1998.

Krop, Henri A., et al., eds. *Post-Theism: Reframing the Judeo-Christian Tradition.* Leuven: Peeters, 2000.

LaCapra, Dominick. "Approaching Limit Events: Siting Agamben." In *Giorgio Agamben: Sovereignty and Life,* edited by Matthew Calarco and Steven DeCaroli. Stanford: Stanford University Press, 2007. 262–304.

———. *Rethinking Intellectual History: Texts, Contexts, Language.* Ithaca, N.Y.: Cornell University Press, 1983.

Landgrebe, Ludwig. "Das philosophische Problem des Endes der Geschichte." In *Kritik und Metaphysik: Festschrift für Heinz Heimsoeth.* Berlin: de Gruyter, 1966. Reprint, *Phänomenologie und Geschichte,* 224–44. Gütersloh: Gütersloher Verlagshaus, 1968.

Lange, Wolfgang. "Über Kafkas Kierkegaard-Lektüre und einige damit zusammenhängende Gegenstände." *Deutsche Vierteljahrsschrift für Literaturwissenschaft und Geistesgeschichte* 60, no 2 (1986): 286–308.

Laughton, Bruce. *Honoré Daumier.* New Haven: Yale University Press, 1996.

Lawson, Richard H. "Kafka's Use of the Conjunction Bis in the Sense 'As Soon As.'" *German Quarterly* 35, no. 2 (1962): 165–70.

Leonhard, Rudolf. "Literarischer Aktivismus." In *Theorie des Expressionismus,* edited by Otto F. Best. Stuttgart: Reclam, 1976. 135–39.

Lilla, Mark. *The Stillborn God: Religion, Politics, and the Modern West.* New York: Knopf, 2007.

Liska, Vivian, Bernd Witte, and Karl Solibakke, eds. *Messianism and Politics. Kabbalah, Benjamin, Agamben.* Würzburg: Königshausen und Neumann, 2008.

Liszt, Franz. *Des Bohémiens et de leur musique en Hongrie*. Paris: A. Bourdilliat, 1859.

Löwith, Karl. *Meaning in History: The Theological Implications of the Philosophy of History*. Chicago: University of Chicago Press, 1949.

Löwy, Michael. "Ernst Bloch and Georg Lukács Meet in Heidelberg." In *Yale Companion to Jewish Writing and Thought in German Culture, 1096–1996*, edited by Sander L. Gilman and Jack Zipes, 287–92. New Haven: Yale University Press, 1997.

———. "Messianism in the Early Work of Gershom Scholem." *New German Critique* 83 (2001): 177–91.

———. "The Modern Intellectual and His Heretical Ancestor: Gershom Scholem and Nathan of Gaza." *Diogenes* 48, no. 2 (June 2000): 105–9.

Lukács, Georg. "Bolshevism as a Moral Problem." Translated by Judith Marcus-Tar. *Social Research* 44 (1977): 416–24.

———. *Dostojewski: Notizen und Entwürfe*. Edited by J. C. Nyíri. Budapest: Akadémiai Kiadó, 1985.

———. "Expressionism: Its Significance and Decline." Translated by David Fernbach. In *Essays on Realism*, edited by Rodney Livingstone. Cambridge, Mass.: MIT Press, 1980. 76–113.

———. "Realism in the Balance." Translated by Rodney Livingstone. In *Aesthetics and Politics*. London: Verso, 2007. 28–59.

Luther, Martin. "The Freedom of a Christian." In *Martin Luther: Selections from his Writings*, edited by John Dillenberger, 42–85. Garden City, N.Y.: Anchor Books, 1962.

Maison, K. E. *Honoré Daumier: Catalogue Raisonné of the Paintings, Water-colours, and Drawings*. Greenwich, Conn.: New York Graphic Society, 1968.

Marion, Jean-Luc. *Being Given: Toward a Phenomenology of Givenness*. Translated by Jeffrey Kosky. Stanford: Stanford University Press, 2002.

———. *In Excess: Studies of Saturated Phenomena*. Translated by Vincent Berraud and Robyn Horner. New York: Fordham University Press, 2004.

———. *Visible and the Revealed*. Translated by Christina Gschwandtner. New York: Fordham University Press, 2008.

Marquard, Odo. "Lob des Polytheismus. Über Monomythie und Poly-mythie." In *Der Abschied vom Prinzipiellen: Philosophische Studien*. Stuttgart: Reclam, 1981.

Marx, Karl. "Der achtzehnte Brumaire des Louis Bonaparte." In *Karl Marx, Friedrich Engels—Werke*. Bd. 8. Berlin: Dietz, 1960. 111–207.

———. *Capital: A Critique of Political Economy*. Translated by Ben Fowkes. London: Penguin Classics, 1990.

———. *A Contribution to the Critique of Political Economy.* Translated by S. W. Ryazanskaya. Moscow: Progress Publishers, 1970.

———. *The Eighteenth Brumaire of Louis Bonaparte.* In *Karl Marx, Frederick Engels: Collected Works.* Translated by Richard Dixon et al. Vol. 11, 99–197. New York: International Publishers, 1979.

———. *Zur Kritik der politischen Ökonomie.* 1859. In *Karl Marx and Friedrich Engels, Werke.* Bd. 13, 7–160. Berlin: Dietz, 1971.

Marx, Karl, and Friedrich Engels. *German Ideology: Including "Theses on Feuerbach" and "Introduction to Political Economy."* Amherst, N.Y.: Prometheus Books, 1998.

Mayer, Hans. *Aussenseiter.* Frankfurt am Main: Suhrkamp, 1975.

———. *Der Weg Heinrich Heines.* Frankfurt am Main: Suhrkamp, 1998.

———. "Walter Benjamin and Franz Kafka: Report on a Constellation." In *On Walter Benjamin: Critical Essays and Reflections,* edited by Gary Smith. Cambridge, Mass.: MIT Press, 1988. 185–209.

Meinecke, Dietlind. *Über Paul Celan.* Frankfurt am Main: Suhrkamp, 1970.

Mendes-Flohr, Paul. *Gershom Scholem: The Man and His Work.* Albany: State University of New York Press, 1994.

Miethe, Helge. *Sören Kierkegaards Wirkung auf Franz Kafka: Motivische und sprachliche Parallelen.* Marburg: Tectum, 2006.

Missac, Pierre. "From Rupture to Shipwreck." In *On Walter Benjamin: Critical Essays and Reflections.* Edited by Gary Smith. Cambridge, Mass.: MIT Press, 1988.

Moltmann, Jürgen. *Theologie der Hoffnung.* Munich: Kaiser, 1964.

Mosès, Stéphane. "Ideen, Namen, Sterne. Zu Walter Benjamin's Metaphorik des Ursprungs." Translated by Andreas Kilcher. In *Für Walter Benjamin: Dokumente, Essays und ein Entwurf,* edited by Ingrid and Konrad Scheurmann, 183–92. Frankfurt am Main: Suhrkamp, 1992.

———. *Spuren der Schrift.* Frankfurt am Main: Athäneum, 1987.

Mühsam, Erich. *Gedichte.* In *Gesamtausgabe: Erich Mühsam,* edited by Günther Emig. Berlin: Verlag Europäische Ideen, 1983.

Munlt, Reinier. "God Reveals Himself in Reason: On Hermann Cohen's Analogy between Logik and Religion." *Archivio di Filosofia* 61 (1993): 269–87.

Murger, Henri. *Scènes de la Bohème.* Paris: M. Lévy Frères, 1851.

Nägele, Rainer. *Theater, Theory, Speculation: Walter Benjamin and the Scenes of Modernity.* Baltimore: Johns Hopkins University Press, 1991.

Nancy, Jean-Luc. *La pensée dérobée.* Paris: Galilée, 2001.

Nietzsche, Friedrich. *Unpublished Writings from the Period of "Unfashionable Observations."* Translated by Richard T. Gray. Stanford: Stanford University Press, 1999.

———. *Werke.* Edited by Karl Schlechta. Frankfurt am Main: Ullstein, 1955.

O'Donnell, James J. *Augustine: A New Biography.* New York: Harper Collins, 2005.

Parker, Robert. *Miasma: Pollution and Purification in Early Greek Religion.* New York: Oxford University Press, 1983.

Pepperell, Nicole. "The Bond of Fragmentation: On Marx, Hegel, and the Social Determination of the Material World." *Borderlands* 10, no. 1 (2011).

———. "Capitalism: Some Disassembly Required." In *Communization and Its Discontents: Contestation, Critique and Contemporary Struggles,* edited by Benjamin Noys. London: Minor Compositions, 2011. 105–30.

———. "The Exorcism of Exorcism: The Enchantment of Materiality in Derrida and Marx." *Ctrl-Z: New Media Mhilosophy* (May 2013).

———. "Handling Value: Notes on Derrida's Inheritance of Marx." *Derrida Today* 2, no. 2 (2009): 222–33.

———. "When Is It Safe to Go on Reading *Capital?*" In *The Devil's Party: Marx, Theory and Philosophy,* edited by Tom Bunyard, 11–21. London: Centre for Cultural Studies, Goldsmiths University of London, 2009.

Pepperell, Nicole and Duncan Law. "Handling Value: Grasping the Fetish in Marx's *Capital.*" Derrida Today International Conference. Macquarie University, Sydney, Australia, July 10–12, 2008.

Perovich, Anthony. "'For Reason . . . Also Has Its Mysteries': Immortality, Religion, and 'The End of All Things.'" In *Kant's Philosophy of Religion Reconsidered,* edited by Philip J. Rossi and Michael Wren, 165–80. Bloomington: Indiana University Press, 1991.

Petuchowski, Elizabeth. "A New Approach to Paul Celan's 'Argumentum e Silentio.'" *Deutsche Vierteljahrschrift für Literatutwissenschaft und Geistesgeschichte* 52 (1978): 111–36.

Pia, Pascal. *Baudelaire par Baudelaire.* Paris: Seuil, 1963.

Pinthus, Kurt, ed. *Menschheitsdämmerung: Ein Dokument des Expressionismus.* Hamburg: Rowohlt, 1959.

Platonov, Andrey. *The Foundation Pit.* Translated by Robert Chandler, Elizabeth Chandler, and Olga Meerson. New York: New York Review of Books, 2009.

Plotinus. *Enneads.* Translated by A.H. Armstrong. 7 vols. Cambridge, Mass.: Harvard University Press, 1968–88.

Riffaterre, Michael. "The Stylistic Approach to Literary History." *New Literary History* 2, no. 1 (Autumn 1970): 39–55.

Robertson, Ritchie. *Kafka: Judaism, Politics, Literature.* Oxford: Clarendon, 1985.

Rosenzweig, Franz. *Stern der Erlösung.* Frankfurt am Main: J. Kauffmann, 1921.

Rubiner, Ludwig. "Die Änderung der Welt." In *Der Aktivismus, 1915–1920,* edited by Wolfgang Rothe, 54–72. Munich: dtv, 1969.

Rumold, Rainer. *The Janus Face of the German Avant-Garde: From Expressionism toward Postmodernism.* Evanston, Ill.: Northwestern University Press, 2002.

Salmony, Hansjörg Alfred. *Kants Schrift: Das Ende aller Dinge.* Zürich: EVZ, 1962.

Samuel, Richard and R. Hinton Thomas. *Expressionism in German Life, Literature, and the Theatre.* Philadelphia: Albert Saifer, 1971.

Sasportas, Jacob. *Sisath Nobel Sevi* (Jerusalem, 1954).

Schmitt, Carl. *The Nomos of the Earth.* Translated by G. L. Ullman. New York: Telos Press, 2003.

———. *Political Theology.* Translated by George Schwab. Chicago: University of Chicago Press, 2006.

Scholem, Gershom. "Confession on the Subject of our Language." Reprinted as an appendix to Derrida, "The Eyes of Language." In *Acts of Religion,* edited by Gil Anidjar. New York: Routledge, 2001.

———. *Die Geheimnisse der Schöpfung.* Berlin: Schocken, 1935.

———. *Lamentations of Youth: The Diaries of Gershom Scholem, 1913–1919.* Edited by Anthony David Skinner. Cambridge, Mass.: Belknap, 2008.

———. *A Life in Letters, 1914–1982,* edited and translated by Anthony David Skinner. Cambridge, Mass.: Harvard University Press, 2002.

———. *The Messianic Idea in Judaism and Other Essays on Jewish Spirituality.* New York: Schocken, 1971.

———. *Sabbatai Sevi: The Mystical Messiah.* Translated by R. J. Zwi Werblowsky. Princeton: Princeton University Press, 1989.

———. *Tagebücher, nebst Aufsätzen und Entwürfen bis 1923.* Edited by Karlfried Gründer, Herbert Kopp-Oberstebrink, and Friedrich Niewöhner unter Mitwirkung von Karl E. Grözinger. Frankfurt am Main: Jüdischer Verlag, 1995–2000.

———. *Über einige Grundbegriffe des Judentums.* Frankfurt am Main: Suhrkamp, 1970.

———. "Walter Benjamin and His Angel." In *On Walter Benjamin: Critical Essays and Reflections,* edited by Gary Smith. Cambridge, Mass.: MIT Press, 1988. 51–89.

———. *Walter Benjamin—die Geschichte einer Freundschaft.* Frankfurt am Main: Suhrkamp, 1976.

Schopenhauer, Arthur. *The World as Will and Representation.* Translated by E. Payne. Indian Hills, Colo.: Falcon's Wing Press, 1958.

Seery, John Evan. *Political Returns: Irony in Politics and Theory, from Plato to the Antinuclear Movement.* Boulder, Colo.: Westview Press, 1990.

Sefer Yetzirah: The Book of Creation. Translated by Aryeh Kaplan. Boston: Weiser Books, 1997.

Steinberg, Michael P. "Walter Benjamin Writes the Essays 'Critique of Violence' and 'The Task of the Translator.'" In *Yale Companion to Jewish Writing and Thought in German Culture, 1096–1996*, edited by Sander L. Gilman and Jack Zipes, 401–11. New Haven: Yale University Press, 1997.

Stump, Eleonore, and Kretzmann, Norman. "Eternity." *Journal of Philosophy* 78 (1981): 429–58.

Suchoff, David. *Kafka's Jewish Languages: The Hidden Openness of the Tradition.* Philadelphia: University of Pennsylvania Press, 2012.

Sullivan, Lawrence E., and Hent de Vries, eds. *Political Theologies: Public Religions in a Post-Secular World.* New York: Fordham University Press, 2006.

Sutherland, Keston. "Marx in Jargon." *World Picture* 1 (2008). 1–25.

Sypher, Wylie. "Aesthetic of Revolution: The Marxist Melodrama." *Kenyon Review* 10, no. 3 (1948): 431–44.

Taubes, Jacob. *Ad Carl Schmitt: Gegenstrebige Fügung.* Berlin: Merve, 1987.

———. *From Cult to Culture.* Edited by Amir Engel and Charlotte Fonrobert. Stanford: Stanford University Press, 2009.

———. *Gespräche mit Peter Sloterdijk.* Typewritten transcript. Bergisch Gladbach, 1987.

———. *Occidental Eschatology.* Translated by David Ratmoko. Stanford: Stanford University Press, 2009.

———. *The Political Theology of Paul.* Stanford: Stanford University Press, 2004.

———. "Walter Benjamin—ein moderner Marcionit? Scholems Benjamin-Interpretation religionsgeschichtlich überprüft." In *Antike und Moderne. Zu Walter Benjamins Passagen,* edited by Norbert W. Bolz and Richard Faber, 138–47. Würzburg: Königshausen und Neumann, 1986.

Taylor, Charles. *A Secular Age.* Cambridge, Mass.: Harvard University Press, 2007.

Thomas Aquinas. *Summa Theologica.* 5 vols. Madrid: Biblioteca de Autores Cristianos, 1951.

Tobias, Rochelle. *The Discourse of Nature in the Poetry of Paul Celan.* Baltimore: Johns Hopkins University Press, 2006.

Toller, Ernst. *Gesammelte Werke.* Edited by John M. Spalek and Wolfgang Frühwald. 5 vols. Munich: Carl Hanser Verlag, 1978.

Vaihinger, Hans. *Die Philosophie des Als Ob: System der theoretischen, praktischen und religiösen Fiktionen der Menschheit auf Grund eines idealistischen Positivismus.* Berlin: Reutheer & Reichard, 1911.

Vattimo, Gianni. "Nihilism: Reactive and Active." In *Nietzsche and the Rhetoric of Nihilism*, edited by Tom Barby et al., 15–21. Montreal: McGill-Queens University Press, 1989.

Vogl, Joseph. *Ort der Gewalt: Kafkas Literarische Ethik*. München: Wilhelm Fink, 1990.

Wagenbach, Klaus. *Franz Kafka: Eine Biographie Seiner Jugend*. Bern: Francke, 1958.

Weber, Max. *Economy and Society: An Outline of Interpretative Sociology*. London: Routledge, 1978.

———. *Gesamtausgabe*. Edited by Horst Baier et al. Tübingen: J. C. B. Mohr, 1992.

Weltsch, Felix. *Gnade und Freiheit: Untersuchungen zum Problem des schöpferischen Willens in Religion und Ethik*. Düsseldorf: Onomato, 2010.

Wedemeyer, Arnd. "'Finally Learning to Walk by Falling a Few Times': Kant's Gait and the King's Gout." Forthcoming. *Eighteenth-Century Studies*.

Wheen, Francis. *Marx's Das Kapital: A Biography*. Vancouver: Douglas & McIntyre, 2007.

Wiedemann, Barbara, ed. *Die Goll-Affäre*. Frankfurt am Main: Suhrkamp, 2000.

Wilson, Edmund. *To the Finland Station: A Study in the Writing and Acting of History*. London: Macmillan, 1972.

Wittgenstein, Ludwig. *Philosophical Investigations*. Translated by G. E. M. Anscombe, P. M. S. Hacker, and Joachim Schulte. 4th edition. West Sussex: Wiley-Blackwell, 2009.

Wohlfahrt, Irving. "Krise der Erzählung, Krise der Erzähltheorie. Überlegungen zu Lukacs, Benjamin und Jauss." In *Erzählung und Erzählforschung im 20. Jahrhundert*, edited by R. Klopfer and G. Janetzke-Dillner, 269–88. Stuttgart: Kohlhammer, 1981.

Wolff, Robert Paul. *Moneybags Must Be So Lucky: On the Literary Structure of Capital*. Amherst: University of Massachusetts Press, 1988.

Wolin, Richard. *Walter Benjamin: An Aesthetic of Redemption*. New York: Columbia University Press, 1982.

Wolosky, Shira. "Mystical Language and Mystical Silence in Paul Celan's 'Dein Hinübersein.'" In *Argumentum e Silentio*, edited by Amy D. Colin, 364–77. Berlin & New York: de Gruyter, 1987.

Zehder, Hugo. "Zeit, Theater und Dichter." *Die neue Schaubühne* 1 (1919): 1–3.

LISA MARIE ANDERSON is Associate Professor of German at Hunter College, City University of New York.

CATHARINE DIEHL is a Research Fellow at Humboldt University, Berlin.

PETER FENVES is Joan and Sarepta Harrison Professor of Literature, Northwestern University.

DAVID FERRIS is Professor of Humanities and Comparative Literature, University of Colorado at Boulder.

OLEG GELIKMAN is Associate Professor of Comparative Literature, Soka University of America.

ANNA GLAZOVA is Max Kade Scholar in Residence, Rutgers University.

WERNER HAMACHER is Professor of General and Comparative Literature, University of Frankfurt, and Emmanuel Levinas Chair, European Graduate School.

VIVIAN LISKA is Professor of German Literature and Director of the Institute of Jewish Studies, University of Antwerp, and Distinguished Visiting Professor, Hebrew University, Jerusalem.

THOMAS MACHO is Professor of Cultural History, Humboldt University, and Codirector of the Center for Literary and Cultural Research, Berlin.

PAUL NORTH is Associate Professor of German, Yale University.

NICOLE PEPPERELL is Program Director Social Science Psychology, School of Global, Urban and Social Studies, RMIT University, Melbourne, Australia.

JOSHUA WILNER is Professor of English and Comparative Literature, City College and the Graduate Center, City University of New York.